The William Morris Chronology

THOEMMES

*Further titles by or about William Morris
are available from Thoemmes Press*

THE WILLIAM MORRIS
CHRONOLOGY

Nicholas Salmon
with Derek Baker

THOEMMES PRESS

© Nicholas Salmon and Derek Baker, 1996

Published in 1996 by
Thoemmes Press
11 Great George Street
Bristol BS1 5RR
England

The William Morris Chronology

ISBN 1 85506 505 3 – Paperback
ISBN 1 85506 504 5 – Hardback

British Library Cataloguing-in-Publication Data

A catalogue record of this title is available
from the British Library

Printed in Great Britain by Bookcraft (Bath) Ltd.

INTRODUCTION & ACKNOWLEDGEMENTS

The original idea for the *William Morris Chronology* dates from the late 1980s when I started the research for my PhD at Reading University on 'William Morris: The Political Vision 1883–1890'. The aim of my thesis was to trace the interrelationship between Morris's propaganda work for the socialist cause and the creative literature he wrote during his period as an activist in the movement. During this research it became clear that the importance of Morris's work for the early socialist movement had been greatly underestimated by many of his biographers. It was my tutor, Professor Patrick Parrinder, who suggested that it might be a useful supplement to my research to compile a list of Morris's day-to-day political activities during the last twenty years of his life. This I did, basing my work on reports in the national and regional press, articles in *Justice* and *Commonweal*, and the archives of the Eastern Question Association, the National Liberal League, the Radical Union, the Social Democratic Federation, the Socialist League and the Hammersmith Socialist Society.

A particularly helpful source for this preliminary work was Eugene LeMire's catalogue of Morris's lecture engagements which formed an appendix to his edition of *The Unpublished Lectures of William Morris* (1969). LeMire's research in this area was extremely impressive as it was undertaken without the aid of a collected edition of Morris's letters. There is no doubt that without LeMire's pioneering work in this area our knowledge of Morris's speaking career would be far from complete. Readers of the *Chronology* who require the full sources for Morris's lecture engagements are recommended to refer back to LeMire's excellent book.

After I finished my PhD in 1992 I began to extend the scope of the *Chronology* by adding in references to all Morris's other activities and details of his private life. When I joined the committee of the William Morris Society in 1994 I showed this expanded version of the *Chronology* to a number of my colleagues all of whom encouraged me to complete the project. I would like to take this opportunity to thank in particular Hans Brill, Peter Faulkner, Dawn Morris, Linda Parry, Christine Poulson and Ray Watkinson. The Hon. Secretary of the Society, Derek Baker, was particularly enthusiastic and offered to help with some of the research into Morris's early life. Derek's subsequent work, especially relating to Morris's diaries, has added substantially to the *Chronology*. We also experienced great satisfaction in making new discoveries about Morris's activities which had been overlooked by previous biographers.

I was extremely fortunate that the final stages of my research coincided with the publication, in early 1996, of volumes 3 and 4 of Norman Kelvin's *Collected Letters of William Morris*. Kelvin had been working on the letters since 1965 and I have been one of the first researchers to enjoy the privileged position of consulting the published version of this monumental work along with his extensive and thorough notation. Without access to the *Collected Letters* it is unlikely that the *Chronology* could have been completed. Those readers eager to extend their reading on Morris are highly recommended to begin with the four volumes of the *Collected Letters*.

Wherever possible the *Chronology* has been based on Morris's own writings. Apart from the *Collected Letters* and the articles in *Justice* and *Commonweal*, which have already been mentioned, other valuable published sources have been Florence Boos' edition of Morris's *Socialist Diary* (1985) and Morris's *Icelandic Journals* introduced by Magnus Magnusson (1996). In addition Morris's unpublished diaries for 1881, 1887, 1893, 1895 and 1896 have been extremely useful in piecing together his activities during the later years of his life. The diary for 1896 is an especially poignant document which charts, in harrowing detail, the final decline of his health. These diaries can be consulted at the British Library. Other manuscript sources include Morris's diary of his work on the 'Cabbage and Vine' tapestry in 1879 (National Art Library) and the log-book of the Ark's voyage up the Thames in 1880 (British Library). The latter was written by Richard Grosvenor, but includes critical notes from – among others – Morris, Jane and Cormell Price. It is a fascinating document full of jokes, quips and anecdotes and deserves to be published in its own right.

The most important supplement to Morris's own writings are those of his immediate family. It is to be regretted that Jane left no reminiscences of her husband. However, some of her letters have been published in John Bryson's *Dante Gabriel Rossetti and Jane Morris: Their Correspondence* (1976) and Peter Faulkner's *Jane Morris to Wilfrid Scawen Blunt* (1986). The British Library also holds her 'Red House Notes'. Morris's oldest daughter Jenny, who was diagnosed with epilepsy in 1876, also left no account of her father. Again this is to be regretted as her work for *The Scribbler*, a home magazine she edited between 1878 and 1880 (and now in the British Library), indicates that she could have been a writer of some talent. Morris's younger daughter May's recollections of her father can be found in her introductions to the twenty-four volumes of *The Collected Works of William Morris* (1910–15) and in the two volumes of her *William Morris: Writer, Artist, Socialist* (1936). She also contributed one or two amusing anecdotes to an appendix which appeared in W. R. Lethaby's *Philip Webb and his Work* (1935).

The *Chronology* has also relied heavily on the personal letters, diaries and recollections of Morris's closest friends and acquaintances. It would be outside the scope of this preface to list all the published sources that have been consulted. However, the following volumes have been of particular use and I thank their authors and editors for their scholarship: H. Allingham and D. Radford (eds.), *William Allingham: A Diary 1824–1889* (1967); Wilfrid Scawen Blunt, *My Diaries* (1919); Georgiana Burne-Jones, *Memorials of Edward Burne-Jones*, 2 vols. (1904); Walter Crane, *An Artist's Reminiscences* (1907); O. Doughty and J. R. Wahl (eds.), *The Letters of Dante Gabriel Rossetti*, 3 vols. (1965–7); H. M. Hyndman, *The Record of an Adventurous Life* (1911); C. Y. Lang (ed.), *The Swinburne Letters*, 6 vols. (1959–62); Dan H. Laurence (ed.), *Bernard Shaw Collected Letters 1874–1950*, 4 vols. (1965–88); P. Lubbock (ed.), *Letters of Henry James* (1920); Viola Meynell (ed.), *Some Friends of a Lifetime, Letters to Sydney Carlyle Cockerell* (1940); Viola Meynell (ed.), *The Best of Friends, Further Letters to Sydney Carlyle Cockerell* (1956); Virginia Surtees (ed.), *The Diaries of George Price Boyce* (1980) and *The Diary of Ford Madox Brown* (1981).

Whenever possible I have tried to check the published sources against the original manuscripts. In this context the following manuscript collections are amongst those which have been consulted: William Scawen Blunt's reminiscences of Morris (British Library); the Blunt Papers (Fitzwilliam Library); the Burne-Jones Papers (Fitzwilliam Library); John Carruthers' reminiscences of William Morris (British Library); the Cockerell Papers (British Library); the Cockerell Letters (National Art Library); R. W. Dixon's reminiscences of William Morris (William Morris Gallery); the Fairfax Murray Papers (John Rylands Library); the John Bruce Glasier correspondence (William Morris Gallery); the Andreas Scheu Papers (International Institute of Socialist History); the Bernard Shaw Papers (British Library); the Warington Taylor letters (National Art Library); the Philip Webb correspondence (National Art Library). I would like to thank the staff of all these institutions, along with those at the National Newspaper Library in Colindale, for their generous assistance. Thanks are also due to the Society of Antiquaries who own the Morris copyright.

The most fascinating of these manuscript sources are undoubtedly the notebooks that J. W. Mackail compiled while writing his book, *The Life of William Morris* (1899), which still remains one of the most authoritative books on Morris. Mackail's book was commissioned by Edward Burne-Jones, and he therefore had unparalleled access to the friends and colleagues who had actually known Morris. Many of his conversations with these people are recorded in the notebooks and they make extremely interesting reading. Dotted amongst their pages are many stories and anecdotes that were omitted from the final biography. Mackail also had access to many letters of Morris and his circle which have subsequently been lost, and his brief summaries of their contents are a useful supplement to Kelvin's work on the *Collected Letters*. Derek and I would particularly like to thank Norah Gillow and Peter Cormack for allowing us to view these notebooks at the William Morris Gallery. Readers are also recommended to visit the Gallery which is the only museum in the country dedicated to Morris and his work.

While these memoirs and manuscript collections have been extremely valuable in compiling the *Chronology*, a work of this kind could not have been written without the scholarship of earlier writers. Mention has already been made of LeMire's work on Morris's lectures. Below is a list of the other specialized works which have been of particular value for my research: Gary L. Aho, *William Morris: A Reference Guide* (1985); H. Buxton Forman, *The Books of William Morris Described, with Some Account of his doings in Literature and in the Allied Crafts* (1897); Peter Faulkner (ed.), *William Morris: The Critical Heritage* (1973); Charles Harvey and Jon Press, *William Morris: Design and Enterprise in Victorian Britain* (1991); David and Sheila Latham, *An Annotated Critical Bibliography of William Morris* (1991); Linda Parry, *William Morris Textiles* (1983); W. S. Peterson, *A Bibliography of the Kelmscott Press* (1984); Charles A. Sewter, *The Stained Glass of William Morris and his Circle*, 2 vols. (1974–5); Ray Watkinson, *William Morris as Designer* (1967). For a comprehensive account of all Morris's work in art, craft and design the reader is recommended to read Linda Parry (ed.), *William Morris* (1996). This is the book which accompanied the V & A's highly successful William Morris Centenary Exhibition.

I am also indebted to the previous biographers of Morris all of whom have contributed something to our knowledge of his life, work and influence. Morris has attracted an amazingly varied – and often unlikely – series of biographers ever since Aymer Vallance published, with Morris's permission, *William Morris: His Art, his Writings and his Public Life* in 1897.

Thereafter books appeared regularly right up to the outbreak of the First World War: J. W. Mackail (1899); James Leatham (1899); Elisabeth Luther Cary (1902); Holbrook Jackson (1908); Alfred Noyes (1908); the Countess of Warwick (1912); Arthur Compton-Rickett (1913); Arthur Clutton-Brock (1914). By contrast the inter-war and immediate post-war years produced very few books of lasting significance with the exception of those by Paul Bloomfield (1934) and Esther Meynell (1947). It was only after the late E. P. Thompson published his masterful *William Morris: Romantic to Revolutionary* (1955) that interest was once again rekindled in Morris. Amongst the books to have appeared since the 1960s have been ones by Andre Tscham (1962), R. Page Arnot (1964), Philip Henderson (1967), Paul Thompson (1967), Jack Lindsay (1975), Ian Bradley (1978), Christine Poulson (1989), Helen Dore (1990) and Stephen Coote (1990). Without doubt the most important new biography has been Fiona MacCarthy's *William Morris: A Life for Our Time* (1994). The success of this book, which won its author the 1994 Wolfson History Prize, has raised the public awareness of Morris's achievement to an unprecedented level.

Finally, I would like to thank the staff at Thoemmes Press for their great enthusiasm and encouragement. Rarely, if ever, can a book have been produced with such efficiency and good humour. In particular I would like to thank Jane Williamson for her meticulous editing of an extremely complex text.

Nick Salmon
Buckinghamshire, 1996

Abbreviations used in the Text:

ACES	Arts & Crafts Exhibition Society
DF	Democratic Federation
EQA	Eastern Question Association
HSS	Hammersmith Socialist Society
ILP	Independent Labour Party
LEL	Labour Emancipation League
LRL	Land Restoration League
NAAA	National Association for the Advancement of Art and its Application to Industry
NLL	National Liberal League
NSS	National Secular Society
SDF	Social Democratic Federation
SL	Socialist League
SLLL	Scottish Land and Labour League
SPAB	Society for the Protection of Ancient Buildings

CHRONOLOGY

14 June 1797: William Morris Snr, the second of four brothers, was born in Worcester. His father is supposed to have come to Worcester from Wales in the late eighteenth century and married Elizabeth Stanley, the daughter of a retired naval surgeon from Nottingham.

24 May 1805: Emma Shelton, William Morris's mother, was born in Worcester. She was the youngest of Joseph Shelton's (1764–1848) children. Her family could be traced back to Henry Shelton (or 'Shilton'), mercer, of Birmingham (c.1450–1520).

1812: Sanderson & Co., brokers, was established by Richard Sanderson.

1816: Richard Sanderson went into partnership with Joseph Owen Harris and Robert Harris to form Harris, Sanderson & Harris.

8 February 1819: John Ruskin was born at 54 Hunter Street, London.

1820: Around this time William Morris Snr moved to London and soon after joined Harris, Sanderson & Harris. The Morrises appear to have been distantly related to the Harrises and both families had Quaker associations.

16 April 1821: Ford Madox Brown was born in Calais.

1824: Emma Shelton became engaged to William Morris Snr. The William Morris Gallery possesses watercolour miniatures of the young couple probably painted at the time of their engagement. The picture of William Morris Snr is signed by T. Wheeler.

20 June 1824: G. E. Street was born in Woodford, Essex.

4 February 1825: Frederick James Furnivall was born in Egham, Surrey.

1826: The Revd F. B. Guy was born. He was later headmaster of Bradfield College (1850–52) and then of the Forest School, Walthamstow (1856–86). He had a passion for painting and architecture.

January 1826: The two Harris brothers were replaced as partners by William Morris Snr and Richard Gard. The firm continued trading as Sanderson & Co. Soon after becoming a partner in the business William Morris Snr married Emma Shelton. The young couple moved into rooms above the business at 32 Lombard Street. They later took a cottage in Sydenham, Kent, where they spent their holidays.

2 April 1827: William Holman Hunt was born in Cheapside, London.

30 August 1827: Charles Stanley, William and Emma Morris's first son, was born at 32 Lombard Street. He died four days later.

16 November 1827: Charles Eliot Norton was born in Cambridge, Massachusetts, USA.

12 May 1828: Dante Gabriel Rossetti was born at 38 Charlotte Street – now Hallam Street – London.

8 June 1829: John Millais was born in Southampton.

29 October 1829: Morris's favourite sister, Emma, was born at 32 Lombard Street, London, over the office of Sanderson & Co.

12 January 1831: Philip[pe] Speakman Webb was born at 1 Beaumont Street, Oxford.

17 July 1833: Morris's sister, Henrietta, was born at 32 Lombard Street, London. At some point shortly after Henrietta's birth the Morris family moved to Elm House, Clay Hill, Walthamstow. This early nineteenth-century building was demolished in 1898.

28 August 1833: Edward Coley Jones – later Burne-Jones – was born at 11 Bennett's Hill, Birmingham.

24 March 1834: William Morris was born at Elm House, Walthamstow. The early nineteenth-century mahogany four-poster bed in which he was born is to be seen at Kelmscott Manor. By this time his father had become senior partner in Sanderson & Co.

25 July 1834: Morris was baptized at St Mary's Church, Walthamstow.

1836: Sanderson & Co. moved from 32 Lombard Street to 83 King William Street. Pugin's *Contrasts* was published.

2 August 1837: Morris's brother, Hugh Stanley, was born at Elm House, Walthamstow.

27 January 1839: Morris's brother, Thomas Rendall, was born at Elm House, Walthamstow.

19 October 1839: Jane Burden – Morris's future wife – was born in a small, three-roomed, insanitary cottage in St Helen's Passage off Holywell Street, Oxford. She was the third child of Robert Burden and his wife Ann (née Maizey). Robert was from the village of Stanton Harcourt and his wife from the neighbouring village of Alvescot. At the time of her birth Robert worked as a stablehand or ostler at Symonds' Livery Stables in Holywell Street. Her mother registered the birth with a cross, indicating she was illiterate. Many years later Morris was to write to the *Daily News* urging the preservation of 'the little plaster houses in front of Trinity College ... [and] the beautiful houses left on the north side of Holywell Street. These are in their way as important as the more majestic buildings to which all the world makes pilgrimage.'

1840: The Morris family moved to Woodford Hall in Essex which they rented for £600 a year. The house was an impressive Palladian brick mansion which had a fifty acre park and a hundred acre farm which bordered Epping Forest. In 1888 Morris was to recall: 'When we lived at Woodford there were some stocks there on a little bit of wayside green in the middle of the village: beside them stood the *Cage* a small shanty some 12 ft sq: and as it was built of brown brick roofed with blue slate, I suppose it had been quite recently in use, since its *style* was not earlier than the days of Fat George. I remember that I used to look at these two threats of law [and] order with considerable terror, and decidedly preferred to walk on the opposite side of the road; but I never heard of anybody being locked up in the Cage or laid by the heels in the stocks.' Morris read *The Arabian Nights* and John Gerard's *Herball*.

30 August 1840: Morris's brother, Arthur, was born at Woodford Hall.

1841: Pugin's *The True Principles of Pointed or Christian Architecture* was published. By this time Morris claimed to have read all Walter Scott's works.

1842: Morris visited Canterbury Cathedral and the Minster at Thanet Church with his father. He later recalled 'thinking that the gates of heaven had been opened to me'. He also went brass rubbing in a number of churches in Essex and Suffolk. Jane's sister, Elizabeth (Bessie) Burden, was born. Tennyson's *Morte d'Arthur* was published.

17 July 1842: Morris's sister, Isabella, was born at Woodford Hall.

1843: Morris went to the Misses Arundale's 'Academy for Young Gentlemen' at Woodford as a day scholar. According to Mackail's *Notebooks*, this school was originally situated opposite Elm House where Morris was born. It later moved to George Lane, Woodford. Mackail also recorded that Morris rode to school on a Shetland pony. Morris's father obtained a Grant of Arms from the Herald's College: 'Azure, a horse's head erased argent between three horse-shoes or, and for crest, on a wreath of the colours, a horse's head couped argent, charged with three horse-shoes in chevron sable.' Pugin's *Apology for the Revival of Christian Architecture in England* was published, as was Carlyle's *Past and Present*.

15 April 1843: Henry James was born in New York.

May 1843: Volume 1 of Ruskin's *Modern Painters* was published.

August 1843: Marlborough College, Morris's future school, was founded in premises at the Castle Inn in the High Street.

6 June 1844: Morris's brother, Edgar Llewelyn, was born at Woodford Hall.

26 July 1844: A new Devonshire mining company agreed a lease with the Duke of Bedford's land agent to sink a mine in Blanchdown Woods, on the Devon bank of the Tamar.

10 August 1844: Work began on the mine known as 'Wheal Maria' named after the Duke of Bedford's wife. The first shaft was named 'Gard's' shaft after William Morris Snr's partner in Sanderson & Co.

November 1844: Rich deposits of copper were found in 'Gard's' shaft just 18 fathoms from the surface. The lode was 40 feet in width and stretched eastwards for over two miles. A whole series of mines were subsequently opened along the seam.

25 March 1845: The Devonshire Great Consolidated Copper Mining Co. was registered as a joint stock company. William Morris Snr and his brother, Thomas, owned 304 of its 1,024 shares. William Morris Snr was appointed trustee and auditor.

15 August 1845: Walter Crane was born in Liverpool.

1846: Volume 2 of Ruskin's *Modern Painters* was published as was Persoz's *L'impression des Tissus* which was one of the volumes Morris was later to refer to in his 'Printer's Notes' of 1883.

May 1846: At the first annual meeting of the Devonshire Great Consolidated Copper Mining Co., William Morris Snr was appointed to the board. Each of the directors were to receive 100 guineas a year for their services. During its first year of operation 13,292 tons of ore were sold for £116,068. A dividend of £71 per share was made. Stockbrokers quoted prices of up to £850 to obtain a share in the business. At this time William Morris Snr's shares were worth approximately £230,000.

5 May 1846: Morris's sister, Alice, was born at Woodford Hall.

1847: A new edition of Paul Henri Mallet's *Northern Antiquities*, translated by Thomas Percy, was published.

8 September 1847: William Morris Snr died, aged 50, at Woodford. His elaborate tomb can be seen in Woodford churchyard bearing the family coat-of-arms.

15 September 1847: Sanderson & Co. suspended business with liabilities amounting to £2,606,569. In the event the company's assets were sufficient to stave off the crisis and the firm recommenced trading as Sanderson, Sandeman & Co.

October 1847: William Morris Snr's estate was valued at £60,000.

Autumn 1847: Morris left the Misses Arundale's school.

1848: A copper mine was named 'Wheal Emma' after Morris's mother. John Henry Newman's Oxford novel *Loss and Gain* was published, as was Marx and Engel's *Communist Manifesto*, Ruskin's *Seven Lamps of Architecture* and G. E. Street and Agnes Blencowe's *Ecclesiastical Embroidery*.

February 1848: Morris went, aged thirteen, to Marlborough College where he acquired the nickname 'Crab'. He was recorded in the school register as 'Morris, William, son of Mrs. Morris, Woodford Hall, Essex, aged 14 [*sic*]'. He spent his first week in the Upper 3rd Form before being transferred to the Fourth Form 1st Remove. His room was in 'A' House of which he became Captain two years later. His housemaster was the Revd Pitman. 'A' House has now been renamed Morris House and serves as a girls residential block. Morris later wrote that it was a 'very rough school. As far as my school instruction went, I think I may fairly say I learned next to nothing there, for indeed next to nothing was taught; but the place is in very beautiful country, thickly scattered over with prehistoric monuments, and I set myself eagerly to studying these and everything else that had any history in it, and so perhaps learnt a good deal' (*c.f.* 14 March 1891). A school friend recalled in the *Marlburian*: 'The Captain of our Dormitory ... made great friends with Morris – not that their tastes were at all similar, but that the former having a passion for listening to tales of romance ... found quite a repertoire of them in Morris.' Another contemporary, G. Ward, recalled Morris as 'a thickset strong looking boy with a high colour and black curly hair, good natured and kind, but with a fearful temper'. Schoolboy gossip was that he was 'Welsh and mad'.

September 1848: The Morris family moved to the Water House, in what is now Forest Road, Walthamstow, Essex. In later life W. Bliss recalled that when he was a child he and Morris used to chase the swans in the moat. (Since 1950 Water House has housed the William Morris Gallery.) The Pre-Raphaelite Brotherhood was founded at 83 Gower Street, London, by John Millais, William Holman Hunt and Dante Gabriel Rossetti. It was later extended to include James Collinson, F. G. Stephens, Thomas Woolmer and William Michael Rossetti. The Brotherhood's aim was to revolutionize the standard of English painting.

1 November 1848: Morris wrote to his eldest sister, Emma, from Marlborough College. This is his oldest surviving letter. At the time he was looking forward with enthusiasm to the Christmas holidays.

Christmas 1848: Morris returned to the Water House for the holidays.

1849: Jane Burden's eldest sister, Mary Anne, died of tuberculosis. Ruskin's *The Seven Lamps of Architecture* was published.

Early 1849: Philip Webb was apprenticed as an architect to John Billing of London Street, Reading.

17 March 1849: Morris was confirmed by the Bishop of Salisbury in Marlborough College Chapel: 'the Bishop himself is very tall and thin and he does not [look] very old though bald on the top of his head.'

18 March 1849: Morris received his first Holy Communion from the Bishop of Salisbury.

19/20 March 1849: Morris wrote to Emma describing his confirmation in the Church of England. He had just sold some baby rabbits to buy a fishing rod. Fishing was to be a passion throughout Morris's life.

9 April 1849: Morris visited Avebury and Silbury Hill 'where there is a Druidical circle and a Roman entrenchment both which encircle the town'.

10 April 1849: Morris paid a second visit to Avebury and visited the church: 'the tower was very pretty indeed it had four little spires on it of the decorated order and ... inside the porch a beautiful Norman doorway loaded with mouldings.'

13 April 1849: In a letter to Emma, Morris described singing the Marlborough anthem on Easter Sunday.

1850: The Pre-Raphaelite magazine *The Germ* appeared. It ran for four issues. Rossetti's *Ancilla Domini* was exhibited at the National Institution. Ford Madox Brown became headmaster of the North London School of Design.

14 May 1850: Morris's sister, Emma, married the Revd Joseph Oldham, curate of Downe, Kent, and later moved to Derbyshire. The couple had two sons (who died in childhood) and a daughter Emmie.

1851: The Great Exhibition was held at the Crystal Palace, Hyde Park, London. F. S. Ellis recalled (in a lecture he gave many years later): 'I remember him speaking many a time of the Exhibition of 1851, at which all the world was struck with unbounded admiration, and telling how, as a youth of 17, he declined to see anything more wonderful in it than that it was "wonderfully ugly," and, sitting himself down on a seat, steadily refused to go over the building with the rest of his family.' At the Exhibition Thomas Welch was awarded a medal for his Printed Table Clothes produced at Merton Abbey (later to be rented by Morris).

March 1851: The first volume of Ruskin's *Stones of Venice* was published.

21 March 1851: Morris's copy of *Quinti Horatti Flacci Opera* (*The Odes of Horace*) bears this date. Inside the cover he drew a pen and ink drawing of a one-legged man holding a placard on which is written 'W. Morris. His Horace'.

2 April 1851: Emery Walker was born at Paddington, London.

5 November 1851: A pupil 'rebellion' began at Marlborough College in which fireworks were let off around the school. The rebellion continued for many days. It is not certain what part, if any, Morris played in this episode.

Late December 1851: After taking his final term's exams, in which he came fifth out of nine, Morris left the 5th form of Marlborough College to study privately with the Revd F. B. Guy in Hoe Street, Walthamstow. Guy was an Assistant Master at the nearby Forest School.

20 April 1852: The Revd F. B. Guy was married. It is probable that Morris attended the wedding.

May 1852: G. E. Street, on the advice of J. H. Parker, moved his architects business from Wantage to Beaumont Street, Oxford.

2 June 1852: Morris sat his matriculation examination for Exeter College, Oxford. Edward Burne-Jones took his examination at the same time. Burne-Jones later recorded how Morris had finished his Horace paper early, folded it, and inscribed it firmly 'William Morris'.

3 July 1852: An article on Welch's Merton Abbey works appeared in *The Illustrated Exhibitor and Magazine of Art*.

Summer 1852: Morris returned to study with the Revd Guy in Walthamstow. He and Guy later spent six weeks in Alphington, Devon. While on holiday Morris visited St Mary's Church, Ottery, which he described as 'certainly one of the most remarkable & beautiful ones in England'.

October 1852: Richard Watson Dixon took up residence at Pembroke College, Oxford. Here he met William Fulford and Charles Faulkner and formed what became known as the 'Set'.

18 November 1852: Morris, to the annoyance of his sister Henrietta, refused to join the rest of the family in going to the Duke of Wellington's funeral. Instead he rode through Epping Forest to Waltham Abbey.

1853: Charlotte M. Yonge's *Heir of Redclyffe* was published, as was Napier's *A Manual of the Art of Dyeing* which was one of the volumes referred to in Morris's 'Printer's Notes' of 1883.

January 1853: Morris went to Exeter College, Oxford, to study theology. Here he made friends with Burne-Jones who also intended to pursue a career in the

Church. Mackail recorded in his *Notebooks* that Burne-Jones told him that: 'Before a week they were inseparable.' He added their 'expenses [were] about £40 a term or say £130 a year, incl. subscriptions to boat and cricket clubs'. Amongst the other things Burne-Jones recalled was that they 'went to St. Thomas's (the church near the station) for early service and plain song: this they practised once a week in [the] Music-room in Holywell College Library'.

1 May 1853: Burne-Jones wrote to Cormell Price: 'I have set my heart on our founding a Brotherhood. Learn Sir Galahad by heart. He is to be the patron of our Order. I have enlisted *one* in the project up here [Morris], heart and soul.' This is the first reference to Morris and Burne-Jones's plan to found a 'monastic brotherhood' and launch a 'crusade and Holy Warfare against the age'.

June 1853: The final volume of Ruskin's *Stones of Venice* was published. This included the chapter on 'The Nature of Gothic' which was to be a crucial influence on Morris's subsequent development.

Summer 1853: Morris spent the long vacation visiting a number of English churches. Burne-Jones also stayed for three days with the Morrises at the Water House at Walthamstow. According to Georgiana Burne-Jones writing in the *Memorials*: '[Morris's] mother welcomed Edward kindly, and seeing his affection for her son would willingly have told many stories of his childhood; but at this Morris chafed so much that the anecdotes had to be deferred.'

Michaelmas Term 1853: Morris moved into rooms at Exeter College in what was known as 'Hell's Quad' overlooking the Fellows garden and the Bodleian Library. Georgiana Burne-Jones noted in the *Memorials* that it was reached by passing 'under an archway called Purgatory from the great quadrangle'. Morris decorated the walls of his rooms with rubbings made from medieval brasses.

6 November 1853: Morris may have accompanied Burne-Jones to hear Pusey preach on 'Justification'.

Late November 1853: What was probably Morris's first poem, *The Dedication of the Temple*, was written. According to May Morris this poem was discovered in the early 1930s in a bureau which had once belonged to Morris's sister Emma. The title was the same as that for an Oxford prize poem, for which Morris was not eligible, which was due in on 1 December 1853.

1854: The Working Men's College was founded by the Christian Socialist, F. D. Maurice. Ruskin was one of the first to teach at the new institution.

Early 1854: Burne-Jones wrote of Morris: 'He is full of enthusiasm for things holy and beautiful and true, and, what is rarest, of the most exquisite perception and judgment in them. For myself, he has tinged my whole inner being with the beauty of his own, and I know not a single gift for which I owe such gratitude to Heaven as his friendship.'

16 May 1854: Philip Webb began work at G. E. Street's office at a salary of £1 a week.

Summer 1854: The publication of Ruskin's *Edinburgh Lectures* introduced Morris and Burne-Jones to the Pre-Raphaelites and the name of Dante Gabriel Rossetti. Georgiana Burne-Jones recorded her husband saying: 'I was working in my room when Morris ran in one morning bringing the newly published book with him: so everything was put aside until he read it all through to me.'

August 1854: Morris, with his sister Henrietta, visited Belgium and Northern France. On this journey Morris viewed pictures by Van Eyck and Memling and visited the Gothic churches at Amiens, Beauvais, Chartres and Rouen. Later he was to write: 'Many times I think of the first time I ever went abroad, and to Rouen, and what a wonder of glory that was to me when I first came upon the front of the Cathedral rising above the flower-market.' He also went to the Musée Cluny, the Tuilleries and the Louvre in Paris.

18 September 1854: Cormell Price's sister recorded in her *Diary*: 'Jones came to tea. He is the most clever and the nicest fellow I ever knew. He says he thinks Fulford will be a "star" and he is sure Morris will be.'

October 1854: The start of the winter term at Oxford was delayed for a week due to the cholera epidemic that was sweeping the country. The delay annoyed Burne-Jones who wrote to Cormell Price saying how keen he was to be back 'with Morris and his glorious little company of martyrs'. At the beginning of the new term Morris moved into rooms adjoining those of Burne-Jones at Old Buildings, overlooking Broad Street, Oxford. In some 'Notes' quoted by Georgiana in the *Memorials*, Burne-Jones recalled that they were 'Tumbly old buildings, gable-roofed and pebble-dashed, little dark passages led from the staircase to the sitting rooms'. While at Old Buildings Morris wrote his poem *The Willow and the Red Cliff* (often cited as his first poem, *c.f.* entry for December 1853). Burne-Jones nicknamed him 'Topsy' after the little slave-girl – who also had unruly curly hair – in Harriet Beecher Stowe's *Uncle Tom's Cabin*. This nickname was often shortened to 'Top' by his friends.

16 October 1854: Burne-Jones wrote to Cormell Price that 'the Monastery ... stands a fairer chance than ever of being founded; I know that it will some day'.

1855: Morris wrote a number of poems including *Blanche*. Tennyson's *Maud* was published as were Browning's *Men and Women* and G. E. Street's *The Architecture of North Italy*.

24 March 1855: On reaching the age of twenty-one Morris inherited thirteen Devon Great Consol shares. These gave him an income of £741 in 1855 and £715 in 1856.

Good Friday 1855: Morris wrote his poem *Kisses* at the Water House, Walthamstow. He dedicated it to Cormell Price.

April 1855: Morris spent some time reading Shelley's poetry. He greatly admired *The Skylark*. He also went brass rubbing in Stoke D'Abernon in Surrey and at Rochester, Kent.

3 April 1855: Morris wrote to Cormell Price from the Water House, Walthamstow, including the text of his poem *Kisses*.

May 1855: Morris and Burne-Jones went to see the Pre-Raphaelite paintings in the Windus Collection. These included Ford Madox Brown's *The Last of England*. Cormell Price recorded that 'Our Monastery will come to nought, I'm afraid; Smith has changed his views to extreme latitudinarianism, Morris has become questionable on doctrinal points, and Ted is too Catholic to be ordained. He and Morris diverge more and more in views though not in friendship.'

18 May 1855: Philip Webb undertook a survey of Holywell Church.

24 May 1855: Cormell Price and Edward Burne-Jones went to London for the short vacation to visit the Royal Academy Annual Exhibition.

June 1855: Morris visited the Royal Academy Exhibition. Here he viewed paintings by Dyce, Leighton, Madox Brown and Millais. It was at this exhibition that he was introduced to Georgiana Macdonald (later Mrs Burne-Jones) by Wilfred L. Heeley as he was viewing Millais picture *The Rescue*. Georgiana Burne-Jones recalled: 'He was very handsome, of an unusual type – the statues of medieval kings often remind me of him – and at that time he wore no moustache, so that the drawing of his mouth, which was his most expressive feature, could be clearly seen. His eyes always seemed to me to take in rather than to give out. His hair waved and curled triumphantly.'

Early July 1855: Morris and Burne-Jones spent four or five days in Cambridge where they discussed plans for the *Oxford and Cambridge Magazine*. Morris was to be proprietor and editor. One of the provisional titles for the paper was the *Brotherhood*. Morris described Cambridge as 'rather a hole of a place'. Burne-Jones recalled that on their first evening in Cambridge they visited St Sepulchre's Church.

18 July 1855: Morris, Burne-Jones and Fulford stayed in an hotel in London prior to embarking on what was originally intended to be a walking tour of Normandy. Cormell Price had intended to accompany them but had to withdraw at the last moment.

19 July 1855: Morris, Burne-Jones and Fulford took the ferry from Folkestone to Boulogne. They arrived in Abbeville at 10.30 pm and walked to the Hotel 'La Tête du Boeuf'.

20 July 1855: The party were up before breakfast sightseeing in Abbeville. They then travelled to Amiens where they visited the cathedral. Fulford wrote 'Morris surveyed it with calm joy and Jones was speechless with admiration. It did not awe me until it got quite dark, for we stayed till after nine, but it was so solemn, so human and divine in its beauty, that love cast out fear.' Morris fell lame at Amiens 'filling the streets', according to Burne-Jones, 'with imprecations on all bootmakers'. He purchased a pair of 'gay carpet slippers' to see if these would make walking easier. The friends stayed the night in Amiens.

21 July 1855: The travellers took the train to Clermont and then walked the seventeen miles to Beauvais. Morris found the carpet slippers did nothing to help his sore feet.

22 July 1855: The party spent the day in Beauvais where Morris attended High Mass at the cathedral. They then took the train to Paris where they arrived at 11.30 pm. Morris, aware of the restoration work being undertaken at Notre Dame, had urged the party to travel straight to Chartres but he was overruled as Burne-Jones wanted to visit the Louvre.

23 July 1855: Morris and his companions visited the Church of St Chappelle, then the Beaux Arts section at the Exposition Universelle in Paris which included Pre-Raphaelite paintings by Hunt, Millais and Collins. Fulford recorded they spent sixteen hours sightseeing around the city. In the evening, at Burne-Jones's instigation, the party went to the opera and heard Madame Alboni in Meyerbeer's *Le Prophete*. Fulford described Morris being 'a good deal bored by the experience'.

24 July 1855: The party spent the day in Paris where they visited the Louvre. According to Georgiana Burne-Jones 'Morris made Edward shut his eyes and so led him up to Angelico's picture of "The Coronation of the Virgin" before he allowed him to look'.

25 July 1855: In the evening Morris and his companions left Paris for Chartres. They arrived at 10.30 pm.

26 July 1855: The friends spent the day sightseeing in Chartres.

27 July 1855: The party spent the day travelling from Chartres to Rouen. On the way they visited the church at Dreux. They stayed the night at the Hotel de France.

28 July 1855: Morris and his friends visited various churches in Rouen and heard vespers at Notre Dame. After dinner they climbed Mont St Catherine.

29–31 July 1855: The party spent these days in Rouen. At some point Morris purchased the Tauchnitz edition of Thackeray's novel *The Newcomes*.

1 August 1855: The party left Rouen on foot and walked the twenty-five miles to Caudebec-en-Caux. Morris suffered greatly with his shoes.

2 August 1855: The party travelled by bus from Caudebec to Yvetot and then by train to Le Havre where they spent the night. According to Burne-Jones 'it was while walking on the quay at Havre at night that we resolved definitely that we would begin a life of art, and put off our decision no longer – he should be an architect and I a painter'.

3 August 1855: The party left Le Havre by steamer for Caen where they visited the church of St Etienne.

4 August 1855: In the afternoon Morris and his friends caught the bus from Caen to Bayeux. In the evening they visited the cathedral.

5 August 1855: The party viewed the Bayeux Tapestry in the Town Hall.

6 August 1855: The friends left Bayeux for St Lô and then Coutances where they visited the cathedral and stayed the night at the Hotel de France.

7 August 1855: The day was spent sightseeing in Coutances.

8 August 1855: The party travelled by bus to Avranches. Here Morris had his first sight of Mont St Michel.

9 August 1855: The friends visited Mont St Michel and then returned to Avranches.

10 August 1855: The day was spent sightseeing in Avranches.

11 August 1855: The party left Avranches in the evening and travelled to Granville.

12 August 1855: The friends took the 11 am boat from Granville to Jersey.

13 August 1855: Morris and his companions reached Southampton.

22 August 1855: By this time Morris was staying in Birmingham with Burne-Jones. On this date they were visited by Fulford, Cormell Price and Heeley. Morris was introduced to Fanny Price, Cormell's sister. Margaret Price, Cormell's younger sister, wrote in her *Diary* that 'F[anny] says Morris is very handsome.'

23 August 1855: Morris, Burne-Jones and Fulford had tea and supper at Cormell Price's home. Margaret Price wrote: 'Morris *is* very handsome.'

26 August 1855: Cormell Price recorded in his *Diary* that he visited Burne-Jones and found Morris there 'wild and jolly as ever'. They had 'much talk about *Maud*'.

27 August 1855: Morris, Price and Burne-Jones visited Dudley Castle. Later they had tea and supper at Cormell Price's home where Morris read poetry out loud. Margaret Price recorded that he was 'a queer reader'.

August/September 1855: Morris and Burne-Jones visited Cornish's bookshop in New Street, Birmingham, where Morris purchased Southey's 1817 edition of Malory's *Morte d'Arthur*. Mackail records in his *Notebooks* that Burne-Jones 'had read great parts of it there [in the shop] but had not money to buy it. M. came to stay with him in a vacation [and] bought it.'

2 September 1855: Burne-Jones and Morris had tea and supper at Cormell Price's home. Margaret Price wrote: 'Morris got so excited once that he punched his own head and threw his arms about frantically.'

7 September 1855: Morris, Burne-Jones, Fulford and Cormell Price had a discussion at the latter's house about architecture, the organization of labour and the proposed *Oxford and Cambridge Magazine*. R. W. Dixon wrote to Cormell Price informing him that Morris – the 'little brick' – had just sent him a copy of Ruskin's *Seven Lamps of Architecture*.

9 September 1855: Morris, Burne-Jones and Cormell Price discussed Aytoun's unsympathetic review of Tennyson's *Maud* which had appeared in *Blackwood's Magazine*.

10 September 1855: Morris visited Malvern – possibly to visit some relatives of his mother – which he described as 'a very splendid place, but very much spoiled by being made into a kind of tea gardens for idle people'. While in Malvern he heard the abbey bells ring to mark the fall of Sebastopol which had occurred the previous day.

11 September 1855: Morris travelled to Clay Cross to stay with his sister Emma and her husband the Revd Joseph Oldham. He was greatly amused that the local people had decorated Clay Cross with Russian flags under the delusion they were French!

28 September 1855: Cormell Price noted in his *Diary* that he had written to Morris 'abusing him roundly for thinking of leaving Oxford [University]'. Morris replied: 'Thank you very much for taking so much interest in me, but make your mind easy about my coming back next term. I am certainly coming back, though I should not have done so if it had not been for my Mother.'

October 1855: In a long letter to his cousin Maria, Burne-Jones claimed that the study of French and German philosophy had 'shivered' Morris's belief in religion and 'palsied' his own.

2 October 1855: Morris began to prepare for his Final Schools exams by reading 'for six hours a day at Livy, Ethics, &c.'. He was coached by Fulford who at the time was hesitating about taking holy orders.

6 October 1855: Morris wrote to Cormell Price once again expressing doubts about taking his university degree as he hoped to take up the study of architecture under G. E. Street.

Autumn 1855: Morris passed his Final Schools exam at Oxford University and took his pass degree. After taking his degree he grew a moustache and long hair.

11 November 1855: Morris wrote to his mother informing her he intended to become an architect. It is apparent from this letter that he had told her some weeks before that he had abandoned the idea of taking holy orders.

17 November 1855: Morris, Cormell Price and Dixon considered the title and other details about the proposed *Oxford and Cambridge Magazine*. They resolved that the magazine should be a 72-page monthly.

22 November 1855: Morris and Cormell Price worked on the prospectus for the *Oxford and Cambridge Magazine* at Pembroke College, Oxford.

1856: Morris took up carving, clay-modelling, illuminating and wood-engraving. Georgiana Burne-Jones recalled 'the long, folded white evening tie which he nailed in loops against his bedroom wall in order to hold his tools'.

1 January 1856: The first number of the *Oxford and Cambridge Magazine* appeared under Morris's editorship. 750 copies were printed by Bell & Daldy of Fleet Street and sold for 1s. They were sent out in green printed wrappers with the contents printed in double columns. The magazine proved so successful that a further 250 copies were later printed. Morris contributed 'The Story of the Unknown Church' and a poem called 'Winter Weather'.

9 January 1856: Margaret Price recorded in her diary that 'Morris does not like being Editor of the O. & C. Magazine'. At around the same time Burne-Jones wrote to Cormell Price saying that if Morris gave up the editorship of the magazine it would 'be a good thing for all of us and a great relief for Topsy'. Shortly after this Morris paid William Fulford £100 to take over as editor.

21 January 1856: Morris was articled to G. E. Street whose office was then in Beaumont Street, Oxford. He paid £5 as a registration fee. Here he met Philip Webb who was Street's senior assistant. Philip Webb later described Morris as 'a slim boy like a wonderful bird just out of his shell'. Morris was to say of Street 'though not an ill-tempered man, he dearly loved a row'. Morris took lodgings which were, according to Philip Webb, 'opposite the Martyr's Memorial, next but one ... to the Randolph Hotel'. According to Webb, Morris was occupied for much of the time during his apprenticeship 'in copying a drawing of the doorway of St. Augustine's Church, Canterbury'. Webb wrote: 'He suffered much tribulation in delineating the many arch mouldings, "and at last the compass points nearly bored a hole through the drawing-board".'

23 January 1856: Cormell Price wrote mysteriously to his father: 'I shall ignore the existence of a female Topsy for the time.'

February 1856: Morris essay on 'The Churches of North France: Shadows of Amiens' appeared in the second number of the *Oxford and Cambridge Magazine* along with a tale called 'The Two Partings'. The latter was attributed to Morris by Buxton Forman.

9 February 1856: Burne-Jones went to stay in Oxford for a few days. The evening he arrived the Oxford set gathered in Morris's rooms where, according to Cormell Price's *Diary*, there was a 'delightful Babel'.

10 February 1856: In the morning Morris and Burne-Jones walked to Summertown where they called on MacLaren.

14 February 1856: Burne-Jones left Oxford for Birmingham by train in the evening. Cormell Price saw him off.

25/26 February 1856: According to Lethaby, Morris and Webb went to sketch churches in Bloxham, King's Sutton, and Adderbury. Webb was amazed by Morris's inability to go without food.

March 1856: Morris contributed 'A Dream' and a review of Browning's *Men and Women* to the third number of the *Oxford and Cambridge Magazine*. Mackail notes a letter from Fulford to Cormell Price which refers to Morris's review of Browning's poems: 'I didn't like Topsy's Review at all ... you men at Oxford must not let your love of Morris carry you away to admire such of his writings as don't deserve admiration.'

6 March 1856: Rossetti recorded in a letter to William Allingham that he had recently been sent a copy of the *Oxford and Cambridge Magazine*. He was flattered by a notice Burne-Jones had given him in his 'Essay on *The Newcomes*'. Rossetti's went on to say that Burne-Jones 'was in London the other day, and whom (being known to some of the Working Men's Coll[ege] council) I have now met; – one of the nicest young fellows in – *Dreamland*'. The same letter also praised Morris's story 'A Dream': 'which really is remarkable, I think, in colour.' There is some confusion about when Burne-Jones actually met Rossetti. The account in the *Memorials* suggests that he was introduced to Frederick James Furnivall and Vernon Lushington at an open evening at the Working Men's College at Red Lion Square, Holborn. Here Rossetti was pointed out to him. Furnivall then invited him to a party at Vernon Lushington's rooms where he was introduced to Rossetti. The latter in turn invited him to view his studio, at Chatham Place, near Blackfriars Bridge, the following day. Burne-Jones recalled Rossetti 'asked much about Morris, one or two of whose poems he knew already, and I think that was our principal subject of talk, for he seemed much interested about him'. Rossetti's letter would suggest that these events took place in late February or early March 1856.

Easter 1856: Burne-Jones began painting in London under Rossetti's guidance.

April 1856: Morris contributed 'Frank's Sealed Letter' to the fourth number of the *Oxford and Cambridge Magazine*.

May 1856: Morris contributed 'A Night in a Cathedral' and a poem 'Riding Together' to the fifth number of the *Oxford and Cambridge Magazine*. Accompanied by Burne-Jones and Cormell Price he visited the Royal Academy Exhibition in London. Here they viewed pictures by Millais, Holman Hunt and Wallis. While at the exhibition Morris greatly admired Arthur Hughes's painting *April Love*.

17 May 1856: Morris wrote to Burne-Jones from Oxford asking him to 'nobble that picture called "April Love," as soon as possible lest anybody else should buy it'.

18 May 1856: Burne-Jones moved into new lodgings at 13 Sloane Terrace, Sloane Street, Chelsea. These lodgings were opposite the chapel where his future wife's father was minister.

20 May 1856: Burne-Jones purchased *April Love* for Morris for £30. Arthur Hughes recalled, near the end of his life, Burne-Jones arriving in his studio with Morris's cheque: 'My chief feeling then was surprise at an Oxford student buying pictures.' The painting is now in the Tate Gallery.

June 1856: Morris is supposed, according to Buxton Forman, to have contributed the article entitled 'Ruskin and the Quarterly' which appeared in the sixth number of the *Oxford and Cambridge Magazine*. It is clear from a letter that Rossetti wrote to John Lucas Tupper that he had still not met Morris.

9 June 1856: Burne-Jones and Georgiana Macdonald became engaged. Morris later presented Georgiana with a copy of Turner's *Rivers of France* as an engagement present. The latter wrote in the *Memorials*: 'I thanked him and he wrote my name in it, but we were not much the nearer for this meeting. The poet who wrote the poem of Guendolen seemed one person and the man

I saw before me another – my eyes were helden that I could not yet see.'

10 June 1856: Burne-Jones presented Georgiana with all the books he possessed written by Ruskin. Charles Faulkner wrote to his mother informing her that he had obtained a Fellowship at University College.

July 1856: Rossetti urged Morris to 'paint'. In a letter to Cormell Price, Morris wrote: 'he says I shall be able; now as he is a very great man, and speaks with authority and not as the scribes, I *must* try.' In the same letter he went on to say: 'I can't enter into politico-social subjects with any interest, for on the whole I see that things are in a muddle, and I have no power of vocation to set them right in ever so little a degree. My work is the embodiment of dreams in one form or another....' Morris contributed the poem 'Hands' and the first part of the story 'Gertha's Lovers' to the seventh number of the *Oxford and Cambridge Magazine*. It is also possible he attended the play *Medea, or the Best of Mothers, with a Brute of a Husband* which was produced at the Olympic starring the burlesque actor Frederick Robson. Morris was later to utilize this play in the plot of his abortive novel.

13 July 1856: Burne Jones wrote to Cormell Price that 'Topsy is here ... the dear little fellow is drawing away in the next room.... [He] wants me to go to Walthamstow on Tuesday to paint some trees on the island behind the house.'

29 July 1856[?]: A self-portrait in pencil by Morris bears the date '29th July'. The year of composition is conjectural. A second self-portrait also probably dates from around this time. Both portraits are now at the V & A.

31 July 1856: Hannah Macdonald – Georgiana's mother – recorded in her *Diary* that Morris had come to tea and 'sat with Georgie on the balcony till 11 o'clock' (*c.f.* 9 June 1856).

August 1856: Morris contributed the second part of 'Gertha's Lovers', 'Death the Avenger and Death the Friend' and 'Svend and His Brethren' to the eighth number of the *Oxford and Cambridge Magazine*.

Mid-August 1856: Morris moved with Street to London where the latter had taken offices at 33 Montagu Place, Russell Square. While in London he and Burne-Jones first took furnished lodgings at 1 Upper Gordon Street. These lodgings were, according to Burne-Jones, decorated by Morris 'with brasses of old knights and drawings of Albert Dürer'.

23 August 1856: Rossetti took Morris to visit Ford Madox Brown at 13 Fortess Terrace, Kentish Town. The following day Ford Madox Brown recorded in his *Diary*: 'Yesterday Rossetti brought his ardent admirer Morris of Oxford, who bought my little hay field for 40 gns.' Ford Madox Brown got the picture back from Morris in 1860 as payment for work done at the Red House.

September 1856: Morris contributed 'Lindenborg Pool', the first part of 'The Hollow Land' and the poem 'The Chapel in Lyonesse' to the ninth number of the *Oxford and Cambridge Magazine*.

Autumn 1856: G. E. Street, after completing his competition drawings for Lille Cathedral, set out with Morris on a tour of the Low Countries. The announcement for the competition had been made in 1855. The chief condition was that the building should be in the French Gothic style. Street's design for the cathedral included two spires with coloured bands. Street wrote: 'We have had about three hours at the Exhibition. We are agreed naturally that I ought to have place No. 1.... I really think I shall have one of the prizes. Morris says the first.' In the event Street came second in the competition, the prize going to Clutton & Burges.

End of Long Vacation 1856: Morris, along with Burne-Jones, Fulford, Faulkner and Vernon Lushington attended Heeley's wedding in Birmingham. During this visit Margaret Price wrote in her *Diary*: 'Fulford was in the most noisy, quizzical humour imaginable, no one could get a word in edgeways for him, and whenever Topsy wanted to say anything he sprang into the middle of the room and flourished his fists till Fulford was silenced.'

October 1856: Morris contributed the second part of 'The Hollow Land' and the poem 'Pray But One Prayer For Me' to the tenth number of the *Oxford and Cambridge Magazine*.

25 October 1856: Cormell Price noted in his *Diary*: 'Ted and Topsy up. To Maclaren's; singlestick with Top. With them before and after hall at Dixon's – then on to Adams' who gave us music. What a difference their coming makes!'

November 1856: Morris and Burne-Jones moved to three unfurnished rooms on the first floor of 17 Red Lion Square. Morris occupied the small room at the rear of the building. Rossetti and Deverell had occupied the same rooms in the days of the Pre-Raphaelite Brotherhood. At the time that Morris and Burne-Jones took the rooms the ground floor of the house was occupied by a French family of feather-dressers called the Fauconniers. Morris and Burne-Jones later designed – and had made – their own furniture for their lodgings. This included Morris's only surviving design for a round table (now to be seen in the Cheltenham Museum). Shortly after they moved in Rossetti wrote: 'Morris is rather doing the magnificent there, and is having some intensely medieval furniture made – tables and chairs like incubi and succubi. He and I have painted the back of a chair with figures and inscriptions in gules and vert and azure, and we are all three going to cover a cabinet with pictures.' Burne-Jones wrote (in November): 'Topsy has had some furniture (chairs and table) made after his own design; they are as beautiful as medieval work, and when we have painted designs of knights and ladies upon them they will be perfect marvels.'

December 1856: Morris's story 'Golden Wings' appeared in the twelfth – and final – number of the *Oxford and Cambridge Magazine*. The twelve issues of the magazine were later bound together and sold as a volume by Bell & Daldy. Some of these contain two photographs from Woolner's medallions of Tennyson and Carlyle. These had been offered to subscribers by the publishers of the magazine.

12 December 1856: Morris and Burne-Jones dined with Ruskin at Denmark Hill.

18 December 1856: Rossetti wrote to William Allingham describing Morris as 'one of the finest little fellows alive – with a touch of the incoherent, but a real man…. In all illumination and work of that kind he is quite unrivalled by anything modern that I know.'

End of 1856: Encouraged by Rossetti, Morris left Street's office and abandoned his career in architecture. Mackail, in his *Notebooks*, recalled Burne-Jones saying that Morris 'began painting directly on leaving Street'.

1857: During the year Morris experimented with sculpture, painting, stained-glass design and embroidery. He finished the 'Bird and Tree' embroidered pattern and the 'If I Can' embroidered wall-hanging worked in wool on linen. The latter is now at Kelmscott Manor. He also produced a great deal of poetry which included an incomplete cycle of Troy poems. These were first published in the *Collected Works* in 1915.

February 1857: In a letter to William Bell Scott, Rossetti described Morris and Burne-Jones as 'now very intimate friends of mine'.

18 February 1857: Morris and Burne-Jones contributed £10 to a subscription fund set up for the artist Thomas Seddon who had died a few months earlier.

3 April 1857: A two-volume edition of Froissart's *Chronicles* – edited by Thomas Johnes (London, Bohn, 1852) – that Morris dedicated to Louisa Macdonald bears this date.

Spring 1857: Burne-Jones painted a wardrobe for 17 Red Lion Square with scenes from Chaucer's *The Prioress's Tale*.

Spring/Summer 1857: Morris saw Keen at the Princess Theatre in Shakespeare's *Richard II*.

June 1857: Rossetti reported that Morris was painting 'Recognition of Tristram by his Dog' (*Tristram and Iseult*). He went on to add: 'It is being done all from nature of course, and I believe will turn out capitally.' This scene is from *Morte d'Arthur* and is described elsewhere as 'Sir Tristram after his illness in the

Garden of King Marko's Palace recognised by the Dog he had given Iseult'.

9 June 1857: Georgiana Burne-Jones recalled in the *Memorials* that she and her fiancé went to see 'The Light of the World' at Mr Combe's house before paying a short visit to the MacLarens. They found 'Morris painting a tree in MacLaren's beautiful garden with such energy that it was long before the grass grew again on the spot where his chair had stood'.

Late June/Early July 1857: Morris went with Rossetti to see Benjamin Woodward in Oxford. Woodward had been chosen to design the University Museum and the Union Debating Hall. Rossetti offered to decorate the apsed upper walls and roof of the Union Debating Hall. The Union Building Committee accepted this offer. Amongst those to take part in the project were Burne-Jones, Arthur Hughes, Spencer Stanhope, Val Prinsep and Hungerford Pollen. Morris subject was 'How Sir Polomydes loved La Belle Iseult with exceeding great love out of measure and how she loved him not again but rather Sir Tristram'. It was generally considered to have been a failure. Morris later described it as 'being extremely ludicrous in many ways'.

July 1857: Morris, Rossetti and Burne-Jones took rooms at 87 High Street, opposite Queen's College, Oxford.

Mid-August 1857: In the *Memorials* Georgiana Burne-Jones wrote that 'the work at the Union was well begun, and the painters then hoped that it would be finished in about six weeks – that is, by the end of the Long Vacation – but it lasted until the spring of the following year'.

September 1857: Morris stayed with Dixon in Manchester and visited the Art Treasures Exhibition. At this Exhibition Morris refused to view the Old Masters, preferring to enjoy the fine collection of carved ivories. While staying at Dixon's he painted a watercolour 'The Soltan's Daughter in the Palace of Glass' (now lost). He also wrote the poem 'Praise of My Lady' which was to appear in *The Defence of Guenevere & Other Poems*.

September/October 1857: Morris was introduced to Jane Burden. There are a number of versions of how this came about. The most popular is that Rossetti and Burne-Jones met Jane and her sister at the theatre. Mackail's account in his *Notebooks* seems to confirm this version: 'DGR and EBJ [met her] at [the] theatre (behind Randolph['s Hotel]) late in [the] summer of [1857]; she and her sister sitting just behind them. After the theatre they followed her and R. asked her to come and sit: she probably did not know what he meant; consented to come the next day, but didn't. EBJ met her again in the street a few days later and spoke with her asking why she hadn't come. Next day she came.' An alternative version of the meeting, given by Georgiana Burne-Jones in the *Memorials*, is that Morris saw Jane in a box above him at the theatre when in the company of Rossetti, Burne-Jones and Hughes.

Morris was later to court her by reading passages from Dickens's *Barnaby Rudge*. Around the same time Morris, Burne-Jones and Rossetti moved to new lodgings in George Street. It was in the first floor sitting-room of these lodgings in early October that Rossetti was to make his first pencil drawing of Jane which is now in the possession of the Society of Antiquaries.

17 October 1857: Cormell Price had breakfast with Morris, Rossetti, Hughes, Prinsep, Burne-Jones and Coventry Patmore at 'Johnson's' in George Street. The friends then visited the Oxford Union frescos.

18 October 1857: Cormell Price wrote in his *Diary*: 'To Rossetti's... Prinsep there; six feet one, 15 stone, not fat, well-built, hair like fine wire, short, curly and seamless – aged only 19. Stood for Top for two hours as a dalmatic.'

24 October 1857: Cormell Price assisted Morris on the Oxford Union frescos by painting black lines on the Union roof. In the *Memorials* Georgiana Burne-Jones quoted her husband as saying: 'Morris ... set to work upon the roof, making in a day a design for it which was a wonder to us for its originality and fitness, for he had never before designed anything of the kind, nor, I suppose, seen any ancient work to guide him.'

25 October 1857: Morris submitted his first volume of poetry – *The Defence of Guenevere & Other Poems* – to the publisher, Alexander Macmillan.

30 October 1857: During the evening Morris entertained Rossetti, Burne-Jones, Cormell Price, Hughes, Swan, Faulkner, Bowen, Bennet, Munro, Hill, Prinsep and Stanhope by reading 'King Arthur's Tomb' and 'Lancelot and Guenevere'.

31 October 1857: Morris worked on the Oxford Union frescos with Cormell Price. In the evening he and Cormell Price played whist at George Street with Rossetti, Faulkner and Ford Madox Brown. Rossetti is supposed to have said of Morris that he 'had the greatest capacity for producing and annexing dirt of any man he ever met with'.

Winter 1857: Morris presented Louisa Macdonald with an illuminated manuscript on vellum of one of *Grimm's Fairytales*.

1 November 1857: Morris met Swinburne for the first time at Hill's house in Oxford. Burne-Jones, Swan, Faulkner and Hatch were also present.

7 November 1857: Morris wrote again to Macmillan this time offering to pay for the publication of *The Defence of Guenevere & Other Poems*.

14 November 1857: Cormell Price recorded in his *Diary* that Rossetti had left Oxford due to Lizzie Siddal falling ill. According to Georgiana Burne-Jones in the *Memorials* he never returned to complete his work.

21 November 1857: Morris wrote to Macmillan about the loss of his manuscript

'Arthur's Tomb'.

10 December 1857: Cormell Price wrote to his father: 'Topsy raves and swares [*sic*] like or more than any Oxford bargee about a "stunner" he has seen.'

26 December 1857: An article by Coventry Patmore in the *Saturday Review* described the Oxford Union Building's frescos as 'so brilliant as to make the walls look like the margin of an illuminated manuscript'.

1858: Morris's *Sir Galahad a Christmas Mystery* – a foolscap 8vo. booklet – was published by Bell & Daldy of 186 Fleet Street. It was possibly in this year that Morris made his first visit to Worcester since being taken there as a baby. In 1888 he wrote to Jenny: 'as to Worcester I have only been there once … when I went to see my Aunts 30 years ago. I … remember Prince Arthur's Chantry and the tombs and also the general look of the Church. The town I don't remember except as a mass of red brick broken by a few half-timber houses.'

January 1858: Ford Madox Brown recorded in his *Diary*: 'Jones is going to cut Topsy, he says his over bearing temper is becoming quite insupportable as well as his conceit.' Rossetti recorded in a letter to Ford Madox Brown that Plint had purchased Morris's painting *Tristram and Iseult* for 75 guineas (*c.f.* 23 April 1861). The painting was later exhibited at the New Gallery, London, in January 1898.

27 January 1858: Ford Madox Brown recorded in his *Diary* that he went to Red Lion Square with a dress bought by his wife on Burne-Jones's instruction for 'a poor miserable girl of 17 he had met in the street at 2 a.m. The coldest night this winter, scarce any clothes and starving, in *spite of prostitution*, after only 5 weeks of London life.'

February 1858: Morris persuaded Jane to marry him. Jane prepared herself for her new role by learning the piano. Rossetti's cartoon of 'Morris presenting Miss Burden with a Ring' could refer to this although the ring is being placed on her right hand. Bell & Daldy published *The Defence of Guenevere & Other Poems* at Morris's expense. The volume was dedicated 'To My Friend, Dante Gabriel Rossetti, Painter'. It contained thirty poems. At the time only 250 out of the original 500 copies were sold. F. S. Ellis recorded that he purchased the copies of the book that remained unsold in 1865 'amounting, if I remember rightly, to some thirty or forty'. Elsewhere, however, it has been stated that Bell & Daldy still had copies available as late as 1871. An unsigned notice relating to *The Defence of Guenevere & Other Poems* appeared in the *Spectator* this month (p. 238). The reviewer wrote: 'To our taste, the style is as bad as bad can be. Mr. Morris imitates little save faults.' This was the first of a series of unfavourable reviews which led Morris to destroy many of the early poems he omitted from the volume.

17 February 1858: Swinburne wrote of how glad he was to hear 'of Morris having that wonderful and most perfect stunner of his to – look at or speak to. The idea of his marrying her is insane. To kiss her feet is the utmost man should dream of doing.' He also wrote: 'Morris's book is really out. Reading it, I would fain be worthy to sit down at his feet.'

March 1858: No further work was done on the Oxford Union Building's frescos. A more positive review of *The Defence of Guenevere & Other Poems* – possibly by Richard Garnett – appeared in the *Literary Gazette* (pp. 226–7). Burne-Jones was taken ill and left Red Lion Square for a year to stay with Mrs Prinsep.

29 March 1858: Ruskin wrote to the Brownings about *The Defence of Guenevere & Other Poems*: 'I've seen his poems, just out, about old chivalry, and they are most noble – very, very great indeed – in their own peculiar way.'

April 1858: An unsigned review of *The Defence of Guenevere & Other Poems* appeared in the *Tablet* (p. 266).

3 April 1858: An unsigned review of *The Defence of Guenevere & Other Poems* – apparently by H. F. Chorley – appeared in the *Athenaeum* (pp. 427–8). Chorley wrote: 'we must call attention to [this] ... book of Pre-Raphaelite minstrelsy as to a curiosity which shows how far affectation may mislead an earnest man towards the fog-land of Art.'

17 April 1858: Edwin Hatch recorded in his *Diary* that he had just arrived in Oxford: 'Called on Swinburne, talked in his window seat in the sunset, and then went to Morris.'

26 April 1858: Swinburne, in a letter to Edwin Hatch, claimed that since the favourable review of *The Defence of Guevenere* in the *Tablet* the *Oxford County Chronicle* had been full of humorous references requesting information relating to Morris's whereabouts. According to Swinburne the town-crier was also going to proclaim the loss the next day: 'Lost, stolen, or strayed, an eminent artist and promising literateur ... Had on when he was last seen the clothes of another gentleman, much worn, of which he had possessed himself in a fit of moral – and physical – abstraction. Linen (questionable) marked W. M. Swears awfully, and walks with a rolling gait, as if partially intoxicated.'

Spring/Summer 1858: The inaugural meeting of the Hogarth Club, a social club for artists and writers, was held at Morris and Burne-Jones's lodgings in Red Lion Square. William Rossetti wrote: 'the original Hogarth Club was so named on the ground that Hogarth was the first great figure in British art, and still remains one of the greatest. Madox Brown (not to mention other projectors of the Club) entertained this view very strongly, and I think it probable that *he* was the proposer of the name.' The Club's headquarters were originally at 178 Piccadilly but it later moved to 6 Waterloo Place, London. It was dissolved in April 1861.

4 May 1858: Boyce wrote in his *Diary*: 'Meeting of the (just formed) Hogarth Club at Jones and Morris's rooms. In the room some interesting drawings, tapestries and furniture, the latter gorgeously painted in subjects by Jones and Morris and Gabriel Rossetti.'

27 May 1858: Philip Webb left G. E. Street's office.

June 1858: William Bell Scott, who visited the Oxford Union Building, found the frescos already much deteriorated. All that could be seen of Morris's picture was Tristram's head over a row of sunflowers.

2 June 1858: Boyce wrote in his *Diary* that he had visited Rossetti in London: 'He made one or two rough sketches while talking, one of a "Stunner" at Oxford which he tore into fragments, but which I recovered from the fire grate.'

17 August 1858: Morris set off to France with Faulkner and Webb.

18 August 1858: Morris, Faulkner and Webb arrived in Amiens. When visiting the tower of the cathedral a shower of sovereigns fell from Morris satchel and were only prevented from disappearing down the mouth of a gargoyle by Webb's boot. Morris then attempted to make a drawing of the choir but this was ruined when he knocked a bottle of ink over his sketch.

20 August 1858: The party visited Beauvais (where Webb drew the transept of St Etienne) and Creil.

21 August 1858: Morris, Faulkner and Webb arrived in Paris where they lodged at Meurice's. Webb recalled rats running around in the gutters. They spent some time sketching at Notre Dame where they drew some of the capitals and the panels of the west porch. During the next few days they rowed and sailed down the Seine in a boat sent over from Oxford. The boat arrived with a large hole in the bottom which had to be repaired. On discovering the damage, according to Webb, Morris was 'transported' and rasped the skin off his hand on the parapet of the river wall in his excitement. The local population jeered as the party set off from the Quai du Louvre with their luggage which consisted of three carpet bags and half-a-dozen bottles of wine. They took Murray's *Guide to France* (1857) which every five miles they marked with the distances from Paris to the sea. At Duclair they encountered an eight-foot high river 'bore'. It engulfed them as they were trying to row to the shore and deposited them high and dry on the bank! It was during this river trip that Morris and Webb began to discuss the building of what was to be the Red House. Webb made a preliminary sketch for the staircase of the house on the back of one of the maps in Murray's *Guide to France*.

24 August 1858: The party visited Chartres. Webb drew 'the noble south-west steeple of the Cathedral and the interior'. They then returned to Paris.

28 August 1858: The party left Paris for Poissy.

1 September 1858: Morris, Faulkner and Webb visited Chateau Gaillard and Petit Andeley. Webb drew the church.

2 September 1858: The party reached Rouen. They were upset to discover the new cast-iron spire for the cathedral was as yet unfinished. Webb wrote: 'the upper part was lying hatefully on the ground.'

6 September 1858: The holiday ended when the party took the boat home from Le Havre to Southampton.

Mid-September 1858: Georgiana Burne-Jones recorded that Morris had returned from his trip 'full of a scheme for building a house for himself'.

Late September 1858: Morris and Webb spent some time looking at possible house sites.

October 1858: Morris went to France on a trip buying 'antiques' for his new house. These included old ironwork, armour, enamel and manuscripts.

Autumn 1858: Morris suffered an illness which his friends attributed to unwise eating. This could have been the first indication of the kidney trouble that affected him in 1861.

20 November 1858: An unsigned review of *The Defence of Guenevere & Other Poems* appeared in the *Saturday Review* (pp. 506–507): 'The later school of pre-Raffaelites and Mr. Morris seem to consider that all art is imitation.'

15 December 1858: Boyce noted amongst Rossetti's new work: 'A most beautiful pen and ink study of Topsy's "Stunner" at Oxford.'

1859: Darwin's *Origin of the Species* was published as was Ruskin's *The Elements of Perspective*. Burne-Jones gave a course on glass painting at the Working Men's College.

January 1859: The Hogarth Club held its first exhibition.

Early 1859: Morris abandoned his attempt to become a painter.

6 March 1859: Faulkner, Burne-Jones and Boyce rowed to Godstow to 'have a look' at Jane Burden. They dined that evening with Morris and Swinburne.

Spring 1859: Morris and Burne-Jones gave up their lodgings at 17 Red Lion Square. Morris returned to 13 George Street, Oxford, while Burne-Jones took lodgings in Charlotte Street, London.

26 April 1859: Morris married Jane Burden at St Michael's Church, Ship

Street, Oxford. The wedding was conducted by Morris's friend R. W. Dixon with Faulkner as the best man. The bride was given away by her father. According to the account that Burne-Jones gave Mackail, 'M. said to Dixon beforehand "Mind you don't call her Mary" but he did'. Dixon mistakenly married them as 'William and Mary'. The entry in the *Register* reads: 'William Morris, 25, Bachelor Gentleman, 13 George Street, son of William Morris decd. Gentleman. Jane Burden, minor, spinster, 65 Holywell Street, d. of Robert Burden, Groom.' The witnesses were Jane's parents and Faulkner. None of Morris's family attended the ceremony. Morris presented Jane with a plain gold ring bearing the London hallmark for 1858. She gave her husband a double-handled antique silver cup.

27 April 1859: Morris and Jane began their six week honeymoon. Jane later told Mackail that she had her first view of the sea on her honeymoon 'at Dover on a grey April day'. She found it 'extremely disappointing'. Later they stayed at the Bruges Hotel du Commerce, Paris. According to May Morris the couple toured France, Belgium, Germany and Switzerland. They visited Basle, Liege, Namur, Mainz, Mannheim, Cologne, Ghent, Bruges, Antwerp and Brussels.

April/May 1859: Webb's designs for the Red House were completed.

June 1859: William Riviere was commissioned to fill the three vacant bays left unfinished when the frescos at the Oxford Union Building were abandoned in March 1858.

Mid-June 1859: Morris and Jane returned from their honeymoon to live in furnished rooms at 41 Great Ormond Street, London. It was here that Burne-Jones introduced Jane to his fiancée Georgiana Macdonald. Work began on building the Red House.

22 June 1859: Rossetti recorded that he had completed one of the two painted panels on a cabinet for Morris's new home at Red House. These panels were later framed and sold in 1865.

19 October 1859: Morris presented Jane with a copy of Chappell's *Popular Music of the Olden Times* for her birthday.

November 1859: Morris joined the Corps of Artist Volunteers. He was to serve until 1862 (or 1864 according to Mackail). He resigned due to ill-health. Amongst the other volunteers were Burne-Jones, Ford Madox Brown and Rossetti. The Secretary of the Corps, William Richmond, remembered the unit being 'supremely comical' in its silver and grey uniform.

1860: Morris's carol 'Masters in the Hall' – written to an old French air – was included in Edmund Sedding's collection of *Nine Antient and Goodly Carols for the Merry Tide of Christmas* (1860). Sedding had at one point also been in the office of G. E. Street. In 1884 Swinburne described this carol as 'one of the co-equal three finest ... in the language'. According to Swinburne the carol was also included, at his suggestion, in A. H. Bullen's *A Christmas Garland; Carols and Poems from the Fifteenth Century to the Present* (1885). The *Daisy* embroidered wall-hanging was designed by Morris and executed by Jane and others. This is now at Kelmscott Manor. Ruskin started the serialization of *Unto this Last* in the *Cornhill Magazine*. These articles were later published in book form in 1862.

31 January 1860: Jane and Morris visited the Hogarth Club. Boyce noted in his *Diary* 'the fine and beautiful character' of Jane's face on this occasion.

6 February 1860: Morris wrote to Mary Nicolson the housekeeper at 17 Red Lion Square requesting that she bring him the brass memorial that used to hang up between the windows in his room (*c.f.* November 1856). Mary Nicolson had been nicknamed 'Red Lion Mary' by Rossetti. In the *Memorials*, Georgiana Burne-Jones recorded her saying 'though he [Morris] was so short-tempered, I seemed so necessary to him at all times, and felt myself his man Friday'. She also recorded 'a never-forgotten' trick that she played on him one day when relations were strained between them, which vastly amused Rossetti, Edward and Madox Brown, all present at the time. Morris was going to Oxford and had asked her before he did so to wind up his watch and set it right, 'on which the wily Mary put it forward nearly an hour, and he "remembered to mention it to her" on his return'. Georgiana Burne-Jones also wrote: 'Morris taught her to embroider his designs for hangings, and being in a fever to see how they looked, often made her bring her embroidery frame into the studio so that she might work under his direction – and many a funny conversation took place as she plied her needle and they painted.'

Spring 1860: Morris and Jane moved temporarily to Aberley (or Aberleigh) Lodge, near the Red House, to supervise the latter's construction. Cormell Price applied for the post of tutor to the family of Count Orloff-Davidoff which he had seen advertised in the *Times*. He was successful in gaining the post and spent most of the next three years in Russia (although he was in London for six to eight months during this period). He described his time in Russia as a 'period of purgatory' (*c.f.* 11 November 1860).

23 May 1860: Rossetti married Lizzie Siddal at St Clement's Church, Hastings. They travelled to Paris for their honeymoon.

June 1860: Morris and Jane moved to the Red House, overlooking the Cray Valley near Bexley Heath, Kent. The house was situated three miles from Abbey Wood Station and only ten miles from the centre of London. The weather vane on the tower has the inscription 'W. M. 1859'. The house cost Morris about £4,000 to build. Rossetti later referred to it as 'the Hole' after some hollow ground nearby known as 'Hog's Hole'.

9 June 1860: Burne-Jones married Georgiana Macdonald in Manchester. The couple later travelled to Chester to attend the service at the Cathedral the next day. Their ultimate plan was to join Rossetti and Lizzie Siddal in Paris.

10 June 1860: Burne-Jones fell ill with a sore throat in Chester and the couple had to abandon their plan to travel to Paris. The two couples finally met when they spent a day at London Zoo on 26 July 1860 at 'The Wombat's Lair'.

Summer/Autumn 1860: The Burne-Joneses stayed with the Morrises at the Red House for several weeks. According to Georgiana Burne-Jones: 'it was by no means on a holiday that Edward had come down, nor only to enjoy the company of his friend again, but that they might consult together about the decoration of the house.' A few days after the Burne-Joneses arrived they were joined by Charles Faulkner. The Burne-Joneses left in October. During this visit many tricks were played on Morris including sending him to Coventry at his own table. Georgiana Burne-Jones recalled that the evenings were spent listening to old English songs 'and the inexhaustible *Echos du Temps Passé*'.

30 July 1860: Boyce noted in his *Diary* that when he visited Rossetti's study: 'Morris and his wife (whom DGR familiarly addresses as Janey) came in.'

September 1860: Morris's sister Isabella married Arthur Hamilton Gilmore at Leyton Church. Morris gave the bride away. They had no children.

October 1860: Lizzie Siddal spent a few days with the Morrises at the Red House.

11 November 1860: Cormell Price took up his tutoring post in Russian.

1861: In the census Morris was recorded as William Morris 'B.A., Artist'. It may also have been in this year that the twelve embroidered figure panels for the Red House were finished. The panels depicting St Catherine and Penelope are at Kelmscott Manor. Three other panels were subsequently made into a screen for the Earl of Carlisle at Castle Howard in 1889. Morris painted the panels on the *George and Dragon* cabinet designed by Philip Webb.

January 1861: Rossetti wrote to William Allingham: 'We are organising (but this is quite under the rose as yet) a company for the production of furniture and decoration of all kinds, for the sale of which we are going to open an actual shop! The men concerned are Madox Brown, Jones, Topsy, Webb (the architect of T[opsy]'s house), P. P. Marshall, Faulkner, and myself.... We expect to start in some shape about May or June, but not to go to any expense in premises at first.' Burne-Jones, in Mackail's *Notebooks*, is recorded as saying 'It was DGR's idea; he saw money in it'.

17 January 1861: Jane Alice ('Jenny') Morris was born at the Red House.

Morris named her Alice after his younger sister. She was – at a later date – christened at Bexley Church in Kent. A celebration dinner was held after the christening at the Red House which was attended by, amongst others, Rossetti, Swinburne, the Browns, the Marshalls and the Burne-Joneses. The centre-piece of the celebration was a lavish medieval banquet set out on a large T-shaped table. The men later spent the night on temporary beds set out in the drawing room.

18 January 1861: Morris reported 'Janey and kid (girl) are both very well'.

21 January 1861: Emma Madox Brown, who had stayed with Jane during the latter stages of her pregnancy, left the Red House.

26 January 1861: George Boyce wrote in his *Diary*: 'Jones told me that he and Morris and Rossetti and Webb were going to set up a shop where they would jointly produce and sell painted furniture.'

25 March 1861: Morris, Marshall, Faulkner & Co. (later referred to as 'the Firm') took premises above a jeweller's workshop at 8 Red Lion Square. The first floor was used as an office and showroom, the third floor as workshops, and the basement to house a small kiln where stained glass was made and tiles fired. Rossetti referred to the new premises as the 'Topsaic Laboratory'. George Campfield, who Morris had met at the Working Men's College in Great Ormond Street, was employed as the Firm's foreman.

11 April 1861: Morris, Marshall, Faulkner & Co. opened for business. The partners – Morris, Burne-Jones, Webb, Faulkner, Hughes (who withdrew soon after), Rossetti, Madox Brown and Marshall – each put up £1 as collateral. The main capital of £100 was loaned by Morris's mother, Emma. The Firm's prospectus was also issued. In its early days the members of the Firm held meetings once or twice a fortnight. Faulkner wrote that these had 'rather the character of a meeting of the "Jolly Masons" or the jolly something else than of a meeting to discuss business. Beginning at 8 for 9 p.m. they open with the relation of anecdotes which have been culled by members of the firm since the last meeting. These stories being exhausted, Topsy and Brown will perhaps discuss the relative merits of the art of the thirteenth and fifteenth century, and then perhaps after a few more anecdotes business matters will come up about 10 or 11 o'clock and be furiously discussed till 12, 1 or 2.'

19 April 1861: Morris wrote to his old tutor, the Revd F. B. Guy, requesting a circulation list of fellow clergy so as to advertise the Firm.

23 April 1861: Mr Plint, annoyed by the delay in receiving his painting by Morris, wrote to Ford Madox Brown to find out how the work was progressing. Madox Brown wrote in reply: 'Morris I have spoken to. His picture is now in my house, and at my suggestion he has so altered it that it is quite a fresh work. There is still a figure in the foreground to be scraped out and another put in its place. It is this sort of work which makes it so difficult for a real artist to say when a painting will be finished. I take as much interest in Morris's picture turning out good as though it were my own, for, though it was not commissioned at my recommendation, I have repeatedly since told you that Morris is a man of real genius.'

2 May 1861: Lizzie Siddal, Rossetti's wife, had a stillborn daughter.

Late June 1861: Morris attended a camp of the Corps of Artist Volunteers on Wimbledon Common.

22 June 1861: While stationed on Wimbledon Common Morris witnessed the fire in the warehouses of the firm of Scovell at Cotton's Wharf. This fire consumed an area of three acres and was considered the worst fire since the Great Fire of London. Later (1881) Morris was to write: 'I always did hate fire works, especially since I saw Cotton's Wharf ablaze.'

23 June 1861: Morris returned to the Red House where the Burne-Joneses were staying for the weekend.

4 July 1861: George Wardle married Madeleine Smith.

5 September 1861: Charles Faulkner recorded that 'Topsy has had very bad kidneys lately'.

October 1861: Lizzie Siddal went to stay at the Red House.

9 November 1861: The Firm advertised in the *Builder* for 'a first-rate fret glazier' to help prepare its glass for the International Exhibition of 1862.

22 November 1861: Morris visited Rossetti to participate in 'oysters and obloquy'. Others present included George Meredith, Val Prinsep and D. G. R. Gilchrist. Gilchrist was to die eight days later of scarlet fever.

24 December 1861: Burne-Jones coughed up blood while in bed with a cold. This was to be the beginning of a period of ill health.

End of 1861: By this stage five men and boys were regularly employed by the Firm. Amongst those taken on at this time were Albert and Henry Goodwin. The boys were recruited from the Industrial Home for Destitute Boys in Euston Road.

1862: The Firm took two stands at the International Exhibition held at the South Kensington Museum. One was for the sole promotion of stained glass (Exhibit no. 6734), the other for embroideries and painted Gothic furniture (Exhibit no. 5783). Both stands were awarded medals of commendation. The prize for the stained glass was given 'for artistic qualities of colour and design' while that for the other exhibits read: 'Messrs. Morris &

Co. have exhibited several pieces of furniture, tapestries, &c., in the style of the Middle Ages. The general forms of the furniture, the arrangement of the tapestry, and the character of the details are satisfactory to the archaeologist from the exactness of the imitation, at the same time that the general effect is excellent.' However, the medal the Firm received for its stained glass was challenged by a petition raised by those in the trade who alleged the seven panels depicting the *Parable of the Vineyard* by Rossetti consisted of genuine medieval glass touched up and remounted. This petition was rejected by the judges. The offending glass was later erected in the east window of St Martin's on the Hill Church, Scarborough. At the Exhibition the Firm sold £150 worth of goods. The Firm undertook its first stained glass commission at All Saints Church, Selsey, Gloucestershire. Morris contributed a number of the designs. The Firm also provided stained glass for St Michael & All Angels Church, Lyndhurst, Hampshire. Morris designed the stained-glass panel depicting St Matthew in the Lady Chapel, Christ Church, Southgate.

January 1862: A further call on the partners of the Firm for £19 per share raised the paid up capital to £140. Morris became General Manager with a salary of £150 per annum. Rossetti wrote to Norton: 'I wish you could see the house which Morris ... has built for himself in Kent. It is a most noble work in every way, and more a poem than a house.'

11 February 1862: Burne-Jones wrote: 'Top ... is slowly making Red House the beautifullest place on earth.' Lizzie Siddal died at Chatham Place from an overdose of drugs. Rossetti put a notebook of poems into her coffin when she was later buried at Highgate Cemetery.

25 March 1862: Mary ('May') Morris was born at the Red House. She was named Mary as she was born on Lady Day, the Feast of the Annunciation.

April 1862: Around this time Faulkner replaced Morris as General Manager of the Firm. Morris was appointed its Business Manager. Rossetti designed the frontispiece of his sister Christina's *Goblin Market*. This was the first identifiable work of the Firm as its initials can be seen in the bottom of the left-hand corner.

16 August 1862: Boyce wrote in his *Diary*: 'Joined Rossetti at Swinburne's rooms where they were looking over "Justine" by the Marquis de Sade, [a] recent acquisition of the latter. We then went on to the International Exhibition.'

22 October 1862: Rossetti took up residence at 'Tudor House', 16 Cheyne Walk, Chelsea.

November 1862: Morris designed the *Trellis* wallpaper. The birds were drawn by Philip Webb (*c.f.* 1 February 1864).

December 1862: Henry Holiday, who was to design stained glass for the Firm, was introduced to Morris and Burne-Jones.

10 December 1862: A *Minute Book* for Morris, Marshall, Faulkner & Co. records a business meeting of the 'Firm' held on this date at 8 Red Lion Square. The entry is signed by Morris.

1863: Morris's sister, Alice, married Reginald Butler Edgecombe Gill. He was one of the partners in the Tavistock firm of Gill & Rundle that acted as bankers to the Devon mines.

7 January 1863: Rossetti invited Ford Madox Brown and Marshall to dinner to discuss the management of the Firm: 'Topsy is excluded by the nature of the meeting.'

1 March 1863: Mackail's *Notebooks* record a letter Morris wrote to the Revd F. B. Guy giving details of the progress of tiles for decorating the Turret School. This work does not appear to have been carried out.

1864: Swinburne introduced Morris to the publisher F. S. Ellis of King Street, Covent Garden. Ellis was later to publish *The Earthly Paradise.* The South Kensington Museum bought four stained-glass panels from the Firm: *Penelope, Chaucer Asleep, Dido & Cleopatra* and *Alcestis & Eros.*

Early 1864: Morris considered moving the Firm from Red Lion Square to the Red House. He also planned to build an extension to the house for the Burne-Joneses to live in.

1 February 1864: The *Trellis* and *Daisy* wallpaper designs were registered. These were the first wallpapers produced by Morris. They were expensive to make as they each required twelve blocks (one for each colour used). Jeffery & Co., of Islington, were employed to print these wallpapers.

May 1864: The Burne-Joneses visited the Red House. Their son, Philip, 'shared the nursery of the Misses Morris, two beautiful children by this time'.

18 July 1864: The poet, William Allingham, visited the Morrises: 'After some wandering, find the Red House and at last in its rose garden, William Morris and his queenly wife crowned with her own black hair.'

19 July 1864: Allingham, who spent the night at Red House, recorded in his *Diary* that he found 'Jenny and May bright-eyed, curly pated ... W. M. brusque, careless, with big shoon'.

September 1864: The Morris and Burne-Jones families took a holiday at Littlehampton, Sussex. During this holiday Morris had one of his rages and threw a pair of broken spectacles out of the window in the belief that he had brought a spare pair with him. It turned out that he had not. He was found the next morning before breakfast searching for them in the street. The holiday ended in disaster when Philip Burne-Jones caught scarlet fever.

28 October 1864: Georgiana Burne-Jones gave birth to a son named Christopher.

21 November 1864: Christopher Burne-Jones died. Soon after this event Morris abandoned the idea of moving the Firm to Red House and building an extension for the Burne-Joneses.

December 1864: Burne-Jones and his family moved to 41 Kensington Square. According to Mackail's *Notebooks* the house was furnished by Burne-Jones and Cormell Price. Morris gave the Burne-Joneses a Persian prayer carpet for one of the rooms.

1865: Morris designed various stained-glass panels for All Saints Church, Middleton Cheney, Northamptonshire. These included St Peter, St Augustine & St Catherine, Eve and Mary Virgin and St Agnes & St Alban. Burne-Jones sketched a cartoon of Morris with his two children. Morris was persuaded to join the board of British Mining & Smelting Ltd, a speculative concern which folded in 1874. G. E. Street published *Some Account of Gothic Architecture in Spain*.

10 February 1865: Morris wrote to Allan Park Patton concerning the Firm's proposed stained glass for the Old West Kirk, Greenock.

3 March 1865: A meeting was held at Philip Webb's house to discuss the appointment of Warington Taylor as Business Manager of the Firm. His appointment was supported by Rossetti – who was not present – as he considered him 'the right man for the purpose'. Warington Taylor was given the job at a salary of £120 per year. Taylor was the son of a Devonshire squire but in 1865 had been 'earning a scanty livelihood as a check-taker at the Opera House in the Hay-market'. May later claimed that Taylor was largely responsible for her father's subsequent conversion to socialism.

12 April 1865: Morris and Jane attended an 'evening party' at Rossetti's. Amongst the other guests were the Burne-Joneses, William Rossetti and the Madox Browns.

May 1865: Burne-Jones noted in his *Account Book* that he paid the Firm £3 4s for eight plain Sussex chairs.

Midsummer 1865: The Firm took a twenty-one year lease on 26 Queen Square, just east of Southampton Row, Bloomsbury. The Firm paid £52 10s per year rent. The ground floor of the house was used as an office and a showroom. The ballroom was converted into a large workshop, while the wooden gallery that connected it to the main building was used for glass painting.

5 July 1865: Rossetti wrote a letter to Jane – apparently postmarked 5 July 1865

('Sunday Night') – in which he said: 'The photographer [John Parsons] is coming at 11 on Wednesday [8 July].' He was to photograph Jane in the garden of 16 Cheyne Walk, Chelsea. However, the 5 July 1865 was not a Sunday. The only years in which 5 July fell on a Sunday during the 1860s were in 1863 and 1868.

Autumn 1865: Bessie Burden, Jane's sister, came to live with the Morrises at the Red House following the death of her father.

14 October 1865: The 'Fine Art Gossip' section of the *Athenaeum* recorded that 'Messrs. Morris, Marshall & Faulkner have been entrusted by the first Commissioner of Public Works with the re-decoration of one of the principal rooms in St. James's Palace... Mr. Cowper, being desirous of obtaining aid of the highest class in such works, has also commissioned the firm above named to design and make two drinking-fountains, which will be placed in prominent positions in London. Messrs. Morris, Marshall & Faulkner have also in hand a stained-glass window for the new church of St. Oswald, Durham, which comprises 6 panels, representing events in the life of St. Oswald, King of Northumbria.'

November 1865: Morris and his family moved from the Red House to the Firm's headquarters at 26 Queen Square. Morris was never to visit the Red House again because, as Mackail wrote, 'the sight of it would be more than he could bear'.

1866: Morris completed the poems 'Orpheus & Eurydice' and the 'Quest of the Golden Fleece'. The poem – 'Aristomenes' – was started but not finished. Morris designed the stained-glass panel depicting the Last Supper at the Church of St Edward the Confessor, Cheddleton, Staffordshire.

16 February 1866: James Arnold Heathcote, a retired commander in the Indian Navy, wrote to Morris asking to know the rent of the Red House.

19 February 1866: Morris wrote to James Arnold Heathcote offering to let the Red House to him for £100 per annum.

7 March 1866: Morris again wrote to James Arnold Heathcote offering to let the Red House for two years at £95 per annum. He also added that Heathcote could have the option of purchasing the freehold after the expiration of this period for £1,800. He concluded: 'I cannot entertain any lower offer than this.'

22 April 1866: Morris and Burne-Jones had dinner with Ford Madox Brown.

June 1866: It is clear from a bill issued by Mr Marsh 'Auctioneer, Surveyor & Land Agent of 2 Charlotte Row, Mansion House' that the Red House was still available for let. This bill described the house as 'Erected in 1859, on an elevated Position, commanding Extensive Views of the surrounding much-admired scenery; it has exceedingly Dry Concrete Foundations, supporting very solidly-built Walls, faced with best Picked Kentish Red Bricks, stands in its own Grounds, approached by a Carriage Sweep... The Grounds are tastefully disposed, the Flower Garden with Plaisances in character with the House, Bowling Green, Orchard, and Productive Kitchen Garden, the whole containing more than an Acre.'

3 June 1866: Margaret Burne-Jones was born.

Mid-June 1866: Morris, Jane, Webb and Warington Taylor went on a holiday tour of the churches in northern France. They visited Sens, Troyes and Paris where Morris searched for books on the quays. Burne-Jones drew a caricature of their departure in which all the party were depicted as seasick. Burne-Jones portrayed himself left on the shore holding his new baby daughter Margaret. Her birth had prevented him accompanying the others on the trip.

3 July 1866: Morris subscribed two guineas to a testimonial fund on behalf of George Cruikshank to defray the expenses of an exhibition of his work.

5 July 1866: Morris travelled to Cambridge with George Frederick Bodley to discuss the decoration of Jesus College Chapel by the Firm.

30 July 1866: William Allingham recorded in his *Diary* that he visited Burne-Jones at his new house in Kensington and found the latter and Morris discussing a book they planned with 'lots of stories and pictures' [the proposed illustrated edition of *The Earthly Paradise*].

1 August 1866: Allingham had dinner with the Morrises. In his *Diary* he recorded that Morris was 'learned about wines and distilling... M. and friends intend to engrave the wood-blocks themselves [for 'the Big Story Book'] – and M. will publish the book at his warehouse. I like Morris much. He is plain-spoken and emphatic, often boisterously, without an atom of irritating matter.'

18 August 1866: William Allingham recorded in his *Diary* that Burne-Jones 'occupies himself, when in the mood, with designs for the Big Book of Stories in Verse by Morris, and has done several from Cupid and Psyche'.

30 August 1866: Morris, Allingham, Webb and the Burne-Joneses visited Winchester where they went to the Cathedral. Allingham recorded that 'Morris talked copiously and interestingly on all things'. In the evening Morris, Allingham and Burne-Jones went to Lymington where Morris stayed at the Nag's Head. Allingham recorded the following conversation between Morris and Burne-Jones: 'When we got to Stanwell House, Ned said, "I'm sorry, but I've been so lazy I've not done a single thing for the book," to which Morris gave a slight grunt. Then Ned produced his eight or nine designs for the wood-blocks, whereupon Morris laughed right joyously and shook himself.'

31 August 1866: Morris, Allingham and the Burne-Joneses took a carriage from the Nag's Head to the sea at Milford where they visited the church. Later they buried Morris up to his neck in shingle on the beach.

September 1866: The Firm began work on the Armoury and Tapestry Room at St James's Palace.

13 September 1866: Morris wrote to Henry Young Darracott Scott stating that the Firm's estimate for glazing the three windows in the Refreshment Room at the South Kensington Museum would be £272.

Autumn 1866: Around this time James Arnold Heathcote purchased the Red House from Morris. Amongst the furniture and effects sold with the house were the tempera paintings executed on the walls, the sideboard designed by Webb and the two great painted cupboards.

26 October 1866: Webb drew the wall design of repeated olive branches for the Green Dining Room at the South Kensington Museum.

November 1866: Work proceeded on Jesus College Chapel, the decoration being undertaken by Frederick R. Leach. Mackail recorded in his *Notebooks* that C. F. Murray went to work for Edward Burne-Jones at Kensington Square around this time 'and soon met Morris there'. Rosalind Howard paid her first visit to Morris and Webb's 'furniture place' at Queen Square.

3 November 1866: Warington Taylor wrote to Philip Webb urging he 'report real visible progress at the palace [St James's], so as to give me some cheering news'. By this time Taylor, who had consumption, was staying at 7 Beach Cottages, Hastings.

6 November 1866: With reference to the work on the Jesus College Chapel, Edmund Henry Morgan wrote to Bodley that 'some astonishment was felt at the employment of a Cambridge workman in the execution of a work which was entrusted to *Mr. Morris*, on the very favourable recommendation given by you'.

8 November 1866: Bodley assured Morgan that 'the figures of angels, in the panels over the wall-cornice, will be executed by Morris' own men. The cartoons are prepared & matters put in hand. I wd. say that Morris finds Leach a very capable & able executant. The design & the exact shades of the colours are all done according to the directions given to him.'

13 November 1866: Warington Taylor complained to Webb about Morris's apparent delay over the Jesus College commission: 'Do see that Morris starts those angels for [the] Cambridge roof now; he will never have them in time, and at the last moment will want others to do the work.' Robinson and Wildman claim 'Morris's own hand is to be seen in the row of stately angels in red, yellow and green around the cove of the ceiling'.

24 November 1866: Morgan, apparently frustrated with the delay over the ceiling of Jesus College Chapel, wrote to Morris setting a deadline for its completion.

27 November 1866: Morris responded to Morgan's letter by stating: 'I must deprecate any hurry with works of this kind; the opportunity (as you probably know) seldom happens to us to paint figures in churches on such a scale, and I am extremely interested in the work and want it to be done in the best possible way.'

30 November 1866: Morris visited Jesus College Chapel, Cambridge, and reported that the work was 'going on satisfactorily'.

3 December 1866: Morris assured Morgan that 'we shall be able to finish the ceiling by the first of April as you have arranged'.

27 December 1866: Warington Taylor wrote to Webb: 'Just remember we are embezzling the public money now – what business has any palace to be decorated at all?'

1867: Edward Burne-Jones began an affair with Mary Zambaco. This relationship was ultimately to devastate his health.

January 1867: According to Buxton Forman, Morris finished writing *The Life & Death of Jason*. Forman claimed that Morris originally intended to publish it under the title of *The Deeds of Jason*.

3 January 1867: Morris wrote to Allan Park Paton with reference to the Firm's work on the proposed vestry windows for the Old West Kirk in Greenock. He suggested the stained-glass windows should depict Nehemiah (cost £41 5s) and Ezra (£48 5s).

Mid-January 1867: The firm completed its work on the Armoury and Tapestry Rooms at St James's Palace.

25 March 1867: Morris went to Cambridge in connection with the work on the Jesus College Chapel.

26 March 1867: Morris wrote to Morgan that following his inspection of the work on Jesus College Chapel: 'I shall not be able to give it up to you this week; it will however be finished by the week after, (week ending April 7th).'

May 1867: *The Life & Death of Jason* was published by Bell & Daldy at Morris's expense in an initial edition of 500 copies. Within five years the poem had gone through seven editions and sold over 3,000 copies.

16 May 1867: A meeting of the Firm was held at which it was decided to offer Philip Webb £80 per annum – backdated to January 1867 – to serve as its consulting manager.

25 May 1867: Robert Browning wrote to Morris thanking him for sending him a copy of *The Life & Death of Jason*: 'What a noble, melodious and most beautiful poem you have written!'

9 June 1867: A favourable unsigned review of *The Life & Death of Jason*, by Joseph Knight, appeared in the *Sunday Times* (p. 7).

15 June 1867: An anonymous review of *The Life & Death of Jason* appeared in the *Athenaeum* (pp. 779 and 780).

20 June 1867: Morris wrote to Burne-Jones expressing himself 'in good spirits after the puffs [ie. the reviews of *The Life & Death of Jason*]'.

30 June 1867: Morris and his family dined with Allingham and Burne-Jones at Queen Square.

1 July 1867: Swinburne's review of *The Life & Death of Jason* appeared in the *Fortnightly Review* (vol. 8, pp. 19–28).

2 July 1867: Morris and Allingham went to the Royalty Theatre to see *Black-eyed Susan*. Allingham recorded in his *Diary* that 'M. seldom goes to the Theatre, and is bored a good deal'.

4 July 1867: Morris and Allingham visited Westminster Abbey.

15 July 1867: Sydney Cockerell was born.

August 1867: The Morrises spent the summer in lodgings in Beaumont Street, Oxford. The Burne-Joneses took lodgings in undergraduate rooms in St Giles. The two families – along with Faulkner – spent most evenings together.

21 August 1867: In a letter to Morgan George Watkins, Morris wrote of Wordsworth that 'his cold unhuman, & sometimes prolix poetry has not much attraction for me, even now I'm grown old'.

22 August 1867: A review of *The Life & Death of Jason* by Professor C. E. Norton appeared in the *Nation* (vol. 5, pp. 146–7): 'By this work Mr. Morris wins a secure place among the chief English poets of the age.'

24 August 1867: Morris, Burne-Jones and Faulkner started out on a river trip from Oxford to Dorchester.

September 1867: Morris and Jane attended the wedding of Charles Howell to his cousin Kate which was held at St Matthew's Church, Brixton. Volume 1 of Marx's *Das Kapital* was published.

October 1867: An unsigned review of *The Life & Death of Jason* by Henry James appeared in the *North American Review* (pp. 688–92). He wrote: 'It is some time since we have met with a work of imagination of so thoroughly satisfactory a character.'

16 October 1867: Morris attended a party at Warington Taylor's lodgings. Allingham recorded Morris reading Tennyson 'with furious emphasis and gestures, making us all shout with laughter'.

18 October 1867: In a letter to Webb, Morris recorded that he had taken Jenny and May donkey riding on Hampstead Heath.

25 October 1867: F. T. Palgrave wrote to W. M. Rossetti about *The Life & Death of Jason*: 'I heard very favourable things about it from A. Tennyson (who came with me for three weeks last autumn to Devonshire), but I have seen no other judge of poetry who knew it except Woolner.'

November 1867: Burne-Jones and his family moved to the Grange, North End Lane, Fulham. The house had previously been occupied by the novelist Samuel Richardson.

25 November 1867: Morris wrote to the Revd F. B. Guy with reference to the proposed decoration of the Forest School, Walthamstow. Guy had introduced *The Life & Death of Jason* to the school curriculum at the Forest School. Morris wrote: 'it makes me laugh to be in the position of nuisance to schoolboys.'

December 1867: A second edition of five hundred copies of *The Life & Death of Jason* was published.

19 December 1867: Morris wrote to Allan Park Paton telling him that the window depicting 'Charity' would be ready to be installed in the Old West Kirk in January 1868.

1868: Morris designed the stained-glass panels depicting Boaz and Ruth in the Church of St Edward the Confessor at Cheddleton, Staffordshire. He also designed the stained-glass panels of Christ as King and Zacharias at Llandaff Cathedral, Glamorgan. Morris's poem 'Captiva Regina' was published in the Forest School Magazine.

February 1868: Burne-Jones noted in his *Account Book* that he paid the Firm £2 16s for twelve Sussex chairs.

2 February 1868: Morris wrote 33 stanzas of 'Pygmalion and the Image' one of the stories for 'August' in *The Earthly Paradise*.

3 February 1868: Morris took the first instalment of *The Earthly Paradise* to the printer.

6 February 1868: Morris finalized the publishing agreement with F. S. Ellis for

The Earthly Paradise.

13 February 1868: William Rossetti wrote in his *Diary*: 'Browning expresses (as I had before been told) a very high opinion of Morris's *Jason*.'

March 1868: Morris commissioned Rossetti to paint a portrait of Jane. This portrait is known as 'Mrs William Morris in a Blue Silk Dress'.

11 April 1868: A review of *The Life & Death of Jason* appeared in the *Times*.

19 April 1868: At some point between this date and 1 May 1868 volume 1 of *The Earthly Paradise* was published by F. S. Ellis. The first edition consisted on a thousand crown 8vo copies (which sold at 14s) and a further twenty-five demy 8vo on Whatman handmade paper. Morris engraved the woodcut, from a design by Burne-Jones, of three female musicians that decorated the title-page (this was also used in later editions of *The Life & Death of Jason*). The volume bore the inscription 'To my Wife I dedicate this Book'.

20 April 1868: Morris wrote to the *Athenaeum* pointing out some inaccuracies in their 'Weekly Gossip' column relating to *The Life & Death of Jason* and the proposed illustrated edition of *The Earthly Paradise*. Morris wrote: 'The time of publication ... of this illustrated edition must, from the magnitude of the work, be very remote.'

May 1868: Warington Taylor wrote to Webb: 'I have lately been quite wonder-fully well – able to read a couple of Morris's poems; how simple and splendid they are!' In a letter to Jane, Rossetti drew a caricature of Morris as 'The Bard and Petty Tradesman'.

16 May 1868: The *Brighton Herald* published an unsigned review of volume 1 of *The Earthly Paradise*.

27 May 1868: Morris held a party at Queen Square. Amongst those present were Allingham, the Burne-Joneses, Rossetti, the Madox Browns and Philip Webb. Allingham suggested the banquet be called the 'Earthly Paradise' and this was written at the top of the menu by Burne-Jones.

30 May 1868: An anonymous review of *The Earthly Paradise* appeared in the *Athenaeum* (pp. 753–4). Another anonymous review of the poem appeared in the *Saturday Review* (pp. 730 and 731).

June 1868: George Eliot wrote to John Blackwood: 'We take Morris's poem into the woods with us and read it aloud, greedily, looking to see how much *more* there is in store for us. If *ever* you have an idle afternoon, bestow it on the *Earthly Paradise*.'

7 June 1868: Robert Browning wrote to Morris thanking him for sending him *The Earthly Paradise*: 'It is a double delight to me – to read such poetry, and know you, of all the world, wrote it.'

Mid-Summer 1868: A second edition – actually a reprint – of volume 1 of *The Earthly Paradise* was published. 750 copies were issued.

August 1868: Warington Taylor introduced Morris to Eiríkr Magnússon. According to Magnússon: 'with a cordial "come upstairs" [Morris] was off at a bound ... [and] I followed until his study on the second floor was reached.'

1 August 1868: Morris's poem 'The God of the Poor' appeared in the *Fortnightly Review* (p. 110).

18 August 1868: Morris and his family were holidaying at Southwold, Suffolk. They were accompanied by Charles and Kitty Howell. It has been suggested that Howell served as a go-between for Rossetti and Jane on this holiday passing on their letters without Morris's knowledge. Morris later described the area round Southwold as 'a mournful place, but full of character'. While on this holiday he visited Blythburgh Church.

24 August 1868: The Morrises returned to London from Southwold.

7 September 1868: The American poet Paul Hayne wrote to Sidney Lanier: 'As for *Wm. Morris*, I – for one, consider him as beyond doubt, the *purest, sweetest, noblest narrative* poet, Great Britain has produced since *Chaucer*. This may sound exaggerated, nevertheless it is simply *true!*'

17 September 1868: Morris wrote to Cowden-Clarke expressing his 'boundless admiration' for Keats 'whom I venture to call one of my masters'.

19 September 1868: Charles Eliot Norton described Morris in a letter to Ruskin as combining 'in a wonderful measure the solid earthy qualities of the man of practical affairs, with the fine perceptions and quick fancy of the poet'.

October 1868: Morris's poem 'The Two Sides of the River' appeared in the *Fortnightly Review* (pp. 54 and 85). He began to learn Icelandic and started some translations with Magnússon. A review of 'Guenevere', 'Jason' and 'The Earthly Paradise' by Walter Pater appeared in the *Westminster Review*, vol. 90, pp. 300–312.

4 October 1868: Octavia Hill, who had just read *The Life & Death of Jason*, wrote to a friend that it was 'true poetry' although she deplored its lack of Christianity.

18 October 1868: Morris visited Charles Eliot Norton, the scholar and art historian, at his home at Keston Rectory, Bromley, Kent.

9 November 1868: Rossetti wrote: 'I called on Top[sy] who was howling and threatening to throw a new piano of his wife's out of [the] window. It unfortunately arrived I believe just at dinner time and the occurrence had poisoned his peace of mind ever since.'

17 November 1868: In a letter to Alice Boyd, Rossetti wrote: 'I met Topsy the other night at a large party of Greeks. He seemed depressed and complained of deafness, but on a large plug of string being taken out of his ear, he revived a good deal and even scratched himself in places apparently inaccessible. The whisky cork had already been got out of his nose, and Janey had nearly succeeded in fishing the paper-knife up from the base of his spine. He was offering to stand on his head that it might drop out, but this was thought unnecessary.'

26 November 1868: William Bell Scott held a dinner party which was attended by the Morrises and Rossetti: 'Gabriel sat by Jeanie [*sic*], and I must say acts like a perfect fool if he wants to conceal his attachment, doing nothing but attend to her, sitting side-ways towards her, that sort of thing.' Bell Scott also recorded that Morris witnessed this behaviour.

29 November 1868: The Revd F. B. Guy had a daughter. Morris agreed to be her godfather.

14 December 1868: Morris wrote to Frederick R. Leach in relation to the organ screens for St Mary's Church, Beddington, Surrey.

1869: Morris designed stained-glass windows for the south aisle of St Mary's Church, King's Walden, Hertfordshire. The panels depicted St Raphael, St Michael, St Gabriel and musician angels. Morris's first decorated calligraphic manuscript – *The Dwellers at Eyr* – was finished. J. S. Mill's *The Subjection Of Women* was published.

January 1869: Morris and Magnússon's translation of 'The Saga of Gunnlaug the worm-tongue and Rafn the Skald' appeared in the *Fortnightly Review* (pp. 54 and 82).

Late January 1869: Mary Zambaco, with whom Burne-Jones was having an affair, tried to drown herself in the Paddington Canal outside Browning's house.

23 January 1869: Rossetti recorded that Morris and Burne-Jones – 'after the most dreadful to-do' – had started from Rome in an attempt to escape Mary Zambaco. Before he left Morris asked Jane to promise to cease her sittings for Rossetti while he was away. She agreed. However, Burne-Jones became so ill that they got no further than Dover before returning to London a few days later. The affair between Mary Zambaco and Burne-Jones continued until 1872.

February 1869: An article on 'William Morris and Matthew Arnold' by J. Skelton appeared in *Fraser's Magazine*, vol. 79, pp, 230–44.

7 February 1869: Rossetti wrote to John Skelton: 'You know Morris is now only

35, and has done things in decorative art which take as high and exclusive a place in that field as his poetry does in its own. What may he not yet do?'

March 1869: Morris wrote the poem 'Bellerophon'.

10 March 1869: Henry James, in a letter to Alice James, described Jane as 'a tall lean woman in a long dress of some dead purple stuff, guiltless of hoops ... with a mass of crisp black hair heaped into great wavy projections on each side of her temples, a thin pale face, a pair of strange sad, deep, dark, Swinburnian eyes, with great thick black oblique brows, joined in the middle of and tucking themselves away under her hair ... a long neck, without any collar and in lieu thereof some dozen strings of outlandish beads'. James, who had recently visited the Morrises, also wrote: 'Morris lives on the same premises as his shop, in Queen's Square, Bloomsbury, an antiquated ex-fashionable region, smelling strong of the last century, with a hoary effigy of Queen Anne in the middle. Morris's poetry, you see, is only a sub-trade. To begin with, he is a manufacturer of stained-glass windows, tiles, ecclesiastical and medieval tapestry, altar-cloths, and in fine everything quaint, archaic, pre-Raphaelite – and I may add, exquisite.'

April 1869: Morris's poem 'On the Edge of the Wilderness' appeared in the *Fortnightly Review* (p. 54).

1 April 1869: Morris's poem 'Hapless Love' appeared in *Good Words* (p. 85).

May 1869: Morris and Magnússon's translation of *The Grettis Saga* was published in an edition of 500 crown 8vo copies by F. S. Ellis. According to Buxton Forman twenty-five copies of the book were printed on Whatman handmade paper.

13 May 1869: Morris sent a copy of *The Grettis Saga* to Charles Eliot Norton.

24 May 1869: Morris had dinner with Burne-Jones and Charles Fairfax Murray. During this meeting there was an argument which may have related to Burne-Jones's affair with Mary Zambaco.

25 May 1869: Morris apologized to Burne-Jones for his behaviour the previous evening: 'we seem to quarrel in speech now sometimes, and sometimes I think you find it hard to stand me, and no great wonder for I am like a hedgehog with nastiness.'

June 1869: Morris and Jane spent some days with Rossetti but Jane was too ill to sit for the portrait Morris had commissioned.

Late-June 1869: Morris completed 'Gudrun's Lovers'.

July 1869: Warington Taylor wrote to Webb complaining about the Firm's failure to collect its outstanding debts: 'Ned, W. M., and Gabriel egg one another on to every kind of useless expense... It is disgraceful such childish conduct.' When Webb passed these comments on to Morris he replied: 'there is a great deal of reason in what he says, though he is not at present quite master of all the details.' A review of Morris's poetry appeared in *Blackwood's Magazine*, vol. 106, pp. 56–73.

16 July 1869: Rossetti wrote to Miss Losh: 'Janey Morris is very ill. She and her husband are going to Ems on the Rhine, where she has been told to go and drink the waters and take baths. Topsy goes on working at a prodigious rate at the second volume of his *Earthly Paradise*, and is making it so bulky that it will have to come out in two divisions, the first of which will appear I suppose about October. One day lately, working from 10 one morning to 4 the morning after (with intervals of meals etc.) he produced 750 lines! – and this of the finest poem he has yet done.'

17 July 1869: Morris and Jane departed for Dover *en route* to Bad Ems via Belgium: 'Ned seemed more moved at my going than I should have liked to have seen him.' The trip was undertaken for Jane's health. May and Jenny were left at Naworth Castle with the Howards.

21 July 1869: Morris and Jane viewed Van Eyck's 'Adoration of the Lamb' in St Bavo's church at Ghent. Rossetti enclosed a cartoon in a letter to Jane which depicted her taking the waters at Bad Ems while she was read poetry by Morris: 'The accompanying cartoon will prepare you for the worst – which ever that may be the seven tumblers or the 7 volumes.'

22 July 1869: The Morrises spent the day in Ghent. Morris purchased soup plates and a number of Delft china oil and vinegar bottles there. In the evening he and Jane left for Mechelen.

27 July 1869: The Morrises probably arrived in Bad Ems. According to May her father had not planned the trip properly and he and Jane arrived at Bad Ems with nowhere to stay: 'they were literally stranded at the station, and I scarcely know which to be sorrier for, mother waiting there alone in a state of collapse, or father, frantically seeking for accommodation and coming back to her in a positively desperate state of mind.' Eventually they found rooms at the Fortuna guest house which overlooked the seventeenth-century Kurhaus.

29 July 1869: Jane visited the doctor and took two baths at the government baths. Morris later took Jane for a ten-mile drive.

30 July 1869: Jane again visited the doctor. Morris later took her for a boat trip on the river. Rossetti wrote to Jane: 'All that concerns you is the all absorbing question with me, as dear Top will not mind my telling you at this anxious time. The more he loves you, the more he knows that you are too lovely and noble not to be loved: and, dear Janey, there are too few things that seem worth expressing as life goes on, for one friend to deny another the poor expression of what is most at his heart.'

31 July 1869: In a letter to Philip Webb, Morris wrote that 'Janey is certainly no worse than when we started'.

August 1869: The *Temple Bar* (vol. 27, pp. 35–50) published an article by Alfred Austin on the poetry of Morris and Matthew Arnold.

1 August 1869: Morris worked on his poem 'Accontius & Cydippe': 'I am not sanguine about it.'

4 August 1869: Rossetti sent a letter to Jane which included a caricature of Morris complaining about his trousers to a German maid: 'I fear that the legitimate hopelessness of the pictorial and ideal Topsy has communicated itself to the german maid in the cartoon.'

6 August 1869: Both Morris and Jane were unwell. Jane was unable to take her usual treatment.

8 August 1869: Morris went on a two-hour walk up a hill road: 'I think the country very jolly I must say.'

9 August 1869: Morris wrote to Webb from Bad-Ems mentioning that he had been reading Carlyle's translation of Goethe's *Wilhelm Meister*. He had also been reading Thackeray to Jane: 'Thackeray's *style* I think so precious bad.'

11 August 1869: Jane recommenced her treatment.

12 August 1869: In a letter to Edward Nicholson, Morris noted that Julia Cameron had 'threatened' to take his picture. There is no record that this actually happened.

14 August 1869: Rossetti drew a cartoon of Morris entitled 'Resolution; or, the Infant Hercules' which depicted him taking a shower. It had a note to Jane: 'Conceive if your cure were now to proceed so rapidly that there remained a glut of surplus baths, and Topsy were induced to express a thanksgiving frame of mind by that act which is next to godliness.' Morris recorded that while out walking he had 'heard a rustle in the dry leaves behind me and out crept one [an adder] as long as my umbrella of a yellowish olive colour and wriggled across the path as though he were expected; I kept feeling the legs of my trousers all the way home after that, and feel a little shy of sitting down on green banks now'.

15 August 1869: By this time Morris was short of cash and wrote to Webb to arrange a loan of £60. In the morning he walked the twelve-mile round trip to Nassau.

19 August 1869: The cash from Webb arrived. Webb offered the money as a gift but Morris wrote: 'I think the money will be much more equally divided by your keeping it, than by your casting it on the dry and thirsty ground of a ne'er-do-well.'

20 August 1869: Morris wrote to Webb: 'I went a walk in the uplands this morning about queer winding cart roads through grain fields dotted over with apple-trees, everything of course being on the slope, and big hills everywhere in the distance, and thought what a delightful country it was if I had any business there.'

24 August 1869: Ellis visited the Morrises at Bad Ems.

25 August 1869: Morris took Ellis on a mule ride in the morning. Later he accompanied Ellis to the Kurhaus where the latter gambled with some success at the card tables: 'his luck has not tempted me to go in there again, it looked too dull.' Ellis left in the evening.

29 August 1869: Morris, who had the 'fidgetts', wrote to Webb outlining a design for a shower that Jane could use once they returned to England: 'Can you get this rigged up for me at once in the dressing-room adjoining our bedroom.'

3 September 1869: Morris, in another letter to Webb, wrote: 'I consider Janey really better now; she is stronger and the local trouble seems so much better, as to be nearly knocked on the head.'

6 September 1869: Morris and Jane left Bad Ems by train for Cologne.

7 September 1869: The Morrises spent the day in Cologne to recover from the journey of the previous day.

8 September 1869: The Morrises travelled to Liege where they spent the night.

9 September 1869: The Morrises travelled to Ghent where they stayed at the Royal Hotel.

10 September 1869: The Morrises spent the day in Ghent.

11 September 1869: At midday the Morrises arrived at Calais. They took the midnight boat to England and had a very stormy crossing.

12 September 1869: The Morrises arrived home at 7 am. The rough weather they experienced crossing the Channel meant that Jane was not as well as Morris had hoped.

21 September 1869: Rossetti wrote to Miss Losh telling her he intended to call his pet Wombat – 'Top' – after Morris: 'He is tremendously strong and heroically good-natured.' Elsewhere he referred to the Wombat as 'A Joy, a Triumph, a Delight, a Madness'. Around this time he drew a caricature depicting Jane taking Morris – as a wombat – for a walk on a lead.

28 September 1869: Rossetti obtained an Order for Exhumation to recover the poems he had buried in Lizzie Siddal's coffin. He nominated Charles Augustus Howell to be present when the coffin was opened.

8 October 1869: Rossetti wrote: 'Topsy goes on writing at a furious rate, but the second volume of the *Earthly Paradise* will not I believe appear till December, and there is to be yet another volume after that.'

13 October 1869: It is clear from a letter Rossetti wrote to his brother William that Morris had found out about the exhumation of Lizzie's body from Charles Augustus Howell. Rossetti had told Jane himself.

14 October 1869: Rossetti went to examine the manuscripts that had been recovered from Lizzie's grave: 'They are in a disappointing state. The things I have already, seem mostly perfect, and there is a great hole right through all the leaves of *Jenny*, which was the thing I most wanted.'

30 October 1869: Paul Hayne, in a letter to Sidney Lanier, wrote: 'Wm. Morris I am ready to swear by. I like him a thousand times better than *Swinburne* – Indeed, often in reading his marvellous tales the question *involuntarily* arises, "has *Chaucer* come back to Earth"?'

November 1869: Part III of *The Earthly Paradise* (dated 1870) was published in an edition of 1,500 copies. This was actually the second volume as in November, during the fifth printing of volume 1, the first book had been divided into Part I and Part II. Morris worked on the unfinished illuminated manuscript – *The Story of the Volsungs & Niblungs* – which contained miniatures painted by C. F. Murray. An unsigned article on Morris's poetry – by Alfred Austin – appeared in the *Temple Bar* (pp. 45–51). Austin described Morris as 'the singer of, perhaps, the most unvarying sweetness and sustained tenderness of soul that ever caressed the chords of the lyre'.

6 November 1869: Rossetti's wombat – 'Top' – died. Rossetti had him stuffed.

December 1869: An unsigned review of *The Earthly Paradise*, possibly by Sidney Colvin, appeared in the *Pall Mall Budget* (pp. 26–7). The reviewer wrote: 'Mr Morris's attitude towards the fabulous, mythical, old-world, or romantic material of his art has been entirely simple, entirely without self-consciousness, the attitude, in a word, of *artistic credulity* – an attitude differing as little as possible from that of Chaucer and the true medieval story-tellers.'

7 December 1869: Swinburne wrote in a letter to William Rossetti: 'I want to read the 'Gudrun's Lovers' – a part I once heard of it seemed to me the most grateful exhalation that has of late emanated from the expanding jaws of that prudential "allegory of the banks of the Nile".'

10 December 1869: In another letter to William Rossetti, Swinburne wrote: 'I have received Topsy's book; the Gudrun story is excellently told.'

21 December 1869: In a letter to Charles Eliot Norton, Morris reported he was working on a translation of the *Nibelungers* (this was abandoned after 216 stanzas).

25 December 1869: The *Athenaeum* reviewed Part III of the *Earthly Paradise* and praised Morris for his Christian viewpoint.

28 December 1869: Swinburne, in a letter to William Rossetti, recorded: 'I wrote to Topsy my congratulations on his promotion by the reviews to the post of Christian laureate, and he responded with much unction and proper feeling.'

1870: Morris designed the stained-glass panels in the Holy Trinity Church, Meole Brace, Shropshire, depicting the 'Marriage Feast at Cana', the 'Healing of Jairus's Daughter', the 'Miracle of the Loaves and Fishes' and 'St Paul Preaching'.

January 1870: A review of Morris's poetry appeared in the *London Quarterly Review*, vol. 33, pp. 330–60.

14 January 1870: Florence Taylor, the wife of Warington Taylor who was suffering from consumption, wrote to Rossetti stating that her husband was 'much worse' and added 'I do not think he will ever recover from this attack'.

19 January 1870: Browning wrote about *The Earthly Paradise*: 'Morris is sweet, pictorial, clever always – but a weariness to me by this time. The lyrics were "the first sprightly runnings" – this that follows is a laboured brew with the old flavour but no *body*.'

21 January 1870: Ruskin wrote in a letter to Miss Joan Agnew: 'Has Isola got Morris's last – 3rd book of the *Earthly Paradise*? I can't understand how a man who, on the whole, enjoys dinner – and breakfast – and supper – to that extent of fat – can write such lovely poems about Misery. There's such lovely, lovely misery in this Paradise.'

22 January 1870: Rossetti wrote to Norton: 'You will be grieved to have heard (as you have doubtless done) how very ill she [Jane] has been since you were in London; nor can I give a good account of her now, though she has been somewhat better just lately.'

30 January 1870: Rossetti wrote to Jane: 'For the last two years I have felt distinctly the clearing away of chilling numbness that surrounds me in the utter want of you; but since then other obstacles have kept steadily on the increase, and its come too late.'

February 1870: Morris began an illuminated book of his poems entitled *A Book* *of Verse* intended for Georgiana Burne-Jones. His translation of the *Volsunga Saga: The Story of the Volsungs & Niblungs* went to the printers. Philip Webb designed the book's cover. A review of Part III of *The Earthly Paradise*, by G. A. Simcox, appeared in the *Academy* (pp. 121–2). Simcox wrote: 'Mr. Morris has always been the poet of moods rather than of passion, of adventures rather than of actions; and this characteristic is still to be traced in the third instalment of his great work; though there is a nearer approach to the familiar sources of human interest.'

4 February 1870: Rossetti wrote to Jane expressing his love: 'more than all for me, dear Janey, is the fact that you exist, that I can yet look forward to seeing you and speaking to you again, and know for certain that at that moment I shall forget all my own troubles nor even be able to remember yours.'

10 February 1870: Morris declined a request from John & Charles Watkins of 34 Parliament Square, London, to have his photograph taken.

12 February 1870: Warington Taylor died of consumption aged thirty-four. He was buried at St Thomas's Church, Fulham. His tombstone was designed by Philip Webb. The Firm met the funeral expenses of £89 19s. Taylor was replaced as Business Manager of the Firm by George Wardle who had been employed as a bookkeeper and draughtsman since about 1866.

March 1870: An unsigned favourable review of Part III of *The Earthly Paradise* appeared in the *Spectator*, pp. 332–4. The writer ended his review with the following observation: 'One quarrel, however, we are inclined to have with Mr. Morris; why will he bring out his poems in winter? So many independent observers have found that they ought to be read in summer, and out of doors if possible, that their combined experience must have sufficient truth in it to deserve the regard of all persons concerned.' A review of Morris's poetry also appeared in *The Christian Observer*, vol. 70, pp. 196–208.

11 March 1870: Rossetti took Scalands, a house in Robertsbridge in Sussex, possibly in order to be close to Jane who was planning to have a holiday with her daughters in lodgings in Hastings. At first Rossetti shared the house with the American journalist, W. J. Stillman, who is supposed to have introduced him to chloral.

12 March 1870: Morris dined with his mother at Leyton. His brother Rendall collected him: 'he is gotten awfully fat: has taken a house at Acton (close to London) and is thinking of setting up a poultry farm there: wh: I think rather a good idea if he will stick to it, and is pretty lucky.'

14 March 1870: In a letter to Jane, Morris wrote that he was about to begin a review of Rossetti's *Poems*. By this time Jane and the children had arrived at Hastings.

26 March 1870: Morris and Jane had dinner with Rossetti at Scalands. They stayed overnight.

27 March 1870: Rossetti recorded that 'Top and Janey are here to-day – the former insolently solid – the latter better than when I last saw her at Hastings.'

11 April 1870: Rossetti wrote: '[Jane] and Morris have been in this neighbourhood lately, and are coming again; and I trust the change may prove eventually of some decided benefit to her.' Morris and Jane probably arrived on 12 April 1870. Jane stayed on at Scalands after this visit.

14 April 1870: Rossetti was at work on a crayon portrait of Jane. The latter was apparently feeling better: 'She is benefiting to a really surprising extent, and walks about like anybody else.'

15 April 1870: Morris wrote to Jane at Scalands. In the afternoon he had his portrait painted by George Frederic Watts – as one of a series the latter was doing on the great men of the age – despite having 'a devil of a cold-in-the-head'. This picture, which was completed in 1871, is now in the National Portrait Gallery.

18 April 1870: Morris visited his mother at Leyton. Rossetti told his mother that Jane was 'benefiting greatly' from her stay at Scalands and that 'Top comes from time to time.'

22 April 1870: Morris spent the evening at Queen Square with Madox Brown, Hueffer and Ellis. At this dinner Hueffer met Catherine Madox Brown – his future wife – for the first time. Morris read his review of Rossetti's book of poems to Ford Madox Brown.

24 April 1870: Morris worked on the 'Hill of Venus' the concluding tale of Part IV of *The Earthly Paradise*.

26 April 1870: Morris dined with Rossetti at Rules restaurant, Maiden Lane, off the Strand. They enjoyed a large meal of oysters.

27 April 1870: Rossetti's *Poems* were published by F. S. Ellis. They were originally intended to appear on 23 April but were delayed due to problems over the binding.

May 1870: *The Volsunga Saga: The Story of the Volsungs & Niblungs* was published. 750 copies of the book were printed. Twelve certificated copies were printed on Whatman handmade paper of demy 8vo size and another twelve on Whatman's handmade paper of crown 8vo size.

5 May 1870: Morris travelled down to Scalands to join Jane. Rossetti recorded 'we shall make some more excursions probably, as there are various things worth seeing'.

7 May 1870: Rossetti wrote: 'Dear old Top is here – not very well. His binding for the *Volsungs* is most lovely – quite perfect.'

9 May 1870: Morris, Jane and Rossetti left Scalands and returned to London.

14 May 1870: Morris's review of Rossetti's *Poems* was published in the *Academy*. Rossetti was pleased with the review describing it as 'direct and complete – an honour and a profit to the book'.

21 May 1870: The *Athenaeum* announced that the first edition of Rossetti's *Poems* had sold out in 'about ten days'.

25 May 1870: Morris and Jane dined with Chariclea Ionides.

June 1870: Morris spent much of the month working on the illuminated manuscript of *A Book of Verse*.

14 June 1870: Morris was photographed by John Parsons in the morning. A carte-de-visite of this photograph printed by Ellis & Green is at the V & A. Morris was accompanied by Charles Fairfax Murray who used Parson's photograph as the basis for a portrait of Morris. This was used in Morris's illuminated manuscript – *A Book of Verse* (*c.f.* 26 August 1870). According to May, Parson's photograph was the earliest of her father except for the daguerreotype taken when he was twenty-three.

22 June 1870: Morris had a second photographic sitting with Parsons.

19 July 1870: The Franco-Prussian war began.

7 August 1870: Cormell Price recorded in his diary that Morris had visited him for dinner. Their discussion centred on the Franco-Prussian War. According to Price, Morris was sympathetic with the Prussian cause.

13 August 1870: An unsigned review of *The Story of the Volsungs & Niblungs* appeared in the *Academy*, pp. 983–4.

26 August 1870: Morris completed *A Book of Verse*. The book included a picture by Burne-Jones (p. 1), a portrait-head of the author by Charles Fairfax Murray (*c.f.* 14 June 1870) and painted letters by George Wardle. All the other pictures were by Murray. The book was given to Georgiana Burne-Jones for her birthday.

October 1870: A review of Morris's poetry appeared in the American journal *The Catholic World*, vol. 12, pp. 89–98.

3 October 1870: Morris and Charles Fairfax Murray visited the Hospital of St John in Bruges where they signed their names in the register (*c.f.* 24 July 1874).

November 1870: An article entitled 'The Later Labours of William Morris' appeared in *Tinsley's Magazine*, vol. 7, pp. 457–65.

24 November 1870: Morris went to buy some new clothes 'but was so alarmed at the chance of turning up something between a gamekeeper and a methodist parson, that I brought away some patterns in my hand to show Webb; but haven't seen him yet'.

25 November 1870: Morris was at 26 Queen Square where he was restless having finished writing *The Earthly Paradise*. In the morning, he told Jane, there was a rumpus: 'May enjoying a good tease and Jenny expressing herself in boo hoo.' At this time Jane was in Torquay where she was staying with Mrs Morris Snr and her sister-in-law Henrietta.

29 November 1870: Jane was still at Torquay. Morris expressed the view that she should stay there if it was doing her good. He went on to write: 'Meantime, one great event has occured – the ordering of a suit of Clothes: Ellis took me to a place in the city: where I was gratified by the tailor complimenting on my great works before he measured me.'

30 November 1870: Morris intended to have a haircut: 'I shall entrust the head wh: accomplished the E. P. to the scissors & comb.'

December 1870: The final volume – Part IV – of *The Earthly Paradise* was published. Buxton-Forman wrote that it was not 'really ready much before December, but at all events it was out well before Christmas'. If Kelvin is right in dating a letter Morris wrote to Jane to 3 December 1870, then it would appear the book was available by 6 December 1870. A review of Part IV of *The Earthly Paradise*, by Sidney Colvin, appeared in the *Academy* (pp. 57–8).

3 December 1870: Jane was still in Torquay where Morris sent her £5. Morris also reported that the picture Rossetti had painted of Jane (*c.f.* March 1868) had been hung on the wall again. This had been altered by Rossetti in 1870. Morris wrote: 'perhaps it looks better, but I can't see much difference.' Rossetti wrote to Alexander Macmillan: 'Why does your magazine resolutely ignore the best things going? It's no business and no meaning of mine to speak for myself ... but why in the world has Morris been left in the lurch till now?'

7 December 1870: Morris travelled to Torquay to spend the week with Jane.

25 December 1870: In the copy of *The Earthly Paradise* that he gave his daughters, Morris wrote the poem beginning 'So many stories written here'.

1871: In the census Morris was described as an 'Artist and Painter, employing 18 men and boys'. Morris began his illuminated manuscript of *The Story of Frithiof the Bold*. The text was completed but not the illustrations. Morris also accepted a directorship of the Devon Mining company. For the purpose of attending the board meetings he purchased a top hat.

January 1871: A review of *The Earthly Paradise*, by G. W. Cox, appeared in the *Edinburgh Review*, vol. 133, pp. 243–66.

11 January 1871: Rossetti reported that 'Morris has at last finished his *Earthly Paradise*, with the most triumphant success, the first 1000 of vol. 4 having been bespoke before publication'. He also added that he had been informed by a servant that it was 'no good knocking at the front door [of Morris's house], as that will not open since Master last banged it.'

27 January 1871: Morris dined with Rossetti at 16 Cheyne Walk. Amongst the other guests were Madox Brown, Burne-Jones and William Rossetti. The latter recorded in his *Diary* that 'Morris has some idea, now *The Earthly Paradise* is done, of writing a drama, or a prose romance – not another narrative poem; he cannot however settle upon any subject'.

February 1871: 'The Dark Wood: A Poem' appeared in the *Fortnightly Review*, p. 79.

1 February 1871: Morris's poem 'The Seasons' was published in the *Academy*. Rossetti described it as 'an exquisite little gem'.

March–April 1871: Morris and Magnússon's translation of *The Story of Frithiof the Bold* was published in the *Dark Blue* [Magazine]. Chapters I–X appeared in March and chapters XI–XV in April.

28 March 1871: The Commune of Paris was proclaimed.

April 1871: Morris completed the manuscript of *The Eyrbyggja Saga*, a folio of 239 pages with some ornamentation but no pictures. At around the same time he began a translation of *The Rubaiyat of Omar Khayyam*. An unsigned notice relating to *The Earthly Paradise* appeared in the *Westminster Review* (p. 581).

Early-May 1871: Morris began to practise riding in preparation for his holiday to Iceland. Rossetti was trying to rent Glottenham for the summer. These negotiations fell through.

10 May 1871: Morris told Edith Marion Story that he was looking for 'a little house out of London' for his family.

16 May 1871: Fairfax Murray wrote in his *Diary*: 'Breakfasted with Mr. Morris. Went with him to Faringdon, lunched at Lechlade and drove over to Kelmscott to look at a house and returned in the evening.'

17 May 1871: Morris wrote to Faulkner about Kelmscott Manor, near Lechlade, which he had found in an Oxfordshire house agent's catalogue. He described it as 'a heaven on earth; an old stone Elizabethan house like Water Eaton, and such a garden! close down on the river, a boat house and all things handy.' This is the first reference to Kelmscott Manor in Morris's surviving letters.

20 May 1871: Morris, Rossetti and Jane visited Kelmscott Manor.

21 May 1871: William Rossetti noted in his *Diary* that Rossetti 'and Morris are now proposing to take an old house near Farringdon, Kelmscott Manor-house, of about the time of Elizabeth: the rent is only £75'.

28 May 1871: The Paris Commune was crushed by Government troops.

9 June 1871: Rossetti wrote to F. S. Ellis from 16 Cheyne Walk requesting him to send a complete set of Scott's novels to Jane.

12 June 1871: Morris wrote to Faulkner reporting that W. H. Evans, who held a commission in the Dorset Yeomanry, was keen to accompany them to Iceland. He also added that he intended to sign the lease for Kelmscott Manor in the coming week and was on the look-out for a suitable boat to use on the Thames.

Mid-June 1871: Morris and Rossetti took the lease on Kelmscott Manor. They rented the property and 68 acres of 'closes' from the executors of James Turner (who died in 1870) as the trustees of his widow, Elizabeth. The main part of the house dated from about 1570. Another block of rooms to the north-east was added about a century later probably by Thomas Turner (1620–82). The house is now owned by the Society of Antiquaries.

July 1871: Emma Morris moved to 'The Lordship', an early eighteenth-century house in Much Hadham, Hertfordshire. She was to live there until her death.

1 July 1871: Morris wrote a letter in support of Magnússon's candidacy for the position of Under Librarian at the University Library, Cambridge. Magnússon was successful and held the post until 1910.

3 July 1871: Morris accompanied Jane and the children to Kelmscott Manor where he spent the day. Later he travelled back to London.

5 July 1871: Morris saw Evans off by boat to Edinburgh. In the evening he had dinner with Burne-Jones, Faulkner and Webb.

6 July 1871: Morris, Magnússon and Faulkner took the 9.15 pm train from King's Cross (3rd Class) to Edinburgh. During the journey Morris was too excited to sleep even though Faulkner bribed the guard to keep other people out of the carriage. Morris was unimpressed with the Scottish capital, writing 'that when I really want to cut my throat I shall go to Edinburgh to do so'!

7 July 1871: Morris, Magnússon, Faulkner and Evans arrived at the Granton Hotel, near Edinburgh, in preparation for their departure for Iceland. They later returned to Edinburgh where Morris had his hair cut: 'Faulkner all the while egging on the hairdresser to cut it shorter.'

8 July 1871: Morris spent the day at Granton. In the morning the party had their first sight of the *Diana* – an ex-gunboat of about 140 tons – that was to take them to Iceland: 'she was a long low vessel with three raking masts ... she carries the swallow-tailed flag with a crown and post horn.' The boat was supposed to depart from Granton at 8 pm but it was delayed until the following day.

9 July 1871: The *Diana* left Granton at 6 am. The party's first day at sea was described by Morris as 'very calm'. Despite this Faulkner was seasick: 'Faulkner is prostrate now but very resigned, and lies without moving on the platform by the wheel.'

10 July 1871: After the *Diana* passed the Orkneys it encountered a very heavy sea for some hours. Morris was seasick: 'I felt as if the ship were going to the bottom at every lurch, i.e. at every two seconds, for she rolled heavily.'

11 July 1871: Morris woke at 6.30 am, half an hour before the *Diana* docked at Thorshaven in the Faroes. The party went ashore for twelve hours and walked across the island of Straumey and visited the little white-washed church at Kirkiuboe (Kirby): 'a most beautiful and poetical place it looked to me, but more remote and melancholy than I can say.' They returned to the *Diana* in time to depart at 7 pm. Rossetti wrote to Philip Webb hoping 'Top is up to his navel in ice by this time and likes it'.

12 July 1871: The party spent 'a very cold bleak day' at sea without once spotting land. Rossetti travelled down to Kelmscott Manor.

13 July 1871: At 3 am Morris was woken by Magnússon and went on deck for his first sight of Iceland. The *Diana* remained at sea all day passing the glaciers at Vatnajökull.

14 July 1871: At 2 am the *Diana* anchored off the Westman Isles to collect mail. The party experienced rough weather on the way to Reykjavik where they arrived in the afternoon. They disembarked soon after their arrival and stayed the night with Magnússon's eldest sister: 'a very clean room in one of the little wooden houses which stands back from the road in its angelica garden.'

15 July 1871: The party spent all day in Reykjavik repacking their luggage. Morris was amused to discover that one unlabelled parcel from the Cooperative Store in the Haymarket contained 2 dozen bottles of scents, 2 dozen bottles of Floriline and 1 large box of violet-powder!

16 July 1871: Another day was spent in Reykjavik. Rossetti told Ford Madox Brown that 'Janey is perfectly well ever since she came here, and takes walks with me of five or six miles at a stretch just as easily as I do'.

17 July 1871: Morris's party set out from Reykjavik on horseback. They spent six and a half hours in the saddle: 'we wriggled into our blankets and so ended our first day of travel.' Jane, Rossetti and the children had begun reading passages from Shakespeare.

18 July 1871: Morris cooked bacon and plovers for breakfast: 'I confess it was with pride that I brought the pan into the tent.' Later the party rode to Eyrarbakki where they stayed with a Mr Thorgrímson.

19 July 1871: Morris and his party rode on to Oddi where they stayed with the local priest: 'it was getting decidedly cold when I came in at last and went to a comfortable bed.' The weather at Kelmscott Manor was so hot that Rossetti was wearing 'a blouse indoors and a wrapper out'.

20 July 1871: The travellers reached Bergthórshvoll.

21 July 1871: Morris spent another day travelling and stayed the night at Lithend: '*I* was cook ... I dealt summarily with all attempts at interference, I was patient, I was bold, and the results were surprising even to me who suspected my own hidden talents in the matter.'

22 July 1871: The party spent the day in Lithend exploring the surrounding countryside.

23 July 1871: The traveller camped at Völlur. Rossetti complained to Murray Marks that the weather was 'provokingly changeable' at Kelmscott Manor.

24 July 1871: Morris and his party travelled on to Stóruvellir where they stayed with the local priest, Síra Gudmundr Jónsson.

25 July 1871: Morris was up at 8 am and spent the day riding through a rainstorm to Geysir.

26 July 1871: Morris and his friends spent the day at Geysir. Jane and Rossetti were supervising the repairs and decoration of Kelmscott Manor.

27 July 1871: Morris spent the afternoon fishing at Geysir: 'I caught two fine trout.'

28 July 1871: The party spent another day at Geysir.

29 July 1871: Morris and his party travelled to Brunnar where they camped.

30 July 1871: The party spent the night at a bonder's house at Kalmanstunga.

31 July 1871: Morris and his friends camped at Búdará. Rossetti was once more complaining about Kelmscott: 'The weather out here is provokingly chilly and windy, with no lack of rain either... I must say that, to my own tastes, the country round is about the most uninspiring I ever stayed in.'

1 August 1871: The weather in Iceland turned colder and Morris and his friends had an unpleasant eight-hour ride to Grímstunga.

2 August 1871: Bad weather prevented the Icelandic party continuing their journey. Morris spent part of the time making a net for the bondsman with whom they were staying in Grímstunga. Rossetti was working on coloured chalk drawings of May and Jenny. The latter are now at Kelmscott Manor. Jane received the first of Morris's letters from Iceland.

3 August 1871: Morris's party arrived at Dr Skaplason's house at Hnausar: 'I wandered around the front of the house and played with a month-old tame fox club, not so very tame either; a pretty little beast he was and really "blue".'

4 August 1871: Morris and his companions reached Vídadalstunga where they stayed the night as Jón Vídalin's house. Rossetti wrote to Charlotte Lydia Polidon saying he hoped to stay a further six weeks at Kelmscott Manor. He described the house as 'as good and genuine a specimen of old middle-class architecture as could be found anywhere'.

5 August 1871: Early in the morning Morris visited the turf-walled church at Vídadalstunga: 'it was all deal inside with a rather elaborate screen, pretty brass chandelier and two old (seventeenth-century?) pictures.' The party camped at Fjardarhorn.

6 August 1871: The party resumed their journey through bog country. At one point a horse had to be hauled out of a hole using ropes. They camped at Hjardarholt.

7 August 1871: The travellers spent the day at Hjardarholt where Morris made an unsuccessful sketch of one of the hills.

8 August 1871: The party spent another day camped at Hjardarholt from which they made an excursion to Ljárskógar and Hvammur: 'I counted [it] one of the best and most memorable days we had.'

9 August 1871: Morris and his friends travelled to Breidabólsstadur on Skógarstrond where they stayed at the priest's house.

10 August 1871: The party spent another day travelling and stayed the night at Stykkishólmur.

11 August 1871: Morris and his companions spent the day at Stykkishólmur resting their horses and rearranging their luggage. Morris wrote to Jane comparing the loose stones on a lava-field to 'a half ruined Paris barricade'. The weather at Kelmscott Manor was so hot that Rossetti wrote to his mother that 'one is tempted to keep indoors altogether'. At some point around this date Rossetti read Browning's *Balaustion's Adventure* out loud to Jane and the children on the lawn.

12 August 1871: Morris's had breakfast on the *Holger*, a boat bound for

Liverpool with a cargo of wool. The party then travelled on to Berserkjahraun where they camped for the night.

13 August 1871: The party travelled to Skerdingsstadur where they spent the night.

14 August 1871: Morris and his companions travelled over the Búlandshöfdi pass: 'I couldn't help feeling rather *light* on my horse every now and then, especially when, as I neared one of the *grooves* in the hillside, Magnússon, who rode before me, looked for all the world as if he were riding straight off into the sea.' They spent the night in the church at Ingjaldshóll: 'on the tombstones of Icelanders dead a hundred and fifty years.'

15 August 1871: Morris and his companions rode on to Stapi where they spent the night: 'a lot of girls and women sat ... to watch us on the bank on the other side of the stream, just as if we were a show they had taken places for.'

16 August 1871: The party arrived at Stadastadur where the local priest killed a lamb in their honour: 'the poor old ewe was bleating and rubbing her nose against the skin in a way to make you forswear fleshmeat for ever.'

17 August 1871: The travellers spent the night in a bonder's house at Miklholt.

18 August 1871: Morris's party arrived at Hítardalu where they spent the night at the priest's house.

19 August 1871: The party rode on to Borg through 'an evil morning of wind and sleet'.

20 August 1871: Morris spent the day in Borg where he peeped in on the service at the church: 'there were candles burning on the altar, and the priest was dressed in chasuble and was intoning the service in Icelandic in doleful key enough: altogether it seemed a dry reminiscence of the Catholic mass and rather depressed me.'

21 August 1871: The travellers rode to Stafholt where they spent the night.

22 August 1871: The party spent the night at the priest's house at Gilsbakki.

23 August 1871: Morris's party arrive at the priest's house in Reykholt.

24 August 1871: The travellers spent the day in Reykholt.

25 August 1871: Morris and his party camped at Thingvellir.

26 August 1871: The party spend the day at Thingvellir.

27 August 1871: Morris's party spent another day at Thingvellir. Rossetti wrote to his uncle – Henry Francis Polydore – putting him off from visiting Kelmscott.

28 August 1871: Morris returned to Reykjavik.

30 August 1871: The party visited the museum in Reykjavik and sold their horses to Geir Zoega.

31 August 1871: Morris and his companions had dinner with Dr Hjaltalin. In a letter to Ford Madox Brown, Rossetti stated that he intended to stay at Kelmscott Manor for another month as 'I don't want ... to be returning just as Top comes here'.

September 1871: An article entitled 'Geoffrey Chaucer and William Morris' appeared in the *New Monthly Magazine*, vol. 149, pp. 280–86.

1 September 1871: The *Diana* set sail from Reykjavik.

4 September 1871: The *Diana* arrived at Thorshaven Firth: 'Magnússon called me out to look at some faint show of the northern lights.'

5 September 1871: The *Diana* made slow progress between the Faroes and the Orkneys: 'I went to a very uneasy bed in which my feet were often much higher than my head.'

7 September 1871: The *Diana* arrived at Granton at about 7 pm. In the evening Morris caught the night mail train to London. He later wrote to his mother that he had returned 'with the complexion of a trading skipper and much thinner'. Rossetti told Fanny Cornforth: 'I have not felt so well lately as at first, but the weather has been very changeable.'

9 September 1871: There is a hint in a letter from Rossetti to Webb that he was not looking forward to the arrival of Morris at Kelmscott Manor due to some scandalous rumours in London: 'your head is doubtless whirling in a cloud of lies, Topsaic and Icelandic, to which the gnats of Kelmscott must be nothing. What the one added to the other may be like I shall know tomorrow! Talk about rest on the Sabbath!'

10 September 1871: Morris arrived at Kelmscott Manor with an Icelandic pony for May and Jenny called Mouse.

11 September 1871: Morris wrote to Magnússon from Kelmscott Manor and stated that his recent holiday had done him 'a great deal of good both mentally & bodily, and increased my debt of gratitude to Iceland'. Rossetti drew a sketch of Morris fishing for gudgeon at Kelmscott Manor. This sketch was inscribed 'Enter Skald, moored in a punt,/And Jacks and Tenches exeunt'.

12 September 1871: Morris read out loud passages from his Icelandic *Journal*.

14 September 1871: Morris returned to London from Kelmscott Manor.

21 September 1871: Morris visited Wimbledon on business.

23 September 1871: Morris went to Kelmscott via Oxford to buy a new boat for use at Kelmscott Manor.

29 September 1871: Morris probably returned to London from Kelmscott Manor.

October 1871: An unsigned article on Morris's poetry appeared in the American journal the *New Englander* (pp. 557–80).

2 October 1871: Rossetti told William Bell Scott that Morris was working on *Love is Enough*: 'The poem is, I think, at a higher point of execution than anything he has done, – having a passionate lyric quality such as one found in his earlier poems, and of course much more mature balance in carrying [it] out. It will be a very fine work.' At the time Morris planned to illustrate it with woodcuts by Burne-Jones.

6 October 1871: Rossetti probably returned to London from Kelmscott Manor. Jane and the children went to London around the same time.

23 October 1871: William Bell Scott sent his wife an account of a dinner party Morris had held at Queen Square. Morris read passages from *Love is Enough*. Jane was not present as she was dining with Rossetti.

1872: The Devon Great Consols ceased to earn a dividend. During his ownership of the shares Morris had received £8,803. Morris designed the 'Larkspur' and 'Jasmine' wallpapers. George MacDonald wrote *The Princess and the Goblin* while living at The Retreat (later Kelmscott House).

January 1872: An unsigned article – by W. J. Courthope – which made reference to *The Earthly Paradise* appeared in the *Quarterly Review*, vol. 132, pp. 75–81. The article was entitled 'The Latest Developments of Literary Poetry' and also discussed Swinburne's *Songs Before Sunrise* and Rossetti's *Poems*.

9 February 1872: Morris travelled down to Kelmscott Manor with Ford Madox Brown. Jane and the children remained in London.

13 February 1872: Morris told Louisa Macdonald that he intended to spend two weeks at Kelmscott Manor to see in the spring.

May 1872: Rossetti became seriously ill.

15 May 1872: Morris wrote to the Royal Literary Fund in support of an application for funds submitted by Martha Jones, a writer of children's books.

23 May 1872: Morris told Magnússon that he was eager to start a translation of the *Heimskringla*. This translation was not completed until 1895.

4 June 1872: Morris wrote to Edmund Henry Morgan with reference to the stained-glass windows for the nave of Jesus College Chapel, Cambridge.

7 June 1872: Rossetti's condition had deteriorated badly and during a cab drive from Cheyne Walk to Hake's house in Roehampton he imagined bells ringing around his head.

8 June 1872: Rossetti attempted to commit suicide by taking an overdose of laudanum. For two days he remained in a coma in the house of Dr Gordon Hake. On hearing the news from Bell Scott, Jane left Kelmscott Manor to be with Rossetti.

11 June 1872: Morris wrote to his mother saying one of his friends was 'very ill, indeed we thought him dying on Sunday'.

20 June 1872 Rossetti was taken by George Hake and Madox Brown to recuperate in Perthshire, Scotland.

22 June 1872: Morris sent Louisa Macdonald a copy of his abortive contemporary novel. This was published in 1982 as *The Novel on Blue Paper*. Morris described it as 'just a specimen of how not to do it'. Morris had previously sent the novel to Georgiana Burne-Jones who had dissuaded him from completing it.

July 1872: In a letter to Alice Boyd, William Bell Scott reported that Rossetti was still suffering from delusions: 'All the birds even on the trees are villains making cat-calls.'

2 July 1872: Allingham spent the night at Queen Square and had dinner with Morris.

3 July 1872: Allingham spent the day with Morris.

24 September 1872: Rossetti spent the day with his mother in London before leaving for Kelmscott Manor.

25 September 1872: Rossetti arrived at Kelmscott Manor: 'here all is happiness again, and I feel completely myself.' Jane and the children were already in residence.

28 September 1872: Morris spent the day at Kelmscott Manor where he went fishing with his daughters and George Hake, Rossetti's companion.

6 October 1872: Morris and Burne-Jones spent some time in Hammersmith looking for a suitable house for Morris to rent as the Queen Square premises where now too small for his family.

7 October 1872: Morris and Burne-Jones again went out searching for a house in Hammersmith: 'we went in great excitement to look at a house in that row of houses in the high road just before you come to North End: but it turned out altogether too small and wretched: Ned was very much disappointed.'

8 October 1872: In a letter to Aglaia Ionides Coronio, Morris stated that he hoped that *Love is Enough* would be published in November. He had just received the last of the proofs of the book. That night he proposed travelling down to Cambridge to spend a day reading Icelandic with Magnússon.

9 October 1872: It is probable that Morris had lunch with the Revd James Porter, Master of Peterhouse, Cambridge, who was taking an active interest in the Firm's restoration of the College Hall and Combination Room. This work had begun in 1868 and was completed in 1874.

16 October 1872: Morris completed his illuminated manuscript on vellum of *The Rubaiyat of Omar Khayyam*. This 23-page book, which included a great deal of ornamentation, was presented to Georgiana Burne-Jones. A second copy of *The Rubaiyat of Omar Khayyam* had been started before this volume was finished. This was on paper and included six pictures by Burne-Jones.

19 October 1872: Morris travelled down to Kelmscott Manor to meet Jane who he had not seen for three weeks. He went fishing with George Hake.

20 October 1872: Morris spent a second day fishing on the Thames. It rained all day with a bitter north-east wind: 'Lord how dull the evenings were! with William Rossetti also to help us.'

22 October 1872: Morris returned to London from Kelmscott Manor.

24 October 1872: Morris complained to Aglaia Ionides Coronio that while the days at Kelmscott Manor had passed 'well enough' the evenings had had been dull mainly due to the presence of William Rossetti. He also complained that he had a pretty 'hardish' time in London on his return being 'all alone with Bessy [Jane's sister], with whom I seldom exchange any word that is not necessary. What a wearing business it is to live with a person with whom you have nothing whatever to do!'

3 November 1872: Rossetti reported he was at work on *Prosperpine* and had finished a chalk drawing of May.

11 November 1872: Sir Richard Francis Burton was present at a gathering at the Grange where Morris read part of *Love is Enough*. Rossetti reported from Kelmscott Manor that he was looking for a new property in which to spend the winter.

16 November 1872: A fellow – unnamed – traveller who Morris had met on the *Diana* on his way to Iceland, brought him a letter from Jón Jónsson and a present of a copy of the *Surlunga Saga*.

18 November 1872: In a letter to Faulkner, Morris stated that he was making plans for a second expedition to Iceland.

20 November 1872: *Love is Enough* was published by F. S. Ellis although it was dated 1873. Twenty-five copies were printed on Whatman handmade paper and four on fine writing vellum.

23 November 1872: Morris sent a copy of *Love is Enough* to his mother. A favourable, although unsigned, review of the poem appeared in the *Athenaeum*, pp. 657–8. Jane returned to Queen Square from Kelmscott Manor. Jenny and May had returned over a week before. In the evening Morris dined with Burne-Jones at the Grange.

25 November 1872: In a letter to Aglaia Ionides Coronio, Morris wrote: 'Rossetti has set himself down at Kelmscott as if he never meant to go way; and not only does that keep me away from that harbour of refuge, (because it is really a farce our meeting when we can help it) but also he has all sorts of ways so unsympathetic with the sweet simple old place, that I feel his presence there as a kind of a slur on it.'

26 November 1872: Morris and Jane went to inspect a house in Theresa Terrace, Hammersmith. This had previously been the home of the painter George Heming Mason who had died earlier in the year.

28 November 1872: Morris attended the Annual General Meeting of the Devon Mining Company of which he was a director.

December 1872: The *Academy* carried a review of *Love is Enough* by G. A. Simcox (pp. 461–2).

2 December 1872: Rossetti suffered violent pain in his eyes and the back of his head.

3 December 1872: Rossetti displayed signs of paranoia when he insisted that all letters addressed to him 'should be *sealed*'. He had started to believe that the local post office officials were reading his mail.

1873: J. H. Dearle joined Morris & Co. He started as an assistant in the showroom, progressed to being a glass-painting apprentice and then turned to tapestry weaving in which he was trained by Morris. Later Dearle was to become the general manager of Morris & Co. Lechlade Station on the Oxford and Fairford line was opened which made it easier for Morris to visit Kelmscott Manor.

January 1873: Morris moved from Queen Square to Horrington House on Turnham Green Road (*c.f.* 23 January 1873). Jane described it as 'a very good sort of house for one person to live in, or perhaps two'. They were to stay there for six years even though – according to May – Morris disliked 'a beastly tin-kettle of a bell in a chapel close by, which ... went *wank, wank, wank*, until he was nearly driven mad'. The house was to be taken on two three-year leases at a rent of £80 per annum. It has since been demolished. One of the advantages of the move for Morris was that Bessie Burden (Jane's sister) was no longer to live with the family. Despite moving house Morris kept on his study and bedroom at Queen Square.

1 January 1873: A review of *Love is Enough* by Sidney Colvin appeared in the *Fortnightly Review* (pp. 147–8).

23 January 1873: It is clear from a letter to Aglaia Ionides Coronio that Morris had by this time taken up residence in Horrington House. He wrote: 'it is a *very* little house with a pretty garden: and I think it will suit Janey & the children: it is some /2 hours walk from the Grange.'

24 January 1873: May and Jenny were due to arrive at Horrington House. This was the first time Morris had seen them for a month.

25 January 1873: Further evidence of Rossetti's paranoia occurred when he wrote to Fanny Cranforth 'Now do buy a sixpenny seal. Letters ought to be sealed, and not with a thimble'.

3 February 1873: Morris dined with the Burne-Joneses at the Grange: 'we had the pleasantest evening that has taken place for this long while.'

9 February 1873: Burne-Jones had breakfast with Morris at Horrington House.

11 February 1873: Morris wrote to Aglaia Ionides Coronio about his hopes for the Firm: 'I should very much like to make the business quite a success, and it can't be unless I work at it myself. I must say, though I don't call myself money-greedy, a smash in that side would be a terrible nuisance.'

18 February 1873: Morris wrote to George James Howard in support of Richard Watson Dixon's candidacy for the living of Lanercost. Dixon was unsuccessful.

9 March 1873: Rossetti told Thomas Gordon Hake that he expected Jane to return to Kelmscott Manor 'either tomorrow or [the] next day'.

18 March 1873: Morris was working on 'The Saga of Olaf Tryggvason' one of the tales in the *Heimskringla*.

26 March 1873: Charles Eliot Norton noted in his *Journal*: 'Leslie Stephen and Morris dined with us. They had never met before. Morris complained of feeling old. Monday was his 39th birthday; his hair, he said, was turning grey. He was as usual a surprising piece of nature; certainly one of the most unconventional and original of men. His talk was much of old Northern stories and sagas, very vivid, picturesque and entertaining from its contents and from its character.'

4 April 1873: Morris and Burne-Jones caught the night train from Paris to Florence via Turin.

5 April 1873: Morris and Burne-Jones arrived in Florence where they stayed at the Lione Bianco (White Lion) Inn.

6 April 1873: Morris and Burne-Jones visited the Duomo and S. Maria Novello in Florence. Mackail wrote that 'Burne-Jones ... found [Morris] a rather exacting companion, and a little determined to make the worst of things'. Morris planned to buy a present for his daughters from a jeweller's shop on the Ponte Vecchio.

8 April 1873: Morris and Burne-Jones visited the church of S. Miniato. Morris condemned its 'barbarous so-called restoration'.

9 April 1873: Morris purchased scents of S. Maria Novella for Jane. He also visited S. Croce which he described as 'the finest church in Florence'.

10 April 1873: The two men took a day trip to Prato and Pistoja. Morris wrote to Webb describing a number of items he had purchased – including pots and flasks – which he hoped could be sold by the Firm. Everywhere in Florence, he wrote, one could see 'change and ruin, recklessness & folly, and forgetfulness of "great men & our fathers that begat us" – it is only in such places as this that one can see the signs of them to the full'.

17 April 1873: Morris probably arrived back in London.

25 April 1873: William Rossetti recorded in his *Diary* that he met Morris who was 'looking uncommonly fresh and vigorous after returning from a brief trip (with Jones) to Florence: he has delighted greatly in Italy'.

6 May 1873: Jane travelled down to Kelmscott Manor.

25 May 1873: Jane returned to London from Kelmscott Manor.

26 May 1873: Morris was making plans for his second trip to Iceland. He was to be accompanied on this occasion by Faulkner as Magnússon had to withdraw at the last moment.

31 May 1873: Rossetti was showing further evidence of his paranoia. In a letter to Ford Madox Brown he wrote: 'Another desirable point is to use envelopes thick enough to prevent letters being read *through* them.'

June 1873: Morris supported Frederick James Furnivall's candidacy for the post of Secretary of the Royal Academy. Amongst those who also supported his application were Tennyson and Kingsley. Furnivall was unsuccessful.

21 June 1873: Morris had planned to go down to Kelmscott Manor but put off the trip. Rossetti wrote to Ford Madox Ford: 'Please don't let it enter your head to suggest him [Morris] coming down with you on Tuesday (when I hope to see you) as it's a bore showing him my work, and not to do so is awkward.'

24 June 1873: Morris apologized to John Westland Marston for being unable to attend his daughter's wedding as Jane was 'too poorly' and he had 'a heap of fidgetty work to do' before he embarked for Iceland.

28 June 1873: Morris visited Magnússon in Cambridge.

8 July 1873: Morris visited Aglaia Ionides Coronio before leaving London by rail for Granton on the first leg of his second visit to Iceland. He also gave Georgiana Burne-Jones a fair copy of his Icelandic *Journal* of 1871.

9 July 1873: Morris and Faulkner spent the day in Granton as the sailing of the *Diana* had been delayed.

10 July 1873: Morris and Faulkner spent a second day in Granton. They were surprised to find four or five ironclads anchored in the harbour: 'queer ugly-looking things.'

11 July 1873: The *Diana* left Granton at 2 pm. Morris and Faulkner had the same cabins as they had on their first voyage. During the voyage Morris made the acquaintance of John Henry Middleton. The two men were to remain lifelong friends.

15 July 1873: The *Diana* was off Iceland at 1 am and sighted Papey at 5 am: 'unimaginably strange it seemed to me to be seeing all this over again on just such a morning as last time.'

17 July 1873: The *Diana* encountered a severe gale as it neared Reykjavik. It was forced to lie under the lea of the land for six hours until the gale abated somewhat. Morris was very seasick.

18 July 1873: The *Diana* arrived at Reykjavik at 11 am in the midst of the gale. Jane and the children arrived at Kelmscott Manor. May was in some pain as she had recently had some teeth extracted.

19 July 1873: Morris and Faulkner left Reykjavik and spent the night camping at Battle Holm, Thingvellir: 'I felt happy and light-hearted and quite at home, to wit, as if there had been no break between the old journey and this.'

20 July 1873: The Icelandic party pitched camp at Snorrastadir in Laugardalur. Jenny fell into the water by the boathouse at Kelmscott Manor. Rossetti wrote: 'Poor Jenny managed to tumble into the water by the boathouse, but somehow got out again. Perhaps this may be the secret of her bedridden state to-day.' This may have been the first of Jenny's epileptic attacks (*c.f.* the entry for Summer 1876).

21 July 1873: Morris and Faulkner travelled on to Skálholt through 'drizzling rain [which] ... hid everything distant: it was charged too with fine dust that half blinded us and we seemed to be riding through a middling London fog'.

22 July 1873: Morris spent the morning visiting 'the departed glories of

Skálholt'. He and Faulkner spent the night on beds set out in the chancel of the church at Stóruvellir.

23 July 1873: Morris and Faulkner left Stóruvellir at noon and travelled to Breidabólsstadur where they spent the night in a tent in the churchyard.

24 July 1873: Morris spent the day at Breidabólsstadur where he sewed 'ten buttons on my breeches'.

25 July 1873: The travellers reached the tún of Eyvindarmúli where they stayed the night.

26 July 1873: Morris and Faulkner reached Thórsmörk where they set up camp.

27 July 1873: The day was spent at Thórsmörk where, amongst other things, Morris and Faulkner amused themselves 'damning up [a] ... little stream to make our bathing-place better'.

28 July 1873: The party travelled to Eyvindarmúli where they made camp. Morris was worried because Faulkner was suffering from a bad toothache.

29 July 1873: Morris visited Keldur where they 'gave me a piece of half salt ling at the stead which I cooked with great care in the midst of about a dozen men, women and children, and then we dined in no great comfort owing to [Faulkner's] toothache'.

30 July 1873: Morris and Faulkner, who was still suffering from toothache, rode back to Stóruvellir.

31 July 1873: Morris and Faulkner, who was slightly better, spent the day fishing at Stóruvellir.

1 August 1873: The party reached Galtalækur where they spent the night.

2 August 1873: The travellers reached Tungnaá where they camped for the night after drinking a bottle of Madeira 'in honour of the waste'.

3 August 1873: Morris and Faulkner rode for seven hours to 'Hvamgil' where they made camp.

4 August 1873: The travellers reached Eyvindarkofaver where they spent the night.

5 August 1873: Morris spent the day at Eyvindarkofaver 'in writing [his] journal, cooking dinner, eating it, and [playing] four games of cribbage'.

6 August 1873: The party set off at 7 am for a day's travel across the wilderness. Morris wrote of the latter: 'It is not a flat but is in great waves, not like hills, not high enough for that and especially having no stability about the look of them; as to the ground you go over, it is all sand indeed but varies as to what

lies on the sand.' He and Faulkner made camp at Fljótsdalur.

7 August 1873: After a further eight hours riding, mainly through the wilderness, Morris and Faulkner reached Miofidal where they made camp.

8 August 1873: Morris had coffee in a house at Miofidal: 'the people I thought seemed depressed and poor, the last tenant had emigrated to America – perhaps this cast an air of gloom on the place.' He and Faulkner later travelled to Halldórsstadir where they made camp.

9 August 1873: Morris and Faulkner spent the day riding on to Gautlönd.

10 August 1873: Morris was up early fishing: 'I caught breakfast in the form of two orange-bellied char.' He and Faulkner then rode on to Grímsstadir where they made camp. At Kelmscott, Rossetti was painting May Morris. Two heads of her, as angels, were later incorporated in *La Ghirlandata*.

11 August 1873: Morris and Faulkner spent the day at Grímsstadir where they made an unsuccessful fishing trip on the lake.

12 August 1873: The travellers spent the day riding over the end of the lava stream 'that flowed from Krabla one hundred and thirty years ago'.

13 August 1873: Morris and Faulkner reached Grenjadarstadur.

14 August 1873: The travellers reached Hals.

15 August 1873: Morris and Faulkner reached Saurbær.

16 August 1873: The travellers camped at Akureyri.

17 August 1873: Morris and Faulkner reached Mödruvellir.

18 August 1873: The travellers arrived at Steinstadir in Öxnadalur.

19 August 1873: Morris made his last entry in his Icelandic *Journal*. At this time he and Faulkner were at Ytrakot Nordardal.

September 1873: Jenny and May started at Notting Hill High School for Girls.

3 September 1873: Morris attended the wedding of Soffia Emilía Einarsdóttir Saemundson, one of Magnússon's sisters, and Sira Sigurður Gunnarsson, in Reykjavik.

12 September 1873: Morris and Faulkner arrived at Granton in the morning. Morris was home at Turnham Green by 10.30 pm. He returned without the Icelandic pony he had promised Louisa Macdonald Baldwin's son.

13 September 1873: In the morning Morris visited the Burne-Joneses at the Grange. Around this time Burne-Jones told Fairfax Murray: 'Mr Morris has come back more enslaved with passion for ice and snow and raw fish than ever

– I fear I shall never drag him to Italy again.'

14 September 1873: In a letter to Aglaia Ionides Coronio, Morris wrote: 'I feel as if a definite space of my life had passed away now I have seen Iceland for the last time.'

6 October 1873: Morris turned down a request from Frederic Every to become a Vice-President of the Trades Guild of Learning. However, he expressed himself willing to subscribe as an 'Associate Member'.

22 October 1873: In a letter to Louisa Macdonald Baldwin, Morris said he was determined to once more take up figure drawing from models. It is clear from the same letter that he had read Dumas's books *Vicomte de Bragelonne* (1848–50) and *Olympe de Cleves* (1852).

24 October 1873: Edmund Henry Morgan requested that the Firm altered one of the panels in the window in the south transept of Jesus College Chapel so that it could be used as a ventilator. In a letter bearing this date George Wardle wrote: 'Mr. Morris is horrified. He says it would be fatal to the window & you must really give it up... What a monster the stove must be to demand such a sacrifice. If it is to be done pray do not ask our connivance. That Mr. Morris will never give.'

28 October 1873: Rossetti reported that Jane had twice telegraphed him dissuading him from going to London.

5 November 1873: Morris was contemplating making another illuminated manuscript of *Lancelot dur Lac*. May describes the original as an incomplete 'manuscript in a very beautiful Italian script'. Morris told Murray that he had again thought of figure painting: 'I have made a step in getting models and have meant to take to drawing again: but I have so little hope about the whole affair that I can scarcely fix my attention on it.' In the event Morris did hire a male model called Colorossi. He later told Charles Fairfax Murray (18 February 1874) that I 'did some very disheartening studies from him, & at last gave it up after making myself a laughing-stock by sending away about every other time.'

12 November 1873: Morris wrote to Buxton Forman thanking him for sending him a copy of his brother Alfred's libretto of Wagner's *Die Walkure*. He went on to add 'I [am not] much interested in anything Wagner does, as his theories on musical matters seem to me as an artist and non-musical man perfectly abominable'. He described opera as 'the most rococo and degraded of all forms of art'.

8 December 1873: Morris wrote to Buxton Forman about his plans for *Three Northern Love Stories and Other Tales*. He had already decided that the three main tales would be the *Story of Gunnlaug the Worm-tongue*, the *Story of*

Frithiof the Bold and the *Story of Viglund the Fair*.

24 December 1873: Morris, Jane and the children attended a party at the Grange. Amongst the other guests were Faulkner, De Morgan and Allingham. Rudyard Kipling, a cousin of Philip and Margaret Burne-Jones, was also present. Amongst the entertainments was a magic lantern show for the children. Georgiana Burne-Jones recalled that 'Mrs Morris, placed safely out of the way, watched everything from her sofa. This is the last time of the kind that I remember. By the following Christmas the children's own world had begun, and it was their turn to amuse us.'

30 December 1873: Morris's textile design – *Tulip & Willow* – was registered. It was his disappointment with the colour of the material produced to this design by Thomas Clarkson of the Bannister Hall Print Works near Preston, that led him to start experiments with dyeing techniques.

12 January 1874: Morris took Jenny and May to a pantomime.

16 January 1874: It is possible that Morris met Walter Theodore Watts-Dunton on this day (or the 17th or 18th) to discuss the proposal to dissolve the Firm. Watts-Dunton was working on behalf of Ford Madox Brown – with the support of Rossetti and Marshall – who opposed Morris taking sole ownership of the business.

Early February: Morris finished his translations of 'The Henthorir Saga', 'The Banded Men' and 'Howard the Halt'. This document, with decorated initials, was given to Georgiana Burne-Jones. It is now in the Fitzwilliam Museum at Cambridge.

8 February 1874: Rossetti reported that both Morris girls had the measles.

12 February 1874: In a letter to Henry Treffry Dunn, Rossetti wrote: 'Jenny *fille* and I shrieked "Creepy" in one of Dizzy's [Rossetti's dog] ears and "Crawly" in the other at the same moment while May drummed on the top of his head. He turned round howling and bit my nose, which has been patched up since!!'

18 February 1874: In a letter to Charles Fairfax Murray, Morris reported that the Firm had been commissioned to provide a window in Christ Church, Oxford. The 'St Cecilia' window was executed by Burne-Jones.

23 February 1874: May and Jenny collected all the flowers in the garden at Kelmscott Manor to send on to Rossetti's mother.

24 February 1874: A letter from Morris to his mother, dated by Kelvin as 'February 1874', was almost certainly written on this date. In it Morris says that Jane and Jenny were due to return to London the next day although May was to remain at Kelmscott Manor to be painted by Rossetti. Morris also makes reference to payments he was making to his brother Rendall. These could have been a subsidy for the latter's poultry business.

4 March 1874: Morris paid a visit to his mother. He stayed overnight and returned to London the next day.

7 March 1874: Philip and Margaret Burne-Jones spent the day with Jenny at Turnham Green. Morris wrote to Charles Fairfax Murray: 'she is not beyond a romp – to judge at any rate by the infernal row that she & Phil & Margery made.' Of May, who was still at Kelmscott being painted by Rossetti, he said 'she is the more grown up, & writes quite like a young lady'.

9 March 1874: Morris had dinner with Burne-Jones, Stanhope and Wallis.

11 March 1874: Rossetti wrote to Henry Treffry Dunn in connection with a theft that Jane was convinced had taken place at Kelmscott Manor.

16 March 1874: Morris received a consignment of vellum from Fairfax Murray.

25 March 1874: Morris and May jointly celebrated their birthdays. Morris had in fact been forty on 24 March 1874.

26 March 1874: Morris was half-way through a transcription on vellum of Horace's *Odes*. This was never completed.

31 March 1874: Morris attended the wedding of William Rossetti and Lucy Brown: 'it enrages me to think that I lack courage to say, "I don't care for either of you & you neither of you care for me, & I won't waste a day out of my precious life in grinning a company grin at you two old boobies".'

4–6 April 1874: Morris spent these three days working on his illuminated manuscripts.

7 April 1874: Morris went to visit his sister Alice in Weybridge. He spent the night there and returned to London the following morning.

9 April 1874: Rossetti wrote to the agent for Kelmscott Manor stating himself willing 'to take a lease of this house for seven or fourteen years'.

16 April 1874: Morris sent Rossetti his share of the rent for Kelmscott Manor adding: 'As to the future though I will ask you to look upon me as offering my share, & not to look upon me as shabby for that, since you have fairly taken to living at Kelmscott, which I suppose neither of us thought the other would do when we first began the joint possession of the house; for the rest I am both too poor &, by compulsion of poverty, too busy to be able to use it much in any case, and am very glad if you find it useful & pleasant to you.'

19 April 1874: William Bell Scott noted he had received a letter from Rossetti requesting the loan of £200. Scott went on to write: 'He had by that time lost nearly every old friend save myself; did he now suspect that I was among his enemies, and had he done this to try me? I fear this semi-insane motive was the true one. A very short time after he suddenly left Kelmscott altogether, having got into a foundationless quarrel with some anglers by the river.'

20 April 1874: Rossetti reported that Morris had requested his boat be sent from Kelmscott to London.

21 May 1874: Morris intended to meet Magnússon in Cambridge. However, he was obliged to put off the trip due to the ill-health of Burne-Jones who was suffering a severe bout of depression at the time.

22 May 1874: Rossetti was expecting Jane to arrive for a holiday at Kelmscott Manor.

June 1874: Morris accompanied Burne-Jones and his son Philip on a visit to Marlborough College. It was arranged that Philip should attend the school after the summer holidays.

3 June 1874: It is clear from a letter that Rossetti wrote to his brother William that he was trying to purchase Morris's unfinished picture of Jane – *La Belle Iseult*.

Early July 1874: Morris spent some days with his mother at Much Hadham near Ware in Hertfordshire.

1 July 1874: Rossetti had begun to look for alternative accommodation.

9 July 1874: Around this time Rossetti left Kelmscott Manor and returned to 16 Cheyne Walk. Morris and F. S. Ellis were to take a joint tenancy on Kelmscott Manor in the autumn.

17 July 1874: Morris and his family travelled by ferry to Calais.

18 July 1874: Morris and his family took the train from Calais to Tournai.

19 July 1874: The Morrises travelled by rail from Tournai to Ghent.

20 July 1874: As the train journey from Tournai to Ghent had been so uncomfortable the Morrises gave up the idea of travelling by train to Antwerp and Mechelen. Instead they spent the day in Ghent.

21 July 1874: Morris hired a charabanc to transport his family the twenty-nine miles from Ghent to Bruges. They entered Bruges 'by the ancient Gate of the Holy Cross'.

23 July 1874: Morris received a letter from Burne-Jones: 'not in high spirits I must say.'

24 July 1874: Morris and his family were staying at the Hotel du Commerce in Bruges. He and Jane occupied the same rooms they had taken when on their honeymoon. They were both suffering from gnat bites. Morris told

Aglaia Ionides Coronio that his wrist was so stiff he could hardly hold a pen. In the morning they visited the Hospital of St John to view *St Ursula* and the other religious paintings of Hans Memling. Morris examined the Visitors Book and discovered that he and Fairfax Murray had last visited the building on 3 October 1870.

27 July 1874: Morris and his family left Bruges for Ypres.

28 July 1874: The party travelled from Ypres to Calais.

29 July 1874: The Morrises left Calais by the evening ferry.

8 August 1874: The *Times* published a petition signed by Morris against the replacement of the tower at Hampstead Church.

10 August 1874: Morris probably travelled to Naworth to stay with the Howards. This is conjecture based on letter 241 in Kelvin actually being dated 8 August 1874. In a letter to Rosalind Howard dated 20 August 1874 Morris referred to 'those few days in the North'. If letter 241 was dated 1 August 1874 – the only other possibility – he would have stayed with the Howards for the best part of a fortnight. Amongst the other guests were Burne-Jones and Richard Dixon. The latter recorded that he found 'Topsy, genial, gentle, delightful'. Rosalind Howard was to write of Morris: 'He talks so clearly and seems to think so clearly that what seems paradox in Webb's mouth, in his seems convincing sense. He lacks sympathy and humanity though – and this is a fearful lack to me – only his character is so fine and massive that one must admire.'

17 August 1874: Morris returned to London from Naworth.

22 August 1874: William Allingham married Helen Paterson.

28 August 1874: Morris wrote to Walter Watts-Dunton claiming that 'two at least of our members wish to be out of the firm'. This was probably a reference to Ford Madox Brown and Peter Paul Marshall.

21 September 1874: Burne-Jones visited Morris at Turnham Green. In a letter to Philip Burne-Jones (dated 28 September 1874) Morris wrote: 'when your father was here last Sunday he pulled down one big web but the spider had it up again by the next morning: I pulled it down again and the next morning there it was again.'

27 September 1874: Morris spent the night at the Grange where he slept in Philip Burne-Jones's bed.

28 September 1874: In a letter to Philip Burne-Jones, who was soon to enter Marlborough, Morris wrote that he was suffering from gout.

13 October 1874: A letter was sent out – signed by 'R. W. S.' – requesting the partners 'attend a meeting of the Firm of Morris & Company at 26 Queen Square on Friday 23rd. inst. to consider what steps are to be taken in consequence of the announcement of withdrawal from the Firm of several members.'

23 October 1874: A meeting was held at 26 Queen Square to discuss the future of the Firm. Morris, Marshall, Faulkner, Burne-Jones and Webb attended. Rossetti and Ford Madox Brown were absent. Faulkner took the chair. It was decided that the Firm should be dissolved and three assessors appointed to evaluate the value of the company. In the event the assessors were never appointed. The meeting was interrupted when Webb burst in and told the others that George Howard was seriously ill with pneumonia.

24 October 1874: Morris wrote to Rossetti enclosing details of the resolutions passed at the meeting at Queen Square the previous day: 'Marshall bore his execution with much indifference and good temper: I suspect he smelt the advent of the golden shower and was preparing to hold his hat under the spout.'

4 November 1874: The last meeting of the Firm was held at 26 Queen Square attended by Morris, Webb, Marshall and Faulkner. It was resolved that a balance sheet should be drawn up as of Michaelmas 1874 in order to ascertain the firm's assets and 'to endeavour if possible to come to an amicable adjustment of the process of dissolution'.

15 November 1874: Morris travelled to Cambridge to view the firm's stained-glass windows in Jesus College Chapel. While in Cambridge he also spent some hours with Magnússon reading Icelandic.

December 1874: An article on 'The Poems of Mr Morris' by Henry G. Hewitt appeared in the *Contemporary Review*, vol. 25, pp. 100–124.

20 December 1874: Rossetti had begun a new painting of *Pandora* with Jane as his model. The progress of the painting was delayed frequently due to Jane's continued ill-health.

End of 1874: Morris began a manuscript version of the *Aeneid* on vellum.

1875: Morris and Burne-Jones read Mommsen's *History of Rome*.

1 January 1875: In a letter to Aglaia Ionides Coronio, Morris said he had been unwell 'but am getting better – cold & – liver – if I may mention that organ to a lady: I beg to state that I have not the least idea where it lives'.

23 February 1875: Morris was working on his translation of the *Aeneid*.

2 March 1875: Hannah Macdonald, Georgiana Burne-Jones's mother, died.

24 March 1875: Morris celebrated his birthday at the Grange.

25 March 1875: In a letter to Louisa Macdonald Baldwin, Morris wrote: 'I am in the second half of my life now, which is like to be a busy time with me. I hope till the very end: a time not lacking content I fancy: I must needs call myself a happy man on the whole.'

Late March 1875: The final arrangements for the dissolution of the firm were agreed. Burne-Jones, Faulkner and Webb waived their claims. Brown, Marshall and Rossetti agreed – after some delay – to be compensated for the loss of interest at £1,000 each. The firm was reconstituted under Morris's management as Morris & Co.

31 March 1875: A circular was issued announcing the final dissolution of the firm. This stated that Burne-Jones and Webb, while no longer partners, would continue to provide designs for stained glass and furniture.

April 1875: *The Defence of Guenevere & Other Poems* was reissued by Ellis and White.

1 April 1875: Morris arrived at Llanidloes at the start of a week's holiday in Wales with Faulkner: 'This town is rather dirty & manufactory but has got a pretty town hall.' They had dinner with a farmer acquaintance of Faulkner's called Jones: 'the farm-house kitchen was such a nice place: there were some very pretty children there, but not a word could they talk of anything but Welsh, except one older girl.' Morris was later to write (1882): 'my mother & father were both Worcester people; but since they were both of Welsh parentage on both sides, I think I may lay claim to be considered one of the Cymry.'

2 April 1875: Morris and Faulkner rode across the mountains to Machynlleth.

4 April 1875: Morris and Faulkner rode from Dinas Mawddwy up the Valley of the Dyfi and then over the mountains to Bala. They had lunch at a 'pot-house' where they were given 'the biggest loaf I ever saw'.

5 April 1875: Morris and Faulkner stayed at the Bull Hotel at Bala: ''tis a queer dull little grey town is Bala.' In the morning Morris went fishing and caught two trout that they had for dinner.

6 April 1875: The two men rode to Dolgellau near Cadair Idris.

7 April 1875: Morris and Faulkner rode to Tywyn. Morris described it as 'a little queer grey Welsh town by the sea-shore on the flats under the mountains in the most Welsh part of Wales'.

8 April 1875: Morris and Faulkner rode back to Dinas Mawddwy.

9 April 1875: Morris and Faulkner returned by rail to London from Wales.

15 April 1875: Morris's *Marigold* wallpaper design was registered as were his

Tulip and *Larkspur* printed cotton designs.

Whitsun 1875: Morris, Burne-Jones and Faulkner spent two days in Oxford '& were very merry together'. Burne-Jones recalled 'Mr Morris and Mr Faulkner and I almost lived on the river, Sunday and Monday… How we teased Mr Morris on the river. We took our lunch one day, and it was a fowl and a bottle of wine and some bread and salt – and Mr Faulkner and I managed to hide the fowl away in the sheet of the sail, and when we anchored at a shady part of the river and undid the basket, lo! there was no fowl. And Mr Morris looked like a disappointed little boy and then looked good, and filled his dry mouth with bread and said it didn't matter much, so we drew out the fowl and had great laughter.'

25 May 1875: Morris expected his brother Arthur in the morning to discuss a forthcoming meeting of the board of the Devon Great Consols. In a letter to his mother he wrote: 'I don't know what may happen at the meeting, but think that nothing will be done: things are looking a little better there, & the last sale was (comparatively) good as I daresay you have heard.' Kelvin tentatively dates this letter to 25 May 1874. It was almost certainly written in 1875.

27 May 1875: Morris attended a meeting of the Devon Mining Company. In a letter to Charles Fairfax Murray he wrote: 'I am up to the neck in turning out designs for paper chintzes & carpets and trying to get the manufacturer to do them.'

7 June 1875: Morris's design for printed linoleum – the first for any floor-covering – was registered as 'Corticine floor cloth'.

Mid-June 1875: Morris took his MA degree at Oxford University.

6 July 1875: Morris wrote to F. W. Farrar, headmaster of Marlborough College, about a stained-glass window for the school's chapel.

17 July 1875: Morris sent his mother one of the large paper copies of his recently published *Three Northern Love Stories & Other Tales*. An unsigned review of the book appeared in the *Athenaeum* (p. 75). There was another review in the *Saturday Review*.

20 July 1875: Morris made his first visit to Leek in Staffordshire where he stayed with Thomas Wardle – brother-in-law of George Wardle – in order to receive instruction in the art of dyeing at the latter's Hencroft Dye Works which had been set up in 1870. Wardle was an authority on dyeing silk and cotton and keen to revive ancient techniques that had gone out of use. He set aside one of his two dye shops for Morris's use. While in Leek Morris stayed with the Wardles in their large house in St Edward's Street.

22 July 1875: Morris's *Acanthus* wallpaper design was registered.

24 July 1875: Morris and Wardle visited Bakewell.

25 July 1875: Morris visited Haddon Hall where he met Katie Moxon.

30 July 1875: In a letter to Rosalind Howard, written from Leek, Morris wrote 'I have been learning several interesting things here, and love art and manufactures, & hate commerce and money-making more than ever'.

31 July 1875: Morris returned to London from Leek.

3 August 1875: Morris wrote to Thomas Wardle complaining that his Prussian blue dyes did not wash well. This was the first of a series of sixty letters Morris wrote to Wardle discussing dyeing techniques. These provide a running commentary on the Leek experiments.

10 August 1875: Morris gave Buxton Forman a copy of Philemon Holland's translation of *Pliny*.

6 September 1875: Morris paid a visit to his mother at Much Hadham.

Mid-October 1875: Rossetti rented Aldwick Lodge, near Bognor, Sussex.

4 November 1875: *The Aeneids of Virgil: Done Into English Verse* was published by Ellis & White (bearing the date 1876). A large paper edition of twenty-five copies was printed on Whatman's handmade paper.

9 November 1875: Morris wrote to Jane from Kelmscott Manor where he had spent the day fishing. Due to a mix-up he was short of food although he did possess a tin of kangaroo meat! Swinburne wrote to Morris thanking him for sending him a copy of *The Aeneids of Virgil* and urging him to do a translation of the *Odyssey*.

13 November 1875: Morris left Kelmscott Manor and returned to London. An unsigned review of the *The Aeneids of Virgil* appeared in the *Athenaeum* (pp. 635–7).

14 November 1875: In a letter to Watts-Dunton, Rossetti said that he expected Jane to arrive shortly at Aldwick Lodge.

23 November 1875: A review of *The Aeneids of Virgil*, by H. Nettleship, appeared in the *Academy*, vol. 8 (pp. 493–4).

24 November 1875: Jane travelled by train with George Hake to stay with Rossetti at Aldwick Lodge. May and Jenny did not accompany her as they were both at Notting Hill High School.

10 December 1875: Jane left Bognor and returned to London. She described Aldwick Lodge as 'dreary' probably because it contained the same furnishings that Rossetti had used at Kelmscott Manor.

24 December 1875: Morris's first designs for carpets were registered. One was

for a border of intertwining poppy-type flower heads and foliage and the other for a repeated motif of acanthus leaves and peonies.

1876: Morris became one of the assessors of students' work at the School of Design at the South Kensington Museum (now the V & A).

20 January 1876: Morris's *Tulip & Rose* textile design was registered.

26 January 1876: Morris was on a brief holiday at Kelmscott Manor.

8 February 1876: Morris's *Anemone* silk and wool fabric design was registered.

11 February 1876: Morris's *Honeycomb* 3-ply carpeting and fabric design was registered.

29 February 1876: Morris's *Pimpernel* wallpaper design was registered.

March 1876: Jane visited Rossetti at Aldwick Lodge to sit for a second version of his *Astarte Syriaca*. She was accompanied by May who sat for the Attendant Spirit. It was probably during this stay that Jane decided to end her relationship with Rossetti after she discovered the extent of his reliance on chloral. Morris was at work on his *Rose* wallpaper design and his poem *The Story of Sigurd the Volsung and the Fall of the Niblungs*.

3 March 1876: Morris and Jenny were in Marlborough presumably in connection with the stained-glass window Morris & Co. were designing for the school chapel.

4 March 1876: Morris and Jenny 'had a delightful drive to Silbury & Avebury ... through a wild stormy afternoon'.

5 March 1876: Morris had dinner with F. W. Farrar, the headmaster of Marlborough College. Jenny was unable to attend as she was suffering from a cold.

6 March 1876: Morris and Jenny left Marlborough for London.

21 March 1876: Morris told May that the old larder at Queen Square had been transformed into 'a make-shift dye-house'.

22 March 1876: Morris left for Leek.

26 March 1876: Morris and Wardle went on a country walk. They first visited Alton Towers, which Morris described as 'a gim-crack palace of Pugin's', then Ellaston – where George Eliot had lived – and finally Norbury and Ashbourne. By this time Jane had returned to London.

29 March 1876: Morris went to Nottingham to visit a wool-dyer called Shelton.

31 March 1876: Four of Morris's carpet designs were registered including *Rose*. These were the last Morris & Co. carpet designs to be registered and

other companies took advantage of this by plagiarizing the designs. The Heckmondwike Manufacturing Company actually registered designs in its own right which were clearly based on Morris's *Tulip & Lily* and *Daisy*.

Easter 1876: Morris spent three days at Kelmscott Manor with Philip Webb.

April 1876: May Morris left Notting Hill High School.

13 April 1876: Morris sent two pieces of 150-year-old Cretan embroidery to Wardle to place in his museum.

25 April 1876: Morris's *Acanthus* printed textile design was registered, as was his *Iris* printed cotton design.

30 April 1876: Rossetti told George Gordon Hake that on his death Jane's letters to him should be burned.

4 May 1876: Morris conducted the first trial printing of his *Bluebell* or *Colombine* cotton and linen design. Parry notes that the design was originally labelled with both names but *Bluebell* was subsequently crossed out.

9 May 1876: Morris wrote to Thomas Wardle asking him to undertake the dyeing of the firm's serges and Utrecht velvets. These were supplied to Morris & Co. by J. Aldam Heaton & Co. of Manchester.

13 May 1876: *The First Foray of Aristomenes* – an extract from an unfinished tale – appeared in the *Athenaeum*, pp. 663–4. Morris received £20 in payment. According to Buxton Forman this was published later in the same year as a private pamphlet along with *The Two Sides of the River* and *Hapless Love*. A longer version was published by May Morris in volume 24 of *The Collected Works*.

18 May 1876: Morris travelled to Northamptonshire on business.

24 May 1876: Morris sent his mother twenty yards of black silk for her birthday.

Summer 1876: Jenny passed her Cambridge Local examinations and appeared destined for one of the women's colleges at either Oxford or Cambridge. But it was at this point that her future was devastated when she developed epilepsy. Her first attack has often been stated to have been triggered by a boating accident on the Thames when she suddenly lost her balance and fell overboard (*c.f.* 20 July 1873).

June 1876: The Bulgarians rose in revolt against Turkish rule.

7 June 1876: In a letter to a Mr Grey, Morris made his first reference to the Eastern Question and pledged himself 'to hang back in no way' if nothing were done.

23 June 1876: The Liberal *Daily News* carried a full account of the atrocities carried out by the mercenary Bashi-Bazouks against the Christian population of Bulgaria.

26 June 1876: It appears from a letter to Thomas Wardle that Morris signed the petition circulated to members of Parliament and public figures calling for non-intervention in the conflict between Turkey and Russia. This petition was presented to Lord Derby on 14 July 1876.

7 July 1876: Morris spent the morning fishing at Kelmscott Manor. Jane and the children had gone down to spend the summer at Deal in Kent.

12 July 1876: Morris returned from Kelmscott Manor to London.

13 July 1876: Jane and the children were joined at Deal by Georgiana and Margaret Burne-Jones.

15–16 July 1876: Over this weekend Morris wrote 250 lines of *Sigurd the Volsung*.

17 July 1876: Morris visited Charles Faulkner's sister Kate in London. He also broke the venetian blind in his room at Queen Square.

18 July 1876: In a letter to Jane, Morris made his first reference to Jenny's epilepsy.

25 or 26 July 1876: Morris planned to travel down to Deal to spend three days with Jane and the children.

19 August 1876: In a letter to Thomas Wardle, Morris expressed himself shocked that the Roebuck, a seventeenth-century inn, had been moved in pieces from Shropshire to Leek: 'It only shows that people now do not care about art and history.'

4 September 1876: Morris drove from Kelmscott to Broadway via Burford. May recalled how the 'sight of Burford Church being pulled down set my father to making notes for a letter of appeal for some united action'. According to Mackail, Morris drafted a letter – which has not survived – 'urging the formation of a Society which might deal with such cases, and, if the destruction done by restorers could not be stopped, might at all events make it clear that it was destruction and not preservation'.

5 September 1876: Morris spent the day at Broadway Tower, on Broadway Beacon. Burne-Jones and his children were also staying at the Tower. May described it as 'a squat thing with turrets that Cormell Price rented ... which overlooked a glorious view of many counties'.

6 September 1876: Morris wrote to Jenny from the Bull Hotel, Burford. Later he travelled to Kelmscott Manor via Northleach and Foss Bridge. Gladstone published his famous pamphlet, *The Bulgarian Horrors and The Question of the East*, which opposed British support for the Turks and demanded the latter's evacuation from the whole Bulgarian province. 200,000 copies of this pamphlet were sold within a month.

8 September 1876: Morris returned to London for 'a few days'.

9 September 1876: Gladstone addressed an enormous anti-Turkish meeting on Blackheath. The crowd was estimated to number 10,000.

26 September 1876: Morris had the proofs of *Sigurd the Volsung* which he forwarded to Cormell Price.

7 October 1876: Morris's *African Marigold* textile design was registered.

10 October 1876: Morris departed by the night mail train for France to visit Paris with Thomas Wardle.

11 October 1876: Morris arrived in Paris at 6.30 am. His *Honeysuckle* block-printed linen design was registered.

13 October 1876: Morris left Paris in a hail storm. He had a smooth crossing of the Channel. While in Paris Morris visited thirteen shops in search of old books on dyeing techniques. He purchased Pierre-Joseph Macquer's *Art de la Teinture en soie* and Hommassel's *Cours de l'Art de la Teinture*.

20 October 1876: Jenny had a slight epileptic fit 'the first for 3 weeks'. The Labour Representation League held a rally of workers at which it was resolved that if Russia made war upon Turkey 'it will be the duty of the English people to oppose any action of the Government which has for its object any defence of the Ottoman Empire'.

22 October 1876: The Patriotic Club held a demonstration of 2,000 working men on Clerkenwell Green to protest against the threatened war with Turkey. Morris referred to this meeting in a letter to the *Daily News* (see next entry) but it is unclear if he actually attended in person.

26 October 1876: The *Daily News* published a letter from Morris – dated 24 October – entitled 'England and the Turks' in which he urged that Britain wage 'no war on behalf of thieves and murderers'.

28 October 1876: Morris carried out dyeing experiments using poplar twigs. At the time these were unsuccessful. However, while visiting Kelmscott Manor the following month he managed to dye a lock of wool 'a very good yellow' using the same material.

9 November 1876: At the Lord Mayor's Banquet Disraeli indicated that the government might contemplate a 'war in a righteous cause'.

10 November 1876: The Tsar responded to Disraeli's remarks by sending an angry reply that seemed to heighten the chances of war.

15 November 1876: Morris wrote to Charles Faulkner about the Eastern Question agitation: 'I do not feel very sanguine about it all ... but since it is started and is the only thing that offers at present, and I do not wish to be anarchical, I must do the best I can with it.' In another letter, addressed to Mundella, he gave a list of his friends – which included Allingham, De Morgan, Ellis, Faulkner and Webb – who supported the agitation.

17 November 1876: Morris had dinner with Allingham. Jane had also been invited but Morris excused her on the grounds that Jenny was due back from her 'school' on this day and 'would not stand her mother's absence'.

18 November 1876: Morris's *Crown Imperial* woven cotton fabric design was registered.

Late November 1876: *The Story of Sigurd the Volsung and the Fall of the Niblings* was published by Ellis & White (dated 1877). Buxton Forman records that he had his copy of the book by 20 November 1876. The first edition consisted of 2,500 copies with an additional twenty-five on Whatman handmade paper. The publication of the book coincided with the first production in Bayreuth of Wagner's *Ring*.

December 1876: A review of *Sigurd the Volsung* by Theodore Watts appeared in the *Athenaeum* (pp. 753–5).

5 December 1876: The *Daily News* published a list of the conveners for the proposed Eastern Question Association (EQA).

8 December 1876: A conference was held at St James's Hall at which the EQA was formed. About 700 people attended including 89 MPs. A. J. Mundella was elected Chairman and Morris Treasurer. Morris was probably introduced to the leaders of the Labour Representation League at this meeting. Ruskin wrote to Burne-Jones in relation to the Eastern Question hoping that 'neither Morris nor you will retire wholly again out of such spheres of effort. It seems to me especially a time when the quietest men should be disquieted, and the meekest self-asserting.'

9 December 1876: A review of *Sigurd the Volsung* by Edmund Gosse appeared in the *Academy* (pp. 557–8).

10 December 1876: Morris suffered an attack of rheumatism.

13 December 1876: Morris's attack of rheumatism had become so severe that he was confined to the house.

24 December 1876: The Morris and Burne-Jones families celebrated Christmas Eve at the Grange '& were very merry'.

28 December 1876: Swinburne, who had just received a copy of *Sigurd the Volsung*, wrote in a letter to Burne-Jones: 'What a feast shall I make of his glorious book when once I fairly tackle it!'

31 December 1876: The Morris and Burne-Jones families visited the Circus.

4 January 1877: Morris was still suffering from rheumatism.

8 January 1877: Morris travelled to Chester to visit the Duke of Westminster (President of the EQA) to discuss the decoration of Alfred Waterhouse's new chapel at Eaton Hall.

9 January 1877: In the morning Morris visited Eaton Hall ''tis a huge place, but not at all a success I think'.

12 January 1877: Morris took May and Jenny to see *Macbeth*: 'I think we all thought it ill done.'

20 January 1877: An unsigned review of *Sigurd the Volsung* appeared in the *Saturday Review* (pp. 81–2).

25 January 1877: Morris probably travelled down to Leek.

February 1877: An unsigned review of *Sigurd the Volsung* appeared in the *Literary World* (pp. 136–7).

4 February 1877: Morris and Thomas Wardle visited Lichfield. Morris described the town as worthy of 'the prize for dullness over every other place in the world'.

5 February 1877: Morris and Thomas Wardle returned to Leek via Needwood Forest.

7 February 1877: Jane was suffering from toothache.

10 February 1877: Morris returned to London from Leek.

16 February 1877: Around this time Morris was approached by Oxford University as a possible successor to F. H. C. Doyle as Professor of Poetry at Oxford. Morris declined: 'I suppose the lectures a Poetry Professor should give ought to be either the result of deep & wide scholarship in the matter; or else pieces of beautiful & ingenious rhetoric, such, for example, as our Slade Professor could give; and in both these things I should fail & do no credit either to the University or myself.'

26 February 1877: Morris and Ellis travelled down to Kelmscott Manor. Morris was suffering from a cold.

27 February 1877: Morris and Ellis spent the day fishing on the Thames: 'but ... my cold made me feel ill & cross now and then.'

28 February 1877: The two men spend a second day fishing on the Thames. By the evening Morris's cold was slightly better.

March 1877: An unsigned review of *Sigurd the Volsung* appeared in the *North American Review* (pp. 323–5).

1 March 1877: Morris returned from his visit to Kelmscott Manor.

6 March 1877: Morris published an attack in the *Athenaeum* (dated 5 March) on the proposed 'restoration' by Sir Gilbert Scott of Tewkesbury Minster. He called for 'an association ... to keep a watch on old monuments, [and] to protest against all "restoration" that means more than keeping out wind and weather'.

9 March 1877: Morris had still not entirely recovered from the cold he had had at Kelmscott Manor.

15 or 16 March 1877: Morris had dinner with F. G. Stephens at Horrington House to discuss the formation of the Society for the Protection of Ancient Buildings (SPAB).

21 March 1877: Morris was photographed by Elliott and Fry.

22 March 1877: Morris was chairman at a meeting held to form SPAB at Morris & Co.'s premises at 26 Queen Square, Bloomsbury. Morris was elected Honorary Secretary and *pro-tem* Treasurer.

25 March 1877: Morris wrote to Thomas Wardle: 'I am studying birds now to see if I can't get some of them into my next design.'

29 March 1877: A second meeting of SPAB was held at which Morris, Webb and George Wardle submitted a programme to be adopted by the Society.

Spring 1877: Morris & Co.'s new showrooms were opened at 264 Oxford Street (later 449), on the corner of North Audley Street. Morris used to entertain clients in the offices above the shop. Curtains and upholstery were handled at 2B Granville Place and furniture-making at Pimlico.

April 1877: Morris & Co. issued a circular announcing that it would no longer supply stained-glass windows for medieval buildings which were being restored. An unsigned review of *Sigurd the Volsung* appeared in the *Atlantic Monthly* (pp. 501–504).

April/November 1877: Morris's translation of the *Odyssey* was published.

3 April 1877: Morris wrote to Rossetti requesting his support for SPAB. It is unclear if Rossetti did join. Michael Rossetti recorded that he 'did not ... take any *active* part in the proceedings of the Society'. Morris also wrote to De Morgan requesting his help in getting Thomas Carlyle to support the Society. Carlyle did take out membership.

7 April 1877: The *Athenaeum* published another letter from Morris (dated 4 April) condemning the 'restoration' of Tewkesbury Minster.

12 April 1877: Another meeting of SPAB was held at Queen Square at which it was resolved that the Secretary should write to the relevant authorities about the proposed restoration of the churches at Cherry Hinton, Ormskirk and Halifax.

18 April 1877: It would appear from a letter that Morris wrote to George James Howard that the SPAB's *Manifesto* was due back from the printers.

24 April 1877: Russia declared war on Turkey after the failure of a conference at Constantinople convened on 20 January 1877. British intervention appeared a real possibility.

May 1877: Morris was introduced to Wagner's wife Cosima when Wagner came to London for his concert series at the Albert Hall. He did not meet Wagner himself. F. G. Guy, one of the sons of Morris's tutor, became Morris's secretary.

2 May 1877: Morris attended a meeting of Henry Broadhurst's 'Workingmen's Political Associations and Trades Societies of the Metropolis' held at the Cannon Street Hotel in support of Gladstone's five anti-Turkish resolutions: 'it was quite a success; they seem to have advanced since last autumn.'

7 May 1877: Morris attended a conference held at St James's Hall under the auspices of the EQA. The meeting demanded parliamentary action on Gladstone's five anti-Turkish resolutions. The *Times* recorded the following day: 'A terrific scene of confusion arose when the Committee made their way to the platform, and they had each and all literally to fight their way in.' Burne-Jones intended to be present at this meeting but the hall was so crowded he was turned away.

11 May 1877: Morris issued his *Manifesto* 'To The Working-men of England' signed 'A Lover of Justice'.

14 May 1877: A meeting was held at Myddelton Hall, Islington, to protest against any action of the Government involving England in a war in the Balkans. Splits in the Liberal Party enabled the parliamentarians to tone down Gladstone's five anti-Turkish resolution only one of which – in a modified form – was taken to a division.

18 May 1877: Broadhurst visited Morris at Queen Square on EQA business.

24 May 1877: The Dean of Canterbury wrote to the *Times* about the proposed restorations to Canterbury Cathedral: 'Mr. Morris's Society probably looks on our Cathedral as a place for antiquarian research or for budding architects to learn their arts in. We need it for the daily worship of God.'

4 June 1877: The *Times* published a letter from Morris on the proposed restoration of Canterbury Cathedral.

7 June 1877: A meeting of SPAB was held at the Oxford Street showrooms of Morris & Co. The *Times* published another letter from Morris on the restoration of Canterbury Cathedral.

13 June 1877: Morris was at the end of a two-day holiday fishing at Kelmscott Manor. At this time Jenny was staying with her grandmother and great-aunt at Much Hadham. Gerald Manley Hopkins stated, in a letter to Robert Bridges, that in his view Morris's *Virgil* was 'very likely a failure, but it cannot be said that Wm. Morris is an ass, no'.

21 June 1877: Morris spent the day at the South Kensington Museum.

22 June 1877: Morris wrote to the Dean of Canterbury Cathedral complaining about the proposed removal of the ancient stalls from the building. The letter was published in the *Athenaeum* on 7 July and appeared as a news item in the *Times* on 8 July 1877. Morris's *Pomegranate* printed cotton fabric design was registered.

25 June 1877: Louis Bazin (nicknamed 'Froggy'), a Frenchman Morris employed as a brocade-weaver, arrived in London from Lyon. He was paid 3,000 francs for his year's work.

30 June 1877: Morris and De Morgan travelled down to Oxford.

July 1877: A review of '*Sigurd*' & the '*Nibelungenlied*' by Henry G. Hewlett appeared in *Fraser's Magazine* (vol. 106, pp. 96–112).

1 July 1877: Morris and Faulkner travelled from Oxford to Bablockhithe and then rowed the twenty miles to Kelmscott Manor.

2 July 1877: The boating party spent the day fishing at Kelmscott Manor where they were joined by Thomas Wardle.

3 July 1877: Morris, Faulkner and De Morgan rowed back to Bablockhithe.

4 July 1877: Morris returned to London.

7 July 1877: The *Athenaeum* published another letter from Morris (dated 22 June) on the restoration of Canterbury Cathedral.

10 July 1877: Morris wrote to Ruskin requesting permission for SPAB to distribute a leaflet containing extracts from *The Seven Lamps of Architecture*.

12 July 1877: By this time Louis Bazin had set up his loom – a Jacquard – in Ormond Yard near Queen Square.

16 July 1877: Morris attended a large fund-raising meeting on behalf of the Bosnian and Hercegovinian refugees held at the Willis rooms.

28 July 1877: Morris reported that Bazin had been taken ill and admitted to St Thomas's Hospital.

August 1877: Morris designed his *Artichoke* wall-hanging.

3 August 1877: Morris collected Jenny from Clay Cross and travelled down to stay with Jane and May at Broadway.

6 August 1877: Cormell Price joined the Morrises at Broadway.

7 August 1877: The Morrises returned to Kelmscott Manor. It was while they where there that Jenny's health deteriorated once again.

14 August 1877: Morris travelled down to London for a few days on business.

17 August 1877: Morris returned to Kelmscott Manor.

20 August 1877: The Morris family were joined at Kelmscott Manor by Cormell Price and the Burne-Joneses: 'Margery is wild with joy at the idea of coming.'

21 August 1877: Jenny's health continued to worry Morris. He was particularly concerned that she had 'got terribly fat'.

September 1877: An unsigned review of *Sigurd the Volsung* appeared in the *International Review* (pp. 696–9).

20 September 1877: Louis Bazin finally began weaving although he experienced problems with his loom.

21 September 1877: Morris went up to London for the day from Kelmscott Manor to inspect the results of Louis Bazin's weaving.

28 September 1877: Morris and his family probably returned to London from their holiday at Kelmscott Manor.

October 1877: F. G. Guy resigned as Morris's secretary in order to go to Oxford University.

6 October 1877: Georgiana Burne-Jones wrote to Rosalind Howard: 'Mr Morris is in roaring health and dined here the other day with two dark blue hands bearing witness that he has plunged into work again.'

8 October 1877: Morris left London by the 8.25 mail train to Holyhead on his first trip to Ireland. He caught the ferry in the evening.

9 October 1877: Morris took the midday train from Dublin to Tullamore. He was unimpressed by Dublin: 'a dirty slatternly city is Dublin, and Guinness seems the only thing of importance there.' He stayed the next few days at the Countess of Charlesville's house at Tullamore, King's County, where he advised 'her as to the doing up of her house'.

12 October 1877: Morris returned from his business trip and travelled to Leek to stay with Thomas Wardle.

22 or 23 October 1877: Morris probably returned from his visit to Leek.

24 October 1877: Morris expressed annoyance that the Windsor Tapestry Works, set up under Queen Victoria's patronage, had received an order that should have gone to Morris & Co.

28 October 1877: In a letter to his mother Morris wrote that he was thinking of letting Horrington House while Jane and the children were in Italy. He later advertised the house 'at $3\frac{1}{2}$ guineas including the cook's wages'.

29 October 1877: The *Times* reported: 'that a ... serious fire broke out on the premises of Messrs. Morris and Co., of 26, Queen-square, Bloomsbury. This extended itself in an alarming manner to the National Hospital for the Paralyzed and Epileptic, at 23, 24, and 25, in the same square. The back workshop of Messrs. Morris, which is 25ft by 25ft, had a floor burned out and the roof off, the basement and contents damaged by fire, heat, and water, and, besides, the ground floor and contents of [the] front house were damaged by fire, heat, and water.' Three fire engines attended the fire. The fire consumed one window for the Jesus College Chapel and part of another destined for the same place. Amongst the other things lost was Morris & Co.'s stock of linoleum. Morris, who had been on the premises when the fire broke out, was well insured, and played down the episode in his correspondence to his friends.

November 1877: A review of *The Story of Sigurd the Volsung* by Henry Morley appeared in the *Nineteenth Century* (vol. 2, pp. 704–12).

21 November 1877: Jane and her daughters left for Italy where they were to take the Villa del Cavo near the Howards at Oneglia. Morris accompanied them as far as the coast. In the evening he had dinner at the Grange.

22 November 1877: Morris had dinner with John James Stevenson, a member of SPAB, before attending 'a small & dullish meeting' of the latter. His *Ceiling* wallpaper design was registered.

24 November 1877: Morris spent the day working on his lecture 'The Decorative Arts'.

25 November 1877: Morris had the sad task of burying Margaret Burne-Jones's cat.

2 December 1877: Morris finished his lecture 'The Decorative Arts'.

3 December 1877: In a letter to Jane, Morris wrote that De Morgan knew someone who might be interested in taking Horrington House. He went on to write that they 'might if we liked perhaps take the lease off our hands: what do you say to this?'

4 December 1877: Morris delivered his lecture 'The Decorative Arts' before the Trades Guild of Learning at the Co-operative Hall – 'a dismal hole near Oxford St' – in London. Prior to his delivery Morris had visited the hall to test the acoustics: 'I went with Wardle to the place, & read Robinson Crusoe to him to see if I could make my voice heard.' Morris wrote later: 'it went off very well, and I was not at all nervous, but made myself well heard.' Webb, who was present, recorded that the lecture had been 'full of truths and knock-me-down blows'.

7 December 1877: Morris accompanied the Burne-Joneses to see a performance of Gilbert & Sullivan's comic opera *The Sorcerer*: 'I doubt if I shall care for it much though.' Morris feared that he would be denied admission to the theatre due to his hands being stained deep blue!

8 December 1877: Morris's lecture on 'The Decorative Arts' was published in the *Architect*, pp. 308–12.

11 December 1877: Morris and Webb travelled down to Kelmscott Manor for a short holiday.

14 December 1877: Morris returned to London from Kelmscott Manor. In the evening he dined with Stopford Brooke.

19 December 1877: Morris gave his first political speech at an anti-war meeting sponsored by the EQA at the Lambeth Baths, Lambeth. He wrote later: 'I made rather a mess of it: the audience was stupid & cold if friendly.'

24 December 1877: Morris attended a meeting of the EQA at which it was agreed to issue a peace manifesto.

25–26 December 1877: Morris spent Christmas with his mother and other members of the family at Much Hadham. During the festivities Morris drank two glasses of port which brought on an attack of gout that was to recur on a number of occasions during the next few months.

28 December 1877: The *Times* printed an address issued by the EQA urging 'a decisive protest against a war for the support of the Turkish Empire'. It was signed by Morris along with seven others.

29 December 1877: The *Spectator* described the communication issued by the EQA as 'a sensible circular'. A pro-Turkish meeting in Trafalgar Square was successfully broken up by those opposed to war.

1878: Morris taught himself the technique of making hand-knotted carpets on a frame he set up at Queen Square. Later, when he had moved to Kelmscott House, carpets were produced for Morris & Co. on the premises. These can be identified by the device of a hammer, the letter 'M' and a wavy line depicting the Thames. Thomas Wardle, in his exhibit at the Paris Exposition Universelle, showed examples of his collaboration with Morris on dyeing and printing fabrics. Morris & Co. made two windows for St Martin's Church, Brampton.

January 1878: *Our Modern Poets: William Morris* by Thomas Bayne appeared in the *St James's Magazine* (vol. 42, pp. 94–107).

1 January 1878: Georgiana Burne-Jones and her children went to spend ten days with Mrs Wyndham at Wilbury House, near Salisbury. Morris wrote: 'fancy her being at a tory house at this crisis!' Percy Wyndham was Conservative MP for West Cumberland.

2 January 1878: A meeting was held at the offices of the Labour Representation League to 'consider what steps should be taken to inform Europe that English artisans or, in other words, the English nation were determined to maintain peace.'

4 January 1878: Morris spent the morning at Broadhurst's preparing plans for the 'Workmen's Neutrality Demonstration' to be held at the Exeter Hall in support of the EQA. It appears from a letter Morris wrote to May that Sophia De Morgan was responsible for one of his favourite epithets, that describing Queen Victoria as 'the Empress Brown'.

5 January 1878: Morris again visited Broadhurst to discuss the 'Workmen's Neutrality Demonstration'.

7 January 1878: Morris delivered an 'Address to English Liberals' before the Chichester Liberal Association.

16 January 1878: In the afternoon Morris attended a small EQA event held at the Willis Rooms, King Street, St James's, London. This was organized by a committee which had been formed to promote free navigation through the Dardanelles. According to LeMire, Morris gave a speech on the 'Opening of the Dardanelles'. In the evening he was on the platform – along with Broadhurst and others – at the 'Workmen's Neutrality Demonstration' at Exeter Hall. This meeting was opened by the singing of Morris's song 'Wake, London Lads' to the tune of 'The Hardy Norseman's Home Of Yore' by a choir from the stonemasons' trade union: 'It went down very well, & they sang it well together: they struck up while we were just ready to come on to the platform & you may imagine I felt rather excited when I heard them begin to tune up: they stopped at the end of each verse and cheered lustily.' The *Times* recorded that 'Mr. W. Morris spoke in strong terms against the action of the "war-at-any-price-party," which he said unfortunately existed in the country.' He went on to criticize the Queen at which point he was interrupted by the audience who demanded 'Three cheers for the Queen'. He was also rebuked by the chairman for introducing the Queen's name into the discussion.

25 January 1878: Morris had dinner at the Grange where he read out loud selections from the works of Dickens.

29 January 1878: 20,000 inhabitants of Sheffield passed a resolution in favour of the Government. This was a major blow to the EQA as Sheffield was Mundella's constituency.

31 January 1878: Morris attended a 'very turbulent' meeting at the Stepney School Hall, Stepney Green, which was disrupted by the war-party: 'we were obliged to leave the hall (at 10 p.m.) in possession of the malcontents.' Another anti-war meeting held at Trafalgar Square was broken up with the aid of a party of 400 workmen brought down from Woolwich Dockyard. This was also the day on which an armistice was signed between Turkey and Russia in Adrianople. However, this news did not reach London until 4 February.

February 1878: Morris was elected President of the Birmingham Society of Arts. By this time Thomas Wardle was printing fourteen designs for Morris & Co.: *Acanthus, African Marigold, Bluebell, Carnation, Honeysuckle, Indian Diaper, Iris, Little Chintz, Marigold, Peony, Pomegranate, Snakeshead, Tulip* and an unnamed acanthus and sunflower pattern.

1 February 1878: Morris attended a meeting at Broadhurst's to consider how best to continue the EQA agitation: 'to say the truth we are floundering rather.'

4 February 1878: Morris's lecture, *The Decorative Arts: Their Relation To Modern Life And Progress*, was published as a 32-page crown 8vo pamphlet. 2,000 copies were printed.

5 February 1878: Morris wrote of his 'shame and anger at the cowardice of the so-called Liberal party'. He went on to praise the steadfastness of 'our working-men allies'.

6 February 1878: Morris went to the House of Commons to lobby Liberal MPs on behalf of the EQA.

8 February 1878: Morris attended a meeting of the Workmen's Neutrality Committee and again went to the House of Commons.

15 February 1878: Morris was one of a delegation representing the Neutrality Committee who in the afternoon visited Mr Gladstone at his home in Harley Street to request he speak to a public meeting of the working men upon the Eastern Question. Gladstone agreed even though by this time the EQA had effectively collapsed with the withdrawal of the parliamentary Liberals. In the event the meeting on 21 February 1878 at which Gladstone was supposed to speak was cancelled as was another at which he was also supposed to appear scheduled to be held at the Agricultural Hall, Islington, on 25 February 1878.

19 February 1878: Morris attended a 'stormy' meeting of the EQA: 'I am out of it now; I mean as to bothering my head about it: I shall give up reading the Papers, and shall stick to my work.'

20 February 1878: In a letter to Jane, Morris wrote 'as to my political career, I think it is at an end for the present; & has ended sufficiently disgustingly, after beating about the bush & trying to organize some rags of resistance to the war-party for a fortnight'.

21 February 1878: Morris delivered an address at the distribution of prizes at the Cambridge School of Art at the Guildhall, Cambridge.

23 February 1878: Morris's address at the Cambridge School of Art was published in the *Cambridge Chronicle and University Journal* under the title 'Cambridge School of Art' (p. 4). Portions of the same lecture also appeared in the *Cambridge Express* (p. 8).

24 February 1878: Another anti-war meeting was held at Hyde Park which was addressed by Auberon Herbert. It was broken up by members of the 'National and Patriotic League' led by a Lieutenant Armit.

25 February 1878: In the morning Morris attended another EQA meeting: 'but I scarcely hope that they will try to do anything.' In the afternoon he travelled down to Kelmscott Manor for a brief holiday with his brother Edgar and F. S. Ellis.

26 February 1878: Morris spent the day fishing at Kelmscott Manor. Ellis caught a 17lb pike.

27 February 1878: Morris returned from his brief trip to Kelmscott Manor.

3 March 1878: Morris was confined to Horrington House due to an attack of gout. Russia and Turkey signed a preliminary peace treaty at San Stefano.

6 March 1878: Morris was unable to go downstairs due to his attack of gout. While he was laid up he read novels by John Galt: 'he wrote about Scott's time, and is certainly good – always as far as his real turn goes.'

7 March 1878: Morris was visited by his mother and sister.

8 March 1878: Morris intended to leave Horrington House for the first time in a week and visit Queen Square although he was still limping as a result of his attack of gout. In a letter to Thomas Wardle, Morris thanked him for sending him a copy of Matthew Arnold's lecture on 'Equality' which had been published in the *Fortnightly Review*. He was not impressed: 'I think myself that no rose-water will cure us; disaster and misfortune of all kinds, I think will be the only things that will breed a remedy: in short nothing can be done till all rich men are made poor by common consent....' He added that Arnold 'though naturally a courageous man, [is] somewhat infected with the great vice of that cultivated class he was praising so much – cowardice to wit'.

10 March 1878: A last attempt by Bradlaugh to galvanize support against the war ended in shambles in Hyde Park. The 'Peace' contingent were hustled by the 'War' party and forced to abandon the meeting. One of the missiles that was thrown amongst the crowd was a dead cat!

12 March 1878: Morris dined with Auberon Herbert: 'we were both chop-fallen enough.' In a letter to Jane, Morris first referred to 'The Retreat' (later renamed Kelmscott House) which he had already visited twice. In the same letter Morris expressed himself 'much distressed' that Jenny had suffered further epileptic fits in Oneglia.

19 March 1878: Morris attended a meeting at Bryce's to discuss the forthcoming Congress of Berlin. This Congress was held from 13 June 1878 to 13 July 1878 and agreed that Armenia was to remain a province of Turkey.

22 March 1878: Morris wrote to George Macdonald requesting details about the healthiness of 'The Retreat'.

24 March 1878: Morris spent his birthday at the Grange with the Burne-Joneses. Jenny sent her father 'a baccy pouch' for his birthday.

25 March 1878: Morris dined with his mother at Much Hadham.

26 March 1878: In the morning Morris had his hair cut 'in the presence of my kinswomen & the parrot: wh. last was delighted, & mewed & barked & swore & sang at the top of his vulgar voice'. He later returned to London from Much Hadham. He also wrote to Jane telling her of the advantages of taking 'The Retreat'. It is clear that Jane had reservations about the house being too far from the centre of London. He also sent Jane a copy of R. D. Osborne's *Islam Under the Khalifs of Baghdad*.

27 March 1878: Morris was reading Victor Hugo's *Histoire d'un Crime: Desposition d'un Temoin*. Sir Gilbert Scott died: 'So Sir G. is gone: I don't suppose it will make much difference either for or against: but I am glad we began before he went off.'

28 March 1878: In the *Times*'s obituary of Sir Gilbert Scott it was stated 'he had encouraged the passion for reckless restoration'. This was one of the first acknowledgements of the change in taste that had been brought about by SPAB.

2 April 1878: Morris wrote to Jane confirming he had arranged to take 'The Retreat'. At the time he was thinking of turning the stable into a gymnasium.

3 April 1878: Morris was one of a national deputation who were received by Lord Granville and the Marquis of Hartington at the Westminster Hotel. The deputation's aim was to find out the Liberal Party's position over the Eastern Question. Morris described the lords' reaction as 'very discouraging, unleader-like &, to use a plain word, cowardly'.

7 April 1878: Morris visited 'The Retreat': 'the tide was high, & the sun was shining, & it looked all very cheerful.'

11 April 1878: Morris attended a meeting of SPAB where he proposed the organization should extend its activities to include buildings outside Britain (*c.f.* 28 March 1879).

17 April 1878: The *Times* published a letter from Morris (dated 15 April) on the destruction of churches in the City of London.

20 April 1878: Morris left London by the night mail for Paris.

21 April 1878: Morris spent the day with Cormell Price, Burne-Jones and his son Philip in Paris. He later caught the evening train from Paris to Turin.

23 April 1878: Morris arrived at Oneglia at 6 pm in the evening: 'I found the place at Oneglia a most beautiful spot to live in: I don't think I should ever have tired of the olive-woods.'

25 April 1878: The Morrises took a drive from Oneglia to Diano Castello.

26 April 1878: The Morris family travelled from Oneglia to Genoa. By this time Morris was suffering a severe attack of gout and had to be carried from the station to the omnibus. During this transfer Morris collapsed 'and enjoyed a dream of some minute and a quarter I suppose'. When he awoke he found himself 'the centre of an admiring crowd'. He was subsequently carried into the Hotel 'chuckling with laughter'.

27 April 1878: The family spent the day in Genoa as Morris could not travel due to his attack of gout.

28 April 1878: The Morrises travelled from Genoa to Venice via Milan. On this trip Morris had his first view of Lake Garda: 'What a strange surprise it was when it suddenly broke upon me, with such beauty as I never expected to see: for a moment I really thought I had fallen asleep and was dreaming of some strange sea where everything had grown together in perfect accord with wild stories.' Here they had to get into separate carriages as the train was full. They took rooms at the Hotel de L'Univers: 'a queer ramshackle old house: very cheap, but attendance bad: it has a nice platform of its own over the water: it is near the iron bridge (damn the iron bridge!) & beside the Academia.'

29 April 1878: Morris, still suffering from gout, enjoyed a ride in a Gondola to the ducal Palace in Venice: 'but I couldn't manage to crawl across the Piazetta.'

30 April 1878: The *Architect* published a letter signed by Morris (dated 17 April) relating to the proposed restoration to be done to the Collegiate Church of Southwell Minster.

4 May 1878: Morris managed to hobble as far as St Mark's Square in Venice. Later the family took a drive to Lido.

14 May 1878: By this time the Morrises had arrived at Padua. Morris described it as 'a most delightful town, as full of character as could be: the precinct of the Arena Chapel is a paradise, and St. Antony & its cloisters is very fine & noble'. In the afternoon Morris and the girls were caught in a shower and sheltered in an arcade until it was over: 'A dyer's hand-cart took refuge by us with a load of blue work (cotton) just done: I was so sorry I could not talk with one of the men, who looked both good-tempered and intelligent.' In the evening they visited the botanic gardens.

16 May 1878: The Morris family had reached Verona. Here Morris visited the church of St Anstasia. Morris wrote of Verona that 'its general beauty & interest is beyond all praise'.

18 May 1878: Morris wrote to George Howard from Verona. He stated that Jane was 'quite poorly' and that he had still not recovered from his attack of gout and this had meant that the family had abandoned its trip to Milan. He went on to add that he had two volumes 'of G[eorge] Sand which I am going to read to punish myself for being so gout-crusty at Venice: I expect this penance will expiate the more part of my sins'.

22 May 1878: The Morris family travelled by train from Turin to Paris. Morris was still lame in one foot as a result of his attack of gout.

23 May 1878: The family left Paris by the night mail and arrived in England early the following morning.

25 May 1878: Morris was still suffering from gout: 'I am still plaguy lame, a very limpet, but I am not so devil-ridden as I was.'

31 May 1878: Rossetti wrote to Jane saying he had 'a feeling far deeper (though I know you never believed me) than I have entertained towards an other living creature at any time of my life. Would that circumstances had given me the power to prove this: for proved it *wd.* have been.'

21 June 1878: The first annual general meeting of SPAB was held at the Willis Rooms, King Street, St James's, London. Morris read the *Annual Report* which drew attention to 'the threatened gradual destruction of all the old churches in the City of London.' He also read out a letter from Thomas Carlyle on the subject. The *Annual Report* was later published as a pamphlet bearing the same date.

Midsummer 1878: Morris took Kelmscott House on a twenty-one year lease. The house had been built in 1790. In 1816 Sir Francis Ronalds had used eight miles of wire in the garden to construct the first electric cable. George MacDonald wrote two of his most popular books while living at the house: *At The Back of the North Wind* and *The Princess and the Goblin*.

6 July 1878: The *Annual Report* of SPAB was published in the *Architect* (pp. 7–8).

30 July 1878: The *Architect* published another letter by Morris (dated 29 July) protesting about the restoration of Southwell Minster.

2 August 1878: The *Times* published a letter from Morris (dated 1 August) on the restoration of the roof of St Albans Abbey.

7 August 1878: Morris received a copy of Sir Rutherford Alcock's book on *Art and Industries in Japan*.

28 August 1878: The *Times* published another letter from Morris (dated 26 August) on the restoration of St Albans Abbey.

8 September 1878: Morris was spending some time at Kelmscott Manor. While at Kelmscott he visited Chastelston House, Oxfordshire: 'I really think the finest Jacobean house I have seen: lots of old furniture & embroidery in it, & 2 rooms hung with their original tapestry.'

9 September 1878: Morris intended to take Jenny and May to Oxford by boat.

21 October 1878: Morris wrote his last surviving letter from Horrington House.

November 1878: According to Jane – as recorded by Mackail – it was in this month that the Morris family moved into Kelmscott House. Georgiana Burne-Jones dates this to October (but *c.f.* 8 November 1878). For a short time after the Morris family took the house they referred to it affectionately by the nickname of 'The Shutters'. It seems likely, as so many of Morris's surviving letters are addressed from Queen Square prior to this date, that Morris stayed there while the house was being refurbished.

8 November 1878: Webb, in a letter to Jane, recorded that he had heard that the Morrises had moved into Kelmscott House 'between the yells and mingled gabble of a full anti-scrape meeting'.

18 November 1878: Morris wrote to Rossetti asking him to sign a memorial protesting against the second British invasion of Afghanistan.

Winter 1878: Jenny began *The Scribbler* a home-made literary magazine of which she was editor and chief writer. Amongst the other contributors were May, Margaret & Philip Burne-Jones and Rudyard Kipling. The magazine continued to appear for the next eighteen months and bore the inscription: 'printed by Messrs Morris & Co. (Junior) and published by them ... NB No connection with a firm of the same name in Oxford Street.'

14 December 1878: A letter from Morris to John Simon is the first that has survived written on Kelmscott House stationery.

1879: In his *Diary* Morris estimated his annual expenses to have been £1,200. Elizabeth Wardle founded the Leek Embroidery Society.

7 January 1879: Morris's *Sunflower* and *Acorn* wallpaper designs were registered.

10 February 1879: A letter written by Morris to Thomas Coglan Horsfall was read at the Manchester Literary Club. This was later published as 'Working Folk and the Future of Art' in *Papers of the Manchester Literary Club*, vol. 5 (1879), pp. 51–5. It contained the famous line, later repeated in his lecture 'The Beauty of Life', 'have nothing in your house that you do not know to be useful or believe to be beautiful'.

19 February 1879: Morris was chairman of the annual meeting of the subscribers to the Birmingham School of Art at the Birmingham and Midlands Institute. Later he delivered 'The Art of the People' as the presidential address before the Birmingham Society of Arts and the Birmingham School of Design. This lecture took place at the annual prize-giving which was held at the Town Hall, Birmingham.

20 February 1879: The *Birmingham Daily Post* published the text of 'The Art of the People' (p. 5).

4 March 1879: Morris wrote to Roberts Brothers in the United States declining their request for him to write a preface to a new edition of *Sigurd the Volsung*.

5 March 1879: Morris wrote to Henry Octavius Coxe in support of Sir William Blake Richmond's candidacy for the Slade Professorship at Oxford. Richmond was successful and held the post from 1879 to 1883.

17 March 1879: Morris wrote to Gladstone on behalf of SPAB urging that the latter reconsider his support for a scheme to restore St Germain's Church on the Isle of Man.

28 March 1879: A 'Foreign Sub-Committee' of SPAB was formed.

8 April 1879: Morris delivered his lecture 'The History of Pattern Design' before the Trades Guild of Learning at the Co-operative Institute, London.

19 April 1879: The *Architect* published a letter from Morris (dated 8 April) in which he reiterated the aims of SPAB.

25–30 April 1879: Morris wrote a letter on behalf of SPAB to the Metropolitan Board of Works protesting at a proposal to 'raise & open up the Water Gate of York House at the foot of Buckingham St: in order to form an entrance to the Embankment Garden'.

May 1879: Jane and her daughters return to England from Italy.

10 May 1879: Morris began work on his *Acanthus & Vine* tapestry (nicknamed *Cabbage and Vine* due to the unruly depiction of the leaves). This was the only tapestry that he wove with his own hands (*c.f.* 17 September 1879). The cartoon from which it was worked is now at the V & A as is the notebook in which he recorded the hours spent on the project.

15 May 1879: Morris's *Acanthus* and *Bird & Vine* fabric designs were registered.

17 May 1879: The *Athenaeum* printed a letter from Morris (dated 12 May) in which he pointed out that his Icelandic translations had been done in collaboration with Magnússon.

28 June 1879: Morris read the annual report of SPAB at a meeting held at the Willis Rooms, King St., St James, London.

August 1879: Morris spent a week in Leeds during the first half of the month in connection with the pirating of his *Lily* design for Kidderminster Carpets.

14 August 1879: Jane and the children travelled to Naworth, in Cumberland, for a holiday.

18 August 1879: Morris and Webb travelled to Salisbury.

19 August 1879: In the morning Morris and Webb spend two or three hours in Salisbury before travelling to Old Sarum and then on to Amesbury. Morris visited Stonehenge for the first time which he found 'a very strange place indeed'. He and Webb stayed the night at the George Inn in Amesbury where Webb taught 'a stranger small-boy cribbage'.

20 August 1879: Morris and Webb left Amesbury and travelled to Marlborough *via* Pewsey: 'We got early in the afternoon to Marlborough & walked out to see the College & so strolled away to the Devil's Den, & back in the dusk.'

21 August 1879: Morris and Webb travelled from Marlborough to Avebury and then Kelmscott Manor. The country all around Kelmscott was flooded and at one point they found themselves 'in deep water enough, right over the axles of the wheels'.

22 August 1879: Morris and Webb spent the day paddling about the floods around Kelmscott Manor.

23 August 1879: Morris and Webb returned to London.

31 August 1879: In the afternoon Morris visited Jonathan Carr at Bedford Park. Morris wrote that 'on the whole the place looked pretty'.

Late Summer 1879: The National Liberal League (NLL) was founded. The NLL was a largely working-class organization formed by radicals who had previously been in opposition to the Eastern policy of the government. Morris was elected Treasurer.

4 September 1879: Morris was asked by the servants to admonish some 'little beasts of girls' who had been helping themselves to apples and pears from the garden at Kelmscott House: 'I nearly burst out laughing, and fortunately had no need to make a long harangue.' This, or a similar episode, was later used as the basis of his dialogue *Honesty is the Best Policy; or, The Inconvenience of Stealing*.

7 September 1879: In the evening Morris travelled up to Naworth to spend a week with Jane and his daughters. He arrived the following morning: 'I ... found my babies flourishing but my wife so, so.' While at Naworth he visited Bewcastle and Thirlwall.

13 September 1879: Morris returned to London from his visit to Naworth.

17 September 1879: The *Cabbage & Vine* tapestry was finished. It took 516 working hours to complete.

21 or 22 September 1879: Morris probably travelled down to Kelmscott Manor for a holiday.

27 September 1879: Morris ordered volume 1 of Charles Kingsley's *Hypatia* be sent to Kelmscott Manor.

October 1879: Photographs of Jenny taken in this month reveal the weight gain she had experienced as a result of her treatment for epilepsy.

3 October 1879: Morris wrote to Georgiana Burne-Jones from Kelmscott: 'Somehow I feel as if there must soon be an end for me of playing at living in the country: a town-bird I am, a master-artisan, if I may claim that latter dignity.'

Mid-October 1879: Morris wrote to Georgiana Burne-Jones from Kelmscott Manor that: 'I have been feeling chastened by many thoughts, and the beauty and quietness of the surroundings, which, latter, as I hinted, I am, as it were, beginning to take leave of. That leave-taking will, I confess, though you may think it fantastic, seem a long step towards saying good-night to the world.'

15 October 1879: Morris returned to London after his holiday at Kelmscott Manor. De Morgan and his sister had stayed at Kelmscott during the preceding week.

18 October 1879: The *Daily News* published a letter from Morris (dated 17 October) in which he outlining the aims of the NLL.

November 1879: A. B. Freeman-Mitford, Secretary of the Board of Works at St James's Palace, commissioned Morris & Co. to provide four Axminster carpets for the two State rooms they had previously decorated at the Palace. These had been installed by March 1880. An anonymous article on *William Morris MA* (with a photograph) appeared in the *Dublin University Magazine* (vol. 2, pp. 552–68). Morris handed over responsibility as case-work secretary of SPAB to Newman Marks.

1 November 1879: The *Daily News* published a letter from Morris (dated 31 October) in which he deplored the proposed restoration of the west front of St Mark's, Venice. The same letter was published in the *Architect* on 8 November.

3 November 1879: Morris wrote to Ruskin suggesting that he write a letter to the *Times* condemning the proposed restoration of St Mark's. This request appears to have been ignored as there is no letter from Ruskin on the subject. Ruskin did, however, provide notes for an exhibition of photographs of St Mark's.

6 November 1879: Morris gave a speech on the restoration of St Mark's, Venice, as a meeting sponsored by SPAB at the SPAB Rooms, 9 Buckingham Street, Strand, London.

7 November 1879: Morris wrote to Robert Browning requesting he attend a meeting scheduled to be held at the Sheldonian Theatre, Oxford, to protest against the restoration of St Mark's. Browning didn't attend but he did write a letter giving his support to the campaign. On the same day Morris wrote to Gladstone requesting he sign a memorial SPAB had prepared on St Mark's. This he did.

12 November 1879: Morris accepted a request to be on the Committee coordinating J. Morley's second – unsuccessful – attempt to enter Parliament as a Liberal.

13 November 1879: Morris gave a speech at a meeting held at the Birmingham and Midlands Institute, Birmingham, to discuss 'the desirability of memoralising the Italian Government on the proposed destruction of St Mark's, Venice'.

15 November 1879: In the afternoon Morris delivered another speech against the restoration of St Mark's, Venice, at a meeting sponsored by SPAB at the Sheldonian Theatre, Oxford. Henry George Liddell, father of Lewis Carroll's

Alice, was in the chair. This was the first time that Morris had spoken in public in Oxford.

19 November 1879: SPAB's memorial against the restoration of St Mark's was published in the *Times*.

24 November 1879: The *Times* published another letter from Morris (dated 22 November) relating to the restoration of St Mark's.

29 November 1879: The *Times* published yet another letter from Morris (dated 28 November) on St Mark's.

December 1879: Morris & Co. were working on the Howards' London house at 1 Palace Green. The dining room was decorated with a series of panels, illustrating the story of Cupid and Psyche, which were painted by Burne-Jones and Walter Crane.

14 December 1879: Morris and Burne-Jones went to inspect the work being undertaken at 1 Palace Green.

22 December 1879: Morris, on behalf of the Executive Council of the NLL, sent a letter to Gladstone congratulating him on reaching the age of seventy. This appeared in the *Daily News* on 23 December. The letter was also signed by George Howell and Henry Broadhurst.

Christmas 1879: Cormell Price spent the Christmas week with the Morrises at Kelmscott House.

7 January 1880: Morris sent his mother four dozen bottles of claret as a New Year gift. Jane was suffering from neuralgia.

8 January 1880: Morris went to Broadwood's to collect a piano which was a Christmas present from his mother.

13 February 1880: By this time Jane and May were staying with the Burne-Joneses at Rottingdean.

14 February 1880: Morris finished writing his lecture 'Labour and Pleasure *versus* Labour and Sorrow': 'I doubt it will be worth reading.'

16 February 1880: Jenny dined with the Miss Cobdens. Morris recorded that Philip Burne-Jones had passed his matriculation exam at University College, Oxford. There is, however, no evidence that he ever took his BA.

18 February 1880: Morris travelled up to Birmingham where he stayed with William Kenrick, Chairman of the Museum and School of Arts Committee, at the Grove, Harborne.

19 February 1880: Morris delivered his lecture 'Labour and Pleasure *versus* Labour and Sorrow' at the Birmingham School of Design at the Town Hall,

Birmingham.

20 February 1880: Morris had breakfast with John Henry Chamberlain, Vice-President of the Royal Society of Artists and Chairman of the Birmingham Society of Arts. He then returned to London from Birmingham by train.

21 February 1880: Morris had dinner with A. J. Mundella and his wife.

28 February 1880: Morris wrote a letter to George Hector Croad recommending Bessie Burden (Jane's sister) to the post of superintendent of needlework of the London School Board.

March 1880: Morris & Co. began work on the decoration and partial furnishing of 1 Holland Park, the home of Aleco Ionides. The work was not finished until October 1888.

3 March 1880: Morris reported that Jane was 'weak & complains of [a] headache'.

17 March 1880: Morris attended a lecture given by Ruskin at the London Institution. The title was 'A Caution to Snakes'.

April 1880: George Wardle travelled to America to promote the activities of Morris & Co.

4 April 1880: Morris wrote a letter to Henry Broadhurst congratulating him on being elected Liberal MP for Stoke-on-Trent in the general election.

7 April 1880: Morris was at the Castle Mona Hotel, Douglas, Isle of Man. It is possible that this trip was in connection with the proposed restoration of St Germain's Cathedral. In the evening he dined with the Governor, Henry Brougham Loch.

8 April 1880: Morris left the Isle of Man by ferry and returned to London by train.

May 1880: The Birmingham School of Art published Morris's lecture 'Labour and Pleasure *versus* Labour and Sorrow' as a pamphlet.

24 May 1880: Morris & Co. began a special Exhibition of their Hammersmith Rugs at 449 Oxford Street. To coincide with this Morris wrote a circular entitled 'The Hammersmith Carpets'. In it he stated that he was trying 'to make England independent of the East for the supply of handmade Carpets which may claim to be considered works of art'. This circular was reissued in 1882. Prior to this date the firm had also issued two other circulars: (i) an account of the twelve departments of artwork they undertook and (ii) an account of 'furniture prints'. These circulars were gathered together in the catalogue to *The Morris Exhibit at the Foreign Fair: Boston 1883–84* published by Robert Brothers.

31 May 1880: Morris gave a speech proposing an international committee be formed with the intention of preserving St Mark's, Venice. This meeting was convened by SPAB and held at the Society of Arts, John Street, Adelphi.

June 1880: Morris wrote to Luigi Federico Menabrea protesting at the proposal to raise the Baptistry at Ravenna.

12 June 1880: The *Times* published a letter from Morris (dated 9 June) on the proposal to raise the Baptistry at Ravenna.

15 June 1880: Morris delivered a speech seconding a resolution for Women's Rights at the Annual Meeting of the Women's Protective and Provident League at the Society of Arts, John Street, Adelphi.

21 June 1880: Morris wrote to Samuel Waddington declining a request to have one of his sonnets included in the latter's *English Sonnets*: 'I have written but one sonnet in my life, and that one was not such as I should care to see reprinted in any Collection.'

28 June 1880: Morris read the Annual Report of SPAB at a meeting held at the Society of Arts, John Street, Adelphi.

Summer 1880: Burne-Jones wrote to Charles Norton: 'Morris … is unchanged – little grey tips to his curly wig – no more; not quite so stout; not one hair less on his head, buttons more off than formerly, never any neck-tie – more eager if anything than ever, but about just the same things; a rock of defence to us all, and a castle on top of it, and a banner on top of that – before meat – but the banner lowered after that.'

July 1880: The *Women's Union Journal* published the text of the speech Morris had given seconding a resolution on women's rights (pp. 69–70).

15 July 1880: Morris visited A. B. Freeman Mitford at the Lord Chamberlain's office to discuss the redecoration of the approaches in the State Apartments at St James's Palace.

22 July 1880: Morris wrote to the Consular Department of the Foreign Office suggesting they employ a British representative in Iceland and recommending Magnússon to the post.

10 August 1880: Jenny and Morris went out before breakfast to examine the *Ark*; a boat in which they were to travel up the Thames towards Kelmscott Manor. Morris described it as 'a biggish company boat with a small omnibus on board, fitted up luxuriously inside with two shelves and a glass-rack, and a sort of boot behind this: room for two rowers in front, and I must say for not many more except in the cabin or omnibus'. The party consisted of Cormell Price, Richard Grosvenor, De Morgan, Morris, Jane, May and Elizabeth Macleod. The *Ark* left Kelmscott House at 2.30 pm and reached

Sunbury, some six miles above Hampton Court, at 10.30 pm. At Sunbury they dined on pickled salmon, poached eggs and ham at the Magpie Inn. Morris and Cormell Price spent the night aboard the *Ark*.

11 August 1880: The *Ark* proceeded up the Thames from Sunbury to Windsor. During the afternoon the party had tea 'on the grass at Runnymead' which Morris described as 'a most lovely place'. They slept that night 'in the inn on the waterside' at Windsor.

12 August 1880: In the morning Richard Grosvenor showed the party round Eton. They then dined just above Bray Lock. Morris wrote: 'cook was I, and shut up in the Ark to do the job, appearing like the high-priest at the critical moment pot in hand.' The meal was rather spoilt by wasps! When they arrived at Maidenhead they found a regatta taking place 'and both banks crowded with spectators, so that we had to drop the tow-rope before our time, and as the Ark forged slowly along towards the Berkshire side with your servant steering on the roof, and De Morgan labouring on the sculls, you may think that we were chaffed a little'. The party spent the night at Marlow: 'Crom and I in the Ark close to the roaring weir, Dick and De M. in the inn (a noisy one) and the ladies up town, over the bridge.' It was on this evening that Morris witnessed the Northern Lights for the first time since he had seen them in the harbour of Thorshaven in 1871 (*c.f.* 4 September 1871).

13 August 1880: The party travelled up the river to Hurley Lock. Here Morris had 'the surprise of seeing a long barn-like building two Gothic arches and then a Norman church fitting on to it and joined into a quadrangle by other long roofs: this was Lady Place: once a monastery, then a Jacobean house, and now there is but a farm-house'. At lunchtime Morris acted as the cook at a meal served at Henley. This was interrupted by an invasion of swans. After being stuck in the mud for twenty minutes at Wargrave they arrived at Sonning at 7.30 pm: 'a village prepensely picturesque and somewhat stuffy that hot night, but really pretty.' Cormell Price and Morris again spent the night on the *Ark*.

14 August 1880: The party left Sonning early in the morning and travelled to Wallingford. After passing Streatley and Goring, Morris wrote 'we were on the Thames that is the Thames, amidst the down-like country and all Cockneydom left far behind, and it *was* jolly'. Everybody spent the night in a 'riverside pothouse'.

15 August 1880: Morris again cooked dinner for the party this time just above Culham Lock. On the way they visited Dorchester to look at the Dykes. They arrived at Oxford a little after nightfall.

16 August 1880: Jane was dispatched to Kelmscott by rail. The others left the *Ark* and carried on up the river towards Kelmscott Manor. Morris noted 'one thing was very pleasant: they were hay-making on the flat flood-washed spits of ground and islets all about Tadpole; and the hay was gathered on punts and the like; odd stuff to look at, mostly sedge, but they told us it was the best stuff for milk'. The party arrived at Kelmscott shortly after 10 pm.

19 August 1880: Morris and his family spent the afternoon in Fairford: 'I was pleased to see the glass and the handsome church once more.'

20 August 1880 : The party travelled to Inglesham to view the church: 'a lovely little building about like Kelmscott in size and style, but handsomer and with more old things left in it.' Morris & Co. submitted plans to redecorate the Visitors' Entrance, the Grand Staircase, the Garden Entrance, the Queen's Staircase and the Ambassadors' Staircase at St James's Palace.

22 August 1880: Morris and his male friends travelled leisurely from Kelmscott Manor to Oxford by river where they arrived at 8 pm. They spent the night in Oxford.

23 August 1880: Morris returned to London.

24 August 1880: Morris recorded that the *Orchard* carpet had been completed although he expressed himself 'a *little* disappointed with it'. The carpet had been copied from figures on the roof of Jesus College Chapel. In a letter he wrote to Georgiana Burne-Jones he said: 'You may imagine that coming back to this beastly congregation of smoke-dried swindlers and their slaves (whom one hopes one day to make their rebels) under the present circumstances does not make me much in love with London.'

27 August 1880: In the evening Morris travelled down from London to spend a few days at Kelmscott Manor.

30 August 1880: Ellis and his daughter Lily joined the Morrises at Kelmscott Manor.

September 1880: Morris and De Morgan visited some abandoned mills in Blockley, near Chipping Camden, as possible new premises from Morris & Co. This was the first of their trips in search of what they humorously referred to as 'the fictionary'. Mackail recorded in his *Notebooks* that De Morgan told him that they went 'all round London; with such a scale of ideas that they were taken as two millionaires'.

2 September 1880: Morris travelled to Rounton Grange on business. The Grange had been designed for Sir Isaac Lowthian Bell by Webb and decorated by Morris and Burne-Jones.

3 September 1880: Morris returned from Rounton Grange to Kelmscott Manor.

6 October 1880: David White, Ellis's partner, wrote to Morris valuing some books he wished to sell at £130.

8 October 1880: Morris planned to entertain William Shedden-Ralston and the Russian novelist Ivan Sergeyevich Turgenev at Queen Square.

November 1880: The St Mark's Committee issued a circular, written by G. E. Street, containing a list of signatures of those opposed to the proposed restoration of the building.

2 November 1880: Morris & Co. were instructed to proceed with the redecoration at St James's Palace.

13 November 1880: Morris delivered his lecture 'Some Hints on House Decoration' before the Trades Guild of Learning in the lecture hall of the Society of Arts, John Street, Adelphi.

20 November 1880: The *Architect* published a summary of Morris's lecture 'Making the Best of It' (p. 318).

December 1880: The *Artist* published a resume of Morris's lecture 'Making the Best of It' (p. 356).

6 December 1880: Morris wrote to Charles Edward Mathews declining an invitation to a dinner organized by the Alpine Club. He excused himself on the grounds that he feared an attack of gout.

8 December 1880: Morris delivered his lecture 'Some Hints on House Decoration' at the Royal Society of Artists, Birmingham.

18 December 1880: The *Architect* printed the first instalment of Morris's lecture 'Making the Best of It' as 'Hints on House Decoration' (pp. 384–7). The second part appeared on 25 December 1880 (pp. 400–402).

1881: May enrolled at the National Art Training School, the precursor of the Royal College of Art, where her special subject was embroidery. During the year Morris kept a scribbling *Diary* (BM.Add.MS.45407B).

1 January 1881: Morris wrote to Georgiana Burne-Jones: 'a word of hope for the new year, that it may do a good turn of work toward the abasement of the rich and the raising up of the poor, which is of all things most to be longed for, till people can at last rub out from their dictionaries altogether those dreadful words rich and poor.'

3 January 1881: Morris entertained Cormell Price and the Richmonds to dinner.

4 January 1881: In his *Diary* Morris wrote: 'to Grange: then pointing Bell's carpet in afternoon. Holland's man putting new gear to big loom: Edgar taking stock of wools. 1100 & more.'

5 January 1881: Morris and Burne-Jones travelled down to Brighton and Rottingdean.

6 January 1881: Morris visited the Grosvenor Gallery and then Queen Square. In his *Diary* he recorded that the Queen's speech at the opening of parliament was 'very shaky'.

10 January 1881: Morris noted in his *Diary* that he 'sketched [an] ornament for a clock case' and that the 'Doyle Carte called about [the] theatre'.

13 January 1881: In the evening Morris attended a meeting of SPAB.

14 January 1881: A Fenian bomb at Salford injured three people.

15 January 1881: Morris spoke at a meeting called for the purpose of establishing The Radical Union at 2 Regent Street, London. This was an attempt to unite the various working-class political clubs in London.

21 January 1881: Morris, Jane and their daughters travelled down to Folkestone where they spent the night.

22 January 1881: At 4 pm Morris and his daughters saw Jane off on the Folkestone-Boulogne ferry on the first stage of her journey to Bordighera on the Italian-French riviera where she was to stay with the Howards. May and Jenny remained in Hammersmith to act as housekeepers for their father.

23 January 1881: Morris had breakfast at the Grange. In his *Diary* he recorded he spent the 'evening designing [a] rug (poor)'.

24 January 1881: Morris received a postcard from Jane saying she had arrived safely in Paris.

25 January 1881: Morris worked on the speech which he was to deliver for the Kyrle Society (*c.f.* 27 January 1881).

26 January 1881: Morris wrote to the Prefect of Florence on SPAB's behalf complaining about the proposed restoration of the Bigallo in Florence.

27 January 1881: Morris spoke at the first public meeting of the Kyrle Society at Kensington Vestry Hall, London. The meeting was called to consider ways of reducing smoke pollution in London and to bring art and music to the people. Later he went to a meeting of SPAB and dinner at the Grange. He also received a postcard from Jane saying she had arrived safely in Bordighera.

28 January 1881: The *Times* (p. 10) carried a report of Morris's speech before the Kyrle Society.

29 January 1881: In his *Diary* Morris wrote: 'at home [and] did a bit of embroidery work'.

30 January 1881: Morris had breakfast at the Grange. In the afternoon he was visited by De Morgan.

31 January 1881: Morris visited Aglaia Ionides Coronio who had just obtained some specimens of dyes from Greece.

February 1881: The *Women's Union Journal* (pp. 13–16) printed the speech Morris had given at the first meeting of the Kyrle Society.

4 February 1881: Thomas Carlyle died. Morris wrote: 'he is off to learn the great secret at last.'

7 February 1881: Morris was at Queen Square even though he was suffering from an attack of gout.

9 February 1881: Morris wrote to Thomas Coglan Horsfall expressing reservation about a plan the latter had to create a workman's model cottage at the museum he was trying to open in Manchester: 'I will have nothing to do with anything, however good the intention, which to my mind tends to keep up the division of men into classes; we shall have neither art nor anything else worth having until we have got rid of that nuisance.'

14 February 1881: In the afternoon Morris travelled down to Devon to visit his sister Alice and her husband Reginald Gill.

15 February 1881: In the morning Morris and his sister walked to where the Tavy joined the Tamar. He returned to London in the evening.

16 February 1881: Morris acknowledged receipt of a copy of Arthur O'Shaughnessy's posthumously published poems: *Songs of A Worker* (London 1881). Jenny and May had dinner at the Grange.

17 February 1881: In a letter to Jane, Morris recorded that Morris & Co.'s work at St James's Palace had been finished '& happily, with good profit'.

18 February 1881: Morris entertained the Burne-Joneses to dinner. Jenny acted as housekeeper.

20 February 1881: In his *Diary* Morris recorded that he had begun a sketch for *The Vase of Flowers* carpet for George Howard. This was the largest carpet that Morris & Co. had undertaken up until this time.

21 February 1881: Edgar Morris went to visit the print-works at Crayford to assess its potential as the site for a new factory for Morris & Co.

23 February 1881: Morris wrote to Jane complaining that 'Tom Wardle is a heap of trouble to us; nothing will he do right and he does write the longest winded letters containing lies of various kinds'. Morris's dissatisfaction with Wardle's dyeing techniques was one of the reasons he decided to go into manufacturing in his own right.

28 February 1881: Morris wrote to George James Howard to congratulate him on being elected MP for East Cumberland.

March 1881: Henry James called on Jane and the Howards in Italy: 'I didn't fall in love with Mrs. William Morris, the strange, pale, livid, gaunt, silent, and yet in a manner graceful and picturesque, wife of the poet and paper-maker ... though doubtless she too has her merits.'

2 March 1881: Morris visited the Grange where he was introduced to Eliot Norton, the son of Charles Eliot Norton. The Liberal Government passed its Irish Coercion Bill which suspended *habeas corpus* and authorized arbitrary and preventive arrest. This was one of the events that destroyed Morris's faith in the Liberal Party.

4 March 1881: Morris travelled down to Hadham to say goodbye to his brother, Colonel Arthur Morris, whose regiment was due to depart for India the following week. Morris's sisters, Isabella and Alice, were also present.

7 March 1881: Morris and De Morgan went to Crayford to view the print-works. They abandoned the idea of using it as a site for new premises for Morris & Co. as it took more than an hour to reach it from London.

10 March 1881: Morris delivered his lecture 'The Prospects of Architecture in Civilisation' at the London Institution, Finsbury Circus, London.

13 March 1881: Czar Alexander II of Russia was assassinated.

16 March 1881: Morris gave a speech before the Nottingham Kyrle Society at 'The Castle', Nottingham: 'my audience at the castle was polite & attentive; but I fear they were sorely puzzled at what I said.' An attempt was made by the Fenians to blow up the Mansion House, the official residence of the Lord Mayor of London. The bomb failed to explode.

17 March 1881: Morris wrote to Jane that he and De Morgan had been to view some premises in Merton, Surrey, earlier that week: 'they seem as if they would do, and if so, and we can get them, then am I for evermore a bird of this world-without-end-for-everlasting hole of a London.' De Morgan later told Mackail that 'Merton was chosen a good deal because of [its] beauty, and [the] remains of [the] abbey'.

18 March 1881: Morris had dinner with William Bell Scott: 'he looked very old: *is* near 70 he told me.'

19 March 1881: Morris attended a meeting of the Radical Union. Wardle and Webb went down to examine the Merton works. They had gone before but had visited the wrong place.

21 March 1881: Morris recorded in his *Diary* that he went to St James's Palace 'to get our work passed'. He also wrote to Henry Broadhurst suggesting that the Radical Union be incorporated with the NLL.

26 March 1881: Morris attended a meeting of the NLL which he described in his *Diary* as 'unsatisfactory'.

31 March 1881: Morris spent the morning pointing the *Case of Flowers* carpet for George Howard. In the evening he was scheduled to give a speech on the restoration of the Campo Santo, Florence, at a meeting sponsored by SPAB in London. In a letter to Jane, Morris noted that he had met Oscar Wilde at a party held at the Richmonds during the preceding week: 'I must admit that the devil is painted blacker than he is, so it fares with O.W. Not but what he is an ass: but he certainly is clever too.' Johann Most, editor of the German socialist paper *Freheit*, was charged with incitement to murder after printing what was claimed to be a 'libel' against Alexander II of Russia.

April 1881: The NLL took the radical step of demanding the replacement of the House of Lords by an elected chamber.

3 April 1881: The census revealed that the Morrises had three domestic servants at Kelmscott House: Annie (38) cook; Elsa (25) housemaid; and Elizabeth (29) parlour maid.

17 April 1881: Morris was visited by De Morgan in connection with the new Merton Works.

21 April 1881: Morris had to call off a dinner engagement at Cecilia Brooke's as he had a cold and feared he was on the verge of an attack of gout.

30 April 1881: Morris left for Paris with Jenny and May. The crossing was calm: 'the sea was grey & hazy with never a wave in it.' They stayed at the Hotel Windsor.

1 May 1881: Morris and his daughters met Jane in Paris early in the morning. While in Paris Morris took the boat to St Germain to visit the Gobelins works where high-warp tapestry was made.

4 May 1881: The inaugural lecture of the English Positivists was held at the opening of the Newton Hall on 4 May 1881. Morris was invited to attend by Frederick Harrison but had to refuse due to his trip to Paris.

6 May 1881: Morris returned to London from Paris.

28 May 1881: The *Radical* carried an announcement inviting delegates from 'advanced political organisations' to form a new federation.

June 1881: Hyndman's *England for All* was published two chapters of which plagiarized, without acknowledgement, *Das Kapital*. This incident was to lead to an estrangement between Marx and Hyndman. Burne-Jones received an honorary degree of D.C.L. from Oxford University. At the ceremony J. W.

Mackail, Morris's future biographer, read the poem that had won him the Newdigate Prize.

3 June 1881: Octavia Hill wrote to Mrs Shaen of a visit to Morris at Kelmscott House: 'He took us all over the garden and into his study, and such an interesting carpet factory… It was just in his own garden. The tapestry he had been making himself in his own study was beautiful!!'

7 June 1881: Morris recorded in his *Diary* that he had signed the lease for the seven acre Merton Abbey Works in Surrey. The rent was £200. The Merton works were on the River Wandle and only seven miles from Charing Cross Station. De Morgan found a separate site at Merton Abbey where he remained until 1884. Prior to taking the site Morris and De Morgan had considered a disused silk mill in Blockley in Gloucestershire. Morris found the last notice of wage reductions still posted to the door.

8 June 1881: The inaugural conference of the Democratic Federation (DF) took place. It soon passed into the control of H. M. Hyndman.

22 June 1881: Morris visited an exhibition of Spanish and Portuguese art at the Spanish Court. This exhibition had opened on 11 June 1881.

24 June 1881: Morris read the Annual Report of SPAB at a meeting held at the Westminster Palace Hotel, London.

27 June 1881: Morris departed for Kelmscott Manor accompanied by Boyce, Stevenson and Jenny. F. S. Ellis, his wife, daughter and friend were already there.

29 June 1881: Morris, Boyce, Stevenson and Jenny went on a boating trip down the Thames from Kelmscott Manor to Oxford before returning to London. Johann Most was sentenced to sixteen months hard labour. Morris wrote: 'These are the sort of things that make thinking people so sick at heart that they are driven from all interest in politics save revolutionary politics: which I must say seems like to be my case.'

2 July 1881: In a letter to Georgiana Burne-Jones, Morris wrote: 'the hope in me has been that matters would mend gradually, till the last struggle, which must needs be mingled with violence and madness.'

5 July 1881: Morris read Thomas Carlyle's *Reminiscences* edited by J. A. Froude: 'I think I never read anything that dispirited me so much.'

16 July 1881: Morris wrote a letter to the *Pall Mall Gazette* on the threatened destruction of Magdalen Bridge at Oxford. It was not published.

18 July 1881: In his *Diary* Morris recorded that he was working on his speech about the restoration of St. Mark's. In the evening he travelled up to Longstone near Manchester.

19 July 1881: Morris returned to London.

25 July 1881: In his *Diary* Morris wrote that he was 'Sick: not able to do anything'.

August 1881: Morris's *St James* fabric design was registered.

4 August 1881: Morris attended a meeting of the Commons Preservation Society.

6 August 1881: In his *Diary* Morris recorded that 'Melinda began silk carpet today'. The latter was finished on 25 August 1881.

8 August 1881: Morris – and a party which included De Morgan, Faulkner, Bessie Macleod and Lisa Stillman – embarked from Kelmscott House on the *Ark* for a second trip up the Thames to Kelmscott Manor.

15 August 1881: The 'Ark' reached Kelmscott Manor at 9 pm: 'Our spirits sank somewhat I think as we neared Kelmscott last night; a thing done and over always does that for people, however well it has gone.'

22 August 1881: Morris returned to London where he spent the week working. He left the others at Kelmscott Manor.

29 August 1881: Morris returned to Kelmscott Manor.

September 1881: Rossetti took a trip to the Lake District with Hall Caine. He was now in a state of extreme paranoia.

9 September 1881: Jane went to visit the Burne-Joneses in Rottingdean. Jenny and May remained at Kelmscott Manor. Morris had by this time returned to London.

13 September 1881: In the morning Morris and Cormell Price travelled down to Kelmscott to join Jenny and May.

14 September 1881: Morris gave Jenny and May a talk on archaeology in Kelmscott Church. Cormell Price left Kelmscott Manor.

15 September 1881: Morris and his daughters visited Langford. De Morgan arrived at Kelmscott Manor in the evening.

17 September 1881: The Kelmscott party travelled by river to Lechlade and then took a trap and drove to Cirencester: 'which turned out a pleasant country town, and to us country folk rather splendid and full of shops.' After 'mooning about' they resumed their journey and travelled along the Foss Way to the foothills of the Cotswolds. Here they visited the Coln villages.

26 September 1881: Morris returned to London from Kelmscott Manor.

13 October 1881: Morris delivered his lecture 'Art and the Beauty of the

Earth' before the Wedgewood Institute at the Town Hall, Burslem. This was later printed as a pamphlet.

26 October 1881: It appears from a letter Morris wrote to Jane Cobden that she had just sent him a copy of John Morley's *Life of Richard Cobden*.

27 October 1881: Morris was attended a meeting held at University College, Oxford, to protest at the proposal to widen Magdalen Bridge. Morris's speech at this meeting – not mentioned by LeMire – was reported in the *Times* the following day. In it he referred to Oxford as 'the most beautiful city, with the ugliest surroundings in England'.

28 October 1881: Morris wrote to Rossetti thanking him for a copy of his *Ballads and Sonnets*. Earlier Rossetti had sent copies of the proofs of this volume to Jane for her approval.

29 October 1881: The *Architect* (pp. 282–4) published the first part of Morris's lecture 'Art and the Beauty of the Earth' under the title 'The Condition and Prospects of Art'. A second instalment appeared on 5 November 1881 (pp. 297–8).

November 1881: Morris resigned as Treasurer of the NLL. He started manufacturing coloured prints, wallpapers and stained glass at Merton Abbey.

13 November 1881: The *Times* published a list of some of the names who had signed a memorial protesting against the widening of Magdalen Bridge.

21 November 1881: A fire at the premises of Jeffrey & Co. destroyed two buildings and damaged others. Morris wrote: 'luckily for us all our blocks were in an unburnt place except the St James Palace ones & one other which made fire-works for the penny a liners.'

29 November 1881: The *Daily News* published a letter from Morris on Ashburnham House (dated 28 November).

8 December 1881: Morris completed the manuscript of his lecture 'Some Hints on Pattern Designing'.

10 December 1881: Morris delivered his lecture 'Some Hints on Pattern Designing' before students of the Working Men's College at the College, Queen's Square, Bloomsbury. The *Athenaeum* also published a letter of his on the proposed rebuilding of High Wycombe Grammar School.

12 December 1881: Morris visited St Peter's Church, Vere Street, Stepney, to inspect the stained-glass window installed by Morris & Co.

17 December 1881: The *Architect* (pp. 391–4) published the first part of Morris's lecture 'Some Hints on Pattern Designing'. A second instalment appeared on 24 December 1881 (pp. 408–410). Rossetti suffered a paralysis of the left arm and leg. His doctor attributed this to his overuse of chloral.

18 December 1881: G. E. Street died.

21 December 1881: Morris and Algernon Foreman-Mitford went to examine the work Morris & Co. had been commissioned to do at St James's Palace.

1882: The DF received a boost from the arrival of the American land reformer, Henry George. Although George was not a socialist his arguments against land monopolies led to a revival of interest in socialism. Ambrose Barker, Frank Kitz, Joseph Lane and Tom Lemon formed the Labour Emancipation League. This was to become affiliated to the DF in the summer of 1884. Also in this year Morris contributed almost half the text to *Lectures on Art* a book published by Macmillan & Co. on behalf of SPAB, and also wrote a circular on Italian restorations which was translated for distribution in Italy. A. H. Mackmurdo established the Century Guild (it disbanded in 1888).

5/6 January 1882: Morris and Jenny probably travelled down to stay for some days at the Burne-Joneses' house in Rottingdean. The Burne-Joneses were not present.

9 January 1882: Morris and Jenny took a trap to Lewes: 'on the whole it is set better than any town I have seen in England: unluckily it is not a very interesting town in itself: there is a horrible workhouse or prison on the outskirts, and close by a hideous row of builders' houses.' Morris also spent some time writing his lecture on 'Some of the Minor Arts of Life'.

10 January 1882: Morris and Jenny went to Brighton. Here they visited the aquarium where Morris complained about the much neglected fish. In a letter to Georgiana Burne-Jones he wrote: 'I think I saw more ugly people in Brighton in the course of an hour than I have seen otherwise for the last twenty years.'

14 January 1882: Morris and Jenny returned to London from Rottingdean.

16 January 1882: The *Times* reported that the plans to widen Magdalen Bridge had been approved.

21 January 1882: Morris delivered his lecture on 'Some of the Minor Arts of Life' before the Birmingham and Midlands Institute at the Institute in Birmingham. It was later printed as 'The Lesser Arts of Life'.

February 1882: Morris's first volume of lectures, *Hopes and Fears for Art* was published priced 4s 6d in an initial edition of 1,000 copies (plus 25 Demy 8vo Whatman handmade paper copies). A second edition of 1,000 copies was issued in 1883.

1 February 1882: Morris was on the platform at a meeting at the Mansion House held to protest at the programs in Russia following the assassination of Alexander II. Burne-Jones was particularly active in this matter through his friendship with Gladstone's daughter.

13 February 1882: Morris wrote to Edward Williams Byron Nicholson to congratulate him on his appointment as the Bodleian Librarian. Nicholson had been appointed on 4 February 1882.

23 February 1882: Morris delivered 'The History of Pattern Designing' as one of a series of lectures sponsored by SPAB at the Kensington Vestry Hall, London.

4 March 1882: The *Atheneaum* reported that Morris's lecture on 'The History of Pattern Designing' had been so successful that SPAB had decided to publish it.

9 March 1882: Morris attended J. T. Micklethwaite's lecture on English Parish Churches.

11 March 1882: By this time Morris & Co. had completed its work on the redecoration of St James's Palace.

17 March 1882: Morris gave evidence before the Royal Commission on Technical Instruction at the South Kensington Museum. This is to be found in volume 3 of the *Second Report of the Commissioners* (1884), pp. 150–61 and *William Morris: Artist, Writer, Socialist*, vol. 1, pp. 205–25.

20 March 1882: Morris visited the lawyers who were conducting the case against a bill which would have enabled the London & South Western Spring Water Company to sink a well at Carshalton which would have greatly affected the flow of the Wandle.

22 March 1882: Morris and Wardle travelled up the river Wandle as far as Carshalton. On the way Morris stopped off at Wallington to visit Arthur Hughes. He also wrote to F. S. Ellis thanking him for bringing up some perch from Kelmscott to stock the water at Merton Abbey.

24 March 1882: Morris, accompanied by Howard and Grosvenor, again went up the river Wandle: 'much of it is quite quiet and unspoiled; it is really very beautiful, crystal clear in spite of all the mills.'

27 March 1882: The bill to enable the London & South Western Spring Water Company to tap the head springs of the Wandle was defeated in Parliament.

30 March 1882: Morris wrote a letter to the *Nineteenth Century* requesting that his name be added to a petition opposing the Submarine Railway Company's plan to build a Channel Tunnel.

2 April 1882: Morris held his annual Boat Race party at Kelmscott House.

8 April 1882: Rossetti's condition, which had continued to deteriorate during the early months of the year, worsened. Dr Marshall and Dr Harris diagnosed blood-poisoning from uric acid. On this day Rossetti asked Hall Caine to make certain that Jane had 'anything of his she cared for'. The objects Jane chose are now in the Victoria and Albert Museum.

9 April 1882: Dante Gabriel Rossetti died at Birchington-on-Sea near Margate. Apparently he 'threw his arms out; screamed out loud two or three times and died'. Morris's assessment: 'what a great man he would have been but for the arrogant misanthropy that marred his work, and killed him before his time: the grain of humility which makes a great man one of the people, and no lord over them, he lacked, & with it lost the enjoyment of life which would have kept him alive, and would have sweetened all his work for him and us. But I say he has left a hole in the world which will not be filled in a hurry.'

12 April 1882: The *Times* published a letter from Morris on 'Vandalism in Italy'.

27 April 1882: Morris wrote to William Bell Scott thanking him for a copy of his recently published *A Poet's Harvest Home*.

May 1882: Morris's name appeared on a list of signatories published in the *Nineteenth Century* opposing the building of a Channel Tunnel.

6 May 1882: A review of Morris's *Hopes and Fears for Art* by Mark Raffalovich appeared in the *Journal de St. Petersbourg* (a Russian publication).

11 May 1882: Harcourt introduced a Prevention of Crimes Bill which increased police powers in Ireland for three years.

20 May 1882: Morris's *Brer Rabbit* or *Brother Rabbit* fabric design was registered.

June 1882: A review of *Hopes and Fears for Art* by Edith Simcox appeared in the *Fortnightly Review* (pp. 771–9).

9 June 1882: Morris read the Annual Report of SPAB at their Fifth Annual Meeting held at the Society of Arts, John Street, Adelphi. He also seconded a motion for a vote of thanks to the chairman. After the lecture he walked back to Bloomsbury with Allingham. The latter recorded in his *Diary* that 'we talked, among other things, of believing or not believing in a God, and he said "It's so unimportant, it seems to me," and he went on to say that all we can get to, do what we will, is a form of words'.

17 June 1882: Morris's *Bird & Anemone* fabric design was registered. It had been designed by Morris prior to April 1881.

July 1882: An anonymous review of *Hopes and Fears for Art* appeared in the *Century Magazine* (vol. 24, pp. 464–5). Tunnelling on the Channel Tunnel was stopped on the grounds that the Company had not complied with the necessary regulations.

6 July 1882: Haymaking began at Merton: 'a sorry haymaking 'tis likely to be amidst all this wet.'

12 July 1882: May was staying with Magnússon in Cambridge.

23 July 1882: Morris travelled down to Kelmscott Manor.

Summer 1882: Morris stated in 'How I Became A Socialist' (*Justice*, 16 June 1894) that by this time he was ready 'to join any body who distinctly called themselves Socialists'. Jenny's condition worsened and she suffered severe and repeated epileptic fits. Mackail wrote: 'This household anxiety coloured all the world to him: and even Kelmscott that year could not charm away his melancholy.'

August 1882: A review entitled *The Poetry of William Morris* by Andrew Lang appeared in the *Contemporary Review* (vol. 42, pp. 200–217).

1 August 1882: Morris returned to London from Kelmscott Manor.

8 August 1882: The *Daily News* published a letter (dated 5 August) from Morris on the 'Impending Famine in Iceland'.

9 August 1882: Morris admitted that he had found it impossible to read Swinburne's latest volume of poetry *Tristram of Lyonesse*.

16 August 1882: The Icelandic Famine Relief Committee was formed. Morris does not appear to have been present at the inaugural meeting but the *Times* (17 August 1882) reported that a letter had been sent to him by the committee. He was later appointed Treasurer.

19 August 1882: The Morrises visited the De Morgans at Witley. They later drove with them – and the Allinghams – to Hind Head Hill on the Portsmouth Road.

23 August 1882: Morris was present at a meeting of the Icelandic Famine Relief Committee.

29 August 1882: Morris attended a meeting of the Icelandic Famine Relief Committee at the Mansion House.

11 September 1882: Morris attended another meeting of the Icelandic Famine Relief Committee this time to organize the distribution of food for Iceland.

16 September 1882: An unsigned review of *Hopes and Fears for Art* appeared in the *Athenaeum* (pp. 374–5).

27 September 1882: Magnússon left London for Glasgow with £3,000 worth of fodder and provisions to ease the famine in Iceland. He sailed on 4

October.

20 October 1882: Morris delivered his lecture 'The Progress of Decorative Art in England' at a banquet celebrating the opening of the Fine Art and Industrial Exhibition at St James's Hall, Manchester. A description of his journey to Manchester on this occasion is to be found in his lecture 'Art a Serious Thing'.

21 October 1882: The *Manchester Guardian* published Morris's lecture – 'The Progress of Decorative Art in England' – as 'Mr William Morris on Art Matters'.

28 October 1882: The *Architect* published Morris's lecture –'The Progress of Decorative Art in England' – as 'Mr William Morris on English Decorative Art'.

7 November 1882: Morris turned down a request from William Cooper, Secretary of the Derby School of Art, to distribute the School's prizes.

13 November 1882: Morris was reading Henry Wallace's *Land Nationalisation*: 'It is not nearly such a good book as George's [*Progress and Poverty*] but there are some things to remember in it.'

15 November 1882: Morris visited the De Morgans. He found them preparing to vote for William Bousfield – 'a pronounced anti-vivisectionist' – for their School Board. Morris wrote: 'I think I put a spoke in *his* wheel.'

16 November 1882: By this time Jane, Jenny and May were staying with a Mrs Toop at 12 Westover Villas, Bournemouth.

30 November 1882: Morris was visiting his family in Bournemouth.

3 December 1882: By this time Morris and Jane had returned to London from Bournemouth.

5 December 1882: Morris spent the day at the South Kensington Museum giving his opinion on some textiles that had been offered for sale by Canon Franz Bock. Morris's report still exists and is titled 'Report on 3 large pieces of tapestry belonging to Conte de Farcy'.

9 December 1882: Morris and Bessie Burden travelled to Bournemouth to spend a few days with Jenny and her companion Miss Casey.

12 December 1882: Morris delivered his lecture 'Art a Serious Thing' at the annual distribution of prizes of the Leek School of Art at the Temperance Hall, Leek.

16 December 1882: The *Leek Times* published portions of Morris's lecture 'Art a Serious Thing'.

19 December 1882: Morris was suffering from an attack of gout. He had to order up a cab to take him from Merton to Hammersmith.

23 December 1882: Morris intended to travel down to Bournemouth to visit Jenny.

28 December 1882: Morris went to Merton to examine the work that was being undertaken on the water-wheel at the works.

30 December 1882: Morris went into town to buy a fairing for Jane. In the afternoon he visited Aglaia Ionides Coronio. He and Aglaia then visited an old lady to buy some lace for May and Jenny.

31 December 1882: Frank Dillon visited Kelmscott House to view some carpets. In the evening Morris entertained W. A. S. Benson to supper.

Winter 1882–83: Morris attended a series of meetings at the Westminster Palace Chambers organized by the DF.

1883: Morris & Co. opened shops in Manchester, first in John Dalton Street and then in Albert Square. They also took a large stand at the Foreign Fair in Boston, USA.

3 January 1883: Morris attended a meeting of the Icelandic Famine Relief Committee.

4 January 1883: Morris dined with Wickham Flowers and his wife: '[I] found to my consternation that it was the *wrong* evening: however I got my dinner, & when I got home I found that Mrs. F. really had asked me for the evening I went.'

6 January 1883: By this time Jane, Jenny and May had moved from Bournemouth to new lodgings at Lyme Regis. May wrote: 'We are staying in a very nice little sea-side town, in the most lovely country imaginable, & our little house looks upon a delightful view of the downs and bay.'

13 January 1883: Morris and Burne-Jones were elected Honorary Fellows of Exeter College, Oxford, a distinction Mackail described as 'generally reserved for old members who have attained the highest official rank in their profession, and implies a tribute to very special distinction in one who is not a Bishop or a Privy Councillor'. Georgiana Burne-Jones stated that the announcement was made in the press on 12 January. May Morris – in the *Collected Works* (volume 19) – maintained that this was also the day on which Morris joined the DF. However, Mackail claimed he joined the organization on 17 January. Both dates are possible. The 13 January was a Saturday and Morris remained in London until 2.30 pm when he caught a train from Waterloo to Axminster on his way to visit Jane and his daughters in Lyme Regis. He arrived back in London at 8.30 pm on Tuesday, 16 January. Morris's membership card was countersigned by H. H. Champion and described him as 'William Morris, designer'.

16 January 1883: Morris returned to London after a brief visit to Lyme Regis.

17 January 1883: Morris may have joined the DF (*c.f.* 13 January 1883). Morris bought some cuffs for Jenny's birthday: 'I think you will suppose me rather barren of imagination in the way of presents, that I must still run upon lace.'

25 January 1883: Morris left for Paris with Mr Armstrong of the South Kensington Museum: 'I had no idea it was going to be so rough a night, till a great dash of spray came right over the pier on to the boat.' They arrived in Paris the following morning at 7.30 am and stayed at an inn on the Rue St Roch. In a letter to May, Morris proposed starting work on an English translation of the Persian epic *Shah Nameh*. A fragment of this exists in the British Library but it was never finished.

26 January 1883: Morris and Armstrong visited the Cluny and 'a new museum of casts of Gothic sculpture at the Trocadero'.

27 January 1883: Morris attended a sale of fifteen thousand patterns in Paris some of which the South Kensington Museum hoped to purchase. Their bid was unsuccessful. The two men had intended to return to London but 'on the way to Calais the wind whistled up against us so that we were cowed, and gave in & so sneaked out at Calais town'.

28 January 1883: Morris and Armstrong spent the morning in Calais before catching the ferry: 'we had only an ordinary rough passage, & I wasn't sick though most were – specially the frogs – and I got back about 7 p.m. in very good condition.'

29 January 1883: Morris was at Merton 'on one of the wettest days I ever saw'.

31 January 1883: Morris started jury service. The case dragged on until April and was an insurance appeal on behalf of some paint-grinders and mixers who had had their premises burnt down (*c.f.* 16 April 1883).

February 1883: Morris served as a referee for the purchase of two carpets offered for sale to the South Kensington Museum by A. Myers. Work progressed on the *Goose Girl* tapestry which was finished in March.

14 February 1883: Morris wrote to Sidney Colvin saying he would be 'delighted' to view the Ashburnham Collection of illuminated manuscripts and early printed books which was being offered to the British Museum.

17 February 1883: Morris intended to visit Aglaia Ionides Coronio 'if I am not leg-fast with gout'. In a letter to Thomas Coglan Horsfall he wrote: 'I am in principle a Socialist, and would be so in practice if there should ever in my lifetime turn up an occasion for action.'

20 February 1883: Morris went to the British Museum to examine the Ashburnham Collection: 'They were very fine & I hope Mr Childers will find the money for them.'

21 February 1883: Morris held a dinner party at Kelmscott House which was attended by the Burne-Joneses.

26 February 1883: The *Daily News* published a letter (dated 23 February) from Morris protesting at the possible demolition of Blundell's School at Tiverton. The school was not demolished.

28 February 1883: In a letter to Jenny, Morris recorded that he had been reading *Dombey & Son*: ''tis after all very amusing, but O, I don't think Mr Dombey was worth taking so much trouble about as his daughter took.'

3 March 1883: Morris wrote to May that 'I am scarcely a sharer in worldly pleasures for 4 days past, for I am leg-fast with gout'.

6 March 1883: Despite suffering from gout, Morris delivered his lecture 'Art, Wealth and Riches' at the Manchester Royal Institution, Mosley Street, Manchester. Although he stopped short of declaring himself a socialist his opinions were immediately denounced by the press.

8 March 1883: Morris's *Campion* fabric design was registered.

14 March 1883: Morris made his first reference to the DF in a letter to Jenny. He also recorded that he was in the process of writing his lecture for the Hampstead Liberal Club. The *Manchester Examiner* published a letter from Morris relating to criticism of his lecture 'Art, Wealth & Riches'. Karl Marx died.

17 March 1883: Morris corrected the proofs of his lecture 'Art, Wealth and Riches' that was to appear in the *Manchester Quarterly* (*c.f.* April 1883). In a letter to Catherine Holiday, Morris acknowledged a letter from her husband electing him an honorary member of 'the Fifteen', a progenitor of the Art Workers' Guild. According to Kelvin 'the Fifteen' had been founded in 1881 and was named after a popular puzzle. Walter Crane played an important part in its inception. In his letter Morris went on to add: 'I fear I shall seldom or ever be able to attend, as I am getting too old to go out in the evening after my days work'! Karl Marx was buried at Highgate Cemetery, London.

30 March 1883: Chamberlain attacked Salisbury as belonging to a class 'who toil not, neither do they spin'. Morris was later to refer to this in the famous frontispiece to *A Dream of John Ball*.

April 1883: 'Art, Wealth & Riches' was published in the *Manchester Quarterly* (pp. 153–75).

1 April 1883: Morris delivered a lecture at a meeting in Hampstead sponsored by the Hampstead Liberal Club: 'the audience if not large was at least as large as the room would hold: they were very polite, and buttered me, as Mr. Jorrocks would say, most plentifully.'

7 April 1883: Morris and Webb visited the South Kensington Museum. Morris's *Violet & Columbine* fabric design was registered.

15 April 1883: Morris was scheduled to give a lecture before the Clerkenwell Branch of the DF at the branch rooms in Clerkenwell.

16 April 1883: Morris finished his jury service. He wrote to Jenny deploring 'the waste of time and money over such matters'.

22 April 1883: Morris's *Corncockle* printed textile was registered.

23 April 1883: In his unpublished *Diary* Cormell Price recorded that 'Top ... was full of Karl Marx, whom he had begun to read in tr.'.

24 April 1883: Ruskin, who had been asked to join the DF by Morris, wrote: 'It is better that you should be in a cleft stick, than make one out of me – especially as my timbers are enough shivered already. In old British battles the ships that had no shots in the rigging didn't ask the disabled ones to help them.'

May 1883: Morris read Auernachs' "*little* tales" (probably *The Earthmother*).

2 May 1883: Morris & Co. prepared an estimate for the decoration of the drawing room and Antiquities Room at 1 Holland Park.

3 May 1883: According to LeMire, Morris delivered a lecture at the Irish National League Rooms in Blackfriars Road, London (*c.f.* 6 May 1883).

6 May 1883: Morris was scheduled to deliver an unnamed lecture at the Surrey Rooms which is not mentioned by LeMire. It is probable, from evidence in a letter Morris wrote to Jenny on 7 May 1883, that the lecture at the Irish National League Rooms actually took place on 6 May 1883, and was the same one referred to as taking place in the Surrey Rooms.

11 May 1883: Morris's *Strawberry Thief* printed cotton design was registered.

13 May 1883: Morris met Andreas Scheu for the first time at Kelmscott House. May described Scheu as a 'fiery and eloquent speaker of striking aspect in his brown close-fitting Jaeger clothing, his fine head like nothing less than one of Durer's careful studies of a curly-bearded German warrior'.

14 May 1883: Morris attended a meeting of the DF and was elected to the Executive as Treasurer: 'without feeling very sanguine about their doings they seem certainly to mean something.' Others elected included Champion, Hyndman, Joynes and Shaw. Morris also recorded that he superintended the first printing of the *Strawberry Thief* design at Merton.

15 May 1883: Morris walked to Merton via Roehampton Lane: 'I am quite sick of the underground, & think I shall often walk to or from Merton.' He returned from Merton by trap. The driver told him about a nunnery on Roehampton Lane so he stopped '& looked over the fence, & lo, a lot of my holy dames, black & white just getting into boats to have a row on the lake there'. A complete house cleaning began at Kelmscott House in preparation for the return of Jenny.

17 May 1883: Morris again walked to Merton from Hammersmith. The journey took two hours 'but you see it is not all pure waste like the sweltering train-business'.

19 May 1883: In a letter to Jenny, Morris said he had just been reading *Underground Russia* by Sergius Stepniak: 'it is a most interesting book, though terrible reading too.' Four days later he was to write to F. S. Ellis: 'Read Underground Russia if you want your blood to boil.' Experiments continued on the printing of the *Strawberry Thief* design at Merton.

23 May 1883: Derby Day. Morris wrote earlier: 'I hope it will rain hard on Derby-day partly out of spite, partly because else we shall be choked with dust.' The Merton Abbey works were on the road to Epsom. In a letter to his mother he wrote: 'I have had so much to pay with Jenny's illness and all that to say truth I have been somewhat pressed.'

30 May 1883: Morris went to visit his mother at Much Hadham.

June 1883: *Socialism Made Plain* was published by the DF. It demanded various palliative measures including better housing for the poor, compulsory education, state ownership of the railways and an eight hour day. It was signed by members of the Executive including Morris. Many radicals were to leave the DF following its appearance.

6 June 1883: Morris read the annual report of SPAB at the Society of Arts, John Street, Adelphi.

8 June 1883: Jenny, and her companion Miss Allen, spent the day with Morris at Merton: 'we have much enjoyed ourselves; though I am a very little lame with a very small touch of gout.'

9 June 1883: Morris wrote: 'I think Jenny is really better & am beginning to feel hopeful about her.'

12 June 1883: Morris gave the first of two lectures on 'Art and the People' at the Vestry Hall, Haverstock Hill, Hampstead. Neither lectures are mentioned by LeMire.

15 June 1883: Morris gave his second lecture on 'Art and the People' at the Vestry Hall, Haverstock Hill, Hampstead. It was probably at this meeting that he met C. E. Maurice and had a conversation about socialism: 'I think that you, like myself, have really been a Socialist for a long time.'

16 June 1883: The *North-Western Gazette* carried a report on the first of Morris's lectures at Hampstead.

23 June 1883: Cobden-Sanderson attended a dinner at the Richmonds at which the Morrises were also present. He noted in his *Journals* (24 June) that Jane had recommended that he take up bookbinding.

25 June 1883: Morris was introduced to Emma Lazarus by the Burne-Joneses at the Grange.

29 June 1883: Morris's *Grafton* wallpaper design was registered.

30 June 1883: The *North-Western Gazette* carried a report on the second of the lectures Morris gave at Hampstead.

July 1883: Morris was on the committee for judging textiles, carpets and lace by students at the government schools of art.

1 July 1883: Morris and Burne-Jones travelled up to Oxford to be received as Fellows of Exeter College.

2 July 1883: Morris and Burne-Jones spent the day in Oxford and in the evening attended a dinner held in their honour at Exeter College.

3 July 1883: Morris and Burne-Jones returned to London by the first train from Oxford.

6 July 1883: Morris entertained Emma Lazarus at Merton. Emma Lazarus later published an article based on her visit, 'A Day in Surrey with William Morris', which appeared in the *Century Magazine* in July 1886, pp. 388–97. At the time of her visit she presented a volume to the circulating library that Morris had established at the Merton Works for the benefit of the employees.

10 July 1883: According to Cobden-Sanderson in his *Journals* Morris delivered a lecture at Islington. This is not mentioned by LeMire.

21 July 1883: In a letter to Jenny, Morris signed himself 'old Proosian Blue'. This was one of Jenny's pet names for her father and referred to his habit of returning home with his hands stained blue from the dye vats.

22 July 1883: 'A great many people' were invited to Kelmscott House by Morris to discuss socialism.

25 July 1883: Morris went to visit an exhibition of pottery and sculpture by

George Tinworth: 'they are very pictury sculpture not beautiful or decorative but certainly with genius in them: puritan works you understand akin to 15th Century German; but certainly *alive*.'

26 July 1883: At this time Jenny was staying near Wheathamstead in Hertfordshire. Her new companion was called Miss Bailey.

August 1883: According to Wilfrid Scawen Blunt, writing in his *Diaries*, he met Jane for the first time at Naworth Castle. He was to become her lover.

2 August 1883: Morris spent the day with Jenny: 'Wheathamstead seemed a pretty village – but O the Church – which has once been a fine one too, 13th & 14th Century mostly I suppose.'

9 August 1883: In a letter to Sarah Anne Unwin Byles, Morris wrote: 'I am in short "one of the people called" Socialists, and am bound as by religious conviction to preach that doctrine whenever I open my mouth in public.'

11 August 1883: Morris visited Jenny in Wheathamstead.

12 August 1883: Morris returned to London from Wheathamstead.

14 August 1883: Morris wrote to Ellis & White requesting them to send him copies of William Cobbett's works: 'any or all of them.'

15 August 1883: Morris and Middleton travelled to Whitney and then drove to Burford via Minster Lovel. The *Daily News* published a letter (dated 14 August) from Morris on 'River Pollution in Putney'.

16 August 1883: Morris and Middleton drove to Chipping Campden and then to Kelmscott Manor where they joined Ellis and his wife.

17 August 1883: Morris returned to London from Kelmscott Manor.

18 August 1883: Morris visited Jenny in Hertfordshire. At this time Bessie Burden was also staying with Jenny. During this visit he and Jenny visited one of the brothers of Philip Webb, possibly Henry.

26 August 1883: It is clear from a letter that Morris wrote to Georgiana Burne-Jones that he already had some reservations about Hyndman: 'Some of the more ardent disciples look upon Hyndman as too opportunist, and there is truth in that; he is sanguine of speedy change happening somehow, and is inclined to intrigue and the making of a party.'

27 August 1883: Morris walked to Merton from Hammersmith. In the evening he attended one of the regular political discussions held by Hyndman at his home.

28 August 1883: Morris visited Aglaia Ionides Coronio before attending a meeting of the DF.

30 August 1883: It is clear from a letter that Morris wrote to Miss Bailey, Jenny's companion, that Jenny had just suffered another epileptic fit.

2 September 1883: Morris's *Evenlode* printed cotton design was registered. This was the first of a series of designs named after tributaries of the Thames.

4 September 1883: Morris, in a letter to Jenny, recorded that he had 'designed a membership card for the Dem: Fed: which I myself did not think much of, but which pleased our "simple people"'. It is clear from the same letter that Morris had also recently completed his first socialist 'chant', 'The Day is Coming'. At this time Morris was working on the blocks for his *Wandle* chintz. He had also received the books he had ordered by Cobbett: 'such queer things they are, but with plenty of stuff in them.'

15 September 1883: Morris gave a brief outline of his life in a letter written to Andreas Scheu. This is often misdated to 5 September 1883.

26 September 1883: Morris delivered a speech in favour of the DF's programme at a meeting held at the Temperance Hall, Temple Street, Birmingham.

16 October 1883: Morris attended a meeting of SPAB possibly to discuss the restoration in progress at Llanenddwyn Church, near Portmeirion, in Wales. His *Kennet* fabric design was registered.

18 October 1883: In a letter Morris commented on a book on lace by Friedrich Fischbach. This was written in German so Morris probably had a working knowledge of the language. Morris's *Pots of Flowers* indigo discharged and block-printed cotton design was registered as were his *Windrush*, *Kennet* and *Flowerpot* fabric designs.

25 October 1883: In a letter to Ingram Baywater, Morris promised to visit him when he came to lecture in November: 'I shall of course make a point of seeing you & bringing my daughter round to lunch or some such entertainment: her state of health I am sorry to say won't allow her to dine out or sit up late.' In another letter to Charles Rowley, Morris described himself as 'an open and declared Socialist, or to be more specific, Collectivist'.

27 October 1883: The Glasgow journal, *The Voice of the People*, included a tribute to Morris written by John Bruce Glasier.

29 October 1883: Morris met Hyndman on SF business. Hyndman published an article, entitled 'Revolutionary Socialism', on behalf of the DF in the *Pall Mall Gazette*. Its topic was the squalor of London and the failure of philanthropy.

November 1883: Hyndman published *The Historical Basis of Socialism in England* an enlargement of his earlier *England for All*. Morris described the book on 8 January 1884 as 'well worth reading & very easy to read'.

4 November 1883: Morris gave a lecture at Merton. This is not mentioned by LeMire.

5 November 1883: May and Jane went with the De Morgans to see Henry A. Jones's play *The Silver King*.

7 November 1883: Morris finished his lecture 'Art Under Plutocracy': 'it isn't my best, have been too careful – I fear mealy-mouthed.'

8 November 1883: In the evening Morris travelled down to Oxford to meet Jenny. They stayed at the King's Arms.

9 November 1883: Morris and Jenny spent the day in Oxford.

10 November 1883: In the morning Morris and Jenny returned to London from Oxford.

14 November 1883: Morris delivered his lecture 'Art Under Plutocracy' at the Russell Club at University College Hall, Oxford. Ruskin also spoke (although he was not chairman as has often been stated). Morris declared himself a socialist and urged his audience to join the DF. The chairman, Benjamin Jowett, was scandalized by Morris's remarks.

15 November 1883: An article by W. T. Stead entitled 'Mr. William Morris on Art and Socialism' appeared in the *Pall Mall Gazette* (p. 4).

16 November 1883: Morris delivered his lecture 'Art under the Rule of Commerce' at the DF's Lecture Hall at Wimbledon. This lecture was almost certainly 'Art Under Plutocracy' given a different title. A letter by an anonymous correspondent appeared in the *Pall Mall Gazette* criticizing one of Morris's lectures claiming the writer 'advocates changes which must affect every person in these islands, and finishes by telling us he does not know what he is talking about'.

17 November 1883: In a letter written to Charles Edmund Maurice, Morris mentioned that he had agreed to deliver his lecture 'Useful Work *versus* Useless Toil' for the DF at the Somerville Club. No further details of this lecture are available and there is no reference to it in LeMire. Morris also wrote to Swinburne urging him to join the DF.

19 November 1883: The *Pall Mall Gazette* published a letter (dated 17 November) from Morris in which he responded to the paper's report of his Oxford lecture on 14 November 1883. In it he clarified his position as a socialist. The *Times* published a hostile response to Morris's lecture 'Art Under the Rule of Commerce'.

20 November 1883: The *Standard* published a letter from Morris in which he explained his position as a socialist who was also a businessman.

21 November 1883: Swinburne declined Morris's invitation to join the DF: 'I must say I don't think you will ... regard me as a dilettante democrat, if I say I would rather not join any Federation.'

23 November 1883: Morris's *Eyebright* indigo discharged and block-printed cotton design was registered

24 November 1883: Morris delivered 'The Origins of Decorative Art' at a meeting sponsored by the Eton College Literary Society in the Lecture Hall, Eton College, Windsor. An anonymous piece entitled *On the Wandle: An Article on Mr Morris's Factory* appeared in the *Spectator* (vol. 56, pp. 1507–1509).

2 December 1883: It would appear from a letter to Cormell Price that Morris gave a lecture at Cambridge. This is not referred to by LeMire but it may be an erroneous reference to the lecture below.

4 December 1883: Morris delivered 'Art Under Plutocracy' before the Cambridge Union Society at the Cambridge Union.

8 December 1883: Morris's pencil and watercolour design for the *Rose* printed fabric was registered.

9 December 1883: Morris travelled to Bournemouth to visit Jenny.

12 December 1883: Morris went to Kelmscott Manor for a few days.

Late December: Morris took Jenny and her nurse-companion, Miss Bailey, down to stay at Much Hadham for Christmas and New Year. Morris spent Christmas at Hammersmith. Here he received a present of a pie from a Mr Diosy which he threatened to bury in the garden!

29 December 1883: Morris visited Charles Fitzgerald to discuss the DF's newspaper *Justice*: 'the prospects of which I am not sanguine over.'

30 December 1883: Scheu visited Morris at Kelmscott House. Here he entertained Morris by singing German revolutionary songs accompanied by May on the mandolin.

1884: An anonymous article on *William Morris at Work* appeared in the *American Architect* (vol. 17, p. 296). Morris wrote a 'Preface' for John Sketchley's *A Review of European Society*. A special loom was built at Merton Abbey to weave the pattern called *Granada*. Morris's younger brother Rendall died at the age of forty-five. He had sold his commission with the intention of setting up a poultry farm in Acton. However, he was almost certainly an alcoholic. He left eight children who were soon deserted by their mother. They were eventually brought up by Morris's sister Isabella. F. S. Ellis gave up his joint tenancy in Kelmscott Manor. The Art Workers' Guild was formed with an initial membership of fifty.

January 1884: Morris's poem *The Three Seekers* was published in the paper *Today*. The *Christian Socialist* reported that a branch of the DF had been formed at Merton 'principally composed of the workers in Morris & Company's establishment at that place, with Mr. J. Simmons as secretary'. The Branch held its meetings in an upper room in the little office building.

1 January 1884: In the morning Morris visited Hyndman on DF business.

9 January 1884: Morris was present when Henry George addressed the Land Reform Union: 'a fine demonstration of discontent, though I thought George weak.'

11 January 1884: Morris spoke against supporting the parliamentary programme of the radicals at a meeting of the DF at Anderton's Hotel, Fleet Street, London. This speech is not mentioned by LeMire.

16 January 1884: Morris delivered 'Useful Work *versus* Useless Toil' before the Hampstead Liberal Club at the Hollybush Assembly Rooms, Hampstead.

17 January 1884: Morris was scheduled to give a lecture in Blackheath. He gave Jenny a broach for her birthday.

19 January 1884: The first edition of the DF's weekly paper, *Justice*, was published with a contribution by Morris entitled 'An Old Fable Retold'. He also signed 'The Principles of *Justice*'. After an initial donation of £300 made by Edward Carpenter was exhausted, Morris subsidized the weekly deficit of the paper. The first editor of the paper was Charles FitzGerald but he was soon ousted by Hyndman.

21 January 1884: Morris delivered 'Useful Work *versus* Useless Toil' before the Ancoats Brotherhood at the Churnett Street Hall, Manchester. While in Manchester he stayed at Bollin Tower at Alderley Edge.

22 January 1884: Morris delivered 'Art Under Plutocracy' at a meeting sponsored by the Ancoats Recreation Committee at the Memorial Hall, Manchester.

23 January 1884: In the afternoon Morris travelled from Manchester to Leicester. In the evening he delivered 'Art and Socialism' before the Leicester Secular Society at the Secular Hall, Humberstone Gate, Leicester. This lecture was later printed as a booklet by W. Reeves. While in Leicester he stayed with Sydney Gimson the brother of Ernest Gimson. Gimson recalled that after supper the Revd J. Hopps said to Morris: 'That's an impossible dream of yours Mr. Morris, such a Society would need God Almighty himself to manage it.' According to Gimson 'Mr. Morris got up and walked round his chair, then going across to Mr. Hopps and shaking his fist to emphasise his words he said "Well, damn it man, you catch your God Almighty – we'll have him"'.

26 January 1884: Morris contributed an article entitled 'Cotton and Clay' to *Justice*.

27 January 1884: Morris gave a speech at a meeting sponsored by the Russell Club at the Clarendon Assembly Rooms, Oxford.

February–March 1884: Macdonald and Williams were sent by the DF to support the great Lancashire cotton strike. Through their efforts the DF secured its first foothold in the north.

3 February 1884: Morris was scheduled to deliver 'Art and Socialism' at a meeting of the LEL at 166 Bethnal Green Road, Bethnal Green.

5 February 1884: Morris took part in a debate, at the Cambridge Union Society, on the proposition that socialism was the only remedy for 'the present anarchy'.

6 February 1884: The *Cambridge Review* (p. 161) carried a report of the debate the previous day.

9 February 1884: Morris contributed an article entitled 'Order and Anarchy' to *Justice*. He and Hyndman also published a joint piece in the paper entitled 'The Bondholders Battue'.

15 February 1884: Morris was scheduled to give a lecture to the Merton Abbey Branch of the DF.

17 February 1884: Morris delivered 'Useful Work *versus* Useless Toil' at a meeting sponsored by the Bradford Sunday Recreation Committee at the Temperance Hall, Bradford. Morris described his audience as 'a sad set of Philistines'.

18 February 1884: Over 1,500 people attended a meeting held in Blackburn which was advertised as 'How the Workers are Legally Robbed'. Morris, Hyndman, Williams and Macdonald all spoke. This is not mentioned by LeMire.

22 February 1884: Morris was scheduled to deliver 'Useful Work *versus* Useless Toil' before the Invicta Club at the Club's rooms in William Street, Woolwich.

23 February 1884: The *Blackburn Times* (p. 3) carried a report of the speech Morris had given on 18 February in Blackburn.

24 February 1884: Morris ordered Thorold Rogers' *History of Agriculture & Prices* and Professor Ely's *French & German Socialism in Modern Times*.

25 February 1884: Morris delivered 'Art under Competitive Commerce' at a meeting sponsored by the West Bromwich Institute at the Town Hall, West Bromwich.

March 1884: Morris's poem 'Meeting in Winter' appeared in the *English Illustrated Magazine*. 'Velvet-weaving' started at Merton.

1 March 1884: Morris contributed 'The Way Out: An Appeal To Genuine Radicals' to *Justice*.

3 March 1884: Morris delivered 'The Gothic Revival – I' at the Birmingham and Midlands Institute, Birmingham.

10 March 1884: Morris delivered 'The Gothic Revival – II' at the Birmingham and Midlands Institute, Birmingham.

15 March 1884: Morris contributed an article entitled 'Art or No Art? Who Shall Settle It?' to *Justice*.

16 March 1884: Morris attended the demonstration to commemorate the anniversary of the Paris Commune and the death of Karl Marx: 'I trudged all the way from Tottenham Court Road up to Highgate Cemetery (with a red-ribbon in my button-hole) at the tail of various banners and a very bad band....' The police refused the marchers entry to the Cemetery so they retired to some waste ground where they sang the 'Internationale'. In the evening Morris had dinner with Hyndman.

19 March 1884: Morris travelled up to Edinburgh by the 5.15 am train from London. In the evening he delivered 'Useful Work *versus* Useless Toil' before the Edinburgh University Socialist Society at the Oddfellows Hall, Edinburgh.

20 March 1884: Morris had lunch with Samuel Henry Butcher, professor of Greek at Edinburgh University. He returned to London by the night mail.

23 March 1884: Morris was scheduled to deliver 'Useful Work *versus* Useless Toil' before the Fabian Society at the South Place Institute, London.

29 March 1884: The first of Morris's *Chants for Socialists*, 'The Day is Coming', was published in *Justice*.

1 April 1884: Morris delivered 'Art and Labour' before the Leeds Philosophical and Literary Society at the Philosophical Hall, Leeds.

5 April 1884: Morris contributed an article on 'Henry George' to *Justice*. The second of his *Chants for Socialists*, 'The Voice of Toil', also appeared in the paper.

8 April 1884: Morris gave a speech at the opening of the Fourth Annual Loan Exhibition sponsored by the Revd Barnett at St Jude's, Commercial Street, Whitechapel.

10 April 1884: Jane returned to Kelmscott House: 'she is very much better, quite able to get about & work and enjoy herself.'

12 April 1884: Morris contributed an article entitled 'Why Not?' to *Justice*.

17 April 1884: Morris was present at a debate between Charles Bradlaugh and Hyndman held at St James's Hall.

19 April 1884: Jenny returned to London from her stay at Kelmscott Manor: 'she is still troubled with those attacks but otherwise seems very well, & quite happy.' The third of Morris's *Chants for Socialists*, 'All for the Cause', appeared in *Justice*.

24 April 1884: Morris subscribed £5 towards the cost of establishing the Social Reform Publishing Company. The venture failed in August 1884.

26 April 1884: Morris contributed an article entitled 'The Dull Level of Life' to *Justice*.

27 April 1884: Morris delivered 'Useful Work *versus* Useless Toil' before the LEL at the Monarch Coffee House, 166 Bethnal Green Road.

Spring 1884: Morris and Hyndman published their 64-page *A Summary of the Principles of Socialism*. It was printed by the Modern Press. Morris designed the wrapper.

9 May 1884: Morris wrote to Henry Cornelius Donavan declining his request to stand as a candidate for the board of Greenwich Zoo.

17 May 1884: Morris contributed an article entitled 'A Factory as it Might Be' to *Justice*. He also published the first of a series of appeals for funds for the paper.

18 May 1884: Morris was scheduled to deliver 'Art and Labour' to the Marylebone Branch of the DF at 95 Hampstead Road, Hampstead.

24 May 1884: Morris contributed an article entitled 'Individualism at the Royal Academy' to *Justice*.

26 May 1884: Morris & Co. sent a bill to Aleco Ionides for £1,330 8s 9d for work done on the drawing room and Antiquaries room at 1 Holland Park.

31 May 1884: Morris contributed 'Work in a Factory as it Might Be – II' to *Justice*.

1 June 1884: Morris estimated his literary income to be £120 per annum.

7 June 1884: The fourth of Morris's *Chants for Socialists* appeared in *Justice*.

14 June 1884: The Hammersmith branch of the DF was set up at Kelmscott House. The committee met once or twice a week and lectures were held every week or so. Morris was present at 21 of the 27 meetings held in 1884. By the end of the year there were thirty-nine members.

26 June 1884: Cobden-Sanderson recorded in his *Journals*: 'I am now the proprietor of a workshop! On Saturday [21 June] I signed an agreement by virtue of which I became on Tuesday last [24 June] the tenant of the second floor of 30 Maiden Lane.'

28 June 1884: Morris contributed 'Work in a Factory as it Might Be – III' to *Justice*.

July 1884: The Scottish Land and Labour League (SLLL) was founded: 'I must say I don't quite like the new name for the Scotch body; it will be looked on here as a secession I am afraid.' The SLLL was accepted as an affiliate of the SDF in August 1884. Morris published an article entitled 'The Exhibition of the Royal Academy' in *To-day*.

1 July 1884: Morris read a paper at the annual meeting of SPAB held at the Society of Arts, John Street, Adelphi.

5 July 1884: Morris published another appeal for funds in *Justice*.

6 July 1884: Morris delivered 'Useful Work *versus* Useless Toil' before the Hammersmith Branch of the SDF at Kelmscott House. Jane wrote to Blunt asking him to contribute an article on Egypt to *To-Day*.

8 July 1884: Morris's earliest surviving letter to George Bernard Shaw bears this date. However, they were already well acquainted. Shaw recorded that he first met Morris at a meeting of the DF. Morris had read a chapter of Shaw's *An Unsocial Socialist* and was keen to be introduced to its author.

11 July 1884: Morris delivered a lecture entitled 'Textile Fabrics' at the International Health Exhibition at the South Kensington Museum, London. This lecture was subsequently published as a pamphlet by William Clowes & Sons on behalf of the International Health Exhibition.

12 July 1884: Morris contributed an article entitled 'To Genuine Radicals' to *Justice*.

13 July 1883: Burns and Williams held a socialist meeting in Hyde Park following a large demonstration in favour of the reform of local government in London. According to Morris 'they got together *five thousand* people who cheered them lustily'. It is not clear if Morris attended this meeting.

15 July 1884: Morris was present at a meeting of the DF held to discuss the distribution of socialist literature at another Hyde Park Franchise meeting to be held on 21 July.

19 July 1884: Morris contributed an article entitled 'The Housing of the Poor' to *Justice*. The *Architect* published the first part of his lecture on 'Textile Fabrics' (pp. 43–5). The second instalment appeared on 26 July 1884 (pp. 50–53).

20 July 1884: Morris entertained Shaw to supper. He was also present when Shaw lectured later that evening on 'Socialism *versus* Individualism' at Kelmscott House.

21 July 1884: A large Franchise meeting was held in Hyde Park organized by the London Trades Council. At the end of the demonstration a socialist meeting was held at which John Burns denounced John Bright as an imposter and 'a silver-tongued hypocrite'. The meeting then broke up in chaos: 'the malcontents began to take us in [the] flank and shove on against the speakers: then whether our people were pushed down partly or wholly or whether they charged down hill I don't rightly know, but down hill they went in the lump banners & all: goodbye to the latter by the way... I heard say that they were for putting Burns in the serpentine.' Morris was present although he did not address the meeting formally: 'I made some remarks to some of the knots of Mr. Bright's lambs, but they kept hands off, & only hooted, being not so many as they had been.'

22 July 1884: The DF held a meeting at which it was decided that in future supporters would be stationed round speakers at large demonstrations in order to protect them from the crowd.

24 July 1884: Morris told Robert Thomson: 'we cannot turn our people back into Catholic English peasants and guild-craftsmen, or into heathen Norse bonders, much as may be said for such conditions of life.'

26 July 1884: Allingham, who was staying with Tennyson, wrote in his *Diary* that 'T. was shocked to hear of William Morris's Democratic Socialism, and asked to see a copy of *Justice* (Morris's *Justice*, I partly agree with and partly detest. It is incendiary and atheistic and would upset everything)'. Morris published another appeal for funds in *Justice*.

28 July 1884: Morris's *Wandle* printed textile design was registered.

29 July 1884: Blunt met Morris for the first time when he visited Kelmscott House.

2 August 1884: Morris published yet another appeal for funds in *Justice*.

4 August 1884: At the Fourth Annual Conference of the DF held at Palace Chambers, Westminster, the organization decided to change its name to the Social Democratic Federation (SDF). It was also decided that parliamentary elections should not be contested. Hyndman was displaced as president in favour of a rotating chairman elected by the Executive Council. Hyndman opposed this and nominated Morris as the new president but he refused.

5/6 August 1884: Morris and Jane probably travelled down to Kelmscott Manor. While at Kelmscott Manor Morris slipped on the grass and was laid up for two days. This accident was followed by an attack of gout. Jane wrote to Blunt (6 August): 'the life is very pleasant here, we spend most of the day in the garden, or reading by the river-side.'

9 August 1884: Morris contributed an article entitled 'Socialism in England in 1884' to *Justice*.

12 August 1884: Morris returned to London. He acted as chairman at an evening meeting of the SDF at which resolutions were passed by the Executive in support of Irish Home Rule and Disestablishment: '[I] hobbled down stairs into the Federation at the rate of a mile in two hours.'

13 August 1884: Morris returned to Kelmscott Manor 'for two days'.

17 August 1884: Morris delivered 'Art and Labour' before the Hammersmith Branch of the SDF at Kelmscott House, Hammersmith.

19 August 1884: Morris was in the chair at a meeting of the DF: 'Hyndman was there ... he seemed rather sulky at me.'

20 August 1884: Morris wrote to Scheu: 'I feel myself very weak as to the science of Socialism on many points; I wish I knew German, as I see I must certainly learn it; confound you chaps!'

22 August 1884: John Carruthers joined the Hammersmith branch of the SDF. He was to become one of Morris's most loyal followers.

26 August 1884: Morris attended a meeting of the SDF chaired by Eleanor Marx-Aveling.

3 September 1884: Morris's growing disillusion with the official policy of the SDF – particularly on Disestablishment and Irish Home Rule – became obvious when the Hammersmith Branch unanimously resolved that any statement on these two issues was 'superfluous'.

5 September 1884: Morris was scheduled to deliver 'Useful Work *versus* Useless Toil' before the Tottenham Branch of the SDF at Stone Bridge Hall, London. Blunt visited Jane at Kelmscott House.

6 September 1884: Morris contributed an article entitled 'Uncrowned Kings' to *Justice*. He also signed a statement which appeared under the title 'Social Democratic Federation to the Trades Unions'.

8 September 1884: Morris delivered 'Misery and The Way Out' before the Borough of Southwark Branch of the SDF at the Queen's Bench Coffee Rooms, 23 Southwark Bridge Road, London.

11 September 1884: Morris travelled down to Kelmscott Manor.

13 September 1884: Morris travelled up to Sheffield: 'Sheffield is a beastly place, but there is lovely country near it.' The *Architect* published portions of Morris's lecture 'Architecture and History' as 'Medieval and Modern Craftsmanship' (pp. 171–3).

14 September 1884: In the afternoon Morris delivered 'Iceland, Its Ancient Literature and Mythology' before the Sheffield Secular Society. In the evening he delivered 'Art and Labour' before the same society.

15 September 1884: Morris returned from Sheffield to London via Clay Cross.

18 September 1884: An article on Morris entitled *A Prophet among the Painters* by W. J. Stillman appeared in the *Nation* (vol. 39, pp. 240–41). A second instalment appeared in the same journal on 25 September 1884 (pp. 261–2).

19 September 1884: Cobden-Sanderson noted in his *Journals* that 'I began to "finish" *Le Capital* for Morris the day before yesterday [17 September]'.

20 September 1884: Morris travelled up to Manchester where he delivered a lecture entitled 'At a Picture Show' at the opening of an Ancoats Recreation Committee art exhibition at New Islington Hall, Ancoats, Manchester. He also contributed an article to *Justice* entitled 'The Hammersmith Costermongers'.

21 September 1884: Morris delivered 'Art and Labour' at a meeting sponsored by the Ancoats Recreation Committee at New Islington Hall, Ancoats, Manchester.

27 September 1884: Morris was scheduled to deliver 'Misery and the Way Out' before the Progressive Association at Ye Old Mansion House, Essex Road, London.

28 September 1884: In a letter to Scheu, Morris stated that Bax was determined to precipitate a quarrel with Hyndman. Morris was at this time trying to act as a peacemaker. He was also scheduled to deliver 'Misery and the Way Out' before the Bayswater and Paddington Branches of the SDF at St John's Temperance Hall, Bell Street, Edgware Road, London.

29 September 1884: Morris wrote a brief introduction to Sketchley's *A Review of European Society*.

1 October 1884: At this time Morris was staying at Kelmscott Manor.

3 October 1884: Morris returned to London. His mother visited him at Merton.

4 October 1884: Morris wrote a letter to the *Manchester Guardian* regarding his recent lectures in Ancoats (it was published 7 October). On the same day he wrote to the *Echo* reaffirming his support for the SDF and defending a lecture he had given on behalf of SPAB (this latter was also published on 7 October).

7 October 1884: Morris and Aveling were requested to write a new *Manifesto* for the SDF: 'my flesh creeps at the difficulties.' This *Manifesto* was eventually published in *To-day* in January 1885, pp. 1–10.

9 October 1884: Cobden-Sanderson finished the binding for Morris's copy of *Le Capital*.

11 October 1884: Morris contributed an article entitled 'An Appeal to the Just' in *Justice*. The paper also published a letter from him in which he reasserted his commitment to the SDF.

12 October 1884: Morris was scheduled to deliver 'Useful Work *versus* Useless Toil' before the Battersea Branch of the SDF at Henley Hall, Henley Street, Battersea, London.

19 October 1884: Morris was scheduled to deliver 'Misery and the Way Out' before the Hammersmith Branch of the SDF at Kelmscott House, Hammersmith.

22 October 1884: Morris delivered his lecture 'A Socialist's View of Art and Labour' at a meeting sponsored by the Preston Eclectic Society at the Unitarian Chapel, Preston.

25 October 1884: In the morning Morris wrote to Cobden-Sanderson thanking him for the 'beautiful binding' he had made for his copy of *Le Capital*. He later travelled down to Kelmscott Manor.

26 October 1884: A meeting of 80,000 protested in Hyde Park at the House of Lord's refusal to approve franchise reform.

27 October 1881: Morris returned to London.

29 October 1884: Morris was chairman at a meeting in Limehouse arranged by the SDF as part of a membership drive in the East End of London.

November 1884: Arguments began to surface in the SDF over the editorial control of *Justice*. Morris again tried to mediate suggesting that the executive should have the right of veto over the articles printed by Hyndman. Hyndman refused.

2 November 1884: Morris delivered 'Useful Work *versus* Useless Toil' at a meeting sponsored by the Rotherhithe Branch of the SDF at the China Hall, Lower Road, Rotherhithe.

8 November 1884: Engels recorded that Morris was due to visit him for 'a long conference'.

9 November 1884: Morris delivered 'Misery and the Way Out' before the Tower Hamlets Radical Club at 13 Redman's Road, Mile End. A select committee of the House of Commons was appointed to consider the restoration of Westminster Hall.

15 November 1884: Morris travelled from London to Newcastle where he stayed the night with Thomas Robert Spence Watson: 'my host is very kind and communicative.' He also contributed an article entitled 'The Lord Mayor's Show' to *Justice*.

16 November 1884: Morris delivered 'Art and Labour' at a meeting sponsored by the Newcastle Branch of the SDF in the Tyne Theatre, Newcastle.

17 November 1884: Morris travelled from Newcastle to Edinburgh. Here he delivered 'Misery and the Way Out' at a meeting sponsored by the Edinburgh Branch of the SLLL at the large hall at the Literary Institute, Clark Street, Edinburgh. He spoke to an audience that numbered 3,000.

19 November 1884: Morris attended a meeting at St James's Hall where Henry George spoke in favour of a single tax on land: 'I seemed to feel that George's nostrum was nearly played out; & that a real socialist would have had a good reception.'

21 November 1884: Morris read his 'The Passing of Brynhild' at an 'Art Evening' sponsored by the SDF at Neumeyer Hall, Hart Street, Bloomsbury. At the same meeting Aveling and Eleanor Marx acted out a play based on their own life. Engels was also present at this entertainment. Morris's *Wild Tulip* wallpaper design was registered.

23 November 1884: Morris was scheduled to deliver a lecture before the Glasgow Branch of the SDF in Glasgow.

26 November 1884: In a letter written to Allingham, Morris clearly described Marx's theory of surplus value (*c.f.* 14 December 1884).

28 November 1884: Mahon visited Engels to discuss the split in the SDF.

29 November 1884: Morris contributed an article entitled 'The Hackney Election' to *Justice*.

30 November 1884: Morris delivered 'How We Live and How We Might Live' before the Hammersmith Branch of the SDF at Kelmscott House, Hammersmith. Dollie Radford, who was present at the lecture, described it as 'a beautiful address'. She later had supper at Kelmscott House: 'His house is beautiful; and his daughter May is *most* beautiful: no wonder that Rossetti painted her so often.'

2 December 1884: A meeting of the SDF approved Morris and Aveling's new *Manifesto*.

5 December 1884: Morris delivered 'Misery and the Way Out' before the Merton Abbey Branch of the SDF at the Branch Rooms, High Street, Merton. Allingham recorded in his *Diary* a conversation that he and Tennyson had about Morris's politics. Tennyson is supposed to have said 'He has gone crazy'.

7 December 1884: Morris delivered 'Misery and the Way Out' at a meeting sponsored by the West Central Branch of the NSS at the Athenaeum Hall, George Street, London.

11 December 1884: Morris was scheduled to deliver a lecture before the Greenock Branch of the LRL at Greenock, Scotland.

13 December 1884: In the afternoon Morris and Scheu took a long walk to Newhaven and then returned by omnibus to Edinburgh: 'the said vehicle was half full of fish-wives and their babies: they were not beautiful ones like Christie Johnson, but were clean and neat, and were dressed in the proper style with jackets of bright chintz.' In the evening Morris delivered 'How We Live and How We Might Live' at a meeting sponsored by the Edinburgh Branch of the SLLL at Picardy Hall, Edinburgh. It was at this lecture that Morris first met John Bruce Glasier. Glasier wrote: 'There he was, a sun-god, truly, in his ever afterwards familiar dark-blue serge jacket suit and lighter blue cotton shirt and collar (without scarf or tie), and with the grandest head I had ever seen on the shoulders of a man.'

14 December 1884: Morris travelled from Edinburgh to Glasgow. In the morning he gave an impromptu speech before the Glasgow Branch of the SDF at the branch rooms in Glasgow. In the evening he delivered 'Art and Labour' before the Glasgow Sunday Society at St Andrew's Hall, Glasgow to an audience of around 3,000. After the lecture Morris addressed the Glasgow branch of the SDF. It was at this meeting that a letter was read out from Hyndman denouncing Scheu. Morris was then heckled by Nairne for his ignorance of Marxist economics. Morris is supposed to have replied, according to Glasier: 'To speak quite frankly. I do not know what Marx's theory of value is, and I'm damned if I want to know' (*c.f.* 26 November 1884). This attack greatly annoyed Morris and he returned to London determined to bring his dispute with Hyndman out in the open.

15 December 1884: In the morning Jenny suffered a slight epileptic fit.

16 December 1884: Morris arrived back in London. After a brief discussion with his supporters he attended a meeting of the SDF. At this meeting Hyndman demanded that W. J. Clarke be expelled from the organization. He was supported by Champion, Quelch, Jack Williams, James Murray, Herbert Burrows and John Burns. The opposition consisted of Morris, Aveling, Eleanor Marx, Bax, Joseph Lane, Sam Mainwaring, Robert Banner and

Mahon (who had come all the way from Scotland for the confrontation). Morris's group won the subsequent vote by eight votes to seven. At the same meeting Morris urged a vote of confidence in Scheu but Hyndman refused.

18 December 1884: In a letter written to Jane, Morris made it clear that he intended to support Scheu, oust Hyndman from the editorship of *Justice*, and force his resignation from the SDF. However, at an evening meeting of the 'cabal' the decision was apparently taken to leave the SDF and found a new organization.

19 December 1884: Morris was scheduled to deliver 'Misery and the Way Out' at the Working Men's Club, Crown Hill, Croydon.

20 December 1884: Morris contributed an article entitled 'Philanthropists' to *Justice*.

21 December 1884: Morris's lecture on 'The Origins of Ornamental Art' was read out by an unnamed speaker at a meeting sponsored by the Hammersmith Branch of the SDF at Kelmscott House, Hammersmith.

22 December 1884: Morris travelled to Chesterfield – 'a queer dingy place' – where he met Edward Carpenter: 'I ... found him very sympathetic and sensible at the same time.'

23 December 1884: At another meeting of the SDF Scheu, who had travelled down from Edinburgh, made a notable defence of his position against Hyndman's allegations.

25 December 1884: In a letter to his mother Morris complained that on Christmas Day he 'was quite fagged and obliged to rest'.

26 December 1884: Morris was scheduled to deliver 'How We Live and How We Might Live' at the Working Men's Club at Crown Hill, Croydon.

27 December 1884: Despite winning a vote on Hyndman's leadership by ten votes to eight, Morris – along with Bax, Aveling, Eleanor Marx and others – handed in his resignation from the SDF.

29 December 1884: In the morning Morris took temporary premises (on the recommendation of Mahon) for what was to be the Socialist League (SL) at 37 Farringdon Street: '[I] authorized the purchase of the due amount of Windsor chairs and a kitchen table: so there I am really once more like a young bear with all my troubles before me.'

30 December 1884: The SL was founded. Morris and Bax began work on its *Manifesto* which was published in January 1885 and signed by the Provisional Council. This document was closely based on *Das Kapital* and made a point of explaining the term 'surplus value'.

31 December 1884: Morris was suffering from a cold.

1885: The SL published two volumes of the *Socialist Platform*. The first an *Address to Trades' Unions* was jointly edited by Morris and Bax. The second was a reprint of Morris's lecture 'Useful Work *versus* Useless Toil'. The *Flora* and *Pomona* tapestries were produced. Morris designed the *Woodpecker* tapestry woven in wool and silk on a cotton warp.

Early January 1885: Shaw recorded that he had no audience at St John's Coffee House in Hoxton 'in consequence of W. Morris being round the corner lecturing'. Cormell Price wrote: 'WM uncomfortable about the split among the Socialists: "feels like a dog with a tin kettle tied to his tail".'

1 January 1885: In a letter to Robert Thomson, Morris explained the *occasion* for leaving the SDF as (i) the attempt to expel W. J. Clarke and (ii) Hyndman's letter to the Glasgow branch in which he accused Scheu of treachery and referred to him as an anarchist. However, he added that the *reason* was Hyndman's autocratic tendencies and opportunism and the pursuit of policies with which he disagreed. Crom Price noted in his *Diary*: 'Dined at Kelmscott House... As I entered the house loud voices in hot discussion audible from W. M.'s study. They were drawing up a programme for the Socialist Federation which is only a week old.'

3 January 1885: Blunt visited Jane at Kelmscott House. He recorded in his *Diary*: 'Her daughter Jenny ... is almost out of her mind with epileptic fits and as Morris will not hear of the girl's leaving home Mrs Morris is taking her other daughter May abroad.' A letter signed by Morris and nine others appeared in *Justice* explaining their reasons for leaving the SDF.

4 January 1885: Morris was scheduled to deliver 'Work as It Is and as It Might Be' at a meeting sponsored by the Hammersmith Branch of the SDF at Kelmscott House, Hammersmith.

7 January 1885: The Hammersmith Branch of the SDF was reconstituted as a branch of the SL. It adopted a folding membership card designed by Walter Crane which depicted Morris as a blacksmith.

8 January 1885: *A Talk with William Morris on Socialism* appeared in the *Daily News*. An unsigned critique of this interview was published in the *Saturday Review* later in the month (pp. 43–4) in which the writer stated 'Mr. Morris cannot look out of his window, or into his looking-glass, or back over his life without seeing how flatly contrary to the whole course of nature and experience – a course with which the arrangements of society have nothing to do – is this cloud castle of his.'

11 January 1885: Morris delivered 'How We Live and How We Might Live' at a meeting sponsored by the Bethnal Green Branch of the LEL at the

Hoxton Academy School, Hoxton.

13 January 1885: The ex-members of the Executive Council of the SDF issued a statement explaining the reasons why they resigned.

17 January 1885: Blunt visited Jane at Kelmscott House where they discussed Swinburne.

18 January 1885: A letter was read at a meeting of the SL outlining the SDF's 'views of the cause of the rupture' between it and the SL.

22 January 1885: Morris reluctantly attended a meeting called by the remaining members of the executive of the SDF to discuss the charges made by those who had resigned. Carpenter – who had visited Morris at some point in January – wrote to Robert Sharland stating that Morris 'has had his mind poisoned against Hyndman and the others by certain schemers, and he has led out into the wilderness a body of men who undoubtedly have done very little in the cause, and several of whom are ambitious and designing. If he can weld them together ... good; but it seems to me probable that he will have ... trouble in doing that.'

24 January 1885: Webb wrote to Kate Faulkner from Rome: 'I should be glad to know how the new [Socialist] League is getting on: I heard from Morris just after the break up, and I should like to know if things are going pretty well in the new form.'

25 January 1885: Morris gave an unnamed lecture to the Woolwich Branch of the SDF in Woolwich. The *Daily News* printed an article in which it was stated that 'Mr. William Morris, the poet of English Socialism – and of other things besides – will issue the first number of his new journal *The Commonweal* next Wednesday.'

27 January 1885: The *Daily News* published a letter from Morris (dated 26 January) on 'The Commonweal'.

28 January 1885: The first issue of the monthly *Commonweal* was published – bearing the date of February 1885 – with articles by Bax, Stepniak, Shaw, Kitz, Engels and the Avelings. Its initial appearance was financed by donations of £300 from Morris and £100 from Faulkner. Morris provided an 'Introductory' and a poem 'The March of the Workers'. As a member of the Provisional Council he also signed the SL's 'Manifesto'.

29 January 1885: Blunt paid his last visit to Jane before she left for Italy. He wrote in his *Diary*: 'There are moments when she is still a beautiful woman and I wish I had known her in [the] old days.'

30 January 1885: Morris read his poem 'All for the Cause' at a Socialist 'Art Evening' at Ladbrooke Hall, London. The entertainment also included a rendition of his song 'The March of the Workers' and a three-act comic drama called *Alone* by Palgrave Simpson and Herman Merivale. Shaw, Aveling, Eleanor Marx and May Morris appeared in the latter. Shaw wrote: 'I do not love her [May Morris] – I have too much sense for such follies; but I hate and envy the detestable villain who plays her lover with all my soul.'

January–February 1885: A constitution was provisionally adopted by the SL. Drafted by the Avelings it was pro-parliamentary in stance and suggested that the SL should assist trade unions and co-operative societies and work towards the formation of a Socialist Labour Party. It was later rejected – at Morris's insistence – at the first Annual Conference of the SL.

1 February 1885: Morris was scheduled to deliver his lecture 'How We Live and How We Might Live' at a combined meeting of Branch 23 of the SDF and the Deutscher Club of the LEL at the latter's club rooms at Featherstone and Moorgate Streets, London.

2 February 1885: According to Cobden-Sanderson, Jane and May left for Bordighera in Italy. Morris's *Lea* block-printed and indigo discharged cotton design was registered.

7 February 1885: Morris spoke at a meeting held to explain the purpose of a series of lectures by Aveling on Karl Marx's *Das Kapital*: 'it went off very well; there were about 200 people there; that's not much; but they were all our supporters.'

8 February 1885: Morris was scheduled to deliver 'How We Live and How We Might Live' at the Hammersmith Radical Club.

10 February 1885: In a letter to Jane – who arrived at Bordighera on this date – Morris stated that the first edition of *Commonweal* had sold 5,000.

11 February 1885: The *Pall Mall Gazette* published a resolution passed by the SL condemning the invasion of the Sudan. The resolution was also published in the *Standard* and *St James's Gazette*. At a meeting of the Hammersmith Branch of the SL it was recorded that Morris promised a number of volumes for the new reading room at Kelmscott House. It was at this meeting that Walter Crane joined the SL.

12 February 1885: Aveling gave the first of his series of lectures on *Das Kapital*: 'it was very successful: 150 audience all attentive many taking notes and answering very well.' Thereafter the lectures were delivered weekly on a Thursday at the South Place Institute and published in *Commonweal*. Jane wrote to Blunt from Bordighera promising to sent him 'a Valentine of violets tomorrow'.

15 February 1885: Morris delivered his lecture 'Slaves and Slave Holders' at the

Hammersmith Branch of the SL at Kelmscott House, Hammersmith.

16 February 1885: A demonstration of between 3,000 to 4,000 unemployed workers assembled on the Embankment and then marched to Westminster to demand that the Local Government Board institute public works: 'I suppose you saw the reports of our would be leader's [Hyndman's] speech on the Thames embankment ... more preposterous humbug I never heard of. However it will answer his purpose for the time and make him notorious.' The SL sent a resolution to a number of papers expressing its pleasure at the recent fall of Khartoum.

19 February 1885: Morris went to Kelmscott Manor.

20 February 1885: Morris wrote to May from Kelmscott Manor: 'I am writing to you in the last (waking) hour of my two days holiday, which I rather wish were longer; not that it has been quite workless: for the floods being out, I have been in, & have designed a carpet, and prepared a speech.'

21 February 1885: In a letter to James Mavor, Morris described 'The March of the Workers' as 'the best short poem I have written'.

22 February 1885: Morris was scheduled to deliver 'Useful Work *versus* Useless Toil' before the Southwark Branch of the SL at the Forester's Arms, 62 Blackman Street, London.

25 February 1885: In the morning Morris travelled down to Oxford with the Avelings. Here he gave a speech at a meeting sponsored by the Oxford Socialist Society at the Music Room, Holywell, Oxford (opposite where Jane had been born). The meeting ended in chaos when one of the students let off a stink bomb.

27 February 1885: Morris wrote his first letter on *Commonweal* stationery.

28 February 1885: Morris recommended *Das Kapital*, Grönlund's *Cooperative Commonwealth* and *Commercial & Communal Economy* by J. Carruthers as books worth reading on socialism. 'On the whole tough as the job is you ought to read Marx if you can: up to date he is the only completely scientific Economist on our side.' *Jackson's Oxford Journal* published a detailed summary of the speech Morris had given before the Oxford Socialist Society.

March 1885: The first instalment of *The Pilgrims of Hope* appeared in *Commonweal* under the title 'The Message of the March Wind'. Morris also published the first of a number of appeals for subscriptions to the paper. The first edition of the *Anarchist* was published: 'a poor little sheet with, it seems to me very little reason d'etre.'

2 March 1885: The *Manifesto of the Socialist League on the Soudan War* was issued. It was signed by Morris – along with a number of others – although it is not clear if he actually wrote it.

3 March 1885: Morris delivered 'Art and Labour' at a meeting sponsored by the Bristol Branch of the SL at the Bristol Museum and Library: '...had a good audience there: earning £4 besides expenses.'

4 March 1885: A meeting of the Peace Society was held to protest against the Sudan War. Blunt invited Morris to attend but he excused himself.

8 March 1885: Morris delivered 'Work as It Is and as It Might Be' before the Manchester Square Branch of the SL at the Westmoreland Arms, George Street, London.

11 March 1885: Morris testified before the Parliamentary Committee on the Restoration of Westminster Hall.

13 March 1885: Morris was scheduled to give a lecture before the Merton Abbey Branch of the SL at Merton Abbey.

16 March 1885: Jenny and Miss Bailey went to Kelmscott Manor.

17 March 1885: Shaw noted in his *Diary* that Aveling visited him to tell him that Morris had rejected an article on 'marriage' he had written for *Commonweal*.

22 March 1885: Morris gave a speech in commemoration of the Paris Commune sponsored by the SL and combined London anarchist groups. The meeting was held at Neumeyer Hall, Hart Street, Bloomsbury.

23 March 1885: Morris attended a similar meeting arranged by the Anarchists at South Place.

24 March 1885: Morris visited Mrs George Brodie Clark at Syon Park House, Brentford, to discuss curtains: 'really when one sells a body porridge one should not be expected to put it into their mouths with a spoon.' He was also working on his lecture called 'Commercial War'.

25 March 1885: Jenny and Miss Bailey attended the marriage of Annie Allen the maid at Kelmscott Manor.

26 March 1885: Jenny and Miss Bailey left Kelmscott Manor and returned to Hammersmith.

27 March 1885: Morris delivered 'Commercial War' before the Croydon Branch of the SDF at Crown Hill, Croydon.

28 March 1885: Morris held his annual Boat Race party at Kelmscott House. Amongst those present were Bax and the Avelings. Prior to this Jane had written to Blunt from Bordighera saying she intended to remain in Italy until the end of the month in order to avoid that 'dreadful thing called a "Boat

Race"'.

29 March 1885: Morris was scheduled to deliver his lecture 'Socialism' before the Mile-End Branch of the SL at 110 Whitehorse Street, Whitechapel. He had tea with E. T. Craig at Kelmscott House.

31 March 1885: Morris, Jenny and 'aunt Bessy' visited an exhibition of Persian art. In the evening he dined at the Howards with Blunt. Blunt wrote: 'William Morris was there in morning dress, for he eschews tail coats, and did most of the talking on his own special subjects – socialism, the evil of capitalism, and the rest. This he does excellently well.'

April 1885: Morris almost certainly read Laveleye's book *Le Socialisme Contemporain* which had appeared in translation (by G. H. Orpen) in 1885. Orpen added a chapter to this work entitled 'Socialism in England' in which he criticized Morris's pamphlet 'Art and Socialism'. Morris contributed 'The Worker's Share of Art', the second part of *The Pilgrims of Hope* and two reviews to *Commonweal*. The latter were of *Socialist Rhymes* by J. L. Joynes and the first edition of the *Anarchist*.

1 April 1885: Scheu came to stay with Morris at Kelmscott House while he searched for work in London. He was still staying with Morris on 14 April and it is possible that he was still there as late as mid-May.

2 April 1885: Morris moved a socialist rider to an anti-war resolution referring to the Sudan at a meeting held at St James's Hall, London. During his speech Morris was cut short by Bradlaugh and the rider declared unacceptable. It was eventually put to the audience and rejected.

3 April 1885: Jenny had an epileptic fit.

5 April 1885: At an 'extraordinary' conference of the SDF it was decided to return to the old pro-parliamentary programme of the DF.

9 April 1885: Morris wrote to Engels suggesting he write a piece for *Commonweal*. An article entitled 'How Not to Translate Marx' subsequently appeared in the paper in November 1885.

10 April 1885: Morris was scheduled to deliver a lecture before the Merton Abbey Branch of the SL at Merton Abbey.

11 April 1885: Jenny and Miss Bailey left Kelmscott House to stay with the Cobden-Sandersons at Abinger, at the foot of Leigh Hill, Surrey.

12 April 1885: Morris was scheduled to deliver his lecture 'Commercial War' before the local LEL at the Academy Schools, Hoxton Street, Hoxton. The SDF held a meeting in Hyde Park where they demanded an eight-hour day in all trades and a public works programme to provide jobs for the unemployed. About 10,000 people attended the meeting.

14 April 1885: Jenny and Miss Bailey returned to Kelmscott House.

18 April 1885: Morris was scheduled to deliver his lecture 'Commercial War' before the Hammersmith Branch of the SL at Kelmscott House, Hammersmith.

23 April 1885: Morris was chairman of an anti-Sudan war meeting sponsored by the SL at South Place Institute, Finsbury, London.

24 April 1885: Morris gave a poetry reading from his own works in aid of the funds of the Glasgow Branch of the SL who sponsored the meeting at Pillar Hall, Queen's Rooms, Glasgow. During the day Morris was taken on a steamboat excursion to Lochgoilhead in order to see some of the scenery on the Clyde. A workman who accompanied Morris on this trip described the conversation 'as good as a university education'. On his railway journey to Scotland Morris read Richard Jefferies' *After London*: 'I rather like it: absurd hopes curled round my heart as I read it.'

25 April 1885: Morris travelled from Glasgow to Edinburgh. Here he delivered 'Work as It Is and as It Might Be' at a meeting sponsored by the Edinburgh Branch of the SLLL at the Free Tron Hall, Edinburgh. He also sat for a bas-relief portrait by J. Pittendreigh McGillivray.

26 April 1885: In the morning Morris travelled from Edinburgh back to Glasgow. Here he delivered 'How We Live and How We Might Live' at a meeting sponsored by the Glasgow Branch of the SL at the Albion Hall, Glasgow. Morris again sat for McGillivray.

27 April 1885: Morris travelled from Glasgow to Chesterfield: 'it was a beautiful journey from Carlisle to Settle ... I think it is the loveliest part of all England.' Morris delivered 'Work as It Is and as It Might Be' at a meeting sponsored by the Chesterfield and District Workingmen's Radical Association at the Stephenson Memorial Hall, Chesterfield. Carpenter was chairman. He spent the night with Carpenter at Millthorpe, half-way between Chesterfield and Sheffield: 'Carpenter seems to live in great amity with the workmen & the women; they all live together in the kitchen, and 'tis all very pleasant.'

28 April 1885: Morris spent the day with Carpenter at Millthorpe. Carpenter presented Morris with a copy of Thoreau's *Walden*.

30 April 1885: Morris inspected some new headquarters – possibly at 20 Chiswell Street – for the SL. In the evening Jane and May returned from their holiday in Italy.

May 1885: Morris published a contribution to 'Sign of the Times', the third instalment of *The Pilgrims of Hope*, an essay entitled 'Unattractive Labour' and an untitled report of an anti-war meeting in *Commonweal*. He also reviewed

Charles Rowley's *Social Politics.*

4 May 1885: Mahon wrote to the Provisional Council of the SL offering his resignation as Secretary. R. Page Arnot suggests that this was due to disagreements over the tactics of the SL but it is more likely to have been as a result of Mahon's ineptitude. Morris was frequently frustrated by the delays associated with the printing of *Commonweal.*

7 May 1885: Morris issued a circular letter to members of the SL in which he stated that the League had found new premises at 20 Chiswell Street. This move never materialized.

8 May 1885: Morris was scheduled to deliver 'How Can We Help?' before the Merton Abbey Branch of the SL at Merton Abbey.

9 May 1885: The first serious attack was made by the police on the socialists' propaganda when they broke up a meeting at the International Socialist Working Men's Club in Stephen's Mews, Tottenham Court Road.

10 May 1885: Morris delivered 'How Can We Help?' at the Hammersmith Branch of the SL at Kelmscott House, Hammersmith.

13 May 1885: In a letter to Georgiana Burne-Jones, Morris expressed himself 'in low spirits about the prospects of our "party"'.

24 May 1885: Morris delivered 'Work as It Is and as It Might Be' before the Mile-End Branch of the SL at 110 White Horse Street, Stepney, London. He described his audience to Georgiana Burne-Jones as 'some twenty people in a little room, as dirty as convenient and stinking a good deal. It took the fire out of my fine periods, I can tell you.'

30 May 1885: In the morning Morris travelled up to York where he made a speech at a meeting called by SPAB to protest against the 'demolition of Churches in York'. The meeting was held at the Corn Exchange.

June 1885: The SL acquired new headquarters at 13 Farringdon Road, Holborn Viaduct. The premises consisted of a large lecture room, reading room, and printing and publishing office. Morris contributed an article entitled 'Attractive Labour', the fourth part of *The Pilgrims of Hope* and some untitled paragraphs to *Commonweal.*

4 June 1885: Morris gave the opening speech at the annual SPAB meeting held in the rooms of the Society of Arts, John Street, Adelphi.

9 June 1885: Morris delivered his lecture 'Socialism' before the Oxford Branch of the SL and the Marx Club in Oxford.

11 June 1885: Morris read his poem 'Socialists at Play' at a social event celebrating the completion of Aveling's lectures on *Das Kapital.* The soirée was sponsored by the SL and held at the South Place Institute, Finsbury, London. The poem was later issued as a pamphlet.

14 June 1885: Morris delivered his lecture 'The Hopes of Civilisation' before the Hammersmith Branch of the SL at Kelmscott House.

22 June 1885: Jane was suffering from rheumatism in her hands.

27 June 1885: Morris was scheduled to give an open-air speech for the Hammersmith Branch of the SL at Weltje Road, Hammersmith.

28 June 1885: In the morning Morris delivered his lecture 'Socialism' before the Northampton Branch of the NSS at Cow Meadow, Northampton. In the evening he delivered 'How We Live and How We Might Live' before the same body at the Secular Hall, Cold Street, Northampton.

July 1885: Morris contributed 'Notes on the Political Crisis', 'Socialism and Politics' and his poem 'Socialists at Play' to *Commonweal*.

5 July 1885: Morris acted as chairman at the First Annual Conference of the SL held at Farringdon Hall, 13 Farringdon Road, London. At the time membership stood at around 230. There were branches at Hammersmith, Bloomsbury, Merton Abbey, Stratford, North London, Leeds, Bradford and Oxford. Sparling was appointed Secretary of the League in place of Mahon. The *Constitution & Rules of the Socialist League* was also published around this time.

6 July 1885: The first of W. T. Stead's articles on child prostitution appeared in the *Pall Mall Gazette*. They continued until 10 July 1885.

8 July 1885: Morris ordered Stepniak's *Russia Under the Tsars*, Bebel's *Woman in the Past, Present & Future* and Thoreau's *Walden*. The first two of these were reviewed in *Commonweal* shortly after.

11 July 1885: Morris delivered 'The Hopes of Civilisation' at a meeting sponsored by the Manchester Socialist Union at the Memorial Hall, Manchester: 'hall not full (about 250) fine evening & great cricket match on.'

12 July 1885: Morris delivered his lecture 'The Depression of Trade' at a meeting sponsored by the Oldham Branch of the SL at the Large Hall, Cucumber Gardens, Royton, Manchester. In the evening he gave an open-air talk in favour of free speech at Thomasfields, Oldham: 'I spoke for about 45 minutes, rather well I think.' LeMire dates this to 13 July but it is clear from a letter Morris wrote to Scheu that it took place on this date.

14 July 1885: In the evening Morris gave an extempore speech at the New Hall, Desborough in Northamptonshire: 'Class-feeling strong here among the workers: wages pretty bad, work precarious: shoemakers tyrannised over by sweaters.'

18 July 1885: Blunt travelled down to Castle Howard with Jane and the Speaker of the House of Commons, Arthur Wellesley Peel.

19 July 1885: Morris gave an open-air speech on the occasion of the 'Revolutionists Excursion' to Epping Forest which was sponsored by the International Club of London.

23 July 1885: Morris sent copies of his poems to Francis Xaver Hueffer who was preparing a volume called *A Selection of the Poems of William Morris* (*c.f.* 1886).

25 July 1885: Jane wrote to Blunt from Castle Howard: 'Lord Houghton is occupying the room next [to] mine, and seems to spend his spare time in tramping up and down and throwing his teeth about.'

26 July 1885: Morris gave an open-air speech in Victoria Park for the SL.

August 1885: At some point during this month Morris visited Sussex. In a letter to Jenny he wrote: 'We have had a nice time so far wandering all over the downs to here [Horrington], a queer out of the way place… The country is very beautiful about here; but the building only so so; we are going on to Pullborough presently & shall wander on to Midhurst & sleep there tonight & so home to Hammersmith.' Morris contributed 'Signs of the Times' and reports on the 'First General Meeting of the Socialist League' and 'The Editors of "Commonweal"' to *Commonweal*. The fifth instalment of the *Pilgrims of Hope* also appeared in the paper.

4 August 1885: Jane returned to Kelmscott House from Castle Howard.

5 August 1885: Morris gave a speech on W. T. Stead's 'recent disclosures' in the *Pall Mall Gazette* regarding prostitution. The meeting was held at Farringdon Hall, 13 Farringdon Road and sponsored by the SL.

8 August 1885: Morris delivered an open-air speech for the Stratford Branch of the SL in Stratford.

10 August 1885: Jane took a river trip to Teddington and back.

16 August 1885: Morris delivered his lecture 'Commercial Depression' before a meeting sponsored by the Hoxton Branch of the SL at the Exchange Coffee House, Pitfield Street, Hoxton.

22 August 1885: A mass meeting took place in Hyde Park to protest against the exploitation of girls in London. Morris was scheduled to speak at this meeting. This is the only demonstration at which Jane was also present. She marched in the procession organized by the Ladies' National Society.

23 August 1885: Morris delivered his lecture 'What's to Become of the Middle Classes?' before the Hammersmith Branch of the SL at Kelmscott House,

Hammersmith.

September 1885: Articles on the SDF and the SL appeared in the *Dispatch*. Morris contributed 'Mr Chamberlain at Hull', 'A New Party', the sixth instalment of *The Pilgrims of Hope* and a short piece on Stead's recent exposure of child prostitution in London to *Commonweal*. He also signed, along with Bax and Theodor, an 'Appeal' for funds for the paper.

1 September 1885: Morris was scheduled to deliver 'The Hopes of Civilisation' before the Mile-End Branch of the SL at Swaby's Coffee House, Mile-End.

6 September 1885: In the evening Morris delivered an unnamed lecture at Rotherhithe: 'the "architecture" there, one of the chief materials of which is filth, will explain why the architecture in middle class quarters is what it is.' This is not mentioned by LeMire.

9 September 1885: Morris delivered his lecture 'The Depression of Trade' at a meeting sponsored by the North London Branch of the SL at Camden Hall, King Street, Camden Town.

10 September 1885: Morris travelled down to Kelmscott Manor to visit Jenny. At the time he was suffering from an attack of 'lumbago' or gout.

20 September 1885: Morris was scheduled to give his lecture 'The Guilds of the Middle Ages' before the Hammersmith Branch of the SL at Kelmscott House, Hammersmith. A meeting held in Dod Street to protest against the recent prosecutions for 'obstruction' was charged by the police. Eight members of the crowd were accused of resisting the police or of obstruction including Mowbray, Kitz, Mahon and Lewis Lyons. The meeting was reported in the *Daily News*, 22 September 1885 (p. 2) and the *Pall Mall Gazette*, 21 September 1885 (p. 6).

21 September 1885: Those accused of 'obstruction' were brought up before a magistrate called Thomas William Saunders at the Arbour Square Police Court. On hearing the verdict Morris shouted out 'shame' and was promptly set upon by the police. One eye-witness wrote: 'William Morris, remonstrating at the hustling and the thumping, became at once the chief thumpee. There has rarely been seen anything more brutal than the way in which two or three able-bodied young men fell upon the author of what one newspaper called the "Paradise League".' Two hours later he was brought before the magistrate accused of assaulting a policeman. When asked who he was Morris replied: 'I am an artist, and a literary man, pretty well-known I think throughout Europe.' He was acquitted. He later wrote: 'There was a funny scene in the police station where they charged me, the inspector and constable gravely discussing whether the damage done to the helmet was 2d or ½d.' Morris's *Medway* fabric design was registered.

22 September 1885: Blunt recorded: 'William Morris was arrested ... at a socialist trial for hissing the magistrate, and I have written to congratulate him.' Eleanor Marx and Aveling visited Engels to ask his advice on the SL's policy during the free speech campaign.

23 September 1885: In the morning Morris travelled to Birmingham on business. In the evening he was scheduled to give a poetry reading at a public entertainment sponsored by the Merton Abbey Branch of the SL at the Branch Rooms, High Street, Merton. He missed this engagement as on his return from Birmingham he 'was rather unwell ... so could not turn up'. The *Daily News* published a letter by Morris (dated 22 September) on his experiences at the Arbour Street Police Court. The *Pall Mall Gazette* published 'The Poet and the Police. An Interview with Mr William Morris'. Morris said: 'I shall probably go to prison yet ... if the authorities maintain their present attitude.'

24 September 1885: Jane, and Jenny – who had 'been very well till quite lately when she had an attack which left her weak' – were still staying at Kelmscott Manor though May had returned to London.

26 September 1885: In the afternoon Morris supported a free speech resolution at an open-air meeting sponsored by the Manchester socialists in Albert Square, Manchester. In the evening he gave a lecture on socialist tactics and organization at a meeting sponsored by the Manchester Socialist Union at the County Forum, Manchester.

27 September 1885: Morris gave a lecture for the Ancoats Recreation Committee at the New Islington Hall, Ancoats, Manchester.

30 September 1885: Morris was scheduled to deliver 'The Larger Hope' at the SL Hall, 13 Farringdon Road, London. Walter Crane wrote to him saying he intended to include a dedicatory sonnet to Morris in his *The Sirens Three*. In this he praised Morris's illuminated *Omar Khayyam* and his socialist activities. Georgiana Burne-Jones wrote a letter to the Editor of *Commonweal* (Morris) stating: 'Please address the Commonweal to *Mrs* Burne-Jones, not to *Mr.*'

Autumn 1885: The first edition of Morris's *Chants for Socialists* appeared. A second edition followed later in the year.

October 1885: Morris read Adam Birkmeyre's pamphlet *Practical Socialism*. He also contributed 'Answers to Previous Inquiries', 'Ireland and Italy: A Warning' and 'Signs of the Times' to *Commonweal*.

1 October 1885: Morris delivered a lecture entitled 'Justice and Socialism' before the Bloomsbury Branch of the SL. This lecture is not mentioned by LeMire but notes pertaining to it were published by Meier. These make reference to

Thomas More, Defoe's *Robinson Crusoe*, Wycliffe and Luther.

3 October 1885: Morris wrote to Thomas Wardle with reference to a suggestion that customers of Morris & Co. could get arsenic poisoning from the lead in the wallpapers they had purchased: 'My belief about it all is that doctors find their patients ailing, don't know what's the matter with them, and in despair put it down to the wall papers when they probably ought to put it down to the water closet, which I believe to be the source of all illness.' Morris went on to add: 'I believe people often get lead-poisoning from eating victuals cooked in tinned vessels, the tin being largely adulterated with lead. In France they are taking to cooking in naked copper: they are so kitchen-clean that they can venture on this, which might not be safe in England owing to our filthy habits.'

10 October 1885: Morris delivered 'Socialism' before the Working Men's College at the College, Great Ormond Street, Bloomsbury.

11 October 1885: In the morning Morris gave an open-air speech welcoming John Williams on his release from prison. The meeting, sponsored by London socialists and radicals, was held in Victoria Park, London. In the evening he delivered an unnamed lecture before the Marylebone Branch of the SL at St John's Temperance Hall, Bell Street, London.

13 October 1885: May went to the printers to collect the second edition of the *Manifesto of the Socialist League*. This had been extensively 'annotated' by Morris and Bax to clarify a number of the points in the original.

15 October 1885: Morris delivered an unnamed lecture before local socialists in Preston.

17 October 1885: Morris wrote to Sparling: 'I am right down ill with cold & rheumatism.'

18 October 1885: Morris was scheduled to deliver 'The Depression of Trade' before the Hammersmith Branch of the SL at Kelmscott House.

20 October 1885: In a letter to Thomas Wardle, Morris described the results of an analysis of the lead content of three of Morris & Co.'s wallpapers: 'the result is not a little curious' but that 'at worst the amount of lead in the whole wall-surface could not be very perilous'.

25 October 1885: Blunt visited Morris at Hammersmith where the latter was laid up with gout. According to Blunt's account Morris 'was inclined to vote for the Tories, but all voting was against socialistic principles'. Morris was also visited by Richmond who had just returned from Egypt: 'he fired my longing to go see the desert there by telling me about his experiences there.'

26 October 1885: Morris was still immobilized by gout. He was so lame that he had to be wheeled from his bedroom to the dining-room at Kelmscott House. He amused himself reading 'trashy novels' including Ouida's *Strathmore* (1865).

27 October 1885: In a letter to John Burns, in which Morris congratulated him for his part in a meeting held in Nottingham on 21 October 1885, he concluded: 'I must ask you to excuse pencil writing as I am tied by the leg by gout & cannot sit up properly.'

28 October 1885: The SL held a public meeting at Farringdon Hall to protest at the threatened British intervention in Burma. Morris had hoped to speak at this meeting but was prevented by gout. However, a letter he had written on the subject was read out to the audience.

29 October 1885: Morris was scheduled to give a lecture at a meeting sponsored by the South London Branch of the SL at the Camberwell Radical Club, Gloucester Road, Peckham. It is unlikely that this lecture was given as he was still suffering from gout.

31 October 1885: In a letter to Georgiana Burne-Jones, Morris complained that he was still laid low with gout and was frustrated that he was prevented from working for the socialist cause: 'in spite of all the self-denying ordinances of us semi-anarchists, I grieve to have to say that some sort of leadership is required, and that in our section I unfortunately supply that want... One must turn to hope, and only in one direction do I see it – on the road to Revolution: everything else is gone now.'

November 1885: It was revealed that two candidates sponsored by the SDF in the first election under the new Reform Act had been backed by 'Tory Gold'. This caused a rift between the SDF and the SL. As his contribution to the election Morris wrote a pamphlet entitled *For Whom Should We Vote?*, addressed 'to the working-men electors of Great Britain', which urged them not to vote at all. This pamphlet was reprinted for use at subsequent elections. Morris published 'Moves in the Game Political', 'Free Speech and the Police', some untitled paragraphs and the seventh part of *The Pilgrims of Hope* in *Commonweal.*

2 November 1885: Morris was unable to attend a general meeting of London members of the SL as he was still suffering from gout. He wrote a letter to the chairman of the meeting apologizing for his absence.

4 November 1885: Morris had just finished reading Francis Marion Crawford's *Mr Isaacs, A Tale of Modern India* (1882): 'which I found despairingly dull.' At the time his foot was so swollen with gout that he could not put on his shoe.

9 November 1885: At the regular Monday meeting of the Executive of the SL Morris's pamphlet *For Whom Shall We Vote?* was read out by May. Morris was unable to attend due to his gout.

10 November 1885: In the afternoon Morris travelled from London to Oxford. He later delivered 'The Rise of a New Epoch' at a meeting sponsored by the Oxford Branch of the SL at the Music Room, Holywell, Oxford: 'the place was crowded, & generally sympathetic; & although there were some dozen or so of Tory young gentlemen, they behaved themselves fairly well.' Morris spent the night at Oxford.

13 November 1885: Morris was scheduled to deliver 'Socialism: the True Road to Individual Development' at a meeting at the Eglesfield Club of Queen's College, Oxford. He also intended to meet Jenny at Kelmscott Manor. It is possible that neither of these engagements were kept due to the continuation of his attack of gout. Blunt visited Jane at Kelmscott House: 'She told me she had seen Swinburne a few days ago, quite well and perfectly happy with his books.'

15 November 1885: Morris was scheduled to deliver 'Socialism' at Kelmscott House, Hammersmith. It appears that he was again too ill to attend in person and instead had May read out his text.

19 November 1885: Morris was in the process of finalizing his agreement with his new publishers Reeves & Turner. They had just sent him copies of some books by James Thomson.

20 November 1885: The *Daily News* published a letter from Morris on the 'Vulgarisation of Oxford'. Morris was scheduled to deliver 'The Rise of a New Epoch' before the Croydon Working Men's Club, at Crown Hill, Croydon. It is probable that this appointment was not kept due to Morris's attack of gout.

22 November 1885: Morris was scheduled to speak at Leicester (not mentioned by LeMire) but his place was taken by Shaw.

23 November 1885: Morris had planned to speak in Birmingham (not mentioned by LeMire) but due to continued ill-health his place was taken by Aveling. Cobden-Sanderson visited him at Kelmscott House to show him some of the new bindings he had produced.

24 November 1885: Morris signed an agreement which confirmed Reeves & Turner as his new publishers. Later he travelled down to Rottingdean, Brighton, to stay with the Burne-Joneses under what May called 'the firm and careful protection of my mother'. Morris finished reading Rider Haggard's *King Solomon's Mines* (1885): '& think [it] amusing if a good deal made of Poe & C. Read.'

25 November 1885: Morris was able to go out twice: 'I was stiffer & weaker than I expected to be but I think I shall soon be all right.' He and Jane spent the day playing forty games of backgammon: 'your mother I regret to state got the best of it.'

26 November 1885: Morris was scheduled to deliver a lecture before the Bloomsbury Branch of the SL at the Eagle and Child Coffee Tavern, 45 Copton Street, Soho. This lecture did not take place as he was still staying at Rottingdean: 'I managed to get out and stumble about for 10 minutes.' He and Jane spent the day playing cribbage.

December 1885: Morris published 'On the Eve of the Elections' and 'To Our Readers' (with Aveling) in *Commonweal*.

1 December 1885: Morris had a recurrence of his gout after taking a day-trip to London from Rottingdean.

2 December 1885: Morris spent the day translating Homer at Rottingdean.

5 December 1885: In the afternoon Morris and Jane returned to London from Rottingdean.

6 December 1885: Morris had to abandon a proposed visited to Sydney Gimson in Leicester due to fears about exacerbating his gout. It appears from a letter he wrote to Gimson on 2 December 1885 that he had intended to lecture – possibly at the Secularist Hall – on this occasion. This lecture is not mentioned by LeMire.

7 December 1885: Morris attended a general meeting of the SL which passed a resolution condemning members of the SDF who had accepted 'Tory Gold' at the general election.

21 December 1885: At a general meeting of the SL it was decided to turn the *Commonweal* into a weekly as soon as £100 was raised to guarantee printing costs (*c.f.* 22 February 1886).

25 December 1885: Christmas Day was a dismal affair in the Morris household as Jenny had been suffering regular attacks of epilepsy, Miss Bailey was ill, and Morris was still suffering twinges of gout.

27 December 1885: The festive entertainment in the Morris household was enlivened by May and Jenny playing duets on the guitar and mandolin. Cobden-Sanderson noted in his *Diary* that Morris had approached him for a subscription to turn the *Commonweal* into a weekly: 'I gave him £5, on consideration that he completed his Horace and Virgil, and allowed me to bind them, and give them to the Bodleian.'

29 December 1885: Morris wrote to Frederick Henderson dissuading him from pursuing a career in the theatre: 'a *professional* actor seems to me as great an absurdity as a *professional* cricketer.'

1886: The Co-operative Printing Company of Edinburgh published Morris's *The Labour Question from the Socialist Standpoint* as no. 5 in their 'Claims of Labour Lectures'. *A Selection of the Poems of William Morris*, edited with a memoir by Francis Hueffer, appeared as one of the Tauchnitz Collection of British Authors (*c.f.* 23 July 1885).

January 1886: Morris met C. R. Ashbee when the latter visited Kelmscott House to hear Carpenter's lecture on 'Private Property'. Morris published 'The Morrow of the Elections', 'Notes', 'The Husks that the Swine do Eat' and the eighth instalment of *The Pilgrims of Hope* in *Commonweal*. He also signed an appeal for funds along with Bax and Theodor.

7 January 1886: Morris was scheduled to deliver 'How We Live and How We Might Live' at a meeting sponsored by the South London Branch of the SL at the Camberwell Radical Club, Gloucester Road, Peckham.

10 January 1886: Morris was scheduled to deliver 'The Political Outlook' before the Hammersmith Branch of the SL at Kelmscott House, Hammersmith.

12 January 1886: Morris delivered 'Socialism' before the Peckham and Dulwich Radical Club at 144 Rye Lane, Peckham.

13 January 1886: Morris delivered 'The Political Outlook' at a meeting sponsored by the SL at the SL Hall, 13 Farringdon Road, London. Shaw also spoke at this meeting and defended parliamentary methods to Morris's annoyance.

15 January 1886: Morris delivered 'How We Live and How We Might Live' before the Working Men's Club and Youth's Institute at the Congregational Hall, Blenheim Road, London. By this time he had raised £70 towards the fund for turning *Commonweal* into a weekly.

24 January 1886: In the afternoon Morris delivered 'Socialism' before a combined meeting of the Hackney and Shoreditch Branches of the SDF at the Hackney Branch Rooms, Goldsmith Row, Hackney Road, Hackney. In the evening he was scheduled to deliver a lecture at a meeting sponsored by the Hammersmith Branch of the SL at Kelmscott House, Hammersmith.

27 January 1886: Morris was scheduled to deliver 'The Political Outlook' before the Clerkenwell (Central) Branch of the SL at the SL Hall, 13 Farringdon Road, London.

February 1886: Morris published 'A Letter from the Pacific Coast' and a further appeal for funds in *Commonweal*.

2 February 1886: Morris's list of his 'Best Hundred Books' was published in the *Pall Mall Gazette*. It was later reprinted in the *Pall Mall Gazette Extra* (no.

24), pp. 10– 11. Morris was scheduled to deliver 'The Political Outlook' before the Mile-End Branch of the SL at the International Working Men's Educational Club at 40 Berner Street, Commercial Road, London.

7 February 1886: By this time Morris had been replaced as Treasurer of the SL by Philip Webb.

8 February 1886: 'Black Monday'. A demonstration by the unemployed in Trafalgar Square organized by the Fair Trade League was highjacked by the SDF. The crowd then marched down Pall Mall and through Piccadilly to Hyde Park. As they passed the Reform Club they were jeered by the members and smashing windows in retaliation. A number of shops were also looted. Hyndman, Burns and Williams were subsequently arrested for sedition. Morris was not present as he was having tea with Blunt at Kelmscott House. During their conversation Morris was to state that 1889 was likely to be the socialists' year as it was the centenary of the French Revolution.

10 February 1886: Morris delivered 'The Political Outlook' at a meeting of the Hammersmith Liberal Club at the Club's Rooms, Hammersmith.

12 February 1886: The *Daily News* published a letter from Morris (dated 11 February) in which he clarified the relationship between the SL and the SDF.

14 February 1886: Morris was scheduled to deliver 'Socialism' at a meeting of the Patriotic Club in London.

20 February 1886: Morris was in the process of writing *A Short Account of the Commune of Paris*.

21 February 1886: A large demonstration organized by the SDF in Hyde Park was brutally dispersed by mounted police. One man received shocking facial injuries when he was stepped on by a horse.

22 February 1886: At a general meeting of London members of the SL it was decided to turn the *Commonweal* into a weekly.

23 February 1886: An unnamed speaker read Morris's lecture 'Misery and the Way Out' at a meeting sponsored by the Bradford Branch of the SL at Laycock's Temperance Hotel, Bradford.

28 February 1886: In the afternoon Morris gave a lecture at a meeting sponsored by Sheffield socialists at the Secular Hall, Sheffield. He delivered another lecture at the same venue in the evening. At this meeting he sold five dozens *Commonweals* and eight dozen pamphlets: 'Both lectures were well received, the evening one, the more plain-spoken and less historical of the two, particularly so: indeed I have never stood before a more sympathetic audience.'

March 1886: Morris published 'Our Policy' and the ninth instalment of *The Pilgrims of Hope* in *Commonweal*.

1 March 1886: Morris attended a small meeting of 'about thirty sympathisers' to discuss the possibility of starting a socialist organization in Sheffield. He urged them to form a branch of the SL but in the end they formed the Society of Sheffield Socialists which remained unaffiliated to the League: 'I found much interest in the subject amongst these friends, also some doubts and hanging back from that step of association, a step undoubtedly harder to take in a provincial town where people are so much more known and as it were ticketted than in London.'

2 March 1886: Morris delivered 'Socialism in Relation to the London Riots' at a meeting sponsored by the Workers' Brotherhood at the Concert Hall, Lord Nelson Street, Liverpool: 'the hall was crowded with an audience mostly of working men, who not only listened with very great attention, but took up all the points which they caught and understood with very hearty applause.'

7 March 1886: An unrecorded speaker read Morris's lecture 'Misery and the Way Out' at a meeting sponsored by the Bradford Branch of the SL.

8 March 1886: Morris delivered 'Socialism' at a meeting sponsored by the Norwich Branch of the SL at the Victoria Hall, Norwich. He had an audience of 800: 'Again the audience was mostly working-class, and was or seemed to be quite in sympathy with the movement.'

11 March 1886: It is possible that Morris lectured before the Bedford Debating Society. If he did this is not mentioned by LeMire.

13 March 1886: The [*Norwich*] *Daylight Supplement* published Morris's lecture on 'Socialism' which had first been delivered on 9 June 1885. This version of the lecture was later printed as a pamphlet.

14 March 1886: Morris delivered 'The Aims of Art' before the Hammersmith Branch of the SL at Kelmscott House, Hammersmith.

18 March 1886: *A Short Account of the Commune of Paris* by Morris, Bax and Victor Dave – price 2d – was published to coincide with a meeting held to commemorate the Paris Commune at the South Place Institute. It was at this meeting that Morris first met Kropotkin.

24 March 1886: Morris had a long talk with Kropotkin at a meeting of the SDF.

25 March 1886: Morris spent the evening with John Hunter Watts and Kropotkin.

28 March 1886: A 'crowded meeting' of the SL was held at Kelmscott House to discuss the recent Belgian strikes.

31 March 1886: Morris delivered 'The Aims of Art' at a meeting sponsored by the Hammersmith Liberal Club at the Club Rooms, Hammersmith.

April 1886: Morris published 'Notes on Matters Parliamentary', 'Socialism in the Provinces' and the tenth instalment of *The Pilgrims of Hope* in *Commonweal*.

4 April 1886: A letter was read from Morris at the Hammersmith Branch of the SL stating that he had been elected to serve on an International Committee formed to support the Belgian miners. According to the *Commonweal* Morris was due to speak in Croydon. This lecture is not mentioned by LeMire.

8 April 1886: The trial of Hyndman, Burns and William for their part in 'Black Monday' began.

9 April 1886: In the morning Morris arrived in Ireland after taking the overnight ferry. It was quite rough and he reported having his spectacles blown off. He roused himself at 5.30 am in time to see the clouds rising over the Wicklow mountains. He was met off the boat by members of the Dublin branch of the SL. In the evening he delivered 'The Aims of Art' at a meeting – mostly of 'ladies and gentlemen' – sponsored by the Dublin Branch of the SL at the Molesworth Hall, Dublin. The speech shocked a number of 'respectables' who walked out early in the proceedings: 'I fear that the "ladies and gentlemen" were disappointed with what I was forced to lay before them, which, as a matter of course, included advocacy of Socialism as a necessity for the new birth of art.' John Butler Yeats made a pencil sketch of Morris at some point during this Irish tour.

10 April 1886: In the afternoon Morris delivered 'The Political Outlook' at a meeting sponsored by the Dublin Branch of the SL in Dublin: 'The audience, mostly working men again, seemed for the most part heartily with me, and the meeting turned out quite a success.' In the evening he opened a debate on 'Socialism: What Is It?' at the Saturday Club in Dublin: 'One slip I unwittingly made by mentioning Sackville Street, which is popularly known as O'Connell Street, a name which the authorities refuse to accept. A great to-do followed this blunder, which, on a hint from the chairman, I corrected with all good will, and so was allowed to go on, with cheers.' The debate ended in a near riot when someone turned out the gas lamps in the hall.

11 April 1886: In the evening Morris met the members of the Dublin branch of the SL: 'It is clear that at present the religious matter is the difficulty; but I cannot help thinking that when Home Rule is established the Catholic clergy will begin to act after their kind, and try after more and more power, till the Irish gorge rises and rejects them.'

12 April 1886: The trial of Hyndman, Burns and Williams ended in their acquittal.

13 April 1886: Morris spent the day up among the Wicklow mountains. In the evening he delivered 'Socialism' at a meeting sponsored by the Dublin Branch of the SL at 30 Great Brunswick Street, Dublin: 'Dublin on the whole I rather like: there is a sort of cosy shabbiness about it which, joined to the clear air, is pleasant.'

14 April 1886: Morris returned from Ireland: 'I had a good passage back.' He translated fifty lines of Homer while on the boat.

17 April 1886: Morris delivered 'The Political Outlook' at a meeting jointly sponsored by the Leeds and Bradford Branches of the SL at the Co-operative Hall in Shipley: 'The hall was not as full as it should have been, considering Shipley is a very Radical place.' Jane returned from the Isle of Wight where she had stayed for a month for health reasons.

18 April 1886: Morris delivered 'Socialism' at a meeting sponsored by the Bradford Branch of the SL at the Temperance Hall, Bradford: 'a full audience, very attentive, and who caught the points well, and seemed pleased by the attack on Bourgeoisdom.' In the evening he was present at a combined meeting of the Leeds and Bradford branches: 'where I had to try to clear up a few difficulties as to principles and tactics which had occurred to two or three members.'

19 April 1886: Morris delivered 'The Present and Future of the Working Classes' at a meeting sponsored by the Leeds Branch of the SL at the Assembly Rooms, New Briggate, Leeds.

23 April 1886: May wrote to Scheu to say that she and Sparling (with whom she had fallen in love) were 'among the brightest and most unsubstantial clouds'.

24 April 1886: Morris wrote to Sparling requesting that he get him a copy of the second report of the Royal Commission on the Depression of Trade and Industry.

25 April 1886: Morris delivered 'Our Policy' at a meeting of the Hammersmith Branch of the SL held at Kelmscott House, Hammersmith.

28 April 1886: Morris was scheduled to deliver 'Competition' as a meeting of the Clerkenwell (Central) Branch of the SL at Farringdon Hall, 13 Farringdon Road, London.

Spring 1886: Karl Theodore Reuss was expelled from the SL when it was discovered that he was a police spy.

1 May 1886: *Commonweal* became a weekly. Morris contributed an 'Editorial', 'Independent Ireland', 'Concerning the "Commonweal"' and a number of untitled paragraphs to the paper. This edition also contained a full-page cartoon by Walter Crane depicting 'Mrs Grundy's Mishap'.

2 May 1886: Morris was scheduled to deliver 'Art and Labour' at a meeting sponsored by the Clerkenwell (Central) Branch of the SL at Farringdon Road, London.

6 May 1886: May wrote to Scheu expressing her 'extreme terror' at the thought of announcing her engagement to Sparling to her parents.

8 May 1886: Morris published 'Notes on Passing Events', 'Socialism in Dublin and Yorkshire', an untitled paragraph on railway monopoly and the eleventh instalment of *The Pilgrims of Hope* in *Commonweal*.

12 May 1886: Morris was scheduled to give a lecture at a meeting sponsored by the Woolwich Branch of the SL at Woolwich.

15 May 1886: Morris published the first chapter of *Socialism From the Root Up*, 'Notes on Passing Events' and a 'Foot-note to "The Commercial Hearth"' in *Commonweal*.

16 May 1886: In the morning Morris delivered 'The Aims of Art' at a meeting sponsored by the Birmingham Branch of the SL at Baskerville Hall, The Crescent, Birmingham. In the evening he delivered 'Socialism' at another meeting held at the same venue.

17 May 1886: Morris delivered 'The Political Outlook' at a meeting sponsored by the Birmingham Branch of the SL at the Exchange Buildings, New Street, Birmingham: 'it was a wretchedly wet night, and there was a counter attraction in the building in the form of the Performing Fleas.'

18 May 1886: M. Sollitt was scheduled to read 'Misery and the Way Out' from Morris's manuscript at a meeting sponsored by the Leeds Branch of the SL at the St James's Cafe, Briggate, Leeds. Morris and Bax were working on chapter II of *Socialism from the Root Up*.

19 May 1886: Morris delivered 'The Origins of the Ornamental Arts' before the Hammersmith Branch of the SL at Kelmscott House: '[it] was not well attended but it went off otherwise well.'

21 May 1886: Morris spent the day at Merton Abbey. In a letter to Jenny he recalled a dream he had had the previous night: 'to wit that we were all together in the high-street near the end of River Court Road, and watching shooting stars which were red & green & yellow like the lights on the new Hammersmith bridge, when all at once one fell to earth in the middle of the road and we all bolted for fear it should burst like a shell; taking it rather coolly though. Why the deuce should one dream such nonsense?'

22 May 1886: Morris published the second chapter of *Socialism from the Root Up* and 'Notes on Passing Events' in *Commonweal*.

24 May 1886: Morris read Jane Austen's *Mansfield Park*.

27 May 1886: Morris travelled down to Kelmscott Manor.

29 May 1886: Morris published the third chapter of *Socialism from the Root Up*, various untitled notes, 'Branch Reports' and 'Notes and Queries: Practical Socialism' in *Commonweal*.

30 May 1886: Wardle and nine others were arrested at Grove Street, Stratford, for obstruction.

31 May 1886: Morris returned to London from Kelmscott Manor. He went almost immediately to the West Ham Police Court to bail Wardle and the others. This cost him £5 17s.

2 June 1886: Morris gave a lecture at a meeting of the Merton Abbey Branch of the SL at Merton Abbey.

3 June 1886: Morris visited the Grange to join in the celebrations for Margaret Burne-Jones's twentieth birthday.

4 June 1886: Morris visited John Faunthorpe at Whitelands College, a training-school for teachers in Chelsea. In the evening he delivered 'Art and Socialism' at a meeting sponsored by the Bloomsbury Branch of the SL at the Arlington Hall, Bloomsbury.

5 June 1886: Morris gave an open-air speech in support of the Stratford Branch of the SL at Grove Street, Stratford. There was an audience of about 300. Despite Wardle's earlier arrest at the same venue the police did not interfere. Morris published the twelfth instalment of *The Pilgrims of Hope*, the fourth chapter of *Socialism from the Root Up*, 'Notes on Passing Events' and 'Instructive items' in *Commonweal*.

6 June 1886: Morris was scheduled to deliver 'The Dawn of a New Epoch' before the Notting Hill Debating Society at the Monarch Tavern, Manchester Street, London.

8 June 1886: Morris gave a speech seconding a resolution to establish a fund for the repair of ancient buildings at the Annual Conference of SPAB at the Society of Arts, John Street, Adelphi.

11 June 1886: Morris delivered 'Whigs, Democrats and Socialists' at the Fabian Conference on Political Action held at the South Place Institute, Finsbury: '[it] ... was very well received: the place was very full.'

12 June 1886: Morris delivered two open-air speeches on behalf of the Marylebone Branch of the SL in Hyde Park near Marble Arch: 'I was quite nervous about it, I don't know why.' Mowbray and Lane were arrested for speaking in Grove Street, Stratford. Morris published 'Notes on Passing Events', 'Correspondence', 'Free Speech at Stratford' and chapter V of *Socialism from the Root Up* in *Commonweal*.

13 June 1886: The Second Annual Conference of the SL was held. Morris was re-elected editor of *Commonweal* but Bax was replaced by Aveling as sub-editor. Bax, Mahon and Henderson spent the night at Kelmscott House.

14 June 1886: Morris went on the SL's annual outing to Box Hill and Dorking. In Dorking they had tea, beer and singing at the Wheatsheaf Inn. The local population mistook the socialists for a band of the Salvation Army as they marched through the town. Mowbray was fined £1 and costs for obstruction.

19 June 1886: Morris published 'Notes on Passing Events' in *Commonweal*.

21 June 1886: Morris travelled to Scotland by the 8 pm train.

22 June 1886: In the morning Morris went for a walk with his host 'a Free Kirk minister and a Socialist'. In the evening Morris delivered a lecture at a meeting sponsored by the Arbroath Lecture Committee in Arbroath, Scotland. He spent the night at the East Tree Manse in Arbroath: 'not a bad sort of town for Scotland: all stone built and all the older houses roofed with stone-slates, right on the sea it is in fact Fairport of the Antiquary [Scott's novel].'

23 June 1886: Morris delivered 'True and False Society' at a meeting sponsored by the Industrial Remuneration Conference Executive Committee at the Oddfellows Hall, Edinburgh: 'the audience seemed sympathetic – nay, enthusiastic.' After the lecture he had a short meeting with the members of the Edinburgh branch of the SL: 'They seemed rather depressed; lack speakers, and so find it difficult to make much way.'

24 June 1886: Morris delivered 'True and False Society' at a meeting sponsored by the Industrial Remuneration Conference Executive Committee at the Waterloo Rooms, Glasgow: 'a good audience, perhaps rather more in assent than at Edinburgh.'

25 June 1886: Morris delivered 'True and False Society' at a meeting sponsored by the Industrial Remuneration Conference Executive Committee in Dundee.

26 June 1886: Morris published 'Whigs, Democrats, and Socialists' and 'Home Rule or Humbug' in *Commonweal*.

27 June 1886: Morris delivered 'The Political Outlook' at a meeting sponsored by the Glasgow Branch of the SL at the Waterloo Rooms, Glasgow: 'The audience was over 600, I should think, and was attentive and sympathetic.' A special tea was held in his honour at which he recited the speech John Ball made in the Market Place in *A Dream of John Ball*. After midnight the members of the branch accompanied Morris to his hotel singing the 'March of the Workers'.

28 June 1886: Morris delivered 'Socialism' at a meeting sponsored by the Glasgow Branch of the SL at the Temperance Institute, James Street,

Bridgeton: 'a most woeful abode of man, crying out from each miserable court and squalid, crowded house for the abolition of the tyranny of exploitation.'

29 June 1886: Morris returned to London from Scotland.

July 1886: *A Day in Surrey with William Morris* by Emma Lazarus (with a portrait by Lisa Stillman and illustrations by Joseph Pennell & W. J. Stillman) appeared in the *Century Magazine* (vol. 32, pp. 388–97).

2 July 1886: Morris delivered 'The Aims of Art' at a meeting sponsored by the Fabian Society at the South Place Institute, Finsbury.

3 July 1886: Morris published 'A Letter from Scotland', 'Whigs, Democrats, and Socialists – II', the thirteenth part of *The Pilgrims of Hope* and chapter VI of *Socialism from the Root Up* in *Commonweal*.

10 July 1886: Morris published 'Notes', 'Notes on the Elections', 'The Sequel of the Scotch Letter' and a review of *Modern Socialism* in *Commonweal*.

11 July 1886: Sam Mainwaring and Jack Williams were arrested for obstruction when addressing a crowd in Bell Street. Morris delivered 'Education' before the Hoxton Branch of the SL at Hoxton.

13 July 1886: In a letter to Alan Summerly Cole, Morris mentioned an Indian embroidered coverlet that he subsequently sold to the South Kensington Museum for £120.

17 July 1886: Morris published 'The Whig-Jingo Victory', 'An Empty Pocket is the Worst of Crimes' and a review of Shaw's *Cashel Byron's Profession* in *Commonweal*.

18 July 1886: Morris addressed an open-air meeting at Bell Street sponsored by the Marylebone Branch of the SL. At this meeting his name was taken by George Draper, Superintendent of Police, for obstructing the highway. In the evening he delivered 'Education' at a meeting sponsored by the Hammersmith Branch of the SL at Kelmscott House.

20 July 1886: Morris received a summons for obstructing the highway at Bell Street. The summons claimed he 'Wilfully [did] obstruct the free passage of the public footway and Highway at Bell Street, Marylebone, by placing yourself upon a stand for the purpose of delivering an address thereby encouraging a crowd of persons to remain upon and obstruct the said Highway and footway at 12 noon.'

24 July 1886: At his subsequent trial before Mr M. Cooke, the magistrate at Marylebone Police Court, Morris was fined 1s on the grounds it was his first offence. Morris published 'What is to Happen Next?' and chapter VII of *Socialism from the Root Up* in *Commonweal*.

31 July 1886: Morris responded to the police harassment by publishing an article entitled 'Free Speech in the Streets' in *Commonweal*. The same edition also included chapter VIII of *Socialism from the Root Up*.

August 1886: Morris approached Hyndman with the intention of healing the breach with the SDF. According to Mackail 'the attempt at peace making proved quite futile'.

1 August 1886: Morris delivered an open-air speech for the Marylebone Branch of the SL at Hyde Park.

2 August 1886: Morris spoke at an open-air meeting sponsored by the Hammersmith Branch of the SL held at Beadon Road, Hammersmith.

7 August 1886: Morris published 'Political Notes' and some untitled paragraphs in *Commonweal*. He was also working on his translation of Homer.

8 August 1886: In the morning Morris went to the Grange and then attended an open-air meeting at Walham Green: 'a good little meeting attentive and peaceable.' He then returned for dinner at the Grange before giving an open-air speech at a meeting sponsored by the Hackney Branch of the SL held at Victoria Park. In the evening he was chairman when Shaw lectured on 'Why We Don't Act Up to Our Principles'.

9 August 1886: Morris gave an open-air speech for the Hammersmith Branch of the SL at Walham Green opposite the railway station.

11 August 1886: The trial of Williams and Mainwaring began at the Middlesex Sessions before Assistant-Judge Peter H. Edlin. Morris and May attended the trial.

13 August 1886: Williams and Mainwaring were sentenced to pay £20 each or serve two weeks in prison. Mainwaring paid the fine but Williams was jailed. May subsequently published a report of the trial in *Commonweal* under the title 'Vindictive Sentence'.

14 August 1886: Morris published 'Notes on Passing Events', 'Mr Chamberlain's Leader' and chapter IX of *Socialism from the Root Up* in *Commonweal*.

15 August 1886: Morris gave another open-air address at a meeting sponsored by the Hammersmith Branch of the SL at Walham Green.

21 August 1886: Morris published 'Notes on Passing Events' and 'The Abolition of Freedom of Speech in the Streets' in *Commonweal*.

22 August 1886: In the morning Morris gave open-air speeches at Walham Green and Beadon Road. In the evening he delivered 'Our Tactics' at a meeting sponsored by the Hammersmith Branch of the SL at Kelmscott

House. Shaw and the Walkers dined with Morris after the lecture.

24 August 1886: Morris delivered 'The Dawn of a New Epoch' at a meeting sponsored by the Mile-End Branch of the SL at Mile-End.

28 August 1886: Morris published 'Notes on Passing Events', 'Misanthropy to the Rescue' and chapter X of *Socialism from the Root Up* in *Commonweal*.

29 August 1886: A large meeting in Trafalgar Square was organized by the SDF to mark Williams's release from prison. The SL were not invited. Morris travelled down to Kelmscott Manor for a few days.

September 1886: The Fabian Society decided to pursue a parliamentary strategy. The Metropolitan Open-Air Temperance Mission and Advocates League came to an agreement with the SL not to hold meetings that interfered with each other.

4 September 1886: In a letter to John Prideaux Lightfoot, written from Kelmscott Manor, Morris made his first reference to the *Adoration of the Magi* tapestry that had been commissioned by Exeter College, Oxford. He also published 'Notes on Passing Events' in *Commonweal*.

5 September 1886: Morris returned to London from Kelmscott Manor in the afternoon. He then visited Burne-Jones at the Grange and discussed the proposed *Adoration of the Magi* tapestry. Later he delivered 'The Labour Question' at a meeting sponsored by the Clerkenwell (Central) Branch of the SL held at the SL Hall, 13 Farringdon Road, London.

6 September 1886: The nineteenth Trades Union Congress began in Hull. Mahon attended this and wrote two articles for *Commonweal*. Morris wrote: 'Yes please do the Trade Union Congress: I think we ought to take the ground that the Unions are not necessarily hostile to Socialism, and might be made use of when we get to reconstruction.'

7 September 1886: In a letter to John Prideaux Lightfoot, Morris estimated the cost of the proposed *Adoration of the Magi* tapestry to be 500 guineas 'including everything'.

8 September 1886: Morris was in the middle of translating the ninth book of the *Odyssey*.

10 September 1886: Morris travelled down to Kelmscott Manor. On the way he stopped off to inspect the proposed site for the *Adoration of the Magi* tapestry at Exeter College, Oxford.

11 September 1886: Morris published 'Notes on Passing Events', 'The Paris Trades' Union Congress' and chapter XI of *Socialism from the Root Up* in *Commonweal*.

14 September 1886: Morris returned to London from Kelmscott Manor.

15 September 1886: Morris delivered his lecture 'Education' at a meeting sponsored by the Clerkenwell Branch of the SL at the SL Hall, 13 Farringdon Road, London.

17 September 1886: During the day Morris was at Merton Abbey. In the evening he delivered a speech 'against the Party of [political] compromise' at a meeting called by the Fabian Society. The event gathered together socialists of various London societies with the object of discussing the formation of a British Socialist Party. The meeting was held at Anderton's Hotel, London. The *Architect* published an extensive summary of Morris's lecture on 'Education' (pp. 170–71).

18 September 1886: Morris published *An Old Story Retold* in *Commonweal*. This was later revised and published as *A King's Lesson* (*c.f.* March 1888).

24 September 1886: Morris was in Edinburgh where he went to visit the Morris & Co. window, 'Crossing the River Jordon', that had recently been installed in St Giles Cathedral: 'Our window is fine & looks a queer contrast with its glittering jewel-like colour to the daubs about it.' On his journey from London he amused himself translating Homer (110 lines) and reading Isabel Florence Hapgood's *The Epic Songs of Russia* (1885). In the evening he stayed at an unidentified hotel 'dull & not over clean' where he witnessed a fight between 'the head waiter and a quarrelsome gentleman more or less in liquor'.

25 September 1886: Morris travelled from Edinburgh to Manchester where he stayed the night with Ford Madox Brown. Earlier he wrote to Charles Rowley: 'there has been a cloud between him & me, & ... I am more than rejoiced it should be cleared off in such a pleasant way by my old friend himself.' Morris published 'Notes on Passing Events' and 'The Reward of "Genius"' in *Commonweal*.

26 September 1886: Morris delivered a lecture on 'The Origin of Decorative Art' at a meeting sponsored by the Ancoats Recreation Committee at the New Islington Hall, Ancoats, Manchester. He spent the night with Charles Rowley.

27 September 1886: Morris delivered 'Socialism: The End and the Means' at a meeting sponsored by the Manchester Branch of the SL at the Ardwick Temperance Hall, Pin Mill Brow, Aston Old Road, Manchester. The *Manchester Guardian* published portions of his lecture on 'The Origins of Ornamental Art' (p. 6).

28 September 1886: Morris travelled from Manchester to Sheffield where he delivered 'Socialism: The End and the Means' at a meeting sponsored by

Sheffield socialists at the Lower Albert Hall.

October 1886: The first edition of Peter Kropotkin and Charlotte Wilson's journal *Freedom* was published.

1 October 1886: Morris was scheduled to give a lecture on pattern designing at the Art Workers' Guild at the Century Club Rooms, London.

2 October 1886: Chapter XII of *Socialism from the Root Up* appeared in *Commonweal*.

3 October 1886: In the morning Morris gave an open-air speech on education jointly sponsored by the Merton and Mitcham Branches of the SL at Mitcham Fair Green. In the afternoon he gave another open-air speech on the same topic at a meeting sponsored by the Metropolitan Radical Association in Trafalgar Square. In the evening he delivered 'The Birth of Feudalism in Scandinavia' at a meeting sponsored by the Hammersmith Branch of the SL at Kelmscott House, Hammersmith.

5 October 1886: Morris travelled down to Kelmscott Manor where he arrived by the last train. He wrote to Jenny: 'you will be abed when I come, but I shall be on the table at breakfast on Wednesday, an excellent substitute for butter.'

9 October 1886: Morris returned to London from Kelmscott Manor.

11 October 1886: Morris delivered 'Socialism: The End and the Means' at a meeting sponsored by the Norwich Branch of the SL held at the Victoria Hall, Norwich.

12 October 1886: Morris travelled back to London from Norwich.

13 October 1886: Morris delivered a lecture at a meeting sponsored by the South West Ham Radical Association at the Congregational Schools, Swanscombe Street, Barking Road, London.

14 October 1886: From a letter written to Shaw it appears that Morris had read Stevenson's *Treasure Island* and *Kidnapped* 'and was much pleased with both'.

15 October 1886: Morris delivered 'Socialism: The End and the Means' at a meeting sponsored by the North London Branch of the SL at Milton Hall, London.

16 October 1886: Jane and Jenny were staying at Kelmscott Manor. Morris published 'Notes on Passing Events' in *Commonweal*. The *Norwich Daylight* printed Morris's lecture 'Socialism: The End and the Means' (pp. 2–4).

17 October 1886: In the morning Morris gave an open-air speech for the Hammersmith Branch of the SL at Walham Green. In the evening he delivered 'Socialism: The End and the Means' at a meeting of the

Hammersmith Branch of the SL at Kelmscott House.

18 October 1886: An anonymous article entitled *Representative Men at Home: Mr William Morris at Hammersmith* appeared in *Cassell's Saturday Journal* (no. 368). Morris delivered 'The Dawn of a New Epoch' at a meeting of a radical debating club at The British Workman, Reading.

19 October 1886: Morris travelled down to Kelmscott Manor.

21 October 1886: Morris returned to London from Kelmscott Manor.

22 October 1886: Morris gave £5 to a subscription fund in aid of Inglesham Church.

23 October 1886: Morris published 'Notes on Passing Events' in *Commonweal*.

25 October 1886: An article appeared in the *Pall Mall Gazette* entitled 'Are Socialists Lunatics?' (p. 9). This made reference to Morris.

29 October 1886: Morris expressed his intention of revising and altering *The Pilgrims of Hope*. However, no significant changes were ever made. By this time he had finished book X of the *Odyssey*.

30 October 1886: Morris published 'Notes on Passing Events' and chapter XIII of *Socialism from the Root Up* in *Commonweal*.

31 October 1886: Morris gave an open-air speech for the Hammersmith Branch of the SL at Beadon Road, Hammersmith.

1 November 1886: The *Pall Mall Gazette* published a letter from Morris on 'English Literature at the Universities'. He also wrote to Julius Chatwin in relation to the East window in St Philip's Cathedral, Birmingham, that Morris & Co. had been commissioned to produce.

2 November 1886: Morris delivered 'Socialism: The End and the Means' at a meeting sponsored by Lancaster socialists at the Palatine Hall, Lancaster.

3 November 1886: Morris delivered 'The Dawn of a New Epoch' at a meeting sponsored by the Preston Eclectic Society in the schoolroom of the Unitarian Chapel, Preston.

4 November 1886: Morris returned to London.

6 November 1886: Morris published 'Notes on Passing Events' in *Commonweal*.

9 November 1886: The SDF organized a demonstration of the unemployed to coincide with the Lord Mayor's Show.

10 November 1886: Morris gave an open-air speech for the Hackney Branch of the SL on the Broadway, London Fields, Hackney.

11 November 1886: Morris visited Burne-Jones to discuss the stained-glass windows for St Philip's Cathedral, Birmingham. One of the original subjects was to have been the Crucifixion but this was rejected. Burne-Jones suggested as alternatives (i) The Agony in the Garden, (ii) The Entry into Jerusalem and (iii) the Baptism. In the event the 'Crucifixion' was reinstated along with the 'Nativity' and 'The Ascension of Christ'.

13 November 1886: The serialization of *A Dream of John Ball* began in *Commonweal*. Morris also published 'Notes on Passing Events' in the paper.

14 November 1886: Morris gave an open-air speech for the Hammersmith Branch of the SL at Beadon Road, Hammersmith.

20 November 1886: Morris published part 2 of *A Dream of John Ball*, 'Mr Jawkins at the Mansion House' and 'The Moral of Last Lord Mayor's Day' in *Commonweal*.

21 November 1886: Morris delivered 'Socialism: The End and the Means' at a meeting sponsored by the Croydon Branch of the SL at the Royal Coffee House, Croydon.

25 November 1886: Morris visited Burne-Jones to discuss the *Adoration of the Magi* tapestry. By this time he had finished book XI of *The Odyssey*. He was also working on *A Dream of John Ball* which he told Jane had 'been much admired by people of various opinions'.

27 November 1886: Morris delivered 'The Dawn of a New Epoch' before the Bedford Park Club at the Club Rooms, Chiswick. It was at this meeting that Morris met Sydney Cockerell. Part 3 of *A Dream of John Ball* appeared in *Commonweal* along with 'The Ten Commandments'.

28 November 1886: In the morning Morris gave an open-air speech in support of the Fulham Branch of the SL at Walham Green. In the evening he delivered a lecture at a meeting sponsored by the Pentonville Progressive Society at Pentonville. The SL also began a series of Sunday meetings which Morris described as aimed at bringing 'out young speakers and try[ing] to cure them of "Stage-fever"; and their wrigglements to avoid speaking are amusing'.

30 November 1886: Morris undertook to start the scale drawings for the *Adoration of the Magi* tapestry.

1 December 1886: Morris delivered 'Socialism: Its Aims and Methods' at a meeting sponsored by the Clerkenwell (Central) Branch of the SL at the SL Hall, 13 Farringdon Road, London.

4 December 1886: Morris published part 4 of *A Dream of John Ball* and 'Notes on Passing Events' in *Commonweal*.

5 December 1886: Morris gave an open-air speech at a meeting organized by the Hammersmith Branch of the SL at Beadon Road, Hammersmith.

11 December 1886: Morris published part 5 of *A Dream of John Ball* and 'Notes on Passing Events' in *Commonweal*.

12 December 1886: Morris delivered 'Early England' at a meeting sponsored by the Hammersmith Branch of the SL at Kelmscott House.

15 December 1886: The *Pall Mall Gazette* published a letter by Morris (dated 14 December) on the 'Civilization of our Germanic Forefathers'. He and May donated a number of items to a raffle to be held in aid of SL funds. Amongst the items they gave were six pieces of Turkish embroidery, a Damascus dish, a copy of *The Earthly Paradise* and two watercolour drawings (one of Kelmscott Manor the other of Naworth Castle).

18 December 1886: Morris published part 6 of *A Dream of John Ball*, 'Notes on Passing Events' and 'Is Trade Recovering?' in *Commonweal*.

19 December 1886: Morris invited Watts-Dunton to Kelmscott House to meet Sparling. By this time Morris was working on book XIII of *The Odyssey*.

20 December 1886: Morris wrote to Thomas Armstrong recommending that the South Kensington Museum purchased the 'Jubinal tapestries' which depicted three episodes of the Trojan War and had originally been part of a single fabric woven by Pasquin Grenier of Tournai in 1472. The Museum followed his advice and purchased the tapestries.

25 December 1886: Morris published part 7 of *A Dream of John Ball* and '"The Law" in Ireland' in *Commonweal*.

1887: Morris's sister, Isabella, founded the Rochester Diocesan Deaconess Institution. One of the latter's functions was to encourage young women deaconesses to do practical work amongst the London poor. The Kelmscott Press later did various printing jobs for the Institution. The *Cherwell* chintz was produced as was the *Willow Bough* wallpaper. During the year Morris kept a small scribbling *Diary* in which he recorded his lecture engagements (BM.Add.MS.45408). Marx's *Das Kapital* was published in an English translation.

1 January 1887: Morris delivered 'The Origins of Ornamental Art' at a meeting sponsored by the Hammersmith Branch of the SL at Kelmscott House, Hammersmith. He also published part 8 of *A Dream of John Ball*, 'Political Notes' and an 'Editorial' in *Commonweal*.

2 January 1887: In the afternoon Morris was scheduled to deliver 'Early England' at the South Place Institute. In the evening he was scheduled to be the chairman at a lecture given by Annie Besant at the Hammersmith Branch of the SL at Kelmscott House, Hammersmith.

4 January 1887: At a meeting of the unemployed in Norwich a deputation tried unsuccessfully to see the Mayor. Some of the crowd then swarmed into the centre of the city and began to loot shops. Mowbray and Henderson, who represented the SL, were among four people arrested.

8 January 1887: Morris published 'Words of Forecast for 1887' and part 9 of *A Dream of John Ball* in *Commonweal*.

15 January 1887: Morris published 'Notes on News', 'The Political Crisis' and part 10 of *A Dream of John Ball* in *Commonweal*.

22 January 1887: Mowbray and Henderson were brought before Justice (*Nupkins*) Grantham and sentenced respectively to nine months and four months in prison. Morris published 'Notes on Passing Events' and ended the serialization of *A Dream of John Ball* in *Commonweal*.

23 January 1887: In the afternoon Morris delivered 'True and False Society' at a meeting sponsored by the Merton Branch of the SL at 11 Merton Terrace, High Street, Merton: 'the little room was pretty full of men mostly of the labouring class: anything attacking the upper classes directly moved their enthusiasm; of their discontent there could be no doubt or the sincerity of their class hatred.' He spent the night at Merton.

24 January 1887: The *Daily News* published a letter from Morris (dated 22 January) on the 'Disturbances in Norwich'.

25 January 1887: Morris started his short-lived *Socialist Diary* (BM.Add.MS.45335). He and Jenny visited the South Kensington Museum to view the 'Tapestry of the Siege of Troy' which had been purchased on his recommendation for £1,250: 'I chuckle to think that properly speaking it was bought for me, since scarcely anybody will care a damn for it.' In the evening he delivered a lecture entitled 'The Labour Question from the Socialist Standpoint' at a meeting of the Hammersmith Radical Club at the Club's Rooms, Hammersmith: 'The frightful ignorance and want of impressibility of the average English workman floors me at times.'

26 January 1887: Morris spent the day at Merton Abbey where he was visited by Cunninghame Graham: 'A brisk bright sort of young man.'

28 January 1887: Morris travelled down to Rottingdean to stay for three or four days with the Burne-Joneses. While there he did some work on his translation of the *Odyssey* as well as an article for *Commonweal*: 'which last was weak, long and no use.'

29 January 1887: Morris published 'Notes on Passing Events' in *Commonweal*.

31 January 1887: Morris 'got a surprise ... by hearing that Janey and Jenny are going to Rome with the Howards'.

February 1887: The SL published Morris's *The Aims of Art* as a pamphlet. It was sold for 3d each or 2s 3d per baker's dozen.

1 February 1887: Morris was chairman at a debate between Annie Besant and George W. Foote: 'she was fairly good, though too Bradlaughian in manner.' The debate was held at the Secular Hall, London.

4 February 1887: Morris opened a debate on the class war held at the Chiswick Club, Chiswick: 'My Socialism was gravely listened to by the audience but taken with no enthusiasm.'

5 February 1887: Morris saw Jane and Jenny off from London on their trip to Italy. He also published chapter XIV of *Socialism from the Root Up* in *Commonweal.*

6 February 1887: Morris gave an open-air speech for the Hammersmith Branch of the SL at Beadon Road, Hammersmith: 'This audience characteristic of small open-air meetings ... quite mixed, from labourers on their Sunday lounge to "respectable" people coming from church: the latter inclined to grin: the working men listening attentively trying to understand, but mostly failing to do so.' He later entertained Bax to dinner at Kelmscott House.

7 February 1887: Morris received a postcard from Jane saying that she and Jenny had arrived safely in Paris.

8 February 1887: Morris was chairman at a meeting held to protest against the 'coming war' between France and Germany. The meeting was sponsored by London socialist and anarchist groups and held at the Cleveland Hall, Cleveland Street, London: 'a wretched place once flash and now sordid in a miserable street.'

9 February 1887: Morris delivered a lecture before an unnamed 'goody-goody literary society' at a schoolroom on Peckham High Street. The meeting started with prayers and ended with a blessing. Canon Ripley was chairman of the meeting.

11 February 1887: Morris spoke at a continuation of the debate on the class war begun on 4 February 1887. A letter of his on art education appeared in the *Manchester Guardian.*

12 February 1887: Morris published 'Notes on News' in *Commonweal.*

13 February 1887: In the morning Morris gave an open-air speech for the Hammersmith Branch of the SL at Walham Green: 'the people listened well though the audience was not large about sixty at most.' In the evening he delivered 'Medieval England' at a meeting sponsored by the Hammersmith Branch of the SL held at Kelmscott House.

15 February 1887: In his *Socialist Diary* Morris wrote: 'to Bax at Croydon where we did our first article on Marx: or rather he did it: I don't think I should ever make an economist even of the most elementary kind: but I am glad of the opportunity this gives me of hammering some Marx into myself.'

16 February 1887: Morris delivered 'Medieval England' at a meeting sponsored by the Clerkenwell (Central) Branch of the SL held at the SL Hall, 13 Farringdon Road, London: 'middling audience.'

17 February 1887: Morris was suffering from an attack of gout.

18 February 1887: The *Architect* published a letter by Morris on the teaching of art. By this time he had finished book XVI of the *Odyssey*.

19 February 1887: Morris visited the Burne-Joneses. A less optimistic feeling can be detected in his writing when he published 'Facing The Worst Of It' in *Commonweal*. The same edition also contained his column 'Notes on News'. In the evening May returned from a short stay in Worthing.

20 February 1887: Morris visited the Grange. Later he gave a lecture on monopoly at a meeting sponsored by the Mitcham Branch of the SL at the Branch Club Room at the corner of Merton Lane and Fountain Place, Mitcham: 'a tumble down shed opposite the grand new workhouse built by the Holborn Union... I wonder sometimes if people will remember in times to come to what a depth of degradation the ordinary English workman has been reduced.' Morris spent the night at Merton.

21 February 1887: Morris spent the day working at Merton.

22 February 1887: The *Pall Mall Gazette* published a letter by Morris in opposition to the Ambleside Railway Bill. This Bill proposed the building of a railway between Windermere and Ambleside. The *Pall Mall Gazette* was leading the opposition against the Bill. Morris spent most of the day with Bax 'trying to get our second article on Marx together: a very difficult job: I hope it may be worth the trouble'.

25 February 1887: Morris spent the day at Merton.

26 February 1887: Morris visited Strangeways & Sons who were to print the *Odyssey* for Reeves & Turner. He spent the rest of the day at Merton. His article 'Fighting for Peace' appeared in *Commonweal*.

27 February 1887: Morris gave an open-air speech for the Hammersmith Branch of the SL at Beadon Road, Hammersmith. In the evening he entertained Shaw and Watts-Dunton to dinner at Kelmscott House: '[Shaw] gave us a comical account of the adventures of a literary man among the publishers.'

1 March 1887: Morris and Bax wrote their third Marx article: 'which went easier'.

5 March 1887: The SL held its bazaar and concert. In the raffle Morris, who did not attend, won a piece of embroidery he had donated and a sixpenny pipe! The bazaar raised £16. Morris published 'Notes on News' in *Commonweal*.

6 March 1887: Morris delivered 'How We Live and How We Might Live' at a meeting sponsored by Hoxton Branch of the LEL at 2 Crondel Street, New North Road, Hoxton.

9 March 1887: In a letter to Jenny, Morris said he hoped his *Socialist Diary* would 'one day be published as a kind of view of the Socialist movement seen from the inside, Jonah's view of the Whale, you know, my dear'. In the same letter he recorded that De Morgan had just got married. In fact De Morgan had written to Morris on 7 March from the Isle of Wight where he was honeymooning: 'Dear Tops: We've been and gone and got splace, me and my wife.'

12 March 1887: Morris published 'Political Notes', 'Notes on News' and chapter XVI of *Socialism from the Root Up* in *Commonweal*. He also wrote some notes about the proposed Ambleside Railway Bill.

13 March 1887: Morris delivered 'Monopoly' at a meeting sponsored by the Hackney Branch of the SL at the Branch Rooms, 23 Audrey Street, Goldsmith Row, Hackney: 'a fresh opportunity (if I needed it) of guaging the depths of ignorance and consequent incapacity of following an argument which possesses the uneducated averagely stupid person.'

14 March 1887: Morris travelled up to Edinburgh. In the evening he delivered 'Socialism: The End and the Means' at a meeting sponsored by the Edinburgh Branch of the SLLL at the Lower Free Tron Hall, Edinburgh: 'The audience … was both attentive and intelligent and very enthusiastic.'

15 March 1887: Morris and Glasse visited Roslin, Midlothian: 'The chapel strange indeed; unquestionably romantic; but the work coarse and quite lacking the deft skill and crispness of medieval work; the romance laid on with a trowel, as if by the amateur determined to be romantic.'

16 March 1887: Morris arrived back in London after taking the all-night train from Edinburgh: '[I woke] at Hatfield [and] found the whole country under a white blanket of snow, and the trees like a father-Christmas toy.'

17 March 1887: The anniversary of the Paris Commune was celebrated at the South Place Institute, Finsbury. Morris wrote: 'I spoke last, and to my great vexation and shame, *very* badly… I tried to be literary and original, and so paid for my egotism.' Kropotkin also spoke.

19 March 1887: Morris published 'Why We Celebrate the Commune of Paris' and 'Political Notes' in *Commonweal*.

20 March 1887: The Annual Meeting of the Hammersmith Branch of the SL took place: 'a dead failure.' Later Morris delivered 'Monopoly' at a meeting sponsored by the Chiswick Club at the Chiswick Hall, London: 'I really did my best; but they hung on my hands as heavy as lead.'

22 March 1887: Morris delivered 'Medieval England' at a meeting sponsored by the Hammersmith Radical Club at the Club's Rooms, Hammersmith. He had an audience of nine.

24 March 1887: Morris wrote in his *Diary*: 'fifty-three years old today – no use grumbling at that.'

26 March 1887: Morris held his annual party to watch the Oxford and Cambridge Boat Race. Some of the guests went up on the roof of Kelmscott House and came down covered in soot. Morris published 'Notes on News' and chapter XVII of *Socialism from the Root Up* in *Commonweal*.

27 March 1887: In the morning Morris delivered 'Monopoly' at a meeting at the Borough of Hackney Club in Haggerston, London: 'the meeting was a full one, and I suppose I must say attentive; but the coming and going all the time [of] … the pie-boy and the pot-boy was rather trying to my nerves.' In the afternoon he spoke in favour of free speech at an open-air demonstration organized by the Hackney Branch of the SL in Victoria Park: 'Dined on the way off three pence worth of shrimps that I bought in a shop, and ate with bread and butter and ginger beer in a coffee shop, not as dirty as it looked from outside.' Morris attended this meeting wearing a grey cape which caused some passers-by to shout after him 'Shakespeare'! In the evening the Hammersmith Branch of the SL passed a resolution proposed by Morris that the question of agitating by parliamentary methods be postponed for a year.

28 March 1887: Morris wrote in his *Diary* that at the weekly meeting of the SL: 'Mainwaring brought up a co-operative scheme, the profits made to go to the funds of the League; I rather agree to this so as to give people something to do; though of course I see the disadvantages.'

April 1887: The first volume of Morris's translation of *The Odyssey of Homer* was published by Reeves & Turner. Volume 2 appeared in November 1887. A review of the first volume by E. D. A. Marshead appeared in the *Academy* (p. 299). A Co-operative Grocery Store was opened at the SL's headquarters at 13 Farringdon Road. It was advertised as 'open on Monday, Wednesday, and Saturday evenings after 8.30 p.m.'. Tennyson's *Carmen Saeculare: An Ode in Honour of the Jubilee of Queen Victoria* appeared in *Macmillan's Magazine*.

2 April 1887: Morris travelled from London to Glasgow by the 10 pm train from Euston: 'I had a very comfortable journey down in a coupe 2/6 to the guard insured my sole holding of it; and my supper was splendid.' He published 'Notes on News' in *Commonweal*.

3 April 1887: Morris arrived in Glasgow at 9.15 am. He was met at the station by Glasier who took him home to his tenement in Crown Street to have breakfast. Morris feasted on ham, eggs, sausage and haddock prepared by Glasier's mother. Glasier left him in the front room to do his daily translation from the *Odyssey*. In the early afternoon Morris and Glasier visited the Cathedral. Here Morris was infuriated when he saw how a white marble sarcophagus had been jammed into the old grey stonework of the aisle. Glasier wrote: '"What infernal idiot has done *that?*" Morris ... demanded, and heedless of the consternation around him poured forth a torrent of invective against the unknown perpetrators of the crime. For a moment I thought he might actually spring upon the excrescence and tear out the hateful thing with his bare fists.' Later Morris gave an open-air speech at a meeting organized by the Glasgow Branch of the SL at Jail Square, Glasgow. According to Glasier: 'He was heartily cheered as he dismounted from the stool.' He then attended a meeting of the branch at which he was embarrassed by the size of the letters on the posters advertising his presence in the town. In the evening he delivered 'True and False Society' at a meeting sponsored by the Glasgow Branch of the SL at Waterloo Hall, Glasgow. The MP, Cunninghame-Graham, presided at this meeting at which there was a paying audience of around 1,000. This was the first time that a British MP had done so at a socialist meeting. While standing drinks at the Grand Central Hotel after this meeting Morris had two sovereigns stolen from his pocket.

4 April 1887: In the afternoon Morris travelled from Glasgow to Dundee where he delivered a lecture from notes at a meeting sponsored by the Revd David Macrea. He later wrote of this meeting: 'I was only *part* of the entertainment; music (which if it had been good I should not have objected to), and a recitation from the parson's self (which I very much objected to) being part of it also.' After the lecture he travelled across the river Tay to stay the night with Macrea.

5 April 1887: In the morning it snowed heavily for three hours. Nevertheless, Morris was still able to travel to Edinburgh in the company of John Gilray. In Edinburgh he delivered 'Monopoly' at an evening meeting sponsored by the Edinburgh Branch of the SLLL held at the Free Tron Hall, Edinburgh. A socialist resolution was passed 'after a rather stormy debate, owing to the stupidity of a cut-& dried opponent one Job Bone, who always opposes everything'. He stayed the night with Revd John Glasse.

6 April 1887: Morris returned to Glasgow stopping on the way to visit the fifteenth-century palace at Linlithgow. In the evening he attended a party arranged by the Glasgow Branch.

7 April 1887: In the morning Morris travelled from Glasgow to Hamilton where he delivered 'Socialism and the Labour Struggle' at a meeting sponsored by the Hamilton Branch of the SL at the Choral Hall. Morris's speech was inter-

rupted by 'a drunken man in the gallery who persisted in taking me for Mr. Mason his M.P. and quarrelling with me on some political subject to which I had never alluded'.

8 April 1887: Morris delivered 'Socialism: The Way and the Means' at a meeting sponsored by Paisley socialists in the Good Templar Hall, Paisley. While in Paisley he visited the old Abbey Church which he found a 'doleful place to look at'.

9 April 1887: Morris travelled with the Glasgow Branch by train to Coatbridge. Due to a misunderstanding the train did not stop at Coatbridge and Morris flared 'up instantly into a amazing state of indignation'. Confronting the astonished guard he began 'a terrible diatribe against railway companies'. According to Glasier the members of the branch were so embarrassed by this outburst that they stealthily crossed the footbridge to the other platform. A few minutes later Morris rejoined the group 'a transformed being'. Later Morris gave an open-air speech at a meeting organized by the Glasgow Branch of the SL at The Cross, Coatbridge on a cinder-heap underneath the Gartsherrie blast furnaces. He built his own stand from a few broken bricks salvaged from the cinder heap. In the evening Morris offered to stand drinks for the comrades but as two were teetotallers they had to go to a temperance establishment where they had lemonade and sandwiches. According to Glasier, Morris's response to this change of plan was 'a whimsical "umph"'. Morris also published 'The Revival of Trade(?)', 'Law and Order in Ireland' and an untitled paragraph on flogging in Egypt in *Commonweal*.

10 April 1887: Morris gave an open-air speech for the Glasgow Branch of the SL on Glasgow Green. He described the audience as 'very sympathetic; but sadly poor & pinched'. He left Glasgow at 5 pm and travelled to Newcastle where he arrived at 11 pm. He was met by Mahon and Donald and also saw Hyndman. He spent the night at a Temperance Hotel.

11 April 1887: Early in the morning Morris left Newcastle and travelled to Northumberland to address the striking miners. Mahon took him to the house of a miner and his family: 'they were very nice people; the man very intelligent & pleasant, talking with that queer Northumbrian smack that makes the talk sound like that of a foreigner; poor man, he had lost one eye in an accident & damaged the other.' Later that morning he made an open-air speech, from a trolley supplied by Mahon, at the Northumberland Miners' Demonstration held in a field outside Horton. The audience at this meeting was estimated to have been between 9,000 and 10,000: 'our meeting was a brilliant success.' He then returned to Newcastle by train. In the evening he gave another open-air speech as part of the Northumberland Miners' Demonstration at Ryton Willows: 'it was successful and the audience stayed till it was nearly dark ... [and] gave three cheers for the Socialists.' In London a huge meeting was held in Hyde Park to protest against the Irish Coercion Bill. It was estimated that between 50,000 to 150,000 attended. Blunt recorded: 'there was … a platform for Morris's section, and I saw May Morris on their cart looking like a French revolutionist going to [her] execution.'

12 April 1887: Morris arrived back in London by the day mail train at 9 pm and later attended the meeting of the League's Council. The *Newcastle Chronicle* carried a report on Morris's speech the previous day.

13 April 1887: Morris delivered a speech at a meeting called by the SL to protest against the 'latest Irish Coercion Bill'. The meeting was held at the SL Hall, 13 Farringdon Road, London.

14 April 1887: May went to 'exhibit' Sparling to her grandmother. The latter wrote (19 April): 'I thought the young gentleman very young, I should have said he was no more than twenty, he seemed good tempered and gentle.'

16 April 1887: Morris told Jane that 250 copies of the first volume of his translation of the *Odyssey* had been sold. Morris's sister, Isabella, was ordained by Bishop Thorold at Park Hill, Clapham.

17 April 1887: In the morning Morris gave an open-air speech for the Hammersmith Branch of the SL at Beadon Road, Hammersmith. In the evening he delivered 'True and False Society' at a meeting sponsored by the Hammersmith Branch of the SL at Kelmscott House, Hammersmith.

19 April 1887: May left for Kelmscott Manor.

22 April 1887: Morris visited his mother and found her 'well but I think a trifle deafer, and perhaps showing her age more than when I last saw her.'

23 April 1887: Morris published 'Notes on News' in *Commonweal*.

24 April 1887: In the afternoon Morris gave an open-air speech at the SL's Northumberland Miners' Demonstration held in Hyde Park: 'a fair success under the circumstances, although a hail storm drove a lot of people out of the Park just as we were beginning.' In the evening he was scheduled to deliver 'Socialism: Its Aims and Methods' at a meeting sponsored by the Hackney Branch of the SL at the Morley Coffee Tavern Lecture Hall, Triangle, Mare Street, Hackney.

25 April 1887: Morris ended his *Socialist Diary*.

26 April 1887: A review of *The Odyssey of Homer* by Oscar Wilde appeared in the *Pall Mall Gazette* (p. 5).

27 April 1887: Morris travelled down to Kelmscott Manor to stay with May.

30 April 1887: Morris was due to return to London from Kelmscott Manor. A review by Edmund Morshead of Morris's translation of the *Odyssey* appeared in the *Academy* (vol. 31, p. 299). Morris published 'Notes on News' and chapter XVIII of *Socialism from the Root Up* in *Commonweal*.

1 May 1887: Morris gave an open-air speech for the Hammersmith Branch of the SL at Beadon Road, Hammersmith. The eight-hour day movement in America called for a nationwide strike to be held on this day.

3 May 1887: The Manchester Royal Jubilee Exhibition opened. It included a number of Morris & Co. designs. Amongst them were two tapestry panels: *St Cecilia* and *St Agnes*. The *Manchester Guardian* (28 June) recorded: 'William Morris, poet, designer, manufacturer and socialist [is showing] his wares... To walk through the rooms which he has furnished is to be converted on the spot to any theories that such a magician may happen to hold.' A meeting of strikers in Chicago was fired on by the police during which people were killed and wounded.

4 May 1887: Morris was scheduled to deliver 'True and False Society' at a meeting sponsored by the Christian Socialist Society at the Industrial Hall, Clark's Buildings, Bloomsbury. A mass meeting in Chicago held to protest at the action of the police the day before ended with a bomb being thrown which killed seven policemen and wounded several others.

7 May 1887: Morris published 'Notes on News' in *Commonweal*. A review of the *Odyssey* appeared in the *Athenaeum* which described it as 'the curiosity of the *dilettante*'.

8 May 1887: Morris gave an open-air speech for the Hammersmith Branch of the SL at Beadon Road, Hammersmith. In the evening he read out a statement by Joseph Lane. This is not mentioned by LeMire.

10 May 1887: Morris was at Kelmscott Manor. In the evening he, along 'with the rest of the youth of the village', helped refloat a launch that had run aground on the ford near the village.

14 May 1887: Morris probably returned from Kelmscott Manor. He also published 'Notes on News' and 'Coercion for London' in *Commonweal*.

15 May 1887: In the morning Morris gave an open-air speech for the Hammersmith Branch of the SL at Beadon Road, Hammersmith. In the evening he delivered 'Art and Industry in the Fourteenth Century' at a meeting sponsored by the Hammersmith Branch of the SL at Kelmscott House, Hammersmith.

16 May 1887: Jane and Jenny returned from their three month visit to Italy. In a letter to an unknown recipient, in which he apologized for missing that evening's SL meeting, Morris wrote: 'if there is to be any outing this year at Whitsuntide ... I give my word and vote for not going anywhere by railway but by *van*.'

17 May 1887: Morris made it clear in a letter to Mahon that he would consider resigning from the SL if it accepted a pro-parliamentary resolution at the Annual Conference.

19 May 1887: Morris wrote a number of letters relating to the Annual Conference of the SL in which he reaffirmed his anti-parliamentary stance. In a letter to John Glasse he wrote: 'I cannot swallow my words and rejoin them [the SDF]; and to have two organisations holding the same tenets and following the same policy seems to me absurd.'

21 May 1887: Morris delivered an open-air speech at a demonstration against Irish coercion. This meeting was sponsored by the Anti-Coercion Demonstration Committee and held in Victoria Park. Morris also published part 1 of 'The Reward of Labour. A Dialogue' in *Commonweal*.

21 May/28 July: The Bax–Bradlaugh debate on socialism appeared in *Commonweal*.

22 May 1887: Morris delivered an open-air speech for the North London and Marylebone Branches of the SL at Hyde Park.

24 May 1887: Morris, in his birthday letter to his mother, wrote that: 'they seem to be really better for the sojourn abroad, especially Janey, who was but poorly when she left, & would have borne this hard winter badly.'

28 May 1887: Morris published 'Notes on News' and the concluding part of 'The Reward of Labour. A Dialogue' in *Commonweal*.

29 May 1887: The Third Annual Conference of the League was dominated by a tussle between the parliamentarists and the anti-parliamentarists when Bax's Croydon branch proposed a motion in favour of putting up parliamentary candidates. This was defeated by seventeen votes to eleven. Those who had been defeated – including the Avelings, Mahon and Bax – refused to stand for the Council. Their places were taken by people like F. C. Slaughter and David Nicoll who had pronounced anarchist views. Henry Barker was elected the new secretary of the SL.

30 May 1887: It was alleged in a handbill – *To the Members of the Socialist League* – issued in 1888 by Lane and Charles that on this date the parliamentarists held a meeting in which they formed themselves into an organized faction within the League. It was claimed that Aveling, Eleanor Marx, Bax, Donald and Binning all attended this meeting.

31 May 1887: Morris sent a copy of the *Odyssey* to Israel Gollancz.

June 1887: Reeves & Turner published a new edition – the fourth – of *Sigurd the Volsung*. This included fifty large paper copies done in crown quarto

Dickinson handmade paper. However, Buxton Forman claimed 'the number printed was, I believe, a hundred'.

1 June 1887: Morris delivered 'True and False Society' at a meeting sponsored by the Clerkenwell (Central) Branch of the SL at the SL Hall, 13 Farringdon Road.

3 June 1887: In a letter written by Jane to Rosalind Howard, shortly after she and Jenny had returned from Italy, she said: 'there is no doubt that Jenny has benefited in every way, her father is delighted with the change in her, she is more like her old self than she has ever been since her illness began 11 years ago.'

4 June 1887: Morris started the serialization of his lecture 'How We Live and How We Might Live' in *Commonweal*. He also wrote to Magnússon asking him whether he could help Sparling learn book cataloguing as the latter was applying for a job as a librarian at the National Liberal Library.

5 June 1887: Morris delivered an open-air speech for the Hammersmith Branch of the SL at Beadon Road, Hammersmith.

7 June 1887: Morris wrote to James Bryce MP asking for his support for Sparling's application for the post of librarian at the National Liberal Library. Engels wrote to Sorge and Laura Lafargue recommending that following the defeat of the parliamentarians at the Third Annual Conference of the SL they should withdraw from the organization.

8 June 1887: Morris was chairman at the annual general meeting of SPAB held in the Old Hall, Staple Inn, Chancery Lane, London. Later he delivered a speech in support of a motion to establish a fund for the repair of ancient buildings.

9 June 1887: Morris delivered 'True and False Society' at a meeting sponsored by the Battersea Branch of the SDF held at the Sydney Hall, 36 York Road, Battersea.

11 June 1887: Morris published 'Notes on News' and continued the serialization of 'How We Live and How We Might Live' in *Commonweal*. He also wrote some untitled paragraphs on the Indian Railways.

12 June 1887: In the morning Morris gave an open-air speech for the Hammersmith Branch of the SL at Beadon Road, Hammersmith. In the afternoon he was scheduled to deliver 'True and False Society' before the Hackney Branch of the SL at the Branch Rooms, 23 Audrey Street, Goldsmith Row, Hackney.

15 June 1887: Morris was scheduled to deliver a lecture at 102 Brompton Road, London.

16 June 1887: Morris gave a speech at a debate sponsored by the Fabian Society at the South Place Institute, Finsbury: 'The debate at the Fabian [Society] last night was a very absurd affair only enlivened by a flare up between me & that offensive snob [Hubert] Bland: otherwise I was as mild as muffin's milk, &, I think, rather more coherent than anybody else.' Annie Besant and George Bernard Shaw also spoke at this meeting.

18 June 1887: Morris published 'Notes on News', 'Notes', 'Common-sense Socialism' and 'The Labour Struggle. Belgium' in *Commonweal*. He also continued the serialization of 'How We Live and How We Might Live'.

25 June 1887: Morris published 'An Old Superstition – A New Disgrace' and 'The North of England Socialist Federation' in *Commonweal*. The serialization of 'How We Live and How We Might Live' also continued.

27 June 1887: In the morning Morris gave an open-air speech for the Hammersmith Branch of the SL at Walham Green, Fulham. In the evening he delivered 'Monopoly' at a meeting sponsored by the Hammersmith Branch of the SL at Kelmscott House, Hammersmith.

28 June 1887: Morris – and a party which included Jane, Jenny, Aglaia Ionides Coronio, Cecil John Opie and Walter Leaf – went on a boating trip. They took the train to Richmond and then a boat to Hampton Court where they arrived just before closing time. They did not get back to Teddington Lock until after 8 pm: 'we mightily enjoyed ourselves.'

July 1887: Morris estimated the League's membership to be around 700.

2 July 1887: Morris published 'Notes' and the last instalment of 'How We Live and How We Might Live' in *Commonweal*.

3 July 1887: In the morning Morris gave an open-air speech for the Hammersmith Branch of the SL at Beadon Road, Hammersmith. In the afternoon he was scheduled to give an open-air speech for the Hackney Branch of the SL at the Broadway, London Fields, Hackney. He also wrote a letter to E. Nesbitt, the writer of children's books, who was active in the Fabian Society.

5 July 1887: Morris visited Hampton Court again 'to look at the tapestries and loaf about the gardens'.

9 July 1887: Morris published 'Notes on News' in *Commonweal*.

13 July 1887: Morris delivered an open-air speech for the Hackney Branch of the SL at London Fields, Hackney.

16 July 1887: Morris published 'Notes on News' in *Commonweal*.

17 July 1887: Morris gave an open-air speech for the Hammersmith Branch of the SL at Beadon Road, Hammersmith.

23 July 1887: Morris delivered an open-air speech on monopoly and socialism for the Mile-End Branch of the SL at Victoria Park, London. He also published his 'Notes on News' column and chapter XX of *Socialism from the Root Up* in *Commonweal*.

24 July 1887: Morris gave an open-air speech for the Hammersmith Branch of the SL at Beadon Road, Hammersmith.

27 July 1887: Morris estimated the circulation of the *Commonweal* to be 'about 2800' and stated that it was 'losing £4 a week'. At the time he was in the process of writing his lecture 'The Policy of Abstention'.

30 July 1887: Morris published his dialogue 'The Boy-Farms at Fault' in *Commonweal*. He had previously referred to the idea of 'boy farms' in a letter he had written to William Sharman in April 1886.

31 July 1887: Morris delivered 'The Policy of Abstention' at a meeting sponsored by the Hammersmith Branch of the SL at Kelmscott House.

6 August 1887: Morris published 'Notes', 'Bourgeois Versus Socialist' and chapter XXI of *Socialism from the Root Up* in *Commonweal*.

7 August 1887: Morris gave an open-air speech for the Hammersmith Branch of the SL at Beadon Road, Hammersmith.

12 August 1887: Morris told Georgiana Burne-Jones that earlier in the week he had visited Tangley Manor: 'It is a very beautiful old house: the old 14th century hall, at least its chief beam, being built up into a house of 1582.'

13 August 1887: Morris published 'Notes' in *Commonweal*.

14 August 1887: Morris gave an open-air speech for the Hammersmith Branch of the SL at Walham Green, Fulham.

15 August 1887: The London members of the SL decided to establish two new open-air pitches and hold a concert in aid of *Commonweal* (*c.f.* 15 October 1887).

17 August 1887: Morris wrote to William Bell Scott thanking him for a copy of his etchings of *The King's Quair*.

20 August 1887: Morris published 'Notes on News' and the first part of the serialization of his lecture 'Feudal England' in *Commonweal*.

21 August 1887: In the morning Morris gave an open-air speech for the Hammersmith Branch of the SL at Walham Green. In the afternoon he gave another open-air speech for the Mile-End and Bethnal Green Branches at Victoria Park. In the evening he delivered 'Monopoly' at a meeting sponsored by the Hoxton Branch of the LEL at the Globe Coffee House, 277 High Street, Hoxton.

23 August 1887: Jane wrote to Rosalind Howard: 'May is away at Kelmscott Manor alone learning cookery and how to live on a few shillings a week. She is bent on marrying without waiting till her future husband gets employment. I have said and done all I can to dissuade her, but she is a fool and persists.'

24 August 1887: Morris delivered 'The Policy of Abstention' at a meeting sponsored by the Clerkenwell (Central) Branch of the SL at the SL Hall, 13 Farringdon Road, London.

25 August 1887: Morris stated in a letter to Georgiana Burne-Jones that he had completed the *Odyssey*.

27 August 1887: Morris published 'Notes on News', 'A Note on Passing Politics', 'Is Lipski's Confession Genuine?' and the second part of his serialization of 'Feudal England' in *Commonweal*.

28 August 1887: Morris gave an open-air speech for the Hammersmith Branch of the SL at Beadon Road, Hammersmith.

September 1887: At some point between 5 September and 11 September Morris spent three days at Kelmscott Manor: 'I had that delightful quickening of perception by which everything gets emphasised and brightened and the commonest landscape looks lovely: anxieties and worrits though remembered, yet no weight on one's spirits – Heaven in short.' Also around this time he visited Burne-Jones to discuss the stained-glass window Morris & Co. were designing for St Martin's Church, Brampton. The *Artist* began a serialization of portions of Morris's lecture 'The Aims of Art'. Further instalments appeared in October and November.

3 September 1887: Morris published 'Notes on News' and the third part of the serialization of 'Feudal England' in *Commonweal*.

5 September 1887: Morris was scheduled to give a speech at the 'Liberal and Radical Fete and Demonstration' at the Alexandra Palace.

9 September 1887: Blunt travelled down to Naworth with Jane.

10 September 1887: Morris published 'Notes on News', 'Artist and Artisan: As an Artist Sees It' and the final instalment of 'Feudal England' in *Commonweal*.

11 September 1887: In the morning Morris delivered an open-air speech for the Hammersmith Branch of the SL at Walham Green, Fulham. In the afternoon he gave an open-air speech for the Mile End and Bethnal Green Branches of the SL at Victoria Park, London. Blunt wrote in his *Diary*: 'Mrs. Morris's daughter May wants to marry a socialist with whom she has fallen in love. She [Jane] describes him as stupid and helpless, but I do not see how she is to prevent it. The girl has been brought up in the mill of socialism. She is 25 and has a will of her own.'

17 September 1887: Morris published 'Notes on News' in *Commonweal.*

20 September 1887: Morris and Jenny had dinner at Thomas Parris's house. A neighbour of Morris, he was Vice-President of the National Secular Society and a socialist. Annie Besant, Scheu and Shaw were there and Morris complained that the latter two 'had so fierce a debate on parliamentarism that I could barely get a word in edgewise'. At this dinner Shaw agreed to act in *The Tables Turned; or, Nupkins Awakened.* In the event he withdrew his offer and attended the first performance in the capacity of a drama critic. A Miss Canthorne was supposed to play Mary Pinch but she was replaced by May Morris (*c.f.* 3 October 1887).

23 September 1887: In a letter to John Glasse, Morris wrote: 'I admit, & always have admitted, that at some future period it may be necessary to use parliament mechanically: what I object to is *depending* on parliamentary agitation.' Jane returned from her holiday at Naworth Castle.

24 September 1887: Morris was hard at work writing *Nupkins Awakened.* He also published 'Notes on News' in *Commonweal.*

25 September 1887: Morris delivered a speech at a demonstration for free speech in Ireland. This meeting was sponsored by the Hoxton Branch of the LEL and held at Hoxton Church, London.

26 September 1887: In a letter to an unknown recipient, Morris recommended Aveling and Moore's recent translation of *Das Kapital* and described Grönlund's *Cooperative Commonwealth* as 'a weakish book, but has much information in it'.

27 September 1887: Morris was scheduled to give an open-air speech for the Mile End Branch of the SL on Mile End Waste, London.

2 October 1887: In the afternoon Morris delivered 'Art and Industry in the Fourteenth Century' at a meeting sponsored by the Ancoats Recreation Committee at New Islington Hall, Ancoats, Manchester. In the evening he delivered 'Monopoly' at a meeting sponsored by the Salford Branch of the SDF at the Temperance Hall, Ford Street, Salford.

3 October 1887: Morris wrote to May, who was at Kelmscott Manor, asking her to help in the production of *Nupkins Awakened.* She subsequently agreed to take the part of Mary Pinch.

4 October 1887: A 'good rehearsal' took place of *Nupkins Awakened*: ''tis thought the play will be a success.'

6 October 1887: Morris gave a speech at a meeting called to protest against the impending execution of the Chicago Anarchists. The meeting was sponsored by combined London socialist and anarchist groups and held at the Communist Club, 49 Tottenham Street, London.

8 October 1887: Morris published 'Notes' and 'Free Speech in America' in *Commonweal.*

9 October 1887: In the morning Morris gave an open-air speech for the Fulham Branch of the SL at Walham Green, Fulham. In the evening he delivered 'The Early Literature of the North' at a meeting sponsored by the Hammersmith Branch of the SL at Kelmscott House, Hammersmith.

11 October 1887: Morris was scheduled to deliver a lecture at a meeting at Lechlade: 'I don't much relish having to speak at Lechlade, as I am coming for a rest: but if I must, you had better hire the Swan as before.'

13 October 1887: Morris returned to London from Kelmscott Manor.

14 October 1887: Another rehearsal of *Nupkins Awakened* took place. Morris gave a speech at a meeting called by combined London socialist and anarchist groups to protest against the impending execution of the Chicago Anarchists. The meeting was held at the South Place Institute, London. It was seriously disrupted by the police.

15 October 1887: The first performance of *The Tables Turned; or, Nupkins Awakened* took place as part of a concert held at the SL Hall in Farringdon Road. Morris played the Archbishop of Canterbury. Shaw claimed he gave a brilliant performance as the pompous prelate 'by obliterating his humour and intelligence, and presenting his own person to the audience like a lantern with the light blown out, with a dull absorption in his own dignity which several minutes of the wildest screaming laughter ... could not disturb.' The play was published later in the year as a pamphlet. Morris also published 'Notes' in *Commonweal.*

16 October 1887: In the morning Morris gave an open-air speech for the Fulham Branch of the SL at Walham Green, Fulham. In the evening he was scheduled to deliver 'Monopoly' at a combined meeting of the Paddington Branch of the SDF and the West Marylebone Working Men's Club at the Club Rooms, 123 Church Street, Edgware Road, London.

17 October 1887: The *Daily News* published a letter from Morris (dated 15 October) in which he protested against the police attack on the meeting of 14 October.

18 October 1887: The *Daily News* published a second letter from Morris (dated 17 October) relating to the police attack on the combined socialist and anarchist groups meeting on 14 October 1887. Walter Crane wrote a letter to the *Daily News* in support of Morris.

22 October 1887: Morris published 'Notes on News' in *Commonweal.*

23 October 1887: Morris delivered an open-air speech for the Fulham Branch of the SL at Walham Green, Fulham. Blunt was arrested at an anti-eviction meeting in Woodford in Galway.

24 October 1887: Blunt was sentenced to two months' imprisonment but was released on bail pending an appeal to the Quarter Sessions.

29 October 1887: Morris travelled by train to Nottingham where he arrived at 5.30 pm. This meant he missed the performance of *Nupkins Awakened* that took place in the evening in London. His part as the Archbishop of Canterbury was taken by Nicoll. Lena Wardle, better known as the suspected poisoner Madeleine Smith, was the ticket seller at this performance. Morris published 'Notes on News' and 'Practical Politics at Nottingham' in *Commonweal*. The SL issued a *Manifesto* stating its views on the renewal of the unemployment agitation.

30 October 1887: In the afternoon Morris delivered 'The Origins of Ornamental Art' at a meeting sponsored by the Nottingham Socialist Club at the Secular Hall, Nottingham. In the evening he lectured on 'Monopoly' at the same venue.

2 November 1887: Morris was scheduled to give a lecture in Highgate, London.

3 November 1887: The *New York Tribune* reported that the United States Supreme Court had rejected an appeal for writ of error in the case of the Chicago Anarchists.

5 November 1887: Morris published 'Notes on News' and the first part of his dialogue 'Honesty is the Best Policy' in *Commonweal.*

6 November 1887: Morris was scheduled to deliver 'What Socialists Want' at a meeting sponsored by the Fulham Liberal Club in Fulham, London.

7 November 1887: Morris was coordinating a petition pleading for clemency on behalf of the Chicago Anarchists. Amongst those he wrote to was Robert Browning. The *Pall Mall Gazette* published a letter he wrote condemning the 'judicial murder' of the Chicago Anarchists.

8 November 1887: Morris delivered 'Socialism' at a meeting sponsored by the Huddersfield socialists at Victoria Hall, Buxton Road, Huddersfield. Sir Charles Warren banned all further meetings in Trafalgar Square on the grounds that it was Crown property.

11 November 1887: Four of the Chicago Anarchists were hanged. The *Pall Mall Gazette* published a letter from Morris commending an article in the paper supporting free speech in Trafalgar Square. Morris also wrote to John Prideaux Lightfoot in relation to the size of the proposed borders round the *Adoration of the Magi* tapestry: 'Mr. Burne-Jones thought it better to have as much picture space as possible so as to get the figures larger, in which view I quite agree.'

12 November 1887: Morris published 'Notes on News' and concluded 'Honesty is the Best Policy' in *Commonweal*. Sir Charles Warren issued a proclamation forbidding the procession to Trafalgar Square planned for the next day.

13 November 1887: A meeting called by the Radicals and Irish at Trafalgar Square to condemn the imprisonment of William O'Brien and affirm the right of assembly led to what became known as 'Bloody Sunday'. Morris and Annie Besant addressed the Clerkenwell contingent of the demonstration on Clerkenwell Green and urged them to be orderly and peaceful. In the event the police broke up the immense crowds with considerable violence. Burns and Cunninghame Graham were arrested. Three people were killed – including a prominent Deptford Radical called William B. Curner – and over one hundred injured. In the evening Morris delivered 'The Future of Society' at a meeting sponsored by the Hammersmith Branch of the SL at Kelmscott House, Hammersmith.

17 November 1887: Around 6,000 special constables were enrolled to prevent future demonstrations. A number of those arrested in Trafalgar Square were arraigned before Sir James Taylor Ingham. Four people were sentenced to six months imprisonment and four others to three months.

18 November 1887: The Law and Liberty League was formed at a meeting at the Memorial Hall, Farringdon Street, with the aim of raising bail for those arrested as a result of the fight for free speech.

19 November 1887: Morris published 'London in a State of Siege' and some untitled paragraphs in *Commonweal*.

20 November 1887: A large demonstration was held in Hyde Park to protest at the action of the police on 'Bloody Sunday'. Alfred Linnell, a Radical law-writer, was ridden down by the police in Northumberland Avenue and later died of the injuries he received. In the morning Morris gave an open-air speech for the Fulham Branch of the SL at Walham Green, Fulham. In the afternoon he delivered 'The Coming Society' at a meeting sponsored by the Clerkenwell (Central) Branch of the SL at the SL Hall, 13 Farringdon Road, London.

21 November 1887: The *Pall Mall Gazette* published a letter from Morris praising the formation of the Law and Liberty League. He pledged himself to stand bail for anyone who was arrested.

23 November 1887: Morris was scheduled to deliver an unnamed lecture in Preston. He left for Preston by the 10 am train from London.

26 November 1887: Morris published 'Notes on News', 'Insurance Against Magistrates' and 'The Liberal Party Digging Its Own Grave' in *Commonweal.*

30 November 1887: Morris and May were present at Bow Street to hear the charges against Burns and Cunninghame Graham. Invitations were sent out to attend the trial by Graham's wife on visiting cards inscribed 'Mrs Cunninghame Graham Bow Street Police Court'. Jane wrote a letter to Blunt in which she said she expected Morris to be arrested at any moment: 'My husband isn't in prison yet, but I should think it would not be long before he will have an opportunity of writing the longest poem ever penned by man.' The *Pall Mall Gazette* published an article in which the author complained about the number of secular entertainments taking place on Sundays: 'Mr. William Morris's Socialist interlude has been performed on several Sundays, when fixed charges were made for admission, but that was unknown to, or in defiance of, the Lord Chamberlain.'

December 1887: Mahon left the SL. C. R. Ashbee visited Morris to discuss the plans for his School of Handicraft. The project received a cool response from Morris.

1 December 1887: Morris delivered 'The Coming Society' at a meeting sponsored by the Bloomsbury Branch of the SL at the Athenaeum Hall, Tottenham Court Road, Bloomsbury. The *Pall Mall Gazette* published a letter from him in which he corrected the false impression that *Nupkins Awakened* had been performed on a Sunday.

2 December 1887: Morris delivered 'Socialism and the London Disturbances' at a meeting sponsored by the Revd Oswald Birchall at Buscot Rectory, Oxfordshire. The meeting should have been held in the schoolhouse but the local gentry refused the socialists use of the building and Morris had to give his talk at the Rectory: 'where we had a very useful meeting, the men listening very attentively and sympathetically.' Jane planned to attend a lecture Blunt was to give in Hampstead.

3 December 1887: A performance of *Nupkins Awakened* was given at the SL Hall 'in aid of the Prisoners' Defence Fund'. Morris published 'Notes on News' in *Commonweal.*

5 December 1887: At the inquest on Alfred Linnell it was claimed that there was no evidence that he had been kicked by a horse. However, four witnesses insisted that he had. The inquest was therefore adjourned in order to re-examine his body.

6 December 1887: C. R. Ashbee drew a picture in his *Journal* entitled the 'Soul of William Morris'. He wrote that Morris was 'a great love rushing through space with a halo of glory round him, but this consuming, tormenting, and goading him on'.

10 December 1887: Morris published 'Notes on News' in *Commonweal.*

11 December 1887: Morris was scheduled to give a lecture for the Hammersmith Branch of the SL at Kelmscott House.

17 December 1887: Morris published 'The Conscience of the Upper Classes' in *Commonweal.*

18 December 1887: In the late afternoon Morris delivered an open-air speech at the funeral of Alfred Linnell. A crowd of over 10,000 attended the procession which preceded the funeral: 'it was the most enormous concourse of people I ever saw; the numbers incalculable: the crowd sympathetic and quite orderly.' He was one of the pallbearers along with Cunninghame Graham, Annie Besant, W. T. Stead, Herbert Burrows and Frank Smith. The hearse was inscribed with the words 'Killed in Trafalgar Square'. As the light failed the crowd sang Morris's *A Death Song* to music arranged by Malcolm Lawson. A penny pamphlet was sold at the funeral to provide funds for Linnell's widow and children. This consisted of Morris *A Death Song*, a design by Walter Crane, and a short description of the circumstances of Linnell's death. Morris described the event as 'a victory'. Later that evening he delivered 'The Present Outlook in Politics' at a meeting sponsored by the Hammersmith Branch of the SL at Kelmscott House, Hammersmith.

21 December 1887: In a letter to John Bruce Glasier, Morris stated that he was 'more likely to write an epic on your (spiritual) birth than that of your namesake of Bannock-burn'. Morris later parodied himself in one of his dialogues as the author of a long poem entitled 'The Birth of the Bruce'.

24 December 1887: Morris published 'Notes on News' in *Commonweal.*

25 December 1887: Morris was scheduled to give an open-air speech for the Fulham Branch of the SL at Walham Green, Fulham.

30 December 1887: In a letter to an unknown correspondent Morris wrote: 'Socialism does not rest on the Marxian theory; many complete Socialists do not agree with him on this point [surplus-value]; and of course the disproving of a theory which professes to account for the facts, no more gets rid of the facts that the medieval theory of astronomy destroyed the sun.' During the day he visited Merton which had just reopened after the Christmas break. Here Debney showed him the new silver coinage with the older effigy of Queen Victoria: 'I think it most frightful; the very ugliest coins that have ever been made.'

31 December 1887: Morris published 'Emigration and Colonisation' in *Commonweal.* He also wrote to W. A. S. Benson expressing reservations about his proposal to stage an arts and crafts exhibition under the title 'The Combined Arts': 'the general public don't care one damn about the arts and crafts … this is of course my private view of the matter, and also of course I wish it success if it comes off.'

1888: Morris contributed a short 'Preface' (dated 5 December 1887) to Frank Fairman's *The Principles of Socialism Made Plain.* An anonymous article entitled *William Morris as a Political Revolutionist* appeared in the *Saturday Review* (vol. 65, p. 607).

January 1888: Blunt was sentenced to two months hard labour which he served in Glawy and Kilmainham jails. The *Bruges* wallpaper was finished. May's first article – 'Chain stitch embroidery' – appeared in the *Hobby Horse* (no. 9).

1 January 1888: In the morning Morris gave an open-air speech for the Fulham Branch of the SL at Walham Green, Fulham. In the evening he lectured on 'The Origins of Ornamental Art' at a meeting sponsored by the Hammersmith Branch of the SL at Kelmscott House, Hammersmith.

4 January 1888: It appears likely that Morris lectured on 'What Socialists Want' as a club run by Thomas Cobden-Sanderson in Hendon. This lecture is not mentioned by LeMire.

7 January 1888: William Curner, who had died on 'Bloody Sunday', was buried. Morris's 'Death Song' closed the proceedings. Morris published 'Notes on News', 'Police Spies Exposed' and 'What 1887 Has Done' in *Commonweal.* In 'Police Spies Exposed' it was suggested that Charles Theodore Reuss was '*now* in the pay of the police-bureau'. On hearing this Reuss threatened a civil action against Morris. For a time Morris feared that this might lead to him paying serious damages. In the event the case never reached court.

8 January 1888: Morris gave an open-air speech for the Hammersmith Branch of the SL at Acton Green, Acton. In the evening he delivered 'The Political Outlook' at a meeting sponsored by the Clerkenwell (Central) Branch of the SL at the SL Hall, 13 Farringdon Road, London.

11 January 1888: Morris was suffering from a slight attack of gout.

14 January 1888: Morris published 'Notes on News' and 'Radicals Look Around You!' in *Commonweal.*

15 January 1888: Morris delivered 'Useful Work *versus* Useless Toil' before the Fulham Branch of the SL at the Branch Rooms, Fulham, London.

18 January 1888: Burns and Cunninghame Graham were imprisoned for their alleged part in the Trafalgar Square riots.

21 January 1888: Morris was scheduled to play the part of the Archbishop of Canterbury in *Nupkins Awakened* at the SL Hall, 13 Farringdon Road, London. He also published 'Notes on News' in *Commonweal*.

22 January 1888: Morris delivered 'The Social Problem' at a meeting sponsored by the Chelsea Branch of the SDF at the Alham Rooms, Kilbolton Row, Fulham Road, London.

25 January 1888: The first general meeting of the Law and Liberty League was held. Morris was elected a member of the executive committee.

28 January 1888: Morris published 'Notes on News' in *Commonweal*. This edition also contained some untitled paragraphs written by Morris.

29 January 1888: Morris delivered 'The Revolt of Ghent' at a meeting sponsored by the Hammersmith Branch of the SL at Kelmscott House, Hammersmith.

February 1888: The New Gallery in Regent Street was opened by Joseph William Comyns Carr and Charles Halle.

5 February 1888: Morris delivered 'What Socialists Want' at a meeting sponsored by the Fulham Branch of the SL at the Branch Rooms, 8 Effie Road, Walham Green, London.

7 February 1888: Morris gave an unnamed lecture at the Parish Hall, Chelsea.

10 February 1888: In a letter to John Glasse, Morris stated that he was keen to deliver art lectures, as well as socialist lectures, on his forthcoming tour of Scotland as these attracted paying audiences.

11 February 1888: Morris published 'Notes on News' and various untitled paragraphs in *Commonweal*.

18 February 1888: Morris had breakfast with Tochatti and his wife before setting off to King's Cross to greet Burns and Cunninghame Graham on their release from Pentonville Prison. However, the authorities let them out early. Luckily Cunninghame Graham was spotted by Morris as he passed in a cab. In the afternoon Morris attended a 'Tea and Public Meeting' arranged for the prisoners by the Law and Liberty League. This was held at the Craven Hall, Regent Street: '*as* a tea-drinking [it] was a confused affair enough; & no wonder as the place was crammed; but as a meeting was as enthusiastic as possible, in fact the audience cheered the prisoners so that they could hardly speak.' On the way back May, Sparling and Morris had supper at the Solferino. Morris also published 'Notes on News' and 'On Some "Practical Socialists"' in *Commonweal*.

19 February 1888: In the morning Morris gave an open-air lecture for the Fulham Branch of the SL at Walham Green, Fulham. In the evening he was scheduled to deliver 'Monopoly' at a meeting sponsored by the Progressive Association at the Penton Hall, Pentonville Hill, London.

20 February 1888: Morris attended a meeting sponsored by the Law and Liberty League at Allan's Riding School, Seymour Place, Edgware Road, to celebrate the release of Burns and Cunninghame Graham. Morris had a great deal of difficulty entering the hall which was packed. He was supposed to move the vote of thanks at this meeting but Michael Davitt, who chaired it, gave time to a number of unscheduled speakers. The meeting ended abruptly without Morris having a chance to give his speech.

22 February 1888: Morris delivered 'Monopoly' at a meeting sponsored by the Thornton Heath Liberal Club at the Seneca Hall, Thornton Heath, London.

25 February 1888: Morris published 'Notes on News' and various untitled paragraphs in *Commonweal*.

26 February 1888: Morris gave an open-air speech for the Fulham Branch of the SL at Walham Green, Fulham.

March 1888: *A Dream of John Ball* was published by Reeves & Turner along with *A King's Lesson*. Both differed from the versions published in *Commonweal*. A review by E. D. A. Morshead of the second volume of Morris's translation of the *Odyssey* appeared in the *Academy* (pp. 143–4): 'There are many translations of the *Odyssey*, and several good ones; but time has brought us the best, from Mr. Morris.'

2 March 1888: Sir Charles Russell moved that Parliament inquire into the right of open-air meetings in Trafalgar Square as it was not in fact within the jurisdiction of the Royal Parks Act of 1872 as Sir Charles Warren had claimed. Bradlaugh also moved that an inquiry be launched into the conduct of the police on 'Bloody Sunday'.

3 March 1888: Russell and Bradlaugh's motions were voted on in the House of Commons and defeated. Morris published 'Notes on News' and 'A Triple Alliance' in *Commonweal*.

4 March 1888: Morris was annoyed when a journal suggested that he had written the poem 'On a Silver Wedding'. This piece had been composed by Lewis Morris to commemorate the twenty-fifth wedding anniversary of the Prince of Wales and Princess Alexandra of Denmark. Lewis Morris was in turn irritated to be referred to as 'a revolutionary socialist'. By this time Jane had returned to Kelmscott House. The Morrises were visited by Mary Howard who had just returned from a trip to Egypt.

6 March 1888: Jenny returned to Kelmscott House. Morris spent the day at Merton. Blunt was released from prison in Dublin.

7 March 1888: Morris delivered an unnamed lecture at the Hammersmith Central Club.

10 March 1888: Morris published 'Notes on News' and chapter XXII of *Socialism from the Root Up* in *Commonweal*.

11 March 1888: Morris delivered 'Monopoly' at a meeting sponsored by the St Pancras Branch of the SDF at the Athenaeum Hall, George Street, London.

16 March 1888: An unsigned review of *A Dream of John Ball* was published in the *Pall Mall Gazette* (p. 3).

17 March 1888: Morris was reading Tolstoy's *War and Peace* 'with much approbation but little enjoyment'. He also published 'Dead at Last' and chapter XXII (cont.) of *Socialism from the Root Up* in *Commonweal*.

19 March 1888: Morris gave a speech at the annual Paris Commune Celebrations sponsored by combined London socialist and anarchist groups at the Store Street Hall, London. The socialists had found it very difficult to arrange a hall for this event due to boycotting.

21 March 1888: Morris delivered 'Monopoly' at a meeting sponsored by the Revd Forrest at Clerk's Lane Church, Kilmarnock, Scotland. In the evening he travelled to Penkill to visit William Bell Scott: 'I was rather comforted by the sight of old Scott still visibly enjoying life though he is 22 years older than I am.'

22 March 1888: Morris spent the day with William Bell Scott at Penkill near Girvan: 'The house at Penkill has been so much spoiled that one can take but little pleasure in the architecture thereof, but the place is lovely: it lies on the hill-side on a spit of ground with a beck running on each side just like Naworth.'

23 March 1888: Morris was scheduled to give a lecture in Leith. However, only five people – excluding the members of the branch – turned up: 'we consoled ourselves by holding a brisk open-air meeting in the open street (Leith Walk) which was very successful.' Here Morris spoke to an audience of 200 people.

24 March 1888: Morris gave a speech for the Edinburgh Branch of the SLLL at West Calder, Scotland: 'a wretched little mining town.' The branch had difficulty gaining an audience for this meeting and had to send a boy round the streets ringing a bell. Morris also published 'Notes on News' and 'A Speech from the Dock' in *Commonweal*. Morris's mother sent him candlesticks for his birthday.

25 March 1888: Morris had intended to give an open-air speech sponsored by the Glasgow Branch of the SL. This had to be postponed due to the weather. Instead in the morning and afternoon Morris spent some hours answering the questions of League members at the branch rooms in St John Street, Glasgow. According to Glasier, Morris said that *Das Kapital* 'had practically no influence in creating Socialist thought in this country'. In the evening Morris delivered 'Art and Industry in the Fourteenth Century' to an audience of 500 at a meeting sponsored by the Glasgow Branch of the SL at Waterloo Hall, Glasgow. Later he was entertained 'with great splendour' by Professor Henry Dyer who regaled him with stories about his time in Japan.

26 March 1888: Morris delivered 'The Society of the Future' at a meeting sponsored by the Edinburgh Branch of the SLLL at the Trades Hall, 142 High Street, Edinburgh. He had nearly finished reading *Anna Karenina* which he thought 'better than "War and Peace" as a work of art, but I find it heavy reading sometimes'.

27 March 1888: Morris delivered an unnamed lecture at a meeting sponsored by the SLLL at Buchan's Hall, Barrack Street, Dundee.

28 March 1888: Morris delivered 'Monopoly' at a meeting sponsored by the Aberdeen Branch of the SLLL at the Lecture Hall, Aberdeen. Morris described the old town in Aberdeen as 'a very pleasant place: it has the Cathedral in it and the College, and the country beyond is very beautiful'. The *Scotsman* published a letter of his (dated 26 March) complaining about the report of his meeting in West Calder on 24 March in which it was claimed he had no audience: 'the audience was as attentive, intelligent, and sympathetic as a lecturer could possibly desire.'

2 April 1888: Morris was scheduled to deliver 'Socialism' at a meeting sponsored by the Fulham Branch of the SL at the Branch Rooms, 8 Effie Road, Walham Green, London.

5 April 1888: Morris gave a speech at an open debate sponsored by the Ball's Pond Radical Club at Ball's Pond, London.

7 April 1888: Morris published 'Notes on News' and 'Socialism Militant in Scotland' in *Commonweal*.

8 April 1888: In the morning Morris gave an address in lieu of an open-air speech at the Fulham Branch Rooms, Walham Green, Fulham. In the evening he delivered 'What Socialists Want' at a meeting sponsored by the Clerkenwell and Islington Branches of the SDF at Claremont Hall, Penton Street, London.

14 April 1888: Morris published 'Notes on News' in *Commonweal*.

15 April 1888: In the morning Morris gave an open-air speech at a meeting sponsored by the Fulham Branch of the SL opposite the Liberal Club in Fulham. In the evening he delivered 'Art and Industry in the Fourteenth Century' at a meeting sponsored by the Hammersmith Branch of the SL at Kelmscott House, Hammersmith.

16 April 1888: The Arts and Crafts Exhibition Society issued its first prospectus. Morris appeared as one of the subscribers.

17 April 1888: Morris delivered 'What Socialists Want' at a meeting sponsored by the Mile-End and Bethnal Green Branches of the SL at the Mile-End Socialist Hall, 95 Boston Street, Hackney Road, London.

21 April 1888: Morris published 'Notes on News' and some untitled verses in *Commonweal*.

27 April 1888: Keir Hardie stood as a member of the Scottish Labour Party in the Mid-Lanark by-election.

28 April 1888: Morris published 'Notes on News' in *Commonweal*.

29 April 1888: Morris gave an open-air speech for the Hammersmith Branch of the SL at Beadon Road, Hammersmith.

May 1888: Morris published 'The Revival of Architecture' in the *Fortnightly Review*. An article entitled 'London as a Literary Centre' by Richard Rogers Bowker was published in *Harper's New Monthly Magazine* (pp. 816–84). This article included an engraving of Morris taken from a picture belonging to the SL. Morris purchased a sixteenth-century notebook written by a Squire's wife. This contained cookery recipes and domestic accounts.

3 May 1888: Morris was staying at Kelmscott Manor.

4 May 1888: Morris returned to London from Kelmscott Manor.

5 May 1888: In a letter to Scheu, Morris spoke of having an engagement on this date. There is no indication what this was but it could have been associated with the forthcoming Annual Conference of the League. Morris was certainly preoccupied with the conference as he left a bundle of *Commonweals* on the train. Morris published 'Notes on News', 'The Reaction and the Radicals' and chapter XXIII of *Socialism from the Root Up* in *Commonweal*.

6 May 1888: Morris gave an open-air speech for the Hammersmith Branch of the SL at Beadon Road, Hammersmith.

8 May 1888: Morris gave an open-air speech for the Fulham Branch of the SL at Walham Green, Fulham.

12 May 1888: Morris published 'Notes on News' in *Commonweal*.

13 May 1888: Morris gave an open-air speech for the Fulham Branch of the SL at Walham Green, opposite the Liberal Club, Fulham. The Hammersmith Branch discussed a resolution calling for the expulsion of the Bloomsbury Branch of the SL.

19 May 1888: Morris published 'Notes on News' and concluded the serialization of *Socialism from the Root Up* in *Commonweal*. Glasier, Emery Walker, Webb and Tareston spent the evening at Kelmscott House discussing the conference the next day. An unsigned review of *Signs of Change* appeared in the *Saturday Review* (pp. 607–608).

20 May 1888: The Bloomsbury Branch put down a pro-parliamentary resolution at the Fourth Annual Conference of the SL. This was defeated and the parliamentarists again refused to stand for election to the Council. This allowed anarchists such as Tochatti and Charles to take their place. Fred Charles replaced Henry Barker as the secretary of the League. In the evening, back at Kelmscott House, Morris read to Glasier from *Huckleberry Finn*. Morris then went on to ask Glasier about his opinions about the art exhibition at the New Gallery that Glasier have visited on 18 May 1888. Glasier apparently made some unintended remarks about one of Burne-Jones's paintings which sent Morris into an 'extraordinary passion' in which he moved 'round the room like a caged lion'. Almost as suddenly his passion subsided and he apologized to Glasier.

21 May 1888: Morris had intended to go on an excursion to Box Hill organized by the Hammersmith Branch of the SL where he was to take part in a cricket match. Instead he took Glasier for a row on the river.

26 May 1888: Morris published 'Notes on News' in *Commonweal*.

28 May 1888: The SL suspended the Bloomsbury Branch for selling an 'illustrated squib' ridiculing Morris and his adherents.

June 1888: C. R. Ashbee's Guild and School of Handicrafts was opened in the East End of London.

2 June 1888: Morris published 'Notes on News' in *Commonweal*.

3 June 1888: In the morning Morris gave an open-air speech for the Hammersmith Branch of the SL at Latimer Road Station, Notting Hill. In the evening he delivered 'The Hopes of Civilisation' at a meeting sponsored by the Hammersmith Branch of the SL at Kelmscott House.

5 June 1888: Morris wrote to Magnússon requesting his help in writing some letters of introduction for Henry Rider Haggard to take with him on a trip to Iceland. According to Haggard's *The Days of My Life* he had visited Morris shortly before requesting these introductions.

8 June 1888: Morris gave a speech proposing the formation of the NAAA at Grosvenor House, London.

9 June 1888: A new policy statement of the League's Council appeared in *Commonweal* which reasserted its anti-parliamentary stance. Morris also contributed an article to the paper on 'Wat Tyler'.

14 June 1888: Henry Rider Haggard sailed for Iceland.

16 June 1888: The *Times* published a letter from Morris on 'Tapestry and Carpet Weaving'. His poem 'The Burghers' Battle' appeared in the *Athenaeum*, p. 761. He also published 'Notes on News' and 'The Skeleton at the Feast' in *Commonweal*.

17 June 1888: In the morning Morris gave an open-air speech for the Fulham Branch of the SL opposite the Liberal Club in Fulham. In the afternoon he was scheduled to give an open-air speech in Victoria Park as part of the SL's East-End agitation.

20 June 1888: Morris delivered 'The Revolt of Ghent' at a meeting sponsored by the Clerkenwell (Central) Branch of the SL at the SL Hall, 13 Farringdon Road.

23 June 1888: Morris told Jane that he had started work on *The House of the Wolfings*. At this time the latter was in the middle of an extended visit to Great Malvern due to her ill-health. Morris published 'Notes on News', 'Pentonville Prison' and 'Counting Noses' in *Commonweal*.

24 June 1888: Morris gave an open-air speech for the Fulham Branch of the SL opposite the Liberal Club in Fulham.

30 June 1888: Morris published 'Notes on News' and 'Thoughts on Education Under Capitalism' in *Commonweal*.

1 July 1888: At midday Morris was scheduled to deliver 'Misery and the Way Out' at a meeting sponsored by the Fulham Branch of the SL at the Branch Rooms, 8 Effie Road, Walham. In the evening he gave an open-air speech for the Fulham Branch of the SL in Fulham.

7 July 1888: Morris published 'Notes on News' and the first part of the serialization of his lecture 'The Revolt of Ghent' in *Commonweal*.

8 July 1888: In the morning Morris delivered an open-air speech for the Fulham Branch of the SL in Fulham. In the early evening he gave a second open-air speech on behalf of the same body at Weltje Road. Later in the evening he delivered 'The Society of the Future' at a meeting sponsored by the Battersea Branch of the SDF at the Sydney Hall, 36 York Road, Battersea.

11 July 1888: Jane wrote to Blunt from Malvern: 'my doctor says I must never again live with Jenny while she is in her present condition, my brain was suffering from it.'

14 July 1888: Morris published 'Notes on News' and continued the serialization of 'The Revolt of Ghent' in *Commonweal.*

21 July 1888: Morris published 'Sweaters and Sweaters', 'Notes on News' and continued the serialization of 'The Revolt of Ghent' in *Commonweal.* He also wrote some untitled paragraphs on the Match Girls' Strike.

22 July 1888: Morris gave an open-air speech at an anti-sweating demonstration sponsored by various socialist bodies at Hyde Park.

24 July 1888: Around this date *True and False Society* was published by the SL priced 1d.

28 July 1888: Morris published 'Notes on News' and continued the serialization of 'The Revolt of Ghent' in *Commonweal.*

29 July 1888: In the morning Morris gave an open-air speech for the Hammersmith Branch of the SL at Starch Green, London. In the evening he delivered 'From Chattel to Wage Slavery' at a meeting sponsored by the Hammersmith Branch of the SL at Kelmscott House. By this time he had nearly completed the first draft of *The House of the Wolfings.*

31 July 1888: Reeves & Turner sent Morris a cheque for sales of the popular edition of *The Earthly Paradise.* Morris described these as 'fairly good all things considered'.

August 1888: The Jack the Ripper murders began in the East End of London.

4 August 1888: Morris published 'Notes on News' and continued the serialization of 'The Revolt of Ghent' in *Commonweal.*

5 August 1888: In the morning Morris delivered an open-air speech for the Hammersmith Branch of the SL at Latimer Road, London. He described the audience as 'small'. In the evening he gave a second open-air speech for the same body at Weltje Road: 'a very fair audience.'

6 August 1888: Morris went on the United Socialist Excursion to Petersham Park organized by the SL and its foreign sections. The *Commonweal* stated that 'A Select Band has been engaged. A Quadrille Party will be presided over by efficient M.C.'s. All the Old English Sports. Boating on the River.' Morris wrote that 'we set off with band and banners through Richmond town to the park which is more than a mile away. I have no doubt the inhabitants sneered as they are mostly Tories; either the villa-abiders or their hangers-on.' The event was somewhat dampened by persistent drizzle. Morris entered one of the foot-races being given a start along with Mainwaring. Unfortunately there was a false start and he and Mainwaring had run halfway around the track before they were called back. 'I came back home about 4.30 and was rather tired.' On his return he was visited by Fairfax Murray who was apparently 'in his usual excellent spirits'.

7 August 1888: In the morning Morris met Edward and Philip Burne-Jones. At the time he had nearly finished re-reading Theodor Mommsen's *The History of Rome*. The book had been translated into English in 1862.

9 August 1888: It is clear from a letter Jane wrote to Blunt that by this time she had returned to Kelmscott House. Her return led to Jenny being sent to a nursing home in Malvern where she stayed for most of the remainder of 1888. Jane wrote: 'Jenny has gone to Malvern ... and the doctor says there is every hope of a complete cure for her so I must hope on. It has been a dreadful grief to us all, worse for me than for any one, as I have been so constantly with her. I never get used to it, I mean in the sense of not minding every time the thing occurs, it is as if a dagger were thrust into me, & I am having a blessed rest now and enjoying it thoroughly.'

10 August 1888: Morris took Jane to stay with his mother at Hadham.

11 August 1888: Morris published 'Notes on News', contributed a footnote to an article on 'The Death of W. Stanley Jevons' and continued the serialization of 'The Revolt of Ghent' in *Commonweal*. Morris travelled down to Norwich in company with Mainwairing, Mrs Schack and Faulkner. They spent the night in 'a clean little Caffee (they call it Caff in Norwich) which had all the virtues except cooking'.

12 August 1888: Morris gave an open-air speech at noon as part of the joint SL and SDF demonstration in the Market Place, Norwich. In the afternoon he gave a second open-air speech near the Wellington Statue in the Market Place. In the evening he delivered 'Monopoly' at a meeting at the Gordon Hall, Norwich. While in Norwich Morris was photographed with the Norwich Branch of the League: 'Item I sat twice (in groups) to a photographer, using many cuss-words.' In the evening he and Annie Besant visited the Cathedral Close but found themselves followed by a group of jeering boys and were forced to take the ferry across the river.

13 August 1888: At noon Morris gave an open-air speech in the Market Place, Norwich. In the early evening he gave another open-air speech at the same venue. In the late evening he was chairman at a lecture given by Annie Besant at St Augustine's Boys Board School, Norwich. During the day the socialists went on a river trip on a branch of the Wensum in five boats which they hired for 15d: 'It was a very pretty water, as clear as crystal, very little stream, banks very nearly awash with the water.' Morris later remarked: 'I always feel in a foreign country when I go to Norwich.'

14 August 1888: Morris returned to London.

15 August 1888: Morris went to Hadham to visit Jane, his mother and his sister Henrietta.

16 August 1888: In the morning Morris and his sister Henrietta went on a short walk around the nearby fields. In the evening Morris left Hadham by chaise and returned to Kelmscott House. Morris wrote to May advising her not to read J. S. Nicolson's *Thoth*: 'it is d — d bad.'

17 August 1888: Morris visited Birmingham to view a new window by Burne-Jones in St Philips's Cathedral.

18 August 1888: Jane returned to Kelmscott House. Morris published 'Notes on News' and finished the serialization of 'The Revolt of Ghent' in *Commonweal*.

19 August 1888: In the morning Morris had breakfast with the Burne-Joneses and Crom Price at the Grange. Here he saw Margaret Burne-Jones for the last time before her marriage. Price wrote in his *Diary*: 'Morris at breakfast – in capital form. Read a large slice of a new Romano-Gothic story [*The House of the Wolfings*] fr. Ms.' Later in the morning Morris gave an open-air speech for the Hammersmith Branch of the SL at Weltje Road. In the evening Morris delivered 'A Chapter in the History of Rome' (a lecture given from notes) at a meeting sponsored by the Hammersmith Branch of the SL at Kelmscott House.

21 August 1888: Morris sent Margaret Burne-Jones a 'Hammersmith Rug' as a wedding present: 'If it should at any time get dirty (as is likely since London will not be pulled down for a few months, I judge) if you send it to Merton we can wash it as good as new.' Morris and Jane travelled down to Kelmscott Manor.

22 August 1888: In the afternoon Morris and Jane walked to a pond near Buscot where Morris caught three perch.

23 August 1888: Morris fried the perch he had caught for breakfast: 'they were done and were not greasy but were not properly crisp.' After tea he and Jane rowed to the weir near Kelmscott.

24 August 1888: In the morning Morris picked gooseberries at Kelmscott Manor. In the evening Cormell Price arrived for a brief stay.

25 August 1888: Morris published 'Notes on News' and 'Socialist Work at Norwich' in *Commonweal*. Ernest Radford arrived at Kelmscott Manor on a bicycle and subsequently spent the night.

26 August 1888: In the morning Morris and the party staying at Kelmscott Manor rowed up the Thames towards Inglesham. After lunch they alighted at the Round House and walked a mile up the nearby canal. In the afternoon Morris, Cormell Price and Jane walked up to Inglesham Church leaving 'Radford & May lazing by the boat': 'It went to my heart on that beautiful afternoon to see the neglect and stupidity that had so marred the lovely building, yet it still looked lovely.' Emery Walker joined them on their return when they reached Buscot Lock.

27 August 1888: Morris returned to London.

28 August 1888: Morris reported to Jenny that a new steamboat pier had been finished opposite Kelmscott House which would 'make Kew & Hampton Court easier to us'. He spent the day at Merton.

31 August 1888: Bax arrived at Kelmscott House and spent the night.

September 1888: Elizabeth and Lily Yeats attended French classes which were being held at Kelmscott House.

1 September 1888: Bax and Morris visited Hampton Court to view the tapestries: 'I wanted to have a good look at the tapestries as we [are] ... beginning the figure of the Virgin in our big tapestry [*Adoration of the Magi*].' They then walked back to Kingston along the river bank. Morris wrote a letter of introduction to Charles Norton in the States on behalf of Sidney Webb. Bax spent another night at Kelmscott House.

2 September 1888: In the morning Morris attempted to give an open-air speech in the rain for the Hammersmith Branch of the SL at Latimer Road, London: 'we tried to hold a meeting at Latimer Road and could not get people together not at all to my surprise.' In the early evening he gave a second open-air speech for the same body at Weltje Road. Although not mentioned by LeMire, he also gave a dramatic reading from one of Joel Chandler Harris's tales at a 'Grand Concert' in aid of funds for S. W. Eden who had been out of work for several months.

4 September 1888: In the morning Morris travelled down to Kelmscott Manor. The *Pall Mall Gazette* published an article he had written entitled 'Ugly London'. Margaret Burne-Jones married J. W. Mackail at Rottingdean. The latter was later to write a biography of Morris – *The Life of William Morris* (1899) – at the request of Edward Burne-Jones.

5 September 1888: Morris organized a boat trip that set off from Kelmscott Manor for Bushey and Bampton at 2.30 pm. The whole Kelmscott Manor party took part except May who had some embroidery to do. At Bampton they visited the church which Morris described as 'shockingly "restored"'. The ladies returned from Bampton by trap while Morris and Walker rowed to Kelmscott. They arrived back at 10 pm.

6 September 1888: Dorothy Walker cooked dinner for the party at Kelmscott Manor.

7 September 1888: Morris and Emery Walker walked to Kencott to get a trap for Mrs Walker and her daughter Dorothy. The trap proved far from satisfactory as it was pulled by what Morris termed 'a little old rat of a pony'. It subsequently overturned when taking Mrs Walker and her daughter to the station. There were no injuries.

8 September 1888: Morris published 'Notes on News' in *Commonweal*.

9 September 1888: Morris was scheduled to give an open-air speech for the Hammersmith Branch of the SL at Weltje Road. It is probable that he missed this appointment as he was still staying at Kelmscott Manor.

10 September 1888: Morris and Jane went for a drive through Langford Broadwell and Kencott to Alvescott where they picked up Sparling.

11 September 1888: Morris returned to London from Kelmscott Manor by 'the *savage* train'. Later he visited Tilbury Docks to discuss carpets for the floor of one of the Orient Line steamers: 'Inside a mere floating hotel for the 1st. & 2nd. class passengers, and pretty much a workhouse for the 3rd. Snobbery rampant over everything.'

12 September 1888: In a letter to Samuel Reeves, Morris described *The House of the Wolfings* as a 'book [which] deals with the life of the Northern tribes while on the move through Central Europe, and the action of the story hangs upon their first hostile meeting with the Romans'.

14 September 1888: Morris called on Aleco Ionides about the decoration at Holland Park. Later he went to Merton.

15 September 1888: Morris published 'Notes on News' in *Commonweal*.

16 September 1888: Morris delivered an open-air speech for the Hammersmith Branch of the SL at Weltje Road.

18 September 1888: Morris left London for Kelmscott Manor. In a letter to James Mavor he wrote: 'women as a rule are very feeble on the artistic side, their line is business & mathematics.' In another letter he described *The House of the Wolfings* as 'not socialistic except by inference'.

21 September 1888: In the afternoon the Revd William Fulford Adams visited Morris at Kelmscott Manor.

22 September 1888: Morris was scheduled to give a poetry reading at an entertainment sponsored by the SL at the International Club, 40 Berner Street, Commercial Road, for the benefit of the Yarmouth Free-Speech Fund. However, it is unlikely that he attended this event as he was still at Kelmscott

Manor. He also published 'Notes on News' and 'A Modern Midas' in *Commonweal*.

23 September 1888: Morris gave an open-air speech for the Battersea Branch of the SDF at Battersea Park, London.

27 September 1888: Morris wrote to Laura Forster, an aunt of E. M. Forster, in connection with some leather bookbindings she had forwarded to him for his comments. A number of Laura Forster's bookbindings were later exhibited at the Arts and Crafts Exhibition Society's show in 1889.

30 September 1888: In the morning Morris gave an open-air speech for the Fulham Branch of the SL opposite the Liberal Club in Fulham. In the afternoon he delivered 'Equality' at an open-air meeting of the Clapham Common Branch of the SDF near the millpond on Clapham Common.

Autumn 1888: A collection of Morris's socialist lectures was published as *Signs of Change*.

October 1888: Charles Faulkner suffered a stroke three days after lecturing at Kelmscott House. Mackail wrote that as a result of this stroke Faulkner was paralysed and 'lingered in a state of living death for upwards of three years, with just so much intelligence as allowed of his being amused a little by the company of friends'. Morris & Co. completed the decoration of 1 Holland Park, London (*c.f.* March 1880).

3 October 1888: Morris was at Kelmscott Manor from where he asked the Chiswick Press to send him proofs of *The House of the Wolfings*. It is clear from this letter that he originally intended the book to have 'an illustration or two'. These never materialized although he did write a poem to be included on the title-page.

4 October 1888: The first Arts and Crafts Exhibition Society show opened at the New Gallery in Regent Street. Morris & Co. exhibited furniture, fabrics, carpets and embroideries. Morris contributed an article on textiles to the catalogue. This was later included in *Arts and Crafts Essays: By Members of the Arts and Crafts Exhibition Society* (Rivington Percival & Co. 1893). The exhibition ran until 15 December.

5 October 1888: Morris spent the day fishing at Kelmscott Manor where he caught 'a few little perch'.

6 October 1888: W. A. S. Benson joined the Morrises at Kelmscott Manor. Morris spent the afternoon fishing. His 'Notes on News' appeared in *Commonweal*.

8 October 1888: The party at Kelmscott visited Fairford. Blunt paid his first visit to Kelmscott Manor where he corrected proofs of the poems he had written in prison. These were published as *In Vinculis*. Jane designed the cover depicting shamrock leaves. It is possible that Morris was referring to Blunt's arrival when he wrote to Ellis that the 'new comer['s] ... short-comings I am not used to like I am to yours and mine; so that we have no standing cause of quarrel; which I think is a necessity to a really good under-standing'. In the same letter he described Mark Twain's *Tom Sawyer* as 'so *very* like Shakespeare, not to say Shelley.'

9 October 1888: Morris returned to London from Kelmscott Manor.

14 October 1888: In the morning Morris gave an open-air speech for the Fulham Branch of the SL opposite the Liberal Club in Fulham. In the afternoon he gave a second open-air speech in Hyde Park.

15 October 1888: Morris travelled down to Surrey on business: 'our client lives on the top of Hind-head; so what Cobbett would have said to him I am sure I don't know.'

20 October 1888: Morris spoke at the opening of the Fine Art and Industrial Exhibition in Manchester. This speech is not mentioned by LeMire.

21 October 1888: Morris delivered an open-air speech in Regent's Park.

25 October 1888: Morris was back at Kelmscott Manor: 'the river has grown small and bright and the fish won't bite.' Trees were delivered for a new orchard. Morris and Jenny visited St George's Church in Kelmscott where they were laying a new floor. During the work on the church thirteenth-century wall-paintings were uncovered.

26 October 1888: Morris had dinner with Mr and Mrs Birchall at Kelmscott Manor. He also received a letter from Webb: 'I thought more hopeful, I mean as to Charles [Faulkner] living, though I am afraid it is a bad job at best.'

27 October 1888: Morris published 'Notes on News' in *Commonweal*.

29 October 1888: Morris returned to London from Kelmscott Manor by the 2.40 pm train in order to attend a Council meeting of the SL.

November 1888: Morris's article 'The Revival of Handicraft' was published in the *Fortnightly Review*. An unsigned review of *Signs of Change* was published in *Today* (pp. 153–4).

1 November 1888: Morris delivered 'Tapestry and Carpet Weaving' at a meeting sponsored by the Arts and Crafts Exhibition Society at the New Gallery, Regent Street, London. Cobden-Sanderson recorded that Morris gave this lecture 'on a raised platform surrounded by products of the loom, at work upon a model loom specially constructed from his design'.

4 November 1888: In the morning Morris gave an open-air speech for the

Fulham Branch of the SL opposite the railway station at Fulham. Later he was scheduled to give another open-air speech for the Hammersmith Branch of the SL at Weltje Road.

9 November 1888: Blunt, and his wife and daughter, travelled to Paris. Jane wrote (8 November): 'I shall love to hear how you are, and what places you go to – the sight of your dear handwriting on the cover cheers me in a way nothing else can.'

10 November 1888: Morris gave a speech welcoming Mrs Albert Parsons, widow of one of the executed Chicago Anarchists, at a meeting sponsored by combined socialist and anarchist groups at St Paul's Cafe. He also published 'Notes on News' and an untitled article on the Chicago Anarchists in *Commonweal*.

11 November 1888: Morris gave an open-air speech at the Bloody Sunday memorial demonstration sponsored by London anarchist and socialist groups in Hyde Park.

12 November 1888: Morris served as chairman at a Bloody Sunday memorial meeting sponsored by London anarchist and socialist groups at the Store Street Hall, London. According to a letter he wrote to Jenny (dated 17 November) he also spoke at this meeting.

13 November 1888: Morris gave an open-air speech for the Clerkenwell (Central) Branch of the SL at Clerkenwell Green: 'there was a bit of a shindy but not till the end when I had gone away.'

14 November 1888: Following the disturbance at the meeting in Clerkenwell Green on the previous day Morris appeared at Clerkenwell Police Court to stand bail for an arrested comrade. This may have been Alfred Powers.

15 November 1888: Morris attended a lecture on 'Letter Press Printing' given by Emery Walker at the Arts and Crafts Exhibition Society's show at the New Gallery. According to May it was this lecture that determined Morris to set up the Kelmscott Press. Oscar Wilde described it in the *Pall Mall Gazette* as the most important lecture in the series. Morris himself said that Walker 'was very nervous and should have written down his words; but of course he knew his subject thoroughly well'. After the lecture an American in the audience came up to Walker and criticized him for some remarks he had made on American printing. Morris immediately came to Walker's defence and gave the American 'some candid speech' on the standard of American printing.

17 November 1888: In a letter to Thomas James Wise, Morris wrote of *The House of the Wolfings*: 'It is a story of the life of the Gothic tribes on their way through middle Europe, and their first meeting with the Romans in war. It is meant to illustrate the melting of the individual into the society of the tribes.'

In the evening Morris travelled up to Nottingham. He also published 'Notes on News' in *Commonweal*.

18 November 1888: In the morning Morris delivered 'Monopoly' at a meeting sponsored by the Nottingham Socialist Club at the Secular Hall, Beck Street, Nottingham. In the evening he delivered 'Equality' at a meeting sponsored by the Nottingham Socialist Club at the same venue.

20 November 1888: Morris was scheduled to deliver an open-air speech for the Hammersmith Branch of the SL outside Walham Green Church.

24 November 1888: A review by Oscar Wilde of the second volume of Morris's translation of the *Odyssey* appeared in the *Pall Mall Gazette* (p. 3).

25 November 1888: Morris was scheduled to deliver 'Equality' at a meeting sponsored by the Fulham Branch of the SL at the Branch Rooms, 8 Effie Road, Walham Green.

29 November 1888: Morris delivered a speech at a farewell meeting for Mrs Albert Parsons sponsored by combined anarchist and socialist organizations at the South Place Institute, London.

1 December 1888: Morris published 'Notes on News' in *Commonweal*.

2 December 1888: In the afternoon Morris delivered 'The Society of the Future' at a meeting sponsored by the Ancoats Recreation Committee at the New Islington Hall, Ancoats, Manchester: 'The audience seemed, as usual, much made up of the "lower middle-class" and the "aristocracy of labour".' In the evening he delivered 'Monopoly' at a meeting sponsored by the Manchester Democratic Club, SDF, at the Manchester Club Rooms, 20 Pilling Street, Rochdale Road, Manchester: 'The members of the branch were almost all of the non-aristocracy of labour, but many of them were as eager and earnest as could be desired.' During his time in Manchester Morris stayed at Mr Hunter Watts lodgings near the City Assize Courts: 'a dreary pretentious heap of buildings (by Waterhouse) built in a Gothic [style] which is an insult to the memory of our forefathers.' During his stay he purchased three postcards for Jenny's scrapbook.

3 December 1888: Morris delivered 'Art and Socialism' at a meeting sponsored by Bolton socialists in Bolton: 'The audience was fair only, the room not being full.'

4 December 1888: Morris delivered 'What Socialists Want' at a meeting sponsored by the Lancashire Council, SDF, at the Spinners' Hall, Saint Peter's Street, Blackburn: 'The audience were very eager, and took up all the points well.' In a letter to Jenny he recorded that he had recently seen *The House of the Wolfings* – all but the title-page – and expected it to be available soon: 'it will be a pretty piece of typography for modern times.'

5 December 1888: Morris delivered 'Art and Its Producers' at the first annual conference of the NAAA at the Rotunda, Liverpool. He arrived in Liverpool too late to hear Walter Crane's address to the conference.

6 December 1888: In the morning Morris was present at Cobden-Sanderson's lecture on 'Craft-Ideals' at the first annual conference of the NAAA in Liverpool: 'he preached Communism pure and simple.' In the evening he travelled to Rochdale where he delivered 'Monopoly' at a meeting sponsored by the Rochdale Social Democratic Club, SDF, at 46 Packer Street, Rochdale. In a conversation that followed this lecture some middle-class members of the audience challenged his claim that the workers in Rochdale were living in poverty. They claimed they were amply provided for by the new co-operative stores. In *Commonweal* Morris wrote: 'this I conclude to be a conventional tradition, the birth of the history of the sham co-operation which began with the good intentions of the Rochdale Pioneers, and has now by the confession of very moderate people become a reactionary force, "Divi" being the one thing looked to, and jobbing in "Co-op" shares being a favourite occupation among the small capitalists created by the system.'

7 December 1888: Morris returned to London.

8 December 1888: Morris published 'Notes on News' in *Commonweal*.

10 December 1888: Elizabeth Yeats recorded in her diary that this was a 'red letter day' as her sister had just been paid ten shillings for a week's embroidery at Kelmscott House.

12 December 1888: Morris was scheduled to deliver 'The Future of the Middle Classes' at a meeting sponsored by the Hammersmith Branch of the SL at Kelmscott House, Hammersmith.

13 December 1888: Jane wrote to Blunt: 'I have been too ill to exert myself much in any way – several attacks of fever closely following each other have weakened me more than usual, so that I can do so very little.'

15 December 1888: According to Buxton Forman the first thousand copies on ordinary paper of *The House of the Wolfings* were available by this time (although dated 1889). Sparling described the font of type 'finally chosen for *The House of the Wolfings* [as] the "Basel" Roman, in which a trial page of the *Earthly Paradise* had been set in 1860. This "Basel" type had been adapted from Froben's [1460–1527] roman letters by Charles Whittingham II [1795–1876].' Morris published 'Notes on News' and 'In and About Cottonopolis' in *Commonweal*.

16 December 1888: Morris delivered a lecture at a meeting sponsored by the

Nottingham Socialist Club at Swan's Buildings, Nottingham.

22 December 1888: Morris visited Stanmore Hall near Harrow on business: 'Our client sent his carriage to meet me and I couldn't help laughing to see the men I met touching their hats, clearly not to me, but to *it*.' Morris & Co.'s work on Stanmore Hall was to continue from 1888 to 1896. In the afternoon Morris saw Bax for the first time since September. He also published 'Notes on News' and 'Talk and Art' in *Commonweal*.

23 December 1888: In the morning Morris gave an open-air speech for the Fulham Branch of the SL at Walham Green: 'the meeting was small: really I think chiefly because the road was so very muddy that standing there was by no means pleasant unless you stood on the curb-stone.' In the evening he was scheduled to deliver 'Equality' at a meeting sponsored by the Hammersmith Branch of the SL at Kelmscott House, Hammersmith.

25 December 1888: Christmas was a low-key affair in the Morris household. Jenny was still staying at a nursing home in Malvern while May, according to Jane, was 'quite absorbed with her love affair' with Sparling. As a Christmas present Morris gave his mother one of the lamps sold by Morris & Co.

28 December 1888: Morris spent the day working at Merton: 'Things are going on rather well in the business and we are scheming several new things in our slow and long manner.' Jane wrote to Blunt: 'one of my sisters-in-law suggested [I should stand] for a Poor Law Guardian.'

29 December 1888: The Hammersmith branch of the SL held its annual Christmas party: 'it threatened at first to be rather dull; partly because we got over our music and recitations so quickly; but at last the good idea struck someone to set them dancing, and then they were happy – and noisy. Mr. Radford acted as master of the ceremonies, so to say, and entered into the fun with great spirit.' Morris published 'Notes on News' in *Commonweal*.

31 December 1888: A further one hundred copies of *The House of the Wolfings* on handmade paper were ready.

1889: An article entitled *The Art Socialists of London* by Mary Bacon Ford (illustrated with a portrait of Morris) appeared in *Cosmopolitan* (pp. 185–90). The *Trent* chintz and *Norwich* wallpaper were produced.

5 January 1889: Morris published 'Notes on News' in *Commonweal*.

6 January 1889: Morris delivered 'Socialism' at a meeting sponsored by the Fulham Branch of the SL at the Branch Rooms, 8 Effie Road, Walham Green, London. 'Clouds', the house that Webb had built for the Hon. Percy Wyndham, was burned to the ground as a result of a maid leaving a lighted candle in a cupboard.

7 January 1889: Morris travelled down to Hadham to visit his mother.

9 January 1889: In the morning Morris and his mother visited the Parish Church in Hadham which was being 'restored'. Later he returned to Kelmscott House where he discussed the destruction of 'Clouds' with Webb.

10 January 1889: Morris visited the Burne-Joneses at the Grange where they discussed the burning of 'Clouds': 'Georgie read me a letter to Margaret from one of the daughters which gave a really good account of the scene'.

12 January 1889: Cormell Price visited Morris at Kelmscott House. Morris published 'Notes on News' in *Commonweal*.

13 January 1889: Morris gave an open-air speech for the Hammersmith Branch of the SL at Weltje Road, London.

15 January 1889: Morris voted at Merton in the first London County Council elections. In the evening he held a dinner party for the De Morgans, Cormell Price and Emery Walker.

16 January 1889: Morris was scheduled to speak at the annual meeting to commemorate the Paris Commune sponsored by the SL and the SDF at South Place. In the evening Kropotkin had dinner at Kelmscott House and then lectured in the coachhouse. Morris described Kropotkin as 'far from well'. Jane wrote to Blunt about Jenny: 'I am cheered ... by the news of Jenny ... I called on her Doctor in London the other day, he said he was more hopeful than ever about her & he expected to cure her entirely in time, she is certainly very much better than she was two months ago, the attacks are getting slighter and she does not quite lose consciousness.'

17 January 1889: Morris sent a four-volume set of Keats' poetry to Jenny for her birthday: 'I wanted you to have a nice parcel on your birthday, because that's a thing I remember I used to like myself.' At this time she was still in the nursing home in Malvern.

19 January 1889: Morris published the first part of his dialogue 'Whigs Astray' in *Commonweal*.

20 January 1889: Morris gave an open-air speech for the Hammersmith Branch of the SL at Weltje Road, London.

21 January 1889: In a letter to Ellis, Morris wrote: 'I am beginning to learn something about the art of type-setting; and I now see what a difference there is between the work of the conceited numskulls of to-day and that of the 15th and 16th century printers.'

26 January 1889: Morris published 'Notes on News' and the final part of his dialogue 'Whigs Astray' in *Commonweal*. An unsigned review of *The House of the Wolfings* appeared in the *Saturday Review* (pp. 101–102).

29 January 1889: In a letter to Jenny, Morris stated that he had just started writing *The Roots of the Mountains*. Jane, who had been visiting her mother-in-law at Much Hadham, returned home in the evening.

30 January 1889: Morris published a letter on Mr Shaw-Lefevre's 'restoration' of the Monumental Chapel at Westminster Abbey in the *Daily News*. He also delivered 'Socialism' at a meeting sponsored by the Hammersmith Branch of the SL at Kelmscott House, Hammersmith.

2 February 1889: Morris published 'Notes on News' in *Commonweal*.

3 February 1889: Morris gave an open-air speech for the Hammersmith Branch of the SL at Walham Green, London.

9 February 1889: A review of *The House of the Wolfings* by Charles Elton appeared in the *Academy* (vol. 25, pp. 85–6). Morris published 'Notes on News' in *Commonweal*. In the evening Morris caught the night train to Glasgow.

10 February 1889: Morris arrived in Glasgow at 8 am. In the evening he delivered 'The Society of the Future' at a meeting sponsored by the Glasgow Branch of the SL at the Albion Hall, Glasgow. According to Glasier there was an audience of 800 people at this meeting.

11 February 1889: Morris delivered 'Gothic Architecture' at a meeting sponsored by the Haldane Trustees at the Corporation Galleries, Glasgow. Afterwards he had dinner at the Arts Club – 'a bore' – and then went to stay the night with Professor John Nichol at 14 Montgomerie Crescent, Kelvinside: 'He is a crony of Watts and Swinburne and talkative & amusing, and was very cordial with me.'

12 February 1889: Morris delivered 'Arts and Crafts' before the Glasgow School of Art at the Corporation Galleries, Sauchiehall Street, Glasgow. Jane wrote of her mother-in-law: 'she is the liveliest old lady possible, she walks and takes drives in an open carriage every day except in the coldest weather, and reads and talks incessantly, she is quite happy and I really think she expects to live another twenty years.'

13 February 1889: At midday Morris caught the train from Glasgow to Edinburgh. In the evening he delivered 'Equality' at a meeting sponsored by the Edinburgh Branch of the SLLL at the Queen Street Hall, Edinburgh: 'We had a good audience … one of the best I have had there.' Morris stayed the night with Glasse at 16 Tantalton Place, Edinburgh.

14 February 1889: Morris delivered a speech 'on art education' at the annual distribution of prizes of the Macclesfield School of Art and Science. He described Macclesfield 'as a shabby town'.

15 February 1889: In the afternoon Morris returned to London.

17 February 1889: In the morning Morris gave an open-air speech for the Hammersmith Branch of the SL at Weltje Road. In the evening he gave a lecture for the West Kensington Park Club in Kensington.

23 February 1889: Morris published 'Notes on News' in *Commonweal*.

24 February 1889: Morris gave an open-air speech for the Hammersmith Branch of the SL at Latimer Road, London.

26 February 1889: Morris wrote to Kropotkin including a cheque for £25 towards the costs of a series of lectures the latter planned to give at Kensington Town Hall. These lectures were never given.

27 February 1889: John Burns wrote to Morris requesting that he and Walter Crane design the seal for the new London County Council. Morris declined and the seal was eventually designed by Walter Crane.

March 1889: Morris's article on 'Westminster Abbey and its Monuments' appeared in the *Nineteenth Century*.

1 March 1889: Morris delivered 'How Shall We Live Then?' at a meeting sponsored by the Fabian Society in Bloomsbury Hall, London.

2 March 1889: Morris published 'Notes on News' and a poem 'Mine and Thine' in *Commonweal*.

3 March 1889: Morris delivered 'How Shall We Live Then?' at a meeting sponsored by the Hammersmith Branch of the SL at Kelmscott House.

9 March 1889: Morris published 'Notes on News' in *Commonweal*.

11 March 1889: Morris was at Kelmscott Manor where he was working on *The Roots of the Mountains*.

13 March 1889: In a letter to an unknown recipient Morris gave his views on tobacco (he was a smoker): 'I should say that tobacco seems to me a more dangerous intoxicant than liquors because people can and do smoke to excess without becoming beastly and a nuisance.'

16 March 1889: Morris published 'Notes on News' and his poem 'All for the Cause' in *Commonweal*. He also wrote a letter to the Chairman of the meeting to celebrate the Paris Commune, apologizing for his absence as a result of an attack of gout.

17 March 1889: Jane wrote to Blunt: 'We came back a few days ago bringing Jenny home, but Alas! she is not as well as we had hoped for – still she is very much better than when she left us in the autumn.'

23 March 1889: Morris published 'Notes on News', 'To Manchester Friends' and a letter apologizing for being unable to attend the celebration of the Paris Commune in *Commonweal*.

26 March 1889: Morris moved a resolution against 'legal monopoly' at a meeting of the Hendon Debating Society. This engagement is not mentioned by LeMire.

30 March 1889: Morris published 'Notes on News' and began the serialization of his lecture 'The Society of the Future' in *Commonweal*.

31 March 1889: Morris was scheduled to deliver 'Equality' at a meeting sponsored by the Southwark and Lambeth Branches of the SDF at the Nelson Coffee Tavern, Westminster Bridge Road, London.

6 April 1889: Morris published 'Notes on News', 'Ducks and Drakes' and continued the serialization of 'The Society of the Future' in *Commonweal*.

8 April 1889: Morris was at Merton.

9 April 1889: Morris delivered 'Gothic Architecture' at a meeting sponsored by the Guild and School of Handicraft which was held in the Lecture Room of Toynbee Hall for students of the University Settlements scheme.

13 April 1889: Morris published 'Notes on News' and concluded the serialization of 'The Society of the Future' in *Commonweal*.

14 April 1889: Morris was scheduled to deliver 'Equality' at the Fulham Liberal Club at Walham Green, London.

17 April 1889: Morris published another letter on the restoration of the monuments at Westminster Abbey in the *Daily News*.

20 April 1889: Morris gave an open-air speech for the Hammersmith Branch of the SL at Bridge End, Hammersmith. He also published 'Notes on News' in *Commonweal*.

22 April 1889: Morris delivered a lecture on architectural restoration at the Art Workers' Guild, at Barnard's Inn Hall, London.

27 April 1889: Morris gave an open-air speech for the Hammersmith Branch of the SL at Weltje Road, London. He also published 'Notes on News' in *Commonweal*.

4 May 1889: Morris published 'Notes on News', a 'Statement of Principles' and an untitled paragraph in *Commonweal*.

5 May 1889: Morris gave an open-air speech for the Hammersmith Branch of the SL at Beadon Road, London.

9 May 1889: Morris travelled to Westbury on a 'grey and stormy' day: 'The town is little and, as I expected, dull, dull, dull.'

10 May 1889: Morris had 'a genuine addled egg' for breakfast at the Lopes Arms in Westbury. In the morning he travelled to Edington where he greatly admired the church: 'one of my dream-churches, so big and splendid.' He then returned to Westbury and in the early afternoon travelled to Bradford: 'Quite a pretty town and as gay as gay.'

11 May 1889: Morris was reading Edward Bellamy's *Looking Backward*. He also published 'Notes on News' in *Commonweal*.

12 May 1889: In the morning Morris gave an open-air speech for the Hammersmith Branch of the SL at Beadon Road, London. In the evening he gave a lecture on Edward Bellamy's *Looking Backward* and Grant Allen's article 'Individualism and Socialism' at a meeting sponsored by the Hammersmith Branch of the SL at Kelmscott House.

13 May 1889: In a letter to Glasier, Morris referred to Grant Allen's article in the *Contemporary Review* on 'Individualism and Socialism' and Edward Bellamy's *Looking Backward*: 'I wouldn't care to live in such a cockney paradise as he imagines.' In a letter to Joseph Lane, written on the same day, Morris was pessimistic about the health of Charles Faulkner: 'after seeming to get a little better he has now taken a turn for the worse, and I am expecting any day to hear of his death.'

18 May 1889: Morris published 'Notes on News' and a letter opposing the anarchists in *Commonweal*.

19 May 1889: In the morning Morris gave an open-air speech for the Hammersmith Branch of the SL at Beadon Road, Hammersmith. In the evening he delivered an open-air speech for the Hammersmith Branch of the SL at Weltje Road, Hammersmith.

21 May 1889: Morris wrote to the actor Henry Irving in support of the application of Joseph Skipsey for the post as Custodian of Shakespeare's House at Stratford. Skipsey was successful and held the post until 1891.

23 May 1889: Morris was staying at Kelmscott Manor. In the afternoon he and his family visited the Revd Oswald Birchall.

2 June 1889: In the morning Morris delivered an open-air speech for the Hammersmith Branch of the SL at Beadon Road, Hammersmith. In the evening he delivered another open-air speech for the same group at Weltje Road, Hammersmith.

4 June 1889: Morris was scheduled to deliver 'Monopoly' at a meeting sponsored by the Northern Radical Club and the Southwark and Lambeth Branches of the SDF at 108 Westminster Bridge Road, London. Jane returned to London from Kelmscott Manor.

7 June 1889: Charles Charrington and Janey Achurch's production of Ibsen's *A Doll's House* opened at the Novelty Theatre amidst great controversy. From a letter written to Blunt on 26 October 1890 it is clear that Jane had seen this play. It is uncertain if Morris also attended although it is possible as he referred to the play in *Commonweal*. Morris wrote to Edmund Henry Morgan undertaking to repair the stained-glass windows the Firm had installed in the Jesus College Chapel.

8 June 1889: Morris published 'Notes on News' in *Commonweal*.

9 June 1889: The fifth annual conference of the SL took place. At this meeting the anarchists on the League's Council were strengthened by the election of H. Davis, Samuels and John Turner.

10 June 1889: Morris was scheduled to give a poetry reading at an entertainment at the SL Hall in aid of the SL Propaganda Fund.

15 June 1889: Morris published 'Notes on News' in *Commonweal*.

16 June 1889: Morris delivered an open-air speech for the Hammersmith Branch of the SL at Beadon Road, Hammersmith.

20 June 1889: Morris and Jenny, who were staying at Kelmscott Manor, visited Great Coxwell, where they saw the thirteenth-century tithe barn, and Little Coxwell, where they viewed the church.

22 June 1889: Morris reviewed Bellamy's *Looking Backward* in *Commonweal*. He also contributed his regular 'Notes on News' column to the paper.

27 June 1889: Morris was scheduled to deliver 'Monopoly' before the New Labour Club at 5 Victoria Park Square, Bethnal Green, London.

29 June 1889: Morris published 'Notes on News' in *Commonweal*.

30 June 1889: Morris was scheduled to give an open-air speech for the Hammersmith Branch of the SL at Weltje Road, London.

6 July 1889: Morris published 'Notes on News' and 'Under an Elm-Tree' in *Commonweal*.

7 July 1889: Morris gave an open-air speech for the Hammersmith Branch of the SL at Weltje Road, London.

13 July 1889: Morris, along with other delegates of the League, met at London Bridge Station at the start of a trip to the International Socialist Working-Men's Congress in Paris. They then travelled to Newhaven by train 'and whiled away the time in singing songs and selling a few numbers of *Commonweal*'.

14 July 1889: The party left Newhaven at 3 am in the morning and arrived at

Dieppe at 10 am. They reach Paris at 1.30 pm and were met at the station by various French comrades. They spent the rest of the day, as Morris put it in *Commonweal*, 'wandering about the city and seeing what I should irreverently call the "fun of the fair"'. It was probably during this sightseeing trip that Morris had his first view of the Eiffel Tower.

15 July 1889: In the morning Morris verified the mandates of the English-speaking delegates. There were so many representatives at the conference that it had to be moved from the Salle Petrelle to a theatre called the Fantasies Parisienne in the neighbouring Rue Rochechouart. It became clear during the day that there were two parties at the conference: those who wished to remain independent and those who wanted to combine with the Possibilist conference which was taking place nearby. This issue dominated the first day's proceeding much to Morris's disgust.

16 July 1889: In the morning Morris gave a speech against the amalgamation of the Possibilist and the International Socialist Conferences at the International Socialist Working-Men's Congress at the Fantasies Parisienne, rue Rochechouart, Paris. In the event it was decided that the possibility of fusing the two conferences should be investigated.

17 July 1889: No agreement could be reached between the two conferences. Morris wrote in *Commonweal*: 'We had thus wasted two whole days in discussing a matter which in the opinion of the delegates of the Socialist League ought never to have been discussed at all.'

18 July 1889: In the morning Morris read a report on the progress and condition of English socialism at the International Socialist Working-Men's Congress at the Fantasies Parisienne, rue Rochechouart, Paris.

19 July 1889[?]: From Morris's account in the *Commonweal* it would appear that on this evening the Paris Municipality held a reception for the delegates of both Congresses at the Hotel de Ville. On the same evening Louise Michel spoke to other delegates at a party at Maxime Lisbonne's 'Taverne dur Bagne' (a hostelry decorated as a prison). Morris was not present at either event as he 'had to spend the night in writing out my report from … notes'. There is some doubt about the date of these events due to an inconsistency in Morris's *Commonweal* article. They may have taken place the evening before.

20 July 1889: After the morning session of the conference Morris, Kitz and Tarleton left for Rouen. In *Commonweal* Morris wrote 'the impression made on me by attendance at the International Congress is that such gatherings are not favourable for the dispatch of business, and their real use is as demonstrations, and that it would be better to organize them as such.'

27 July 1889: Morris published 'Impressions of the Paris Congress – I' in *Commonweal.*

29 July 1889: Morris gave an open-air speech for the Hammersmith Branch of the SL at Weltje Road, Hammersmith.

August 1889: A review of *The House of the Wolfings* by Henry Hewlett appeared in the *Nineteenth Century* (vol. 26, pp. 337–41). Hewlett wrote: 'None of his recent writings will be generally read, I think, with more unqualified pleasure.'

3 August 1889: Morris published 'Notes on News' and 'Impressions of the Paris Congress – II' in *Commonweal.*

11 August 1889: In the morning Morris gave an open-air speech for the North Kensington Branch of the SL at Latimer Road, London. In the evening he was scheduled to give an open-air speech for the Hammersmith Branch of the SL at Walham Green, Fulham.

13 August 1889: Morris purchased a copy of *Lorna Doone*, which he had read before: 'It really isn't bad.'

16 August 1889: Morris spent the day at Merton where he was visited by Annie Catherwood.

17 August 1889: Morris published 'Trial by Judge v Trial by Jury' and a letter on anarchism in *Commonweal.*

21 August 1889: Morris travelled down to Kelmscott Manor.

24 August 1889: Morris published 'Notes on News' in *Commonweal.*

26 August 1889: Morris visited Inglesham and then went to Lechlade to see Cormell Price off at the station.

28 August 1889: In the afternoon Morris travelled to Yarmouth where he delivered 'Monopoly' at a meeting sponsored by the Yarmouth Branch of the SL at the Cora Hall: 'I got there on the most beautiful evening with the low sun setting over the great flats.' After the meeting he spent the night in Yarmouth.

29 August 1889: In the morning Morris visited St Nicholas's Church, Yarmouth – which he recorded had been 'woefully restored' – and walked two miles along the beach before returning to London by train.

2 September 1889: The twenty-second Trades Union Congress met in Dundee. It continued until 6 September 1889. Jane wrote to Blunt: 'How I wish I had the real close companionship of either of my children.'

3 September 1889: John Henry Middleton came to stay at Kelmscott Manor. At the time Jane and Jenny were alone at the house.

7 September 1889: Morris published 'The Lesson of the Hour' in *Commonweal*. He returned to Kelmscott Manor.

10 September 1889: Morris published a letter on 'The Preservation of Peterborough Cathedral' in the *Pall Mall Gazette*. According to Mackail, Morris had known the building since he was a child 'and felt towards it as though he had been one of its own builders.'

14 September 1889: An unsigned review – actually by Theodore Watts-Dunton – of *The House of the Wolfings* appeared in the *Athenaeum* (vol. 2, pp. 347–50). Watts-Dunton described the book as 'a delight to those who in literature are alone worth delighting, the cultivated students of all that is sweet and light and noble in literary art'. Morris published 'Notes on News' in *Commonweal*.

16 September 1889: The London Dock Strike ended when the dock directors agreed to the strikers' demand for a wage rate of 6d an hour.

20 September 1889: The *Pall Mall Gazette* published another letter from Morris on Peterborough Cathedral.

21 September 1889: Morris published 'Notes on News' in *Commonweal*.

28 September 1889: Morris published 'Notes on News' in *Commonweal*.

5 October 1889: Morris contributed some untitled notes to *Commonweal*.

11 October 1889: Morris finished *The Roots of the Mountains*.

13 October 1889: Morris was scheduled to deliver 'The Class Struggle' at a meeting sponsored by the Hammersmith Club in Hammersmith.

15 October 1889: Morris visited Georgiana Burne-Jones who was suffering from toothache. His attitude to Victorian autograph hunters can be guaged from the following response to one such request: 'I don't much sympathise with the autograph-hunter; but I have no excuse to give for not writing my name for you except that I don't like the trouble of doing so, which perhaps would make my refusal seem churlish, so take this scrawl since you want it.'

16 October 1889: Morris went to see the printers about the final arrangements for *The Roots of the Mountains*.

17 October 1889: Morris had sprats for dinner: 'I bought them myself (3d. per lb.).'

19 October 1889: Morris published 'Notes on News' in *Commonweal*.

20 October 1889: Morris was scheduled to give an unnamed lecture at a meeting sponsored by the Yarmouth Branch of the SL at Yarmouth. He stayed the night.

21 October 1889: Morris returned to London from Yarmouth.

22 October 1889: Morris travelled down to Kelmscott Manor to stay with Jane and Jenny.

26 October 1889: In the afternoon Morris returned from Kelmscott Manor to London. He published 'Notes on News' in *Commonweal.*

27 October 1889: Morris delivered 'Why Working Men Ought To Be Socialists' at a meeting sponsored by the North Kensington Branch of the SL at the Clarendon Coffee Tavern in London.

28 October 1889: The Second Annual Art Congress sponsored by the National Association for the Advancement of Art was officially opened.

29 October 1889: Morris delivered 'The Art of Dyeing' at a meeting sponsored by the NAAA as part of its annual Art Congress. The meeting was held at the Museum of Science and Art, Edinburgh.

30 October 1889: In the morning Morris delivered 'The Arts and Crafts of Today' as the presidential address to the Applied Art Section of the NAAA at a meeting held in Queen Street Hall, Edinburgh. Glasse recorded that 'our comrade Morris drew the largest gathering of the week. Nothing could have been better than the effect produced, for the audience not merely admired its ability, but were moved by its reasoning.' In the afternoon Morris was chairman of a meeting of the Applied Art Section of the NAAA at the National Portrait Gallery, Edinburgh: 'I was in the chair at some monumentally dull papers; and you may imagine how I fidgetted.'

31 October 1889: Morris acted as chairman of the general conference of the NAAA sections at the National Portrait Gallery, Edinburgh.

Late October 1889: Jane went to stay with R. W. Hudson and his wife at Tyny-Coed, Bettws-y-Coed, in North Wales. She had certainly arrived by 31 October.

November 1889: *The Roots of the Mountains* was published by Reeves & Turner. Morris described it as 'just out' in a letter he wrote to his mother dated 16 November 1889. 'Day Dreams', a drawing by Rossetti, was reproduced in James Mavor's *Scottish Art Review* with Morris's permission.

1 November 1889: Morris delivered a lecture on socialism at a meeting sponsored by the Edinburgh branch of the SLLL at the Oddfellows' Hall, Forrest Road, Edinburgh.

2 November 1889: In the afternoon Morris, Crane, Walker and Cobden-Sanderson travelled from Edinburgh to Glasgow. Here Morris delivered 'On the Origins of Ornamental Art' at a meeting sponsored by the Glasgow Branch of the SL and the Edinburgh Branch of the SLLL at the Albert Hall, Edinburgh. It is possible that it was on this occasion, as Walter Crane recorded in *An Artist's Reminiscences*, that the scheme to establish the Kelmscott Press was first discussed.

3 November 1889: In the afternoon Morris spoke at a reception organized by the Edinburgh socialists at the Waterloo Rooms, Edinburgh. This speech is not mentioned by LeMire. Morris also acted as chairman – and gave a short speech – at a lecture given by Walter Crane before the Glasgow Branch of the SL at the Waterloo Hall, Glasgow.

7 November 1889: Morris delivered 'Gothic Architecture' at a meeting sponsored by the Arts and Crafts Exhibition Society at the opening of their second exhibition at the New Gallery, Regent Street, London. The exhibition continued until 7 December.

9 November 1889: Morris travelled to Liverpool. He wore a red ribbon in his buttonhole so that he could be easily recognized by anyone who met him at the station in Liverpool. He published 'Notes on News' in *Commonweal*.

10 November 1889: In the afternoon Morris delivered 'Monopoly' at a meeting sponsored by the Liverpool Secular Society at the Lower Concert Hall, Lord Nelson Street, Liverpool. In the evening he delivered 'The Class Struggle' at a meeting held at the same venue.

11 November 1889: Morris gave a speech at a Bloody Sunday memorial meeting sponsored by various London socialist groups at the South Place Institute, Finsbury, London.

16 November 1889: In a letter to his mother Morris wrote: 'I go to Merton now by a new line which takes less time and saves me the underground part of the journey, which is much more comfortable.' He published 'Notes on News' in *Commonweal*. In the evening he travelled up to Derbyshire where he stayed with his sister Emma and her husband Joseph Oldham at North Wingfield Rectory.

17 November 1889: Morris delivered 'Monopoly' at a meeting sponsored by the Chesterfield Discussion Society in Chesterfield. Morris opened the meeting by reading from his poem 'The Message of the March Wind'.

18 November 1889: Morris delivered 'Socialism' at a meeting sponsored by Sheffield socialists at the Cambridge Hall, Sheffield: 'I had a large and enthusiastic audience.'

20 November 1889: The *Pall Mall Gazette* published a review of *The Roots of the Mountains* (p. 3) in which it parodied Morris's style as 'Wardour Street English': 'A goodly book in sooth it is which William the Hall-Bedecker, by some called the Folk-Fellowship-Furtherer, and others Will o' the Wildgoose-Chase, hath put forth in these days to gladden this our winter-tide withal.'

Morris was scheduled to deliver 'Gothic Architecture' at a meeting sponsored by the Hammersmith Branch of the SL at Kelmscott House, Hammersmith.

21 November 1889: It is clear from a letter to F. S. Ellis that Morris was already considering the possibility of designing his own print-face: 'Walker and I both think Jenson's the best model.'

23 November 1889: Morris published 'Notes on News' and his poem 'A Death Song' in *Commonweal*.

24 November 1889: Morris was scheduled to deliver 'Socialism' at a meeting sponsored by the Star Radical Club at 8 Mayall Road, Herne Hill, Brixton, London.

29 November 1889: Jane wrote to Blunt from North Wales: 'I have had a weary time this past fortnight, feeling unusually depressed and out of health.'

30 November 1889: Morris travelled to Manchester where he was met by Charles Rowley. In the evening he delivered 'The Class Struggle' at a meeting sponsored by the Manchester Social Democratic Club at the Secular Hall, Rusholme Road, Manchester. He also published 'Notes on News' in *Commonweal*.

1 December 1889: In the afternoon Morris delivered 'The Revolt of Ghent' at a meeting sponsored by the Ancoats Recreation Committee at the New Islington Hall, Ancoats, Manchester. In the evening he gave a speech at a meeting sponsored by the Ancoats 'At Home' Committee at the New Islington Hall, Ancoats, Manchester.

3 December 1889: Jane probably returned to London from North Wales. Referring to her return in a letter to Blunt she wrote: 'I found Jenny very ill ... she scarcely spoke for some days.'

7 December 1889: Morris published 'Notes on News' in *Commonweal*.

8 December 1889: Jenny had an epileptic fit.

10 December 1889: Morris was scheduled to give a lecture for the New Fellowship at the SDF Hall, 337 The Strand, London.

11 December 1889: Jenny saw the doctor. Jane wrote: 'she seemed to gain fresh hope and began to talk of her chances of a complete recovery.'

14 December 1889: Morris published 'Notes on News' and began the serialization of his lecture 'Monopoly' in *Commonweal*.

21 December 1889: Morris concluded the serialization of 'Monopoly' in *Commonweal*.

23 December 1889: Jenny and a friend went to visit the Chiswick Horticultural

Gardens. Morris wrote: 'I remember as clearly as if it were yesterday going with father there when I was quite a little boy, and have never been inside the place since.'

28 December 1889: Morris published 'Notes on News' in *Commonweal*.

29 December 1889: Jane wrote to Blunt: 'Jenny got better quite suddenly and has had no attacks since of a serious nature; her's is certainly the most mysterious illness.'

1890: Morris's participation in the work of Morris & Co. began to diminish when Wardle retired and the Oxford Street Showroom managers became partners. George Washington Henry Jack was appointed Chief Designer for Morris & Co. He introduced some new types of furniture in a quasi-eighteenth-century style. Morris and Burne-Jones presented the *Adoration of the Magi* tapestry to Exeter College, Oxford.

January 1890: Morris's lecture, 'Art and Industry in the Fourteenth Century', was published in *Time*.

11 January 1890: Chapter I and part of chapter II of *News from Nowhere* appeared in *Commonweal*.

18 January 1890: Chapter II of *News from Nowhere* was concluded in *Commonweal*.

19 January 1890: Morris delivered an open-air speech for the Hammersmith Branch of the SL at Weltje Road, Hammersmith.

22 January 1890: Morris delivered 'How Shall We Live Then?' at a meeting sponsored by the North London Branch of the SL at 6 Windmill Street, Tottenham Court Road, London.

25 January 1890: Morris published a long review of the *Fabian Essays* in *Commonweal*. The first part of chapter III of *News from Nowhere* also appeared in the paper.

February 1890: Morris's poem 'The Hall and the Wood' appeared in the *English Illustrated Magazine*. While Morris and Jane were away from Kelmscott House, Lily Yeats was asked to stay with May as her chaperone. Morris is supposed to have said, after she agreed, 'What a joke if May does not want you'. Lily Yeats was later to refer to May as 'the Gorgon'.

1 February 1890: The second part of chapter III and chapter IV of *News from Nowhere* appeared in *Commonweal*. Morris also published 'Notes on News' in the paper.

2 February 1890: In the afternoon Morris delivered 'How Shall We Live Then?' at a meeting sponsored by the Leicester Radical Club at the Club

Rooms, Vine Street, Leicester. In the evening he delivered 'What Socialists Want' at a meeting sponsored by the Leicester Branch of the SL at the Co-operative Hall, Leicester.

4 February 1890: Morris sent John Burns a copy of *A Dream of John Ball.*

8 February 1890: An unsigned review of *The Roots of the Mountains* appeared in the *Spectator* (vol. 64, pp. 208–209). Morris published 'Notes on News' and chapter V or *News from Nowhere* in *Commonweal.*

9 February 1890: Morris was scheduled to deliver 'Equality' at a meeting sponsored by the Hammersmith Branch of the SL at Kelmscott House.

11 February 1890: Jane wrote to Blunt: 'my husband is writing and publishing in "Commonweal" another story [*News from Nowhere*] giving a picture of what he considers likely to take place later on, when Socialism shall have taken deeper roots.'

12 February 1890: Morris was scheduled to act as chairman of the semi-annual meeting of the Socialist Co-operative Federation at the SDF Hall, 337 The Strand, London.

15 February 1890: Morris published 'Notes on News' and chapter VI of *News from Nowhere* in *Commonweal.*

18 February 1890: Morris wrote to Bernard Quaritch agreeing to purchase a first edition of Cicero's *Orationes* (1471) and Flavius Josephus's *Opera* (c.1478) for £45.

22 February 1890: Morris wrote to John Oldrid Scott, on behalf of SPAB, complaining about the repairs the latter was carrying out at St Mary's Church, Thame. He also published 'Notes on News' and chapter VII of *News from Nowhere* in *Commonweal.*

26 February 1890: Morris wrote to Oliver Elton thanking him for sending him a copy of his Icelandic translation of Einar Haflidason's *The Life of Laurence, Bishop of Holar in Iceland.*

1 March 1890: Chapter VIII of *News from Nowhere* appeared in *Commonweal.*

2 March 1890: Morris delivered 'How Shall We Live Then?' at a meeting sponsored by the North Kensington Branch of the SL at the Clarendon Coffee Tavern, London.

8 March 1890: The first part of chapter IX of *News from Nowhere* appeared in *Commonweal.* Morris also published 'Coal in Kent' and 'Christianity and Socialism' in the paper.

11 March 1890: Morris delivered 'The Class Struggle' at a meeting sponsored by the Leicester Branch of the SL at the Co-operative Hall, High Street,

Leicester.

14 March 1890: Morris wrote to Ford Madox Brown agreeing to second the election of George Wooliscraft Rhead to membership of the Art Workers' Guild. The latter was elected a member on 11 April 1890.

15 March 1890: The second part of chapter IX of *News from Nowhere* appeared in *Commonweal.*

16 March 1890: Morris delivered an open-air speech for the Hammersmith Branch of the SL at Walham Green, Fulham.

19 March 1890: Morris delivered a speech at a Paris Commune memorial meeting sponsored by combined London socialist and anarchist groups at the South Place Institute, Finsbury, London.

20 March 1890: Morris travelled down to Torquay.

22 March 1890: Morris sent a letter of support to the workers on strike at Cours in France. He also published 'Notes on News' and 'The Great Coal Strike' in *Commonweal.* Chapter IX and the first part of chapter X of *News from Nowhere* also appeared in the paper.

24 March 1890: Morris spent the day at Merton.

25 March 1890: Morris delivered 'The Class Struggle' at a meeting sponsored by Leeds socialists at the Grand Assembly Rooms, Leeds.

29 March 1890: Morris published 'Notes' and the second part of chapter X of *News from Nowhere* in *Commonweal.*

30 March 1890: Morris purchased from Bernard Quaritch a copy of Gerard Leeu's 1480 edition of the *Dialogus Creaturarum.*

31 March 1890: Morris purchased a rare edition of Aesop (Augsburg 1498). He also delivered an open-air speech for the Hammersmith Branch of the SL at the Bridge-End, Hammersmith.

2 April 1890: Morris, Jenny and May travelled down to Kelmscott Manor to spend Easter. Jane did not accompany them as she was 'far from well'.

5 April 1890: The party at Kelmscott Manor – but not May – travelled by boat as far as Donkey Reach. Morris published 'Notes on News' and concluded chapter X of *News from Nowhere* in *Commonweal.*

9 April 1890: Morris was due to return to London from Kelmscott Manor.

12 April 1890: Morris delivered 'Gothic Architecture' before the Artists' Club at the Club Rooms, Eberle Street, Liverpool. Chapter XI of *News from Nowhere* appeared in *Commonweal.* Morris also published 'Notes on News' in the paper.

13 April 1890: In the afternoon Morris delivered 'The Development of Modern Society' at a meeting sponsored by the Liverpool Socialist Society at the Rodney Hall, Liverpool. In the evening he delivered 'The Social Outlook' at the same venue.

19 April 1890: Chapter XII of *News from Nowhere* appeared in *Commonweal.*

26 April 1890: Chapters XIII and XIV of *News from Nowhere* appeared in *Commonweal.*

27 April 1890: Morris gave an open-air speech for the Hammersmith Branch of the SL at the Bridge-End, Hammersmith.

1 May 1890: The SL held its May Day celebrations on Clerkenwell Green. Only a few thousand turned up. This contrasted with the meeting held by the London Trades Council on Sunday, 4 May 1890, which attracted more than 100,000.

2 May 1890: Morris delivered 'Gothic Architecture' at a meeting sponsored by the Fabians at the St James's Hall.

3 May 1890: Morris published 'Labour Day' and 'Notes on News' in *Commonweal.* The first part of chapter XV of *News from Nowhere* also appeared in *Commonweal.*

10 May 1890: The conclusion of chapter XV and the first part of chapter XVI of *News from Nowhere* appeared in *Commonweal.*

11 May 1890: Morris gave an-open-air speech for the Hammersmith Branch of the SL at the Bridge-End, Hammersmith.

12 May 1890: Morris appeared as the invalid in the one act play *The Duchess of Bayswater & Co.* which was performed in aid of *Commonweal* at a hall in Tottenham Court Road. Shaw was also in the cast. Morris afterwards read the 'Tar Baby' from Uncle Remus.

13 May 1890: Blunt visited Jane at Kelmscott House: 'Sitting in the garden on a bench she told me more about Rossetti than I had yet heard from her.'

17 May 1890: Morris published 'The "Eight Hours" and the Demonstration' in *Commonweal.* The conclusion of chapter XVI and the first part of chapter XVII of *News from Nowhere* also appeared in the paper.

18 May 1890: Morris gave an open-air speech for the Hammersmith Branch of the SL at the Bridge-End, Hammersmith.

19 May 1890: Jane wrote to Blunt: 'Jenny is causing great anxiety again.'

23 May 1890: Morris and Jenny spent the day at Merton.

24 May 1890: The *Speaker* published a letter from Morris (dated 19 May) complaining about the changes that had taken place in Oxford during the previous thirty years. The second part of chapter XVII of *News from Nowhere* appeared in *Commonweal*.

25 May 1890: At the Sixth Annual Conference of the SL the anarchists took control of the Council leaving Morris isolated. Morris and Sparling were forced to resign from the editorship of *Commonweal* and were replaced by Nicoll and Kitz. According to May, Morris got increasingly bored at this meeting which lasted from 10 am to 10 pm. At one point he is supposed to have said: 'Mr Chairman *can't* we get on with the business. I want my TEA!'

29 May 1890: Cockerell recorded in his *Diary* that Morris was in 'Lincoln with Thackeray Turner'. While in Lincoln Morris visited the Cathedral: 'The whole place is chock full of history.'

30 May 1890: According to Blunt's *Diary* Jane and May had spent the last three days at Crabbet.

31 May 1890: The third part of chapter XVII of *News from Nowhere* appeared in *Commonweal*.

June 1890: The four-part serialization of *The Story of the Glittering Plain* began in the *English Illustrated Magazine*. The last instalment appeared in September. An unsigned review of *The House of the Wolfings* appeared in the *Atlantic Monthly* (pp. 851– 4).

1 June 1890: In the morning Morris gave an open-air speech for the Hammersmith Branch of the SL at the Bridge-End, Hammersmith. In the afternoon he was scheduled to open a discussion on 'The Effects of the Socialist Movement on Imperial Politics' for the Hammersmith Branch of the SL at Kelmscott House, Hammersmith.

4 June 1890: Morris travelled down to Kelmscott Manor with Jane and Jenny.

7 June 1890: The fourth part of chapter XVII of *News from Nowhere* appeared in *Commonweal*. Morris also published 'Anti-Parliamentary' in the paper.

8 June 1890: Morris acted as chairman at the fifth anniversary celebration of the International Working Men's Club at 40 Berner Street, London.

13 June 1890: Jane wrote to Blunt: 'I heard from May that she wished to be married this week instead of next – it has all been like a bad dream, but it must end sometime like all dreams – the wedding will be tomorrow (Saturday) and then May and her husband go to Kelmscott Manor for about a fortnight.' The *Arbeter Fraint* included a report on the fifth anniversary celebration at the International Working Men's Club.

14 June 1890: May and Sparling were married at Fulham Register Office. Jenny and Morris signed as witnesses after a long wait in 'a dismal little cell'.

The couple spent their honeymoon at Kelmscott Manor. They later lived at 8 Hammersmith Terrace, one of a small row of terraced houses situated to the west of Kelmscott House. The couple divorced in February 1898 (*c.f. Daily Mail*, 8 February 1898). Chapter XVII of *News from Nowhere* was concluded in *Commonweal*.

15 June 1890: Morris gave an open-air speech for the Hammersmith Branch of the SL at Bridge-End, Hammersmith.

16 June 1890: Jane planned to take Jenny to see the sights of London.

20 June 1890: In a letter to Georgiana Burne-Jones, Morris recorded that he had finished *The Story of the Glittering Plain* and 'begun another'. This was probably the unfinished romance, *The Story of Desiderius*, which was identified by Cockerell on its manuscript cover as 'written about 1890'. The latter may well have been intended as part of a trilogy that began with *The House of the Wolfings* and *The Roots of the Mountains*.

21 June 1890: Morris travelled down to join May and her husband at Kelmscott Manor. Chapter XVIII of *News from Nowhere* appeared in *Commonweal*. Morris also published 'Notes on News' in the paper.

22 June 1890: Morris spent the day fishing at Kelmscott Manor.

23 June 1890: Morris, May and her husband probably went on an excursion to visit the White Horse.

24 June 1890: Morris returned to London from Kelmscott Manor.

25 June 1890: Morris gave a speech seconding the adoption of the SPAB Annual Report at the Old Hall, Barnard's Inn, Holborn.

28 June 1890: The first part of chapter XIX of *News from Nowhere* appeared in *Commonweal*. Morris also published 'Notes on News' in the paper.

5 July 1890: The conclusion to chapter XIX along with chapter XX and XXI of *News from Nowhere* appeared in *Commonweal*. Morris also published 'Notes on News' in the paper.

11 July 1890: Morris opened a discussion on 'The Present Strikes of Police, Postmen & Guards' at the Hammersmith Branch of the SL at Kelmscott House, Hammersmith.

12 July 1890: Nicoll began to fill the *Commonweal* with inflammatory anarchist copy. Morris as owner and publisher of the paper was forced to write to him and urge caution: 'I must say that I think you are going too far: at any rate farther than *I* can follow you... I never bargained for this sort of thing when I gave up the editorship.' The first part of chapter XXII of *News from Nowhere* appeared in the paper.

13 July 1890: Morris delivered an open-air speech for the Hammersmith Branch of the SL at Walham Green, Fulham.

14 July 1890: Morris travelled down to Kelmscott Manor with Jane and Jenny.

19 July 1890: Morris returned from Kelmscott Manor to keep an engagement with Magnússon. Chapter XXII of *News from Nowhere* was concluded in *Commonweal*. The serialization of Morris's lecture 'The Development of Modern Society' also began in the paper.

21 July 1890: Morris was at Merton Abbey. He also purchased a copy of Caxton's translation of *The Golden Legend* (1527).

22 July 1890: Morris travelled back to Kelmscott Manor.

26 July 1890: Morris returned to London from Kelmscott Manor. He contributed the last of his 'Notes on News' columns to *Commonweal*. Chapter XXIII of *News from Nowhere* and the second instalment of 'The Development of Modern Society' also appeared in the paper.

27 July 1890: Morris and Burne-Jones were photographed by Frederick Hollyer in the garden of the Grange.

28 July 1890: Morris was due to serve on the grand jury at the Central Criminal Court in the Old Bailey. However, he had a stomach ache the evening before and was able to obtain a doctor's certificate. One of his clerks took the certificate round to the Old Bailey (*c.f.* 10 September 1890). In the evening he had supper with May 'who looked well and happy'. Jane wrote to Blunt from Kelmscott Manor: 'Mrs De Morgan and her daughter are with us now, both great friends of mine, the former is an extraordinary old lady, she is over 80, and takes the greatest interest in all that goes on.'

29 July 1890: Morris spent the day at Merton.

1 August 1890: Morris returned to Kelmscott Manor.

2 August 1890: The first part of chapter XXIV of *News from Nowhere* appeared in *Commonweal*. The paper also contained the third instalment of 'The Development of Modern Society'.

3 August 1890: A 'Revolutionary Conference' was organized by the new Executive of the SL at the Autonomic Club. Here anarchist doctrines were preached openly. Mowbray's proposal, in the event of a revolutionary uprising, was 'to fire the slums and get the people into the West-end mansions'. It was resolved 'to dispense with any such quasi-constitutional official as a chairman, and all red-tapeism and quasi-authoritarianism were banished'.

6 August 1890: Morris and his family, accompanied by Ellis, Mary Abbey and

Katherine Birchall, hired a waggonette and pair and travelled to Fairford, Quennington, Coln St Aldwyn's, Bibury, Ablington, Winsom, Colne Roger, Colne St Denis and Fosse Bridge. They had dinner at Fosse Bridge before visiting the Roman Villa at Chedworth.

8 August 1890: Morris spent the day fishing with Ellis at Buscot.

9 August 1890: Chapter XXIV of *News from Nowhere* appeared in *Commonweal* along with the fourth instalment of 'The Development of Modern Society'.

12 August 1890: Morris returned to London from Kelmscott Manor.

15 August 1890: Morris travelled to view the recently installed reredos – made by Morris & Co – at the Whitelands College Chapel. The *Times* also published a letter of his on Stratford-on-Avon Church.

16 August 1890: An article entitled *Free Studies from Life: William Morris* (with a portrait) appeared in the *Star*. Chapter XXV of *News from Nowhere* appeared in *Commonweal* and the serialization of 'The Development of Modern Society' was concluded.

18 August 1890: Blunt went to stay with the Morrises at Kelmscott Manor.

21 August 1890: Blunt wrote: Morris's 'appearance is that of a merchant sea captain with a rollicking bon homie [*sic*] and quick Welsh temper. He is withal an excellent talker, discoursing always of the thing uppermost in his mind and [has] little respect of his company.'

23 August 1890: The first part of chapter XXVI of *News from Nowhere* appeared in *Commonweal*.

25 August 1890: Morris returned to London from Kelmscott Manor.

30 August 1890: The second part of chapter XXVI of *News from Nowhere* appeared in *Commonweal*.

1 September 1890: Blunt returned to Kelmscott Manor after spending a short time in Paris. He accompanied the Morrises on a boat trip to the highest navigable point on the Thames: 'a lovely day and it was pleasant to see Jenny well enough to row the whole six miles home. Her devotion to her father is very pretty, for when he in his rough way lays about him and one responds she is almost angry in her defence of him, though in truth he needs no protection for he is a hard, a too hard, hitter.'

2 September 1890: Blunt wrote in his *Diary* that Morris's socialism was 'antiquarian rather than a true doctrine of the future'.

6 September 1890: Chapter XXVI of *News from Nowhere* was concluded in *Commonweal*.

7 September 1890: Morris delivered an open-air speech for the Hammersmith Branch of the SL at the Bridge-End, Hammersmith.

10 September 1890: Morris served on the jury at the Central Criminal Court of the Old Bailey: 'This Jury business is a sad waste of time: nothing useful possible to be done and a mass of degrading twaddle to be waded through.' In the afternoon he planned to visit Chiselhurst in Kent. Morris's letter (dated 6 September) on the 'Hanseatic Museum at Bergen' appeared in the *Times*.

11 September 1890: Morris was at Merton and later attended a meeting of SPAB. An agreement was signed between Bernard Quaritch and Morris for the publication of Caxton's *Golden Legend*. Morris was 'to have absolute and sole control over choice of paper, choice of type size ... and selection of the printer'. Quaritch was to pay for the printing and the binding of the book.

12 September 1890: Morris travelled down to Kelmscott Manor to stay with Jenny.

13 September 1890: Morris and Jenny went for a drive: 'Langford, Broadwell, Kencote, Alvescott, Black Burton, Bampton, Aston and at last Cote.' Chapter XXVII of *News from Nowhere* appeared in *Commonweal*.

14 September 1890: In a letter to F. S. Ellis, written from Kelmscott Manor, Morris recorded that eleven letters of the 'Golden' type had been cut.

20 September 1890: Morris returned from Kelmscott Manor. In the evening he was visited by Emery Walker. Chapter XXVIII of *News from Nowhere* appeared in *Commonweal*.

21 September 1890: Morris was scheduled to deliver 'The Hope of the Future' at a meeting sponsored by the North Kensington Branch of the SL at the Clarendon Coffee House, Clarendon Road, London.

27 September 1890: Chapter XXIX of *News from Nowhere* appeared in *Commonweal*.

4 October 1890: Chapter XXX of *News from Nowhere* appeared in *Commonweal*. This concluded the serialization of the book.

7 October 1890: In his *Diary* Blunt noted he wanted to have made 'a replica of the piece at Exeter College [*Adoration of the Magi*] with the addition of an Arab horse and a Camel'. Morris told Glasier that he intended to 'begin to touch up News from Nowhere for its book form'.

11 October 1890: Morris wrote to Blunt saying he would be delighted to make him a replica of the *Adoration of the Magi* tapestry.

17 October 1890: Morris attended Bernard Quaritch's yearly trade-sale. He was also the special guest at a lavish dinner held that evening at the

Freemason's Tavern, London. Blunt spent the day with Jane: 'the last I fancy in a quite intimate way – we felt this and said it.' Morris told Ellis that all twenty-six lower case letters for the 'Golden' type had been completed.

18 October 1890: Blunt departed for France on his way to Egypt.

20 October 1890: Morris delivered 'Art for the People' (better known as 'Of the Origins of Ornamental Art') at a meeting sponsored by the 'Commonweal' Branch of the SL at the Athenaeum Hall, Tottenham Court Road, London.

22 October 1890: According to Mackail, Morris travelled down to Joseph Batchelor's paper mill at Little Chart in Kent with Emery Walker to examine paper on which to print Caxton's *Golden Legend*. Mackail wrote: 'With unabated interest in any form of manual art, he must take off his coat and try to make a sheet of paper with his own hands. At the second attempt he succeeded in doing very creditably what it is supposed takes a man several months to master.'

23 October 1890: Morris wrote to Joseph Batchelor enclosing a copy design for the 'Flower' watermark – also known as 'Primrose' – to be used on the paper for the Kelmscott Press. Two other watermarks were to be used on paper produced by Batchelor: 'Perch' and 'Apple'.

26 October 1890: In a letter to Blunt, Jane wrote that she was going to a performance of Ibsen's *The Lady from the Sea*. This play was translated by Eleanor Marx and published by Fisher Unwin in 1890. However its first performance, under Aveling's direction, is not supposed to have taken place until May 1891 at Terry's Theatre. Was Jane referring to a private production?

November 1890: Morris's poem 'The Day of Days' appeared in *Time*.

1 November 1890: Morris delivered an open-air speech at a meeting called by the combined London socialist and anarchist groups to protest against 'the persecution of Jews in Russia'. This meeting had originally been planned for the Great Assembly Hall, Mile End, but was forced out to Mile End Waste as a result of a police ban. Morris's article 'Workhouse Socialism' appeared in *Commonweal*.

7 November 1890: Morris opened a discussion on 'Thrift from a Socialist Standpoint' at the Hammersmith Branch of the SL at Kelmscott House.

11 November 1890: Morris delivered a speech at a Bloody Sunday memorial meeting sponsored by combined London socialist and anarchist groups held at the Milton Hall, London.

15 November 1890: Morris's association with *Commonweal* ended when his final article for the paper – 'Where Are We Now?' – was published: 'I meant it as a "Farewell." It was, and was meant to be, directly opposed to anything the Anarchist side would want to say or do.'

17 November 1890: Morris signed an agreement with Quaritch for the publication of the *Eyrbiggia Saga* and the *Heimskringa* in the Saga Library.

21 November 1890: The Hammersmith Branch left the SL. Before leaving Morris made over the type, plant and copyright of *Commonweal* to the League's Council.

23 November 1890: An organizing committee, including Morris, met with the intention of establishing a new political group.

26 November 1890: Morris circulated a letter to all the Secretaries of the Branches of the SL explaining the reason why the Hammersmith Branch had taken the decision to leave the organization.

28 November 1890: The first meeting of the Hammersmith Socialist Society (HSS) was held at which the *Statement of Principles* was approved. Emery Walker was appointed secretary of the Society and Morris treasurer. In the evening Morris delivered 'Gothic Architecture' at a meeting held at Barnard's Inn. The lecture was illustrated with lantern slides. This is not mentioned by LeMire.

Winter 1890: The first edition of *News from Nowhere* was published – without Morris's permission – by Robert Brothers in the United States. This reproduced the text as it had appeared in *Commonweal*.

1 December 1890: Morris thanked Bernard Quaritch for sending him a copy of volume 1 of the Saga Library.

5 December 1890: Cobden-Sanderson and his wife Annie joined the HSS. Scheu and his wife joined at the same time.

9 December 1890: Morris was working on a *Manifesto* for the new HSS.

11 December 1890: Morris gave a speech on the protection of ancient buildings at a meeting sponsored by SPAB and the Master of Trinity College at Trinity College, Cambridge.

13 December 1890: A review of the Saga Library appeared in the *Pall Mall Gazette* (p. 2).

15 December 1890: Morris wrote a letter to the *Pall Mall Gazette* (dated 13 December) in which he cleared up some errors in the paper's review of the Saga Library.

19 December 1890: Scheu gave the first lecture under the auspices of the HSS. His subject was 'The Essence of Freedom and Servitude'.

22 December 1890: Morris declined Hyndman's invitation to write for *Justice*.

'I have come to the conclusion that no form of journalism is suited to me.'

23 December 1890: Morris sent Horace Meeres, vicar of Bradwell with Kelmscott, £5 to be distributed among the poor of Kelmscott.

26 December 1890: Bax joined the HSS.

1891: The first British edition of *News from Nowhere* was published by Reeves & Turner. This differed quite significantly from the version published in *Commonweal*. The Arts and Crafts Exhibition Society held its first Exhibition on the continent in Brussels.

January 1891: Morris's article 'The Socialist Ideal I – Art' appeared in the *New Review*. This was later reprinted as a pamphlet.

2 January 1891: The 'Rules' and 'Statement of Principles' of the HSS were published, both drafted by Morris.

5 January 1891: Morris probably interviewed William Bowden at Kelmscott House for the post of compositor and pressman for the Kelmscott Press. Bowden accepted the post. His daughter, Mrs Pine, was also to join the Press. Shaw noted in his *Diaries* (p. 685) that May had made him a present of the first volume in the Saga Library 'the other day'.

12 January 1891: According to Mackail this was the date when Morris rented a cottage at 16 Upper Mall as the first premises of the Kelmscott Press. However, in a letter Jane wrote to Blunt dated 29 December 1890 there is evidence that the decision may have been made earlier: 'he has taken a little place where he can set up the press.' The cottage was equipped with a proof-press and a second hand Albion printing press.

20 January 1891: In a letter to William Bowden, Morris said he was 'expecting the cases &tc. from Reeds today'. This was a reference to the Golden type which was cast at the Fann Street Foundry of Charles Reed & Sons.

23 January 1891: Webb joined the HSS.

27 January 1891: Morris acknowledged receipt of some trial paper he had ordered from Joseph Batchelor.

30 January 1891: Jane wrote to Blunt: 'I [have] had rheumatism and inter-mittent fever which often kept me in bed.'

31 January 1891: The first trial page of *The Story of the Glittering Plain* was printed at the Kelmscott Press.

February 1891: A poem *On William Morris* by A. E. Cross appeared in the *New English Magazine* (vol. 3, p. 731). It was accompanied by an article entitled *William Morris* by W. Clarke (vol. 3, p. 740).

2 February 1891: Morris sent James Tegaskis £35 in payment for Galiot du Pre's *Meliadus de Leonnoys* (Paris 1528).

6 February 1891: Morris participated in a discussion on the 'non-economical side of Socialism' held under the auspices of the HSS.

7 February 1891: The *Liverpool Daily Post* published a letter from Morris praising Holman Hunt's painting the *Triumph of the Innocents* as 'the greatest of his latest works'.

8 February 1891: Walter Crane visited Morris to discuss the planned illustrations for *The Story of the Glittering Plain*.

11 February 1891: The *Times* published a letter from Morris (dated 5 February) concerning the proposal to build a memorial chapel at Westminster Abbey.

12 February 1891: Morris wrote to Walter Crane declaring himself 'red hot' to begin the works of the Kelmscott Press. On the same day Sparling noted that ten reams of the 'Flower' paper were delivered by Batchelor.

13 February 1891: Morris opened a discussion on the 'legal Maximum [price] and Minimum [wage]' for the HSS at Kelmscott House, Hammersmith.

15 February 1891: Morris was scheduled to give two deliveries on 'Idiots and Idiocy', the first in the morning at Bridge-End, Hammersmith, the second in the evening at the lecture hall of the HSS at Kelmscott House.

18 February 1891: Cockerell recorded that a 'good supply of type' was delivered to the Kelmscott Press.

19 February 1891: In his *Diary* Cockerell recorded that Morris was unable to go to a SPAB meeting 'owing to Jenny's illness'. This was a reference to a sudden attack of meningitis suffered by Jenny. This greatly affected Morris whose health broke down soon after (*c.f.* 1 March and 4 March).

20 February 1891: Morris wrote to an unknown recipient: 'I would have called on you this morning, but the grievous illness of my daughter keeps me in the house.'

21 February 1891: Morris, in a letter to John Pincher Faunthorpe, recorded that he had 'very serious illness in the House and am not able to leave it for the present'. A notice in the *Athenaeum* that *The Story of the Glittering Plain* was for sale led to a rush on Reeves & Turner who sold every copy before the price was announced.

28 February 1891: Jane told Blunt: 'We are in great sorrow, our poor Jenny has had an attack of brain-fever and though all immediate danger is past, she is still very ill, with two nurses attending her day and night.'

1 March 1891: Morris was house-bound due to an attack of gout.

2 March 1891: Printing began on the Kelmscott edition of *The Story of the Glittering Plain*. Cockerell recorded that by this date a pressman, called Giles, had been hired. He was to leave soon after *The Story of the Glittering Plain* was finished.

3 March 1891: Batchelor visited Morris at Kelmscott House to discuss the paper for the Kelmscott Press.

4 March 1891: Morris, in a letter to Ellis, claimed 'my hand seems lead and my wrist string'.

8 March 1891: The Revd Guy, Morris's old tutor, died. Morris was not told immediately as he was too ill at the time.

14 March 1891: Morris wrote of his schooling: 'I was educated at Marlborough under clerical masters, and I naturally rebelled against them. Had they been advanced men, my spirit of rebellion would have probably led me to conservatism ... as a protest. One naturally defies authority.'

28 March 1891: Cobden-Sanderson made his first visit to the Kelmscott Press. He wrote of Morris: 'He looked – despite his supper! – a little empty, his clothes hanging somewhat loosely upon him.'

4 April 1891: Morris left London for Folkestone where he stayed with William Vincent – a printer-compositor – and his wife: 'I hope while there to begin a little work again, which has been stopped now for five weeks: that is the worst of being ill.' *The Story of the Glittering Plain* was the first book to be finished by the Kelmscott Press. Two hundred paper copies were produced and a further six on vellum. The book was reissued three years later with illustrations by Walter Crane. This was the only Kelmscott Press book to be printed twice (*c.f.* 13 January 1894). Cobden-Sanderson recorded in his *Journals* that he had just received a dummy binding for *The Story of the Glittering Plain* done by Leighton.

8 April 1891: Morris wrote to Emery Walker from Folkestone: 'my hand is much firmer yesterday & today. In fact I am getting on altogether; nothing but the cold weather keeps me back now I think.'

10 April 1891: Morris wrote to Emery Walker: 'I am getting on I think; but slowly: the pain flits about me, but I sleep well & can walk a bit.'

13 April 1891: Morris returned to London. Jane wrote to Blunt: 'My husband has been very ill, the shock of Jenny's illness was too much for him, and he broke down entirely a few days afterwards – he is much better, but not nearly recovered... Jenny has made a miraculous recovery.'

22 April 1891: Batchelor made a second delivery of ten reams of the 'Flower' paper to the Kelmscott Press.

29 April 1891: Morris returned to Folkestone.

30 April 1891: Morris wrote to Cobden-Sanderson: 'I have managed to get down here to keep Jenny company. But though I am otherwise quite strong, and feeling fairly well; the gout has descended upon me somewhat, and I cannot shake it off.' During the day he drove to St Leonard's Church, Hythe: 'terribly restored by Street and Pearson, but still well worth seeing.'

May 1891: The *Commonweal* was subtitled 'A Revolutionary Journal of Anarchist Communism' and was issued from a temporary address in Lamb's Conduit Street. An unsigned review of *News from Nowhere* appeared in *Review of Reviews* (vol. 3, p. 509).

1 May 1891: Morris wrote to Fairfax Murray about the selection of the poems to be included in *Poems by the Way*. The last sheets of *The Story of the Glittering Plain* were sent to Mr Bowden for binding.

6 May 1891: Morris returned to London from Folkestone.

7 May 1891: In his *Diary* Blunt recorded visiting the Morrises at Kelmscott House where Morris had 'been at death's door through gout'. It was during this meeting that Blunt purchased the first volume of *The Story of the Glittering Plain* that had just been brought to Morris by the printer. The book was inscribed 'I sold this book to Wilfrid Scawen Blunt May 7th 1891. William Morris.'

8 May 1891: According to Cockerell this was the day that subscribers received their copies of *The Story of the Glittering Plain*.

10 May 1891: Morris gave Walter Crane a signed copy of *The Story of the Glittering Plain*.

11 May 1891: Cockerell recorded that fifty pages of *The Golden Legend* were in type by this date.

12 May 1891: The first page of *The Golden Legend* was printed at the Kelmscott Press. Morris entertained Blunt at Merton Abbey. The latter wrote: 'It is a charming 18th century house with an old fashioned garden, and the buildings beyond it, where the cotton and silk fabrics are made and dyed and the tapestry is woven.'

20 May 1891: Morris wrote 'Goldilocks and Goldilocks' to fill up *Poems by the Way*. He read the completed poem to Emery Walker when he came to dinner that evening.

23 May 1891: Lionel Johnson's review of *News from Nowhere* appeared in the *Academy* (vol. 39, pp. 483–4).

25 May 1891: The Kelmscott Press moved into larger premises at 16 Upper

Mall. Morris referred to it as 'the Doggeries' as it had previously been used as kennels. The other part of the building was occupied by Emery Walker's process-engraving firm.

30 May 1891: Morris gave Kate Faulkner a signed copy of *The Story of the Glittering Plain.*

June 1891: Work began on designing the Troy type for the Kelmscott Press.

4 June 1891: Blunt visited the Morrises at Kelmscott Manor. In his *Diary* he wrote: 'I have been reading Morris's "News from Nowhere"... It is written just as he talks and the conversations on the river are precisely his own; only in real life he never discusses women's character or makes himself in the smallest manner agreeable to them.'

7 June 1891: Morris travelled to Folkestone to visit Jenny.

10 June 1891: Morris gave a speech moving a vote of thanks to W. B. Richmond for a paper the latter gave at the Fourteenth Annual Meeting of SPAB at the Old Hall, Barnard's Inn, London.

26 June 1891: Morris opened a discussion on gambling at a meeting sponsored by the HSS at Kelmscott House, Hammersmith. LeMire misdates this 21 July 1891. The *Minutes* record that there 'was a good audience and many members of the society spoke'.

12 July 1891: Morris probably travelled down to Folkestone to visit Jenny.

15 July 1891: Morris and Jenny visited Rye and Winchelsea: 'They are delightful places, especially Winchelsea, and we had a beautiful sunny day for our outing to them.'

16 July 1891: Jane wrote to Blunt: 'I have good news of Jenny, her father is with her for a week which gives her the greatest pleasure possible, they wander about the downs together like two happy babies.'

17 July 1891: Morris returned from his visit to Folkestone.

26 July 1891: Morris, who had returned to Folkestone, and Jenny climbed to the top of the downs in a sea-fog: 'we ... got clean above the fog into a beautiful calm sunny evening, and looking down saw the sea blotted out as it were by a mass of rolling clouds: it almost reminded me of one of the great glacier fields in Iceland except that was grey instead of glittering white.'

28 July 1891: Morris and Jenny visited 'Caesar's Camp', an early earthwork fortification, situated to the north of Folkestone: 'as to Caesar, I rather suppose it to have been made a good many centuries before him, & that it was a city of the ancient people.'

29 July 1891: Morris stated in a letter to Georgiana Burne-Jones: 'I am ashamed to say that I am not as well as I should like, and am even such a fool as to be rather anxious – about myself this time.'

30 July 1891: Morris returned from Folkestone to attended a SPAB meeting.

August 1891: The lower case alphabet for the Troy type was finished early in the month. A review of *News from Nowhere* by Maurice Hewlett appeared in the *National Review* (vol. 17, p. 818–27).

2 August 1891: Cockerell recorded in his *Diary* that he visited Morris in the afternoon and found 'Emery Walker there & Dr Hogg part of the time'. In the evening Morris read from – and opened a discussion on – *News from Nowhere* at a meeting sponsored by the HSS at Kelmscott House.

4 August 1891: Jane visited the dentist. Morris spent the day at Merton.

6 August 1891: Morris travelled down to Folkestone to see Jenny.

7 August 1891: Morris and Jenny travelled by ferry to France: 'I feel very loth to go, though I shall like it when I get there no doubt.' Blunt recorded in his *Diaries* that he had lunch with Jane at Kelmscott House.

8 August 1891: Morris and Jenny reached Abbeville. In the morning they travelled to St Riquier where they visited the church: 'a quite unrestored church; mostly flamboyant & very fine.' While in Abbeville Morris purchased for Jane 'a wide-mouthed jug with comic lady & gentleman on it, rude modern, but traditional pottery'.

8 August 1891: Morris and Jenny travelled to Amiens.

11 August 1891: Morris and Jenny visited the Cathedral at Beauvais: 'Certainly the Cathedral here is one of the wonders of the world: seen by twilight its size gives one an impression almost of terror; one can scarcely believe in it.'

12 August 1891: Jenny and Morris visited the churches at Gournay-en-Bray and St-Germer-de-Fly: 'both early & interesting, the second exceedingly beautiful.'

13 August 1891: Morris and Jenny visited St Stephens in Beauvais 'to read the late stained glass'.

14 August 1891: Morris and Jenny travelled to Soissons via Compiegne where they stayed for two or three hours: 'We went … through Pitou's forest by a sort of omnibus train in the cool of the evening.'

15 August 1891: Morris and Jenny spent the day in Soissons: 'Soissons is a jolly town; beautiful country all about; not many *ancient* houses, but (in the town itself) all *old* ones of stone. As to the church, it is a wonderful work.'

16 August 1891: Morris and Jenny visited Rheims Cathedral: 'though a wonderful place, is, if I am right, not so great a work as Amiens, Beauvais, or

Soissons.'

18 August 1891: Morris and Jenny arrived in Laon where they stayed at the Hotel de la Hute.

19 August 1891: Morris and Jenny spent the day at Laon. It was probably on this day that they visited the Church of St Martin: 'I did not see the inside of the Cloisters, because I quarrelled with the sacristan who wanted to sell me photos: as soon as I came into the church, telling him I didn't want photos of restored churches.'

20 August 1891: Morris and Jenny travelled to Noyon: 'quite a delightful place.'

22 August 1891: Morris and Jenny returned to Beauvais.

23 August 1891: Morris and Jenny travelled to Amiens.

25 August 1891: Morris and Jenny took the ferry to Folkestone: 'roughish passage but nobody sick.' They spent the night in Folkestone.

26 August 1891: In the afternoon Morris and Jenny returned to London from Folkestone.

27 August 1891: The first proof sheets of Blunt's *The Love Lyrics and Songs of Proteus* were ready.

30 August 1891: Morris lectured on 'the last seven years of the movement' at a meeting sponsored by the HSS at Kelmscott House, Hammersmith. The *Minutes* record an audience of sixty.

5 September 1891: Morris's lecture 'Seven Years Ago and Now' was published in *Justice* (p. 1).

8 September 1891: Morris was at Kelmscott Manor.

9 September 1891: Morris was back in London where he spent the day at Merton. In the evening he dined with Edward Burne-Jones.

22 September 1891: Morris was visited by 'a stout man' who used to keep the dogs at the Doggeries who wanted to rent the kennels back.

24 September 1891: *Poems by the Way* was finished by the Kelmscott Press. There were 300 copies on paper and thirteen on vellum. The book was sold by Reeves & Turner. This was the first Kelmscott Press book to be printed using two colours.

25 September 1891: In the morning Morris visited Walter Crane to discuss the illustrations for the second Kelmscott Press edition of *The Story of the Glittering Plain*. In the evening he held a dinner party for Ellis, his daughter Phyllis, and Sparling.

26 September 1891: Morris returned to Kelmscott Manor.

28 September 1891: *Poems by the Way* was sent to the binders.

30 September 1891: In his *Diary* Blunt wrote: 'I have been away for two nights to Kelmscott to see Morris about the printing and to wish Mrs. Morris goodbye for the winter. It was very perfect weather, and we did our gudgeon fishing and walks as usual and I made a little love to Mrs. Morris, poor woman, for quite the last time (*c.f.* 11 August 1892).'

October 1891: The HSS published the first issue of a four-page monthly called the *Hammersmith Socialist Record*.

2 October 1891: Morris delivered an 'Address on the Collection of Paintings of the English Pre-Raphaelite School' at a private showing of the exhibition arranged by the Birmingham Museum and Art Gallery Committee at the Corporation Gallery, Birmingham.

4 October 1891: In the afternoon Morris delivered 'Socialism Up-To-Date' at a meeting sponsored by the Ancoats Recreation Committee at the New Islington Hall, Ancoats, Manchester. In the evening he lectured on French and English cathedrals at a meeting sponsored by the Ancoats 'At Home' Committee at the New Islington Hall, Ancoats, Manchester.

9 October 1891: Morris returned to Kelmscott Manor.

20 October 1891: Morris returned to London from Kelmscott Manor. *Poems by the Way* was published by Reeves & Turner.

21 October 1891: Morris was visited by his daughter May: 'I thought her looking much better, & she said that she was so and had slept well except on the night of the storm.' He inscribed a copy of *Poems by the Way* to Phyllis Marion Ellis.

22 October 1891: In the morning Morris visited the Burne-Joneses at the Grange. He then worked on *The Well at the World's End* before going to a SPAB meeting in the afternoon. After this meeting he spent some time at Gatti's with, amongst others, Webb and Cockerell. The latter recorded in his *Diary*: 'W. M. at S.P.A.B. & Gatti's. He talks of getting another press. One volume of the Golden Legend is printed. The black letter fount is almost ready, & he thinks of making a beginning with John Ball, Chaucer to follow, & also perhaps the Gesta Romananorum.'

27 October 1891: The *Pall Mall Gazette* published a letter from Morris (dated 22 October) on the proposed restoration of Westminster Abbey.

2 November 1891: Morris & Co. were responsible for the stage-decoration of Henry Arthur Jones's play *The Crusader* which opened on this day and enjoyed a run of three months at the Avenue Theatre, London. This included

'Mrs Greenslade's Drawing Room in Mayfair' in Act I and 'The Rose Cottage & Rose Farm at Wimbledon' in Act II.

6 November 1891: The *Illustrated London News* praised Henry Arthur Jones for mounting his play 'luxuriously and in excellent taste'.

12 November 1891: An anonymous article entitled *Poet as Printer: Interview with William Morris* appeared in the *Pall Mall Gazette*.

15 November 1891: Morris wrote to Thomas Hardy saying he would 'be very pleased' to receive a copy of *Tess of the D'Urbervilles*. It is clear from this letter that Morris had already read *Far from the Madding Crowd* and *The Return of the Native*.

18 November 1891: Morris was scheduled to give an unnamed lecture at a meeting sponsored by the HSS at Kelmscott House, Hammersmith.

19 November 1891: Morris was interviewed at Kelmscott House by another correspondent from the *Pall Mall Gazette*.

20 November 1891: Morris lectured 'On the Influence of Building Materials on Architecture' at a meeting sponsored by the Art Workers' Guild at Barnard's Inn, London.

9 December 1891: Jane and Jenny travelled to Tunbridge Wells to stay first at the Mount Ephraim Hotel and then lodgings at 67 Mount Ephraim. Morris lectured on 'Real Socialism' at a meeting sponsored by the HSS at Kelmscott House.

17 December 1891: Morris inscribed a copy of *Poems by the Way* to F. S. Ellis.

19 December 1891: By this time Morris was staying with Jenny in Tunbridge Wells: 'not such a bad place, I mean the place itself; plenty of open common & the like, though Podsnap very busy in villa building.' During the day he went to visit the Morris & Co. stained glass in the Church of St Mary the Virgin in Speldhurst.

25 December 1891: May and Sparling spent Christmas at Tunbridge Wells. Jane wrote: 'they both looked almost robust before they went away.'

29 December 1891: Morris returned to London from Tunbridge Wells.

1892: An article by G. Francis Watt Lee entitled *Some Thoughts upon Beauty in Typography suggested by the Work of Mr William Morris at the Kelmscott Press* appeared in the *Knight Errant* (vol. 1, no. 2, pp. 53–63). Morris was appointed Master of the Art Workers' Guild.

January 1892: Morris's article on 'The Influence of Building Materials upon Architecture' appeared in the *Century Guild Hobby Horse*.

8 January 1892: Morris was back in Tunbridge Wells with Jenny.

9 January 1892: A review of *Poems by the Way* by Richard Garnett appeared in the *Illustrated London News* (p. 50).

11 January 1892: Morris returned to London from Tunbridge Wells.

25 & 28 January 1892: Two letters by Morris appeared in the *Times* 'On the Woodcuts of Gothic Books'.

26 January 1892: *The Love Lyrics & Songs of Proteus* by Wilfrid Scawen Blunt was finished by the Kelmscott Press. Three hundred copies were printed on cloth. This was the only Kelmscott Press book in which the initials were printed in red. Morris lectured on 'The Woodcuts of Gothic Books' at a meeting sponsored by the Applied Art Section of the Society of Arts at the Society's Rooms at John Street, Adelphi, London. Sir George Birdwood, who introduced the lecturer, said: 'It is not only as a poet and an art critic that he is one of the first Englishmen of the Victorian age. When the decorative arts of this country had, about the middle of the present century, been denationalised, it was Mr. William Morris "who stemmed the torrent of a downward age," and, by the vigour of his characteristic English genius, upraised those household arts again from the degradation of nearly two generations, and carried them to a perfection never before reached by them.'

30 January 1892: The Kelmscott Press printed an invitation to the annual gathering of the HSS.

February 1892: A review of *Poems by the Way* by Oliver Elton appeared in the *Academy* (p. 197). Edward Prince began cutting the 'Chaucer' type.

2 February 1892: Morris was once again staying in Tunbridge Wells.

5 February 1892: Morris, accompanied by Jane and Jenny, returned to London from Tunbridge Wells.

7 February 1892: Cockerell spent the afternoon at Kelmscott House: 'Saw a number of old books, including a magnificent copy of the first book printed at Abbeville, also proof sheets of "The Nature of Gothic," and of the Golden Legend, both now nearing completion. A young Edinburgh anarchist at tea who had been imprisoned for a fortnight in Paris for chaining himself to a lamp-post and addressing the passers-by.'

12 February 1892: An illustrated article by Morris appeared in the *Journal of the Society of Arts* entitled 'Paper on the Woodcuts of Gothic Books'.

15 February 1892: *The Nature of Gothic* by John Ruskin was finished by the Kelmscott Press. Five hundred copies were produced on paper. It was subsequently published by George Allen. Morris provided the 'Preface'.

17 February 1892: The first sheet of *The Defence of Guenevere* was printed by the Kelmscott Press.

20 February 1892: Charles Faulkner died.

21 February 1892: Morris was scheduled to deliver a lecture at a meeting sponsored by the North Kensington Branch of the SDF at the Clarendon Coffee Palace, Clarendon Road, London.

27 February 1892: Jane reported that she had just received from Reeves & Turner the first bound copy of Blunt's *The Love Lyrics & Songs of Proteus*.

4 March 1892: Cockerell wrote: 'Meeting of Art-Workers' Guild. Subject, "London Improvements." W. M. in the chair and at his very best. I was never more impressed with his greatness.'

9 March 1892: Morris wrote to Glasier: 'I sometimes have a vision of a real Socialist Party at once united and free. Is it possible? Here in London it might be done, I think, but the S.D.F. stands in the way.'

12 March 1892: An untitled review – actually by Theodore Watts-Dunton – of *Poems by the Way* appeared in the *Athenaeum* (pp. 336–8).

22 March 1892: *The Nature of Gothic* was issued.

31 March 1892: In a letter to Cunninghame Graham, Morris wrote of Sir Joshua Reynolds: 'I hate Reynolds so heartily that I never look at his pictures except when I am compelled, and partly therefore, I suppose, am no judge whatever as to whether some beastly sleasy daub is by him or some other imposter of the period.' Cobden-Sanderson finished a binding for a copy of *A Dream of John Ball*. The trial of the Walsall Anarchists began.

2 April 1892: *The Defence of Guenevere* was finished by the Kelmscott Press. There were 300 copies on paper and 10 on vellum.

8 April 1892: Morris entertained Emery Walker and Ellis to dinner.

9 April 1892: In the morning Morris was up at 6 am working on *The Well at the World's End*. In the afternoon he held his annual Boat Race party at Kelmscott House. He wrote to Jenny: 'Oxford won the race; but I suppose that you care for that as little as I do.' Nicoll published an inflammatory editorial in *Commonweal* in support of the Walsall Anarchists.

11 April 1892: Morris gave Ruskin a signed copy of *The Nature of Gothic*.

13 April 1892: Morris travelled down to Kelmscott Manor.

18 April 1892: The police raided the offices of *Commonweal* and arrested Nicoll and Mowbray. Mowbray's wife had died only a few hours before his arrest but he was refused permission to attend her funeral until Morris subsequently came before the court and entered into surety for him for £500. According to Cockerell in his *Diary*, when Morris heard that Ruskin had described him as 'the ablest man of his time' he had opened a bottle of his favourite Imperial Tokay to celebrate.

20 April 1892: Morris returned to London from Kelmscott Manor.

21 April 1892: Morris spent the morning fair-copying *The Well at the World's End*.

22 April 1892: Morris was in the chair at a lecture given by Webb at the Art Workers' Guild, Barnard's Inn, London.

May 1892: In an article in the *Hammersmith Socialist Record* Morris strongly condemned the anarchists.

2 May 1892: Morris finished one of the borders for *The Golden Legend*.

4 May 1892: Morris returned to London from Kelmscott Manor.

5 May 1892: Blunt wrote in his *Diary*: 'To Mrs. Morris at Hammersmith and stopped a couple of hours with her in the gloomy old house. We talked about Rossetti, and I asked her whether she had been very much in love with him. She said, "Yes, at first, but it didn't last long".'

6 May 1892: Nicoll and Mowbray were tried at the Central Criminal Court at the Old Bailey for inciting violence by publishing an article in *Commonweal* entitled 'The Walsall Anarchists Condemned to Penal Servitude'. Nicoll was sentenced to eighteen months hard labour but Mowbray was acquitted. During Nicoll's imprisonment *Commonweal* was edited by Henry Benjamin Samuels whose brother-in-law, Henri Bourdin, died in a bomb explosion outside the Greenwich conservatory on 15 February 1894. This incident later formed the basis of Joseph Conrad's *The Secret Agent*.

10 May 1892: Blunt visited the Morrises at Kelmscott House where he found Morris hard at work on *The Well at the World's End*.

13 May 1892: *A Dream of John Ball and A King's Lesson* was finished by the Kelmscott Press. There were 300 copies on paper and 11 on vellum.

17 May 1892: By this time Morris was staying at Kelmscott Manor. In the evening he worked on *The Well at the World's End*.

18 May 1892: Morris spent most of the day working on *The Well at the World's End*.

19 May 1892: *The Defence of Guenevere* was issued by Reeves & Turner.

25 May 1892: Morris spent the evening at Kelmscott Manor working on *The Well at the World's End*: 'I had a beautiful vegetarian dinner today: sparrow grass and poached eggs and pan-cakes!'

26 May 1892: Morris went to Buscot Wood 'and saw the harebells beautiful just within'.

28 May 1892: Morris returned to London from Kelmscott Manor.

29 May 1892: Morris delivered 'Town and Country' at a meeting sponsored by the HSS at Kelmscott House, Hammersmith. He also signed a copy of *The Defence of Guenevere* which he presented to Swinburne.

June 1892: An article entitled *Three English Poets: William Morris* by Louise C. Moulton appeared in *Arena* (vol. 6, p. 46).

4 June 1892: Blunt and his daughter had lunch at Kelmscott House.

13 June 1892: Morris travelled down to Kelmscott Manor.

20 June 1892: In the morning Morris returned to London.

21 June 1892: Morris spent the day at Merton.

28 June 1892: Morris delivered a speech at the annual conference of SPAB at Barnard's Inn, London. At the same meeting he also gave a speech moving a vote of thanks to the chairman, Judge Lushington.

29 June 1892: Morris travelled down to Kelmscott Manor.

July 1892: An article entitled *William Morris* by F. Richardson appeared in the *Primitive Methodist Quarterly Review* (vol. 34, p. 414).

4 July 1892: Blunt visited the Morrises at Kelmscott Manor: 'we played dominoes in the old way. Morris was in fine spirits.'

8 July 1892: Morris probably returned to London from Kelmscott Manor.

9 July 1892: Morris had dinner with Emery Walker, Madame Kropotkin and Miss Philpot at Kelmscott House.

10 July 1892: Morris visited Bax to work on the revision of *Socialism from the Root Up*: 'hard labour till about 11pm.'

12 July 1892: Morris 'worked hard' on *The Well at the World's End*.

15 July 1892: Morris held an 'afternoon tea' at Merton: 'Our party at Merton Abbey went off very well. There were about 40 I think, and we had our drinks in the carpet room after we had gone round.'

16 July 1892: Morris went to Rottingdean to discuss the designs for the Kelmscott *Chaucer* with Burne-Jones. He stayed the night.

17 July 1892: In the evening Morris returned to London from Rottingdean.

19 July 1892: Morris travelled down to Kelmscott Manor.

26 July 1892: Morris returned to London from Kelmscott Manor. He had dinner with Ellis at 17 Hammersmith Terrace.

29 July 1892: Morris spent the day at Merton.

August 1892: In the *Hammersmith Socialist Record* Morris reaffirmed his opposition to the institution of Parliament.

2 August 1892: Morris travelled down to Kelmscott Manor.

5 August 1892: Cockerell visited Morris at Kelmscott Manor: 'Reached Kelmscott Manor about 6. W. M. was at the door, and the first thing he did was to take me over the house and through the garden and down to the Thames.'

6 August 1892: Morris and Cockerell visited Inglesham Church which was being repaired 'mainly at W. M.'s expense'. The two men then walked to Buscot and back to Kelmscott Manor across the meadows.

7 August 1892: In the morning Morris, Jenny and Cockerell went out on the Thames fishing in a punt. Morris caught fifty gudgeon and a perch. In the afternoon they walked to Buscot Woods. In the evening Morris spent some time working on *The Well at the World's End*.

8 August 1892: In the morning Cockerell helped Morris by washing in a blue background to one of the latter's new wallpaper designs. In the evening Middleton joined Morris and Cockerell for dinner.

9 August 1892: Morris, Jenny, Cockerell and Miss Strick walked to Eaton Hastings. In the afternoon the party, which also included Jane and Middleton, visited Kelmscott Church. The day was rounded off by playing 'Twenty Questions'.

10 August 1892: Morris, Jane, Jenny, Miss Strick and Cockerell took a drive to Great Coxwell to visit the tithe barn. According to Cockerell, Morris declared 'that it was the finest piece of architecture in England, and [he] wanted to build a house like it'. Cockerell went on to add that they then visited the church 'which has some pretty tracery, and two 15th century brasses to William Morys and Johane, wyf of William Morrys'.

11 August 1892: In the morning Morris and Cockerell travelled back to London. On the way Morris 'pointed out the house that they were rebuilding in the 26th chapter of News from Nowhere'. Later Morris attended a meeting of SPAB. Blunt visited Jane at Kelmscott Manor. He wrote: 'We slept together, Mrs. Morris and I, and she told me things about the past which explain much in regard to Rossetti. "I never quite gave myself," she said, "as I do now".'

13 August 1892: Morris and Magnússon spent the afternoon working on the first volume of the *Heimskringla*.

14 August 1892: Morris and Magnússon continued working on the *Heimskringla*. Morris delivered an unnamed lecture at a meeting sponsored by the HSS at Kelmscott House, Hammersmith. Afterwards he had supper with the Sparlings: 'I thought May looking much better.'

18 August 1892: Morris travelled down to Kelmscott Manor.

21 August 1892: Morris was scheduled to deliver 'Communism' at a meeting sponsored by the HSS at Kelmscott House.

25 August 1892: Morris returned to London from Kelmscott Manor.

31 August 1892: Morris travelled down to Kelmscott Manor.

4 September 1892: Morris visited the Grange. In the evening he had dinner with the Sparlings, Emery Walker and Murray. Later he attended Henry Gaylord Wilshire's lecture 'The American Revolution, No. 2' at Kelmscott House.

5 September 1892: Morris attended the annual Kelmscott Press 'Wayzegoose' (an entertainment held by a master printer for his workmen). The Kelmscott Press printed the programme for the event.

12 September 1892: *The Golden Legend* by William Caxton was finished by the Kelmscott Press. There were 500 copies on paper. It was subsequently sold by Bernard Quaritch.

14 September 1892: *A Dream of John Ball and A King's Lesson* was issued by Reeves & Turner.

15 September 1892: Cockerell recorded in his *Diary* that after attending a meeting of SPAB he had supper with Morris and Webb and there was 'talk about Munera Pulveris etc.'.

1 October 1892: Morris spent the day working on the proofs of the *Heimskringla* with Magnússon.

5 October 1892: Morris returned to Kelmscott Manor possibly in the company of Emery Walker.

6 October 1892: Tennyson died. Morris was subsequently approached as a possible candidate for the laureateship but indicated he did not want to be considered for the post (*c.f.* 17, 27, and 29 October). According to Cockerell, Morris said that he could not contemplate 'sitting down in crimson plush breeches and white stockings to write birthday odes in honour of all the blooming little Guelfings and Battenburgs that happen to come along'.

7 October 1892: It is clear from a receipt written by Morris that the total cost of the 500 copies of *The Golden Legend* was £1,350. In a letter to Shaw, Morris wrote: 'Don't you think Lord Lorne ought to be made Laureate. Wouldn't that please all parties?' Morris visited Inglesham Church where he found 'that the bell-turret has been mended & put up again; and that the nave roof is nearly finished'.

12 October 1892: Morris returned to London from Kelmscott Manor. He declined an invitation to attend Tennyson's funeral. Despite this the *Daily Chronicle* (13 October) recorded – in error – his attendance at Westminster Abbey: 'A not less conspicuous figure was that of William Morris, with his bright clear eyes and broad forehead.' Jane wrote to Blunt: 'my nerves have given way under the great pressure of being continually in the house with her [Jenny]. Dr. R. Rouse says that if I don't make a change now, either to go away for the winter or at least for 3 or 4 months, I shall break down entirely, and pass beyond the help of any doctor.'

13 October 1892: Morris and Jane visited Dr Rouse to discuss the latter's illness. Cockerell recorded in his *Diary*: '[Morris] said he didn't see why the queen shouldn't choose her laureate just as much as her butler & that Sir Theodore Martin, being a courtier, would be a suitable man for the post.'

14 October 1892: Blunt recorded in his *Diary* that Jane's health had broken down and she 'was threatened with melancholia'. Morris wrote to Glasier cancelling a proposed lecture tour in Scotland: 'The fact is, my dear fellow, that at present the absolute *duties* of my life are summed up in the necessity for taking care of my wife and my daughter, both of whom in one way or other are in bad health: my *work* of all kinds is really simply an amusement taken when I can out of my duty time.' William Caxton's *The Recuyell of the Historyes of Troye* was finished by the Kelmscott Press. There were 300 copies on paper and 5 on vellum. This was the first book printed using Troy type.

17 October 1892: Cockerell visited Morris at Kelmscott House where he admired 'a newly acquired Italian choir-book (dated 1295)' that Morris had bought. The two men then travelled down to Kelmscott Manor. They played whist in the evening before Morris began work on one of the borders he was designing for *The Well at the World's End*. During the evening Cockerell suggested that a frontispiece depicting Kelmscott Manor should be used for the Kelmscott Press edition of *News from Nowhere*: 'W. M. seemed to like the idea (*c.f.* 5 November 1892).' Gladstone, after considering Ruskin and Swinburne for the laureateship, turned his attention to Morris. He wrote to Acton: 'I understand Mr. W. Morris is an out and out socialist.' Acton replied: 'he is quite a flaring Communist, with unpleasant associations.'

19 October 1892: Morris spent the morning fishing and caught a pike which was cooked for supper. In the afternoon Cockerell read the proofs of the first 200 pages of *The Well at the World's End*.

20 October 1892: According to Cockerell, Morris 'donned his best clothes and went to pay a society call on Mr. and Mrs. Hobbs'. Mr Hobbs was the son of the landlord of Kelmscott Manor. Blunt wrote: 'Mrs Morris came to lunch with me... She cannot bear being with many people, especially when her daughter Jenny is there, and is happiest alone (which I believe is a symptom of that form of madness).'

22 October 1892: The *Biblia Innocentium* was finished by the Kelmscott Press. Two hundred paper copies were printed. This was the last Kelmscott Press book to be issued with untrimmed edges.

27 October 1892: In a letter to James Bryce, who had sounded him out about the laureateship on Gladstone's behalf, Morris wrote: 'I am a sincere republican, and therefore could not accept a post which would give me even the appearance of serving a court for compliance sake.'

28 October 1892: Morris attended a dinner at the Blue Posts Restaurant to celebrate the publication of *The Golden Legend*. He also presented Jenny with a signed copy of *A Dream of John Ball*.

29 October 1892: Morris wrote a letter to the *Daily Chronicle* (published 31 October): 'Will you kindly contradict the report that I have been offered the Laureateship, as it is not true.'

3 November 1892: *The Golden Legend* was issued. Cockerell recorded in his *Diary* that Morris engaged him for 'two guineas a week and a copy of the Golden Legend' to catalogue his books.

5 November 1892: Morris wrote to Charles March Gere asking him to go to Kelmscott Manor to make some drawings of the house to be used as the frontispiece for *News from Nowhere*.

7 November 1892: Cockerell wrote in his *Diary* of a visit to Kelmscott House: 'When I went up into the drawing room to say goodnight Morris and his wife were playing at draughts, with large ivory pieces, red and white. Mrs. M. was dressed in a glorious blue gown, and as she sat on the sofa, she looked like an animated Rossetti picture or pages from an old MS of a king and queen.'

10 November 1892: William Caxton's *The Order of Chivalry* was finished by the Kelmscott Press. There were 250 copies on paper and 10 on vellum. This was the first book published using Chaucer type. Quaritch purchased for Morris a first edition of St Augustine's *De Civitate Dei* and Conrad Botha's *Cronecken der Sassen* at the Apponyi Sale. According to Cockerell, Morris was greatly impressed by the compressed type of the *De Civitate Dei*: 'He at once designed a lower-case alphabet on this model, but was not satisfied with it and did not have it cut.'

11 November 1892: Cockerell recorded in his *Diary*: 'Saw proofs of some drawings of Kelmscott made by Gere, who is to make an illustration for News from Nowhere.'

12 November 1892: Jane gave Blunt the love letters she had received from Rossetti for safe keeping. Her instructions were that they should 'not be published till 50 years after my death'. She later asked for them back.

15 November 1892: Morris and Jane left London at 9.30 am at the start of their journey to Bordighera.

17 November 1892: In the evening Morris and Jane arrived at Bordighera. Jane wrote to Blunt (22 November): 'My husband ... was so unwell that I had to look after him instead of his looking after me.'

18 November 1892: Morris wrote to Jenny: 'From my window it is all olives & olives & the sea beyond; from the balcony I can just see a bit of the coast-line handsome enough.'

20 November 1892: Morris left Bordighera.

21 November 1892: Morris arrived back in London. The *Star* (p. 2) published an article 'William Morris Designs and Produces "the most Beautiful Book" Ever Published'.

22 November 1892: *News from Nowhere* was finished by the Kelmscott Press. There were 300 copies on paper and 10 on vellum. It was decorated with a woodcut engraved by W. H. Hooper from Gere's design.

December 1892: The HSS held a discussion on the subject: 'Is it now desirable to form a Socialist Federation?' The question was answered in the affirmative and approaches were made to the SDF and the Fabian Society.

3 December 1892: In the afternoon Morris was visited by the illustrator Arthur Joseph Gaskin.

15 December 1892: *The History of Reynard the Foxe* was finished by the Kelmscott Press. There were 300 copies on paper and 10 on vellum. This was the last of the large books printed by the Kelmscott Press to be issued through a publisher.

18 December 1892: The HSS appointed a special sub-committee – including Morris – 'to promote the alliance of Socialist organisations in Great Britain'.

21 December 1892: Macmillan & Co. wrote to Morris proposing that the Kelmscott Press produce an edition of Tennyson's *Maud* for them (*c.f.* 11 August 1893).

23 December 1892: Morris wrote a testimonial for Cockerell who was a candidate for the curatorship of Sir John Soane's Museum. Later he travelled down to Kelmscott Manor to spend Christmas. Amongst the others present were Shaw, the Sparlings, Jenny and Mary De Morgan.

28 December 1892: Jane wrote to Blunt: 'I have taken part in some "tableaux vivants" at George Macdonald's, people seemed pleased, some characters are to be played tomorrow where I believe I am to be chief lover as I am so much taller than anybody else.'

29 December 1892: Shaw and May returned to London from Kelmscott Manor. Sparling had returned the previous day. The *Biblia Innocentium* was published by Bernard Quaritch.

1893: A revised version of *Socialism from the Root Up* was published in book form as *Socialism: Its Growth and Outcome* by Swan Sonnenschein & Co. Morris provided a 'Preface' to *Arts And Crafts Essays* published by Rivington, Percival & Co. May's book *Decorative Needlework* was published. The Arts and Crafts Exhibition Society's magazine – the *Studio* – was founded. Morris kept a *Diary* (BM.Add.MS.45409).

January 1893: An article entitled *William Morris and the Meaning of Life* by F. W. Myers appeared in the *Nineteenth Century* (vol. 33, p. 93).

2 January 1893: An exhibition of Burne-Jones's work opened at the New Gallery. It ran until 15 April 1893.

5 January 1893: Morris wrote to Oscar Wilde requesting permission to publish Lady Wilde's *Sidonia the Sorceress*.

13–14 January 1893: The first Conference of the Independent Labour Party (ILP) was held at Bradford. A number of ex-Leaguers – including J. L. Mahon and A. K. Donald – played a prominent part at the Conference. Blatchford, in the *Clarion*, later called for Morris to take his rightful place amongst the leadership of the ILP.

17 January 1893: *The Poems of William Shakespeare* was finished by the Kelmscott Press. There were 500 copies on paper and 10 on vellum. The book was sold by Reeves & Turner.

20 January 1893: In his *Diary* Morris recorded that *The Poems of William Shakespeare* was sent to the binders.

24 January 1893: Morris travelled down to Kelmscott Manor.

25 January 1893: Morris was visited by Gere at Kelmscott Manor. *The History of Reynard the Foxe* was issued.

26 January 1893: Morris returned to London from Kelmscott Manor.

31 January 1893: Morris gave F. S. Ellis an inscribed copy of *The History of Reynard the Foxe*.

February 1893: Keir Hardie of the ILP lectured on 'The Labour Movement' at Kelmscott House and Shaw Maxwell (also of the ILP) on the 'Programme of the Labour Party'.

3 February 1893: Morris opened a discussion on 'the attitude of trades unions to Socialism' at a meeting sponsored by the HSS at Kelmscott House, Hammersmith.

5 February 1893: Morris visited the Grange where he met the Burne-Joneses' grandson – Denis Mackail – for the first time: 'He is a dear little baby; and looks so *good*. That joined with the fact that his ears stick out very much make me think he will grow up into something.' He became a popular novelist.

8 February 1893: Morris invited Cobden-Sanderson to Kelmscott House to discuss the binding of some of his medieval books.

9 February 1893: Morris attended a meeting of SPAB and later an Arts & Crafts supper.

11 February 1893: The Kelmscott Press printed an invitation for the annual gathering of the HSS.

16 February 1893: Morris recorded in his *Diary* that he had just finished the design for the first page of the *Chaucer*.

19 February 1893: Morris delivered 'Communism' at a meeting sponsored by the HSS at Kelmscott House. The audience numbered 'about 150'.

21 February 1893: Morris began his translation of *The Tale of Beowulf* with A. J. Wyatt.

22 February 1893: The *Daily Chronicle* published an article entitled 'Master Printer Morris: Interview with Mr. William Morris'.

23 February 1893: Morris attended the first meeting of the Joint Committee of Socialist Bodies held at Kelmscott House, Hammersmith. He was elected chairman for three months.

March 1893: Shaw Maxwell returned to Kelmscott House to lecture on the 'Aims and Objects of the Labour Party'. Despite these talks the ILP was not asked to join the joint committee as Hyndman did not regard it as a truly socialist body. An article by Professor O. L. Triggs entitled 'The Socialist Thread in the Life and Work of William Morris' appeared in *Poet Lore* (vol. 5, p. 116).

10 March 1893: Morris delivered 'Communism' at a meeting sponsored by the 'Freedom' Publication Fund Committee at the Grafton Hall, London.

20 March 1893: Cobden-Sanderson established the Doves Bindery in a house opposite the Kelmscott Press in the Upper Mall, Hammersmith. He let the attic and the first floor room to Morris as additional accommodation for the Kelmscott Press.

24 March 1893: *News from Nowhere* was issued by Reeves & Turner.

30 March 1893: George Cavendish's *The Life of Thomas Wolsey* was finished by the Kelmscott Press. There were 250 copies on paper and 6 on vellum. It was sold by Reeves & Turner.

5 April 1893: The *Journal of the Derbyshire Archaeological and Natural History Society* (p. 97) published a letter from Morris on tapestry.

7 April 1893: Morris gave Ellis a signed copy of *News from Nowhere*.

20 April 1893: Morris met Robert Blatchford: 'and rather liked the looks of him.'

25 April 1893: Morris travelled to Kelmscott Manor.

27 April 1893: William Caxton's *The History of Godefrey of Boloyne and of the Conquest of Jerusalem* was finished by the Kelmscott Press. There were 300 copies on paper and 6 on vellum. This was the first book to be printed *and* sold by the Kelmscott Press.

29 April 1893: Morris returned to London from Kelmscott Manor.

30 April 1893: Morris gave an open-air speech at a meeting organized for the benefit of the striking Hull dockers at Ravenscourt Park, London.

1 May 1893: *The Manifesto of the English Socialists* was issued written by Morris, Hyndman and Shaw. It was sold for a penny.

7 May 1893: Morris gave an open-air speech at the May Day celebrations sponsored by combined London socialist and anarchist groups in Hyde Park, London. Morris spoke from the SDF platform. A letter of his to Joseph Edwards was read at the Labour Church Service in Liverpool.

18 May 1893: Blunt wrote in his *Diary*: 'To Hammersmith. Mrs Morris tells me that Jenny really went mad a year and a half ago, thought she had murdered her father and tried to throw herself out of the window. She was so violent that she had to be tied down to her bed.'

24 May 1893: *The History of Godefrey of Boloyne* was issued.

June 1893: The last edition of the *Hammersmith Socialist Record* was published.

6 June 1893: Morris gave a speech opposing the restoration of St Mary's Church, Oxford, at a convocation called by the University's Vice-Chancellor at Oxford.

15 June 1893: Morris attended a meeting of SPAB and later went on to Gatti's. Cockerell recalled in his *Diary*: 'He had a superb little 13 c. Psalter (Liege) which he brought into New Gallery in the afternoon and has since bought from Ellis & Elvey.'

19 June 1893: Morris lectured on 'The Ideal Book' at the Bibliographical Society, London.

20 June 1893: Blunt wrote: 'Lunched with Mrs Morris, whom I really love a great deal better.'

22 June 1893: Morris gave a signed copy of *The History of Godefrey of Boloyne* to Arthur Hughes.

July 1893: The Fabian Society withdrew from the Joint Committee of Socialist Bodies.

12 July 1893: In the afternoon Morris wrote the preface to the Kelmscott Press edition of Thomas More's *Utopia*.

13 July 1893: Morris had lunch with Georgiana Burne-Jones at the Grange.

14 July 1893: Morris visited the 'Toothster' [dentist].

16 July 1893: Cockerell recorded in his *Diary*: 'Went to tea at K. H. Saw another B-J drawing for the Chaucer, the cutting of which had been unsuccessful.'

18 July 1893: Morris was chairman at the annual meeting of SPAB held at Barnard's Inn, London.

Summer 1893: The HSS published *The Reward of Labour: A Dialogue* which had originally appeared in *Commonweal*. It was sold for a penny. Around the same time a pamphlet entitled *Concerning Westminster Abbey* by Morris was published by SPAB.

4 August 1893: Sir Thomas More's *Utopia* was finished by the Kelmscott Press. There were 300 paper copies and 8 on vellum. This was the last book to be sold through Reeves & Turner.

9 August 1893: In a letter to Emery Walker, Morris wrote: 'More and more at any rate I want to see a due Socialist party established.'

11 August 1893: *Maud* by Alfred Lord Tennyson was finished by the Kelmscott Press. There were 500 copies on paper and 5 on vellum. It was published by special arrangement with Macmillan & Co.

14 August 1893: Morris travelled down to Kelmscott Manor.

16 August 1893: Morris, Jane and Middleton visited Burford.

22 August 1893: By this time Morris had returned to London. In the evening he was visited by George Bernard Shaw.

23 August 1893: Jane wrote to Blunt telling him that Lisa Stillman was staying at Kelmscott Manor: 'Lisa began a drawing of me in the summerhouse, she did a very good one of me two years ago, it was not quite finished, but very like.'

8 September 1893: The Kelmscott Press held its annual 'Wayzegoose'.

15 September 1893: *Sidonia the Sorceress* was finished by the Kelmscott Press. There were 300 copies on paper and 10 on vellum.

25 September 1893: In the morning Morris visited the preparations at the New Gallery for the exhibition of the Arts and Crafts Exhibition Society. He later travelled to Much Hadham to visit his mother who was ill.

26 September 1893: Morris wrote to Jenny: 'Your poor dear Granny is certainly much changed for the worse since I saw her more than a year ago; but on the whole she is better than I expected to see her.'

30 September 1893: Morris travelled to Kelmscott Manor. The Kelmscott Press edition of Tennyson's *Maud* was issued.

5 October 1893: Morris returned to London to be at the opening of the Arts and Crafts Exhibition Society's show at the New Gallery.

6 October 1893: Blunt, who was at Kelmscott Manor, wrote: 'Morris in excellent spirits. Judith has made him give his "visual memory" for her collection, but he has none except for names.' Ford Madox Brown died.

9 October 1893: The *Daily Chronicle* published an article entitled 'Art, Craft and Life: An Interview with Mr. William Morris'.

14 October 1893: Rossetti's *Ballads and Narrative Poems* was finished by the Kelmscott Press. There were 310 copies on paper and 6 on vellum. It was published by Ellis & Elvey.

16 October 1893: The *Sun* published an article by Morris 'On the Coal Struggle'.

21 October 1893: Morris lectured on 'Printed Books, Ancient and Modern' at a meeting sponsored by the Manchester Technical Instruction Committee at the Lord Mayor's Parlour, Manchester.

22 October 1893: Morris lectured on 'The Dangers of Restoration' at a meeting sponsored by the Ancoats Recreation Committee at the New Islington Hall, Ancoats, Manchester.

2 November 1893: Morris lectured 'On the Printing of Books' at a meeting sponsored by the Arts and Crafts Exhibition Society at the New Gallery at 121 Regent Street, London.

5 November 1893: An article on Morris by Alfred Henry Miles appeared in *The Weekly Dispatch* (p. 2).

6 November 1893: Morris's article 'On the Printing of Books' appeared in the *Times*.

10 November 1893: A letter from Morris on the 'Deeper Meaning of the Struggle' was published in the *Daily Chronicle*. This appeared soon after as a pamphlet. In the afternoon he lectured on 'Waste' at a meeting sponsored by the Burnley Branch of the SDF at the St James Hall, Burnley. In the evening he delivered 'What Shall We Do Now?' at the same venue. Both lectures were given in support of Hyndman's contest for the Burnley Parliamentary seat.

18 November 1893: An untitled review of *Socialism: Its Growth and Outcome* appeared in the *Athenaeum* (p. 965).

20 November 1893: Morris travelled to Rottingdean to visit the Burne-Joneses: 'I got here about 6 after a long dark drive, and ate so much buttered toast at tea that I was good for very little supper afterwards.' Later he did some work on *The Wood Beyond the World*.

21 November 1893: In the morning Morris went for a walk before returning to work on a border for one of his books.

27 November 1893: Cockerell wrote in his *Diary*: 'W. M. came to the N[ew] G[allery] looking much the better for his week in Rottingdean.'

12 December 1893: Morris wrote to James Tochatti in reply to his invitation to write for *Liberty*: 'considering the attitude which some anarchists are taking up about the recent anarchist murders, & attempts to murder I could not in conscience allow anything with my name attached to it to appear in an anarchist paper, (as I understand yours is to be) unless you publish in said paper a distinct repudiation of such monstrosities.' Tochatti did this and Morris contributed to the paper (*c.f.* February 1894 and May 1895).

16 December 1893: *Of King Florus and the Fair Jehane* was finished by the Kelmscott Press. There were 350 copies on paper and 15 on vellum.

18 December 1893: Morris gave Oscar Wilde a signed copy of *Sidonia the Sorceress*.

1894: Morris's *Letters on Socialism* was privately printed in a limited edition of 34 copies by Thomas J. Wise. Morris's *Why I Am a Communist* was printed by Tochatti and sold for a penny.

January 1894: Morris's article 'Some Notes on the Illuminated Books of the Middle Ages' appeared in the *Magazine of Art*. Morris contributed an article to the *Labour Prophet*. The first edition of Tochatti's paper *Liberty* appeared.

2 January 1894: An unsigned review of Morris's lecture 'Gothic Architecture' appeared in the *Daily Chronicle*.

7 January 1894: Arnold Dolmetsch had lunch with Morris and Burne-Jones to discuss the prospect of the Kelmscott Press publishing an edition of early English songs (this project was never completed). Dolmetsch introduced Morris to early instrumental music around this time. He wrote: 'One memorable day, in 1894, Burne-Jones brought Morris to one of my old English performances in Dulwich. He understood this music at once, and his emotion was so strong that he was moved to tears! He had found the lost art!' (*c.f.* 21 September 1896).

13 January 1894: The second – illustrated – edition of *The Story of the Glittering Plain* was finished by the Kelmscott Press. There were 250 copies on paper and 7 on vellum.

14 January 1894: Morris lectured on 'Early England' at a meeting held at the South London Art Gallery, Peckham Road, London.

20 January 1894: Morris was probably visited by Octave Muse in connection with exhibiting at the first Salon of *La Libre Esthetique* which was due to open in Brussels in February (*c.f.* 17 February 1894).

22 January 1894: Morris gave a signed copy of *The Tale of King Florus and the Fair Jehane* to Walter Swinburne.

26 January 1894: According to Cockerell in his *Diary*, F. S. Ellis visited Kelmscott House to discuss with Morris the possibility of the Kelmscott Press doing an edition of the *Border Ballads*. This was never to materialize although Mackail recalled that during the final stages of his illness Morris 'when he was too ill to do anything else ... amused himself by having the ballads read aloud to him and beginning to form his own version'.

27 January 1894: 'A Socialist Poet on Bombs and Anarchism: An Interview with William Morris' signed 'Wat Tyler' appeared in *Justice*. In it Morris dismissed anarchism as 'a social disease caused by the evil condition of society'. He also gave guarded approval for palliatives.

Late January 1894: Burne-Jones accepted a baronetcy from Gladstone. He was too embarrassed to tell Morris even though he dined with him the previous evening. Morris found out by reading the morning papers.

February 1894: Morris spoke in favour of George Lansbury the SDF candidate at Walworth. An unsigned review of *Socialism: Its Growth & Outcome* appeared in the *Critic* (p. 107). Morris's article 'Why I Am a Communist' appeared in *Liberty*.

4 February 1894: Morris began work on *The Waters of the Wondrous Isles*.

14 February 1894: Cockerell recorded in his *Diary* that Morris was translating 'Amis and Amile'. Morris later told Ellis that he translated the poem 'in one day and a quarter, it was *very* easy'.

15 February 1894: Morris was visited by a Mr. Holst: 'I thought [him] a jolly sort of a chap, & really with some good discrimination about work, which all our foreign friends have not got.' This was probably a reference to the first visit of Gustav Holst to Kelmscott House. Holst was to join the HSS in 1894 and become director of the Hammersmith Socialist Choir. However, Kelvin in *The Collected Letters* suggests that the caller was Richard Nicolas Roland Holst a Dutch painter and writer.

16 February 1894: Morris wrote to Swinburne praising an ode which had appeared in the *Athenaeum* (10 February 1894, p. 179) under the title 'To William Morris/Dedication of a Forthcoming Volume of Poems'. This poem was the concluding one in Swinburne's volume *Astrophel and Other Poems* which was issued by Chatto and Windus on 26 April 1894.

17 February 1894: The first Salon of *La Libre Esthetique* opened in Brussels. Morris was one of the exhibitors.

20 February 1894: Rossetti's *Sonnets and Lyrical Poems* was finished by the Kelmscott Press. There were 310 copies on paper and 6 on vellum. It was sold by Ellis & Elvey. Morris gave a speech at the Jesmond Street School, Walworth, London. This was in support of the candidature of George Lansbury for the Walworth seat.

21 February 1894: In the afternoon Morris lectured on 'The Woodcuts of Gothic Books' at a meeting sponsored by the Birmingham Municipal School of Art at the Birmingham and Midlands Institute. In the evening he gave an address at the Distribution of Prizes at the same venue.

24 February 1894: Morris's speech in support of the candidacy of George Lansbury was published in *Justice* (p. 1).

27 February 1894: Morris's letter on the 'Proposed Addition to Westminster Abbey' appeared in the *Daily Chronicle*.

March 1894: The Kelmscott Press printed a four-page leaflet for the Ancoats Brotherhood. This had a frontispiece from the Kelmscott Press edition of *A Dream of John Ball*.

1 March 1894: Morris attended a meeting of SPAB and then went on to Gatti's. Cockerell recalled in his *Diary* that 'W. M. had a splendid bible,

French, c.1300, which he had just bought of Quaritch'. Morris had purchased it for £190.

7 March 1894: *The Poems of John Keats* was finished by the Kelmscott Press. There were 300 copies on paper and 7 on vellum.

9 March 1894: In response to an inquiry from A. Momberger, Engels supplied a bibliography of socialist publications – from a more or less Marxist standpoint – in English. The list was headed by Morris and Bax's *Socialism: Its Growth and Outcome*.

10 March 1894: The first part of Morris's lecture 'What Shall We Do Now?' was published in *Justice*.

11 March 1894: In the morning Morris delivered 'What Shall We Do Now?' at an open-air meeting near Trafford Bridge, Manchester, sponsored by the South Salford Branch of the SDF. James Leatham was at this meeting and wrote: 'The last time I saw Morris he was speaking from a lorry pitched on a piece of waste land close to the Ship Canal... It was a wild March Sunday morning, and he would not have been asked to speak out of doors, but he had expressed a desire to do so, and so there he was, talking with quiet strenuousness, drawing a laugh now and then from the undulating crowd, of working men mostly, who stood in the hollow and on the slopes before him... Many there were hearing and seeing the man for the first time, most of us were hearing him for the last time; and we all looked and listened as though we knew it.' In the evening he lectured on 'Waste' at another meeting sponsored by the South Salford Branch of the SDF at the Free Trade Hall, Manchester.

13 March 1894: *Of the Friendship of Amis and Amile* was finished by the Kelmscott Press. There were 500 copies on paper and 15 on vellum.

17 March 1894: The second part of Morris's lecture 'What Shall We Do Now?' was published in *Justice*.

30 March 1894: Morris was visited 'unexpectedly' by Magnússon who stayed the night at Kelmscott House.

31 March 1894: The *Clarion* published a poem entitled 'On Hearing William Morris Address an Open-Air Meeting on Trafford Bridge': 'Like an archangel in the morning sun/He stood with a high message, and men, heard.'

April 1894: An unsigned article entitled 'An English Socialist: William Morris' appeared in the *London Quarterly Review* (vol. 22, pp. 84–8).

2 April 1894: Cockerell recorded in his *Diary* that 'W. M. finished the first verso border for the Chaucer'.

10 April 1894: According to Cockerell in his *Diary*, Morris finished his translation of *The Tale of Beowulf*. However, Morris and A. J. Wyatt continued to revise the text during the next few months.

11 April 1894: Morris wrote a letter in support of Fairfax Murray's candidature for the Directorship of the National Gallery. The latter was unsuccessful and Sir Edward Pounter was appointed to the post.

23 April 1894: Morris declined an invitation from H. A. Jones to attend the opening of the latter's play *The Masqueraders* at the St James Theatre on 28 April 1894.

24 April 1894: Morris was 'working hard' at Kelmscott Manor designing the borders for the *Chaucer*.

30 April 1894: Blunt recorded that he went to Hammersmith 'where I found Morris, very scornful of an American imitation of his Kelmscott Press, though it was good enough to have taken Mrs. Morris in'.

4 May 1894: *Atalanta in Calydon: A Tragedy* by Algernon Charles Swinburne was finished by the Kelmscott Press. There were 250 copies on paper and 8 on vellum.

8 May 1894: Morris visited an exhibition at the New Gallery where he viewed Charles Gere's *Hermia and Helena*: '[I] liked it very much; I congratulate you on it.' *The Poems of John Keats* was issued.

10 May 1894: Morris, Cockerell, Emery Walker and Carruthers travelled from Victoria to New Haven. According to Cockerell in his *Diary* they then 'had a calm crossing to Dieppe'. This was the start of a week's holiday visiting the churches and cathedrals in northern France.

17 May 1894: Morris, Cockerell, Walker and Carruthers returned to London after their short holiday in France.

24 May 1894: Jane wrote to Blunt: 'I have been in a heart-broken condition. May's married life has come to an end.'

26 May 1894: Jane wrote to Blunt: 'May's position is this, she has been seeing a good deal of a former lover [George Bernard Shaw], and made her husband's life a burden to him, he refuses to bear it any longer.'

28 May 1894: Cockerell wrote in his *Diary*: 'Went up to Oxford Street with W. M. to see the Lancelot tapestry which is just off the loom.' Later Morris and Jenny travelled down to Kelmscott Manor.

30 May 1894: *The Wood Beyond the World* was finished by the Kelmscott Press. There were 350 copies on paper and 8 on vellum. It contained a frontispiece by Burne-Jones.

7 June 1894: Morris was elected a Fellow of the Society of Antiquaries.

16 June 1894: Morris dined with the Cobden-Sandersons at their home in Hampstead. Amongst the other guests were Lady Airlie, Mrs J. R. Green, Benjamin Kidd and Kropotkin. Morris's article 'How I Became a Socialist' was published in *Justice*. It was issued as a pamphlet in 1896.

27 June 1894: Morris wrote to Blunt quoting a price of £544 for the tapestry he had ordered (*c.f.* 29 May 1896).

30 June 1894: The Kelmscott Press printed an address to Sir Lothian Bell from his employees.

July 1894: An illustrated article by Aymer Vallance entitled 'On the Revival of Tapestry-Weaving: An Interview with William Morris' appeared in the *Studio* (vol. 3, p. 99).

3 July 1894: Morris was at Kelmscott Manor. Middleton and his family were also staying at the house. They left on 19 July 1894.

5 July 1894: Morris returned to London from Kelmscott Manor.

15 July 1894: Jane, who was staying at Kelmscott Manor, wrote of Middleton: 'Mr Middleton is so very ill, hopelessly to my thinking.'

16 July 1894: The Kelmscott Press printed the invitation for the unveiling of Keats's bust in Hampstead Parish Church which took place on this day. Jane returned to London from Kelmscott Manor.

24 July 1894: The *Daily Chronicle* (dated 20 July) printed a letter from Morris relating to the Kelmscott Press *Chaucer*. He hoped the book would be issued 'about the middle of next year'. *Atalanta in Calydon* was issued.

27 July 1894: Morris dined with Fairfax Murray at an Italian restaurant near Leicester Square.

31 July 1894: Morris appeared as a character witness at the trial of Thomas Cantwell of the SL held at the Old Bailey, London. Cantwell was charged with incitement to murder members of the Royal Family. According to the *Times*, Morris described him as 'a good-natured man, perhaps rather rash'. Cantwell was sentenced to six months imprisonment with hard labour. Later Morris travelled down to Kelmscott Manor.

2 August 1894: Cockerell recorded in his *Diary* that he bought 'a 13th c Italian MS for W. M. at Sotheby's. Gregory's Decretals.'

5 August 1894: Morris was scheduled to give an open-air speech at a universal suffrage demonstration sponsored by combined London socialist and radical groups in Trafalgar Square.

7 August 1894: Morris returned to London from Kelmscott Manor. He sent Swinburne a signed copy of the Kelmscott Press edition of *Atalanta in*

Calydon. In the evening he entertained Emery Walker to dinner.

8 August 1894: Cockerell recorded that the first page of the Kelmscott *Chaucer* was printed.

9 August 1894: Morris visited Stanmore Hall presumably to see the *San Graal* tapestries woven by Morris & Co.

14 August 1894: Blunt arrived at Kelmscott Manor: 'I feared for a moment they were all away, but Mrs Morris and Jenny were there, and later Morris himself arrived from London.'

15 August 1894: Blunt recorded that 'In the afternoon ... we all went out for a walk along the roads for Kelmscott has no walks except in the meadows by the river and they were drenched... I found a pansy on the floor of my room when I went to bed. But it is too late, alas, and I slept soundly.' Blunt claimed it was Jane's habit to leave a pansy on the floor of his room when she wished him to share her bed. An illustrated article by Jean Lahor (Dr Henri Cazalis) entitled 'M. William Morris et l'Art decoratif en Angleterre' appeared in the *Revue Encycopedique* (vol. 4, no. 89, pp. 349–59).

16 August 1894: Blunt left Kelmscott Manor.

18 August 1894: An article entitled 'The Poetry of William Morris' by G. Saintsbury appeared in the American journal *The Critic* (vol. 25, p. 101).

21 August 1894: Morris returned to London from Kelmscott Manor in the company of Lord Dillon: '(who can't help being a lord) and is otherwise a good antiquary & an agreeable man.' On the way back he mislaid the inscription Blunt had given him to be used in the *Primavera* tapestry. He had to write to Blunt the following day asking for another copy of the inscription.

22 August 1894: Morris told Jenny that the *Chaucer* 'is all sold except 3 vellum copies & people are quarrelling over the privilege of buying it'.

30 August 1894: By this time Morris had returned to Kelmscott Manor. *The Tale of the Emperor Coustans and of Over Sea* was finished by the Kelmscott Press. There were 525 copies on paper and 20 on vellum.

September 1894: Morris wrote an 'Introduction' to Dr Neale's *Good King Wenceslas* which was published in 1895.

4 September 1894: Morris, who was back in London, had lunch with Burne-Jones and showed him the rose border he had been designing for the *Chaucer*. In the evening Emery Walker came to Kelmscott House to bid farewell as he along with Shaw, Cockerell, Wardle and Gere were travelling to Italy on a trip sponsored by the Art Workers' Guild. They left the following day and returned on 23 September 1894.

14 September 1894: Charles and Jane Rowley visited Morris and Jane at Kelmscott Manor. They stayed until 18 September.

19 September 1894: Morris left Kelmscott Manor and travelled to Wolverhampton to visit Mr Hodson at Compton Hall. Morris & Co. designed the Compton wallpaper for this house in 1896.

20 September 1894: Morris returned to London from Wolverhampton.

Last Week in September 1894: Mackail recorded that he and his wife and their baby son Denis spent a week at Kelmscott Manor. Mackail wrote that in his 'favour Morris discarded any prejudices which he might have against children other than his own; for outside his own family he was not a lover of children, and seldom took any notice of them'.

29 September 1894: *The Book of Wisdom and Lies* by Sulkhan-Saba Orbeliani was finished by the Kelmscott Press. There were 250 copies on paper.

Autumn 1894: Aymer Vallance approached Morris with the proposal of writing a book on his life and art. According to Vallance, Morris 'told me frankly that he did not want it done either by myself or anybody else so long as he was alive, but that if I would only wait until his death I might do it'. Morris did, however, insist the work be illustrated and authorized the use of pictures in the possession of Morris & Co. The book eventually appeared as *The Life and Work of William Morris* (George Bell & Sons 1897). The 'Preface' is dated 'LONDON, *August*, 1897'.

October 1894: *Liberty* published a letter from Morris under the title 'Between Ourselves' (p. 76).

3 October 1894: Morris wrote to Georgiana Burne-Jones about his encounter with Denis Mackail: 'he is the dearest little chap, and as merry as the day is long – all that a gentleman of his age should be: everybody paid him the attention which he deserves.'

4 October 1894: According to Cockerell's *Diary*: 'W. M. returned from K. not feeling very well.'

5 October 1894: Morris was visited by the doctor: '[He] told me he would send me a bottle which will set me all right; though indeed there is very little that is wrong.'

6 October 1894: Morris wrote to Chris Healy in response to the latter's suggestion that he should dramatize *A Dream of John Ball*. Morris wrote: 'I am not of the timber from which playwrights are hewn. Why not have a try at it yourself to see what you can make of it?'

9 October 1894: Morris held a dinner party for Emery Walker, Catterson-Smith and an Icelander he referred to as Guomundr of Stóruvellir. According to

Morris the latter and his father had 'entertained us with much hospitality in /73: put us to bed in the Church [and] … dined us (off Brent Goose) also in the church' (*c.f.* 22 July 1873).

11 October 1894: Morris, in a letter to Shaw, wrote of Aubrey Beardsley: 'I can only say that the illustrations to the M.D.A. [*Morte D'Arthur*] which *I* saw were quite below contempt: absolutely *nothing* in them, except an obvious desire to be done with the job.' Morris's hostility to Beardsley had begun when he had rejected the latter's drawings for *Sidonia the Sorceress*. Later Morris travelled down to Kelmscott Manor.

14 October 1894: Carruthers and his daughter Amy Jane visited the Morrises at Kelmscott Manor. They left the following day.

16 October 1894: *The Well at the World's End* was issued.

21 October 1894: May had 'tea and crumpets' with her father. In the evening Morris entertained Emery Walker to dinner.

25 October 1894: Morris, Catterson-Smith and Webb travelled down to Kelmscott Manor. During this trip Webb visited the tithe barn at Great Coxwell. On 29 October Morris wrote: 'Webb was delighted with the barn.'

27 October 1894: Webb left Kelmscott Manor.

29 October 1894: *The Book of Wisdom and Lies* was issued.

30 October 1894: Morris wrote to Emery Walker from Kelmscott Manor: 'I have been a little gouty but it seems passing off, & I am quite well otherwise.'

1 November 1894: Morris returned to London with Jane and Jenny.

3 November 1894: A letter from Morris (dated 25 October) on a proposed 'United Socialist Party' appeared in the *Clarion*. Morris argued that minor differences within the Socialist movement should be forgotten in order to aim for the nationalization of the means of production.

4 November 1894: Swinburne wrote to Morris thanking him for a copy of the Kelmscott edition of *The Wood Beyond the World*: '*The Wood Beyond the World* makes my mouth water – I only wish I had had it to read a month or two ago at Dursley, when I was spending some weeks with my mother and sisters in one of the most delicious corners of England.'

14 November 1894: Morris issued a circular announcing that the number of copies of the proposed volume of *Chaucer* was to be increased from 325 to 425. Subscribers were offered the opportunity of cancelling their orders if they did so before 31 December 1894.

15 November 1894: *The Psalmi Penitentiales* was finished by the Kelmscott Press. There were 300 copies on paper and 12 on vellum.

18 November 1894: Morris delivered 'Makeshift' at a meeting sponsored by the Ancoats Recreation Committee at New Islington Hall, Ancoats, Manchester.

23 November 1894: Morris sent copies of the Kelmscott Press editions of *Godefrey of Boloyne* and *Sidonia the Sorceress* to the Exeter College Library.

28 November 1894: Morris and Emery Walker went to the Bodleian to view the manuscript known as the *Douce Apocalypse*. Morris hoped the Kelmscott Press would be able to publish a facsimile edition. It never did.

6 December 1894: Cockerell recorded in his *Diary* that 'W. M. [was] at home with a bad cold'.

7 December 1894: Morris's mother, Emma, died aged eighty-nine. She had been ill for four years. Webb designed her tombstone. The inscription reads: 'In memory of Emma, widow of William Morris, who fell asleep in Jesus on 7 December 1894 in the 90th year of her age. Thine eyes shall see the King in his beauty.'

10 December 1894: The *Psalmi Penitentiales* was issued.

11 December 1894: Morris attended his mother's funeral: 'I went to bury my mother, a pleasant winter day with gleams of sun. She was laid in earth in the churchyard close by the house, a very pretty place among the great wych-elms, which, if it were of no use to her, was softening to us. Altogether my old and callous heart was touched by the absence of what had been so kind to me and fond of me.'

15 December 1894: Jane wrote to Blunt: 'I have the anxiety of my husband's health, he was in the doctor's hands for several weeks, but is now better – his mother's death a week ago was a shock to him although she had been ill so long, she passed away quite suddenly at the last.'

29 December 1894: Morris wrote to Angela Mackail thanking her for a pen she had given him for Christmas. Under her married name of Angela Thirkell she became a well-known novelist. Her first book, called *Three Houses*, includes descriptions of Sunday visits to the Grange.

1895: Morris was invited by the South Salford Branch of the SDF to stand as their parliamentary candidate. He declined. *News from Nowhere* was translated into Italian by Ernestina d'Errico under the title *La Terra Promessa*. Morris lent £6,000 to Robert William Hobbs to purchase Kelmscott Manor from his father's executors. This loan was made on the condition that Morris was granted a twenty-year lease on the house and its grounds (which by this time extended to 275 acres). Edward F. Strange's *Alphabets: A Handbook of Lettering with Historical, Critical and Practical Descriptions* was published. The first edition of this work contained a specimen sheet showing the three types used at the Kelmscott Press. Strange wrote in the Preface that 'this country owes an enormous debt [to Morris] for the revival of interest in artistic typography'.

Early 1895: Morris & Co. provided the stage decoration for Acts I and III of Henry Arthur Jones's play *The Case of Rebellious Susan* which opened at the Criterion Theatre, London.

January 1895: 'The Aesthetes', an article by Thomas F. Plowman (with a portrait of Morris after a drawing by Miss C. M. Watts), appeared in the *Pall Mall Gazette* (pp. 27–44).

5 January 1895: Morris gave an unnamed lecture at a meeting sponsored by the HSS at Kelmscott House, Hammersmith.

8 January 1895: A second Albion press was set up at 21 Upper Mall to speed up the production of the Kelmscott *Chaucer*. Morris met the family solicitor, Charles Gayton, to discuss the probate of his mother's will.

10 January 1895: *The Tale of Beowulf* was finished by the Kelmscott Press. There were 300 copies on paper and 8 on vellum.

11 January 1895: Morris was granted probate on his mother's will.

2 February 1895: *The Tale of Beowulf* was issued.

4 February 1895: Morris and Webb travelled to Much Hadham to discuss with Morris's sister Henrietta a plan to convert two existing cottages into a single building to serve as her new home. This was because she was obliged to leave the 'Lordship' as a result of her mother's death. The work was subsequently done to Webb's design.

16 February 1895: *Syr Perecyvelle of Gales* was finished by the Kelmscott Press. There were 350 copies on paper and 8 on vellum.

18 February 1895: Morris was writing *The Waters of the Wondrous Isles*.

2 March 1895: A review of *The Wood Beyond the World* by Theodore Watts appeared in the *Athenaeum* (pp. 273–4).

8 March 1895: Jane, in a letter to Blunt, wrote: '[W]e are all at this moment rather disturbed in temper, our next-door neighbour has sent in to ask us to cut down our biggest and most cherished tree, saying it spoils her view of the river.' On the same day Morris wrote to this neighbour, Mary Philpott, refusing to allow the tree to be cut down.

19 March 1895: Morris and Cockerell attended the sale at Sotheby's of the Library of Sir Thomas Phillips.

31 March 1895: Morris delivered 'What We Have to Look For' at a meeting sponsored by the HSS at Kelmscott House, Hammersmith.

April 1895: An anonymous article entitled 'William Morris at the Kelmscott Press' appeared in the *English Illustrated Magazine* (vol. 13, p. 47).

2 April 1895: A letter by Morris on the storm damage to Peterborough Cathedral appeared in the *Times, Standard, Daily Chronicle, Morning Post* and *Daily News*. By this time Morris was staying at Kelmscott Manor where he was working on one of the designs for the *Chaucer*. Later he was visited by an aged labourer: 'A poor old chap called to thank me for my dole this morning: he said his name was Jones; he didn't seem to me fit to work, was very frail and said he was 83. I spoke to him with impressive dignity till I found that he was *very* deaf, after which I had to bellow into his ear; which spoilt the dignity, but was no doubt more impressive – to him.'

4 April 1895: Morris returned to London from Kelmscott Manor.

22 April 1895: Morris and Jenny travelled down to Kelmscott Manor.

23 April 1895: A letter by Morris (dated 22 April) on 'Tree-felling in Epping Forest' appeared in the *Daily Chronicle*.

29 April 1895: Morris and Jenny returned from Kelmscott Manor. W. Irving Way visited the Kelmscott Press. He recorded that the last sheets of Morris's romance, *Of Child Christopher and Goldilind the Fair*, had just been pulled and were about to go to the press. Way later visited Morris at Kelmscott House where Morris showed him some of his medieval manuscripts. He also offered to sell Way a copy of one of his romances that he had had specially illuminated by Reuter for £105.

30 April 1895: Another letter from Morris on the felling of trees in Epping Forest (dated 27 April) appeared in the *Daily Chronicle*. In this Morris admitted that he had not visited the Forest during the last nine years.

May 1895: Morris contributed an article entitled 'As to Bribing Excellence' to Tochatti's paper *Liberty*.

1 May 1895: Morris gave an open-air speech at the May Day celebrations sponsored by the SDF and other London socialists at Hyde Park.

2 May 1895: According to Cockerell's *Diary* 'W. M. went to Quaritch's with F. S. Ellis and bought the Huntingfield Psalter'. The book cost £800 and Morris wrote his initials and date on the flyleaf of the volume.

5 May 1895: It is probable that Morris gave a lecture at a meeting sponsored by the HSS at Kelmscott House, Hammersmith.

7 May 1895: Morris visited Epping Forest with Webb, Lethaby, Walker, Ellis and Cockerell to examine the amount of tree-felling. They went to Loughton first before travelling to Monk Wood, Theydon Woods, Fair Mead Bottom and then Bury Wood. According to Cockerell in his *Diary* during this visit 'We heard a nightingale and W. M. declared that he had never heard one before'.

9 May 1895: Yet another letter by Morris on 'Tree-felling in Epping Forest' (dated 8 May) appeared in the *Daily Chronicle* this time under the title 'Epping Forest. Mr. Morris's Report'.

13 May 1895: Morris gave a speech at a meeting sponsored by the George Lansbury Campaign Committee held at the Browning Hall, Walworth.

24 May 1895: Cockerell noted in his *Diary* that the ink supplied by the English firm of Shackell, Edwards & Co. had been found to leave a yellow stain behind some of the borders in the Kelmscott *Chaucer*.

25 May 1895: *The Life & Death of Jason* was finished by the Kelmscott Press. There were 200 copies on paper and 6 on vellum.

26 May 1895: Morris wrote a letter to Henry Joseph Wilson MP giving his support to the campaign to get the Walsall Anarchists released. In this he wrote: 'I should mention, to show that I am not biased in this matter, that I am not an anarchist, but disagree both with the theory and tactics of Anarchists.' The appeal for clemency was unsuccessful.

1 June 1895: Morris travelled down to Kelmscott Manor. A letter of his (dated 31 May) on the 'Royal Tombs in Westminster Abbey' appeared in the *Times*.

5 June 1895: Morris returned to London from Kelmscott Manor.

8 June 1895: Morris wrote to the German firm of Gebruder Janecke and Fr. Schneenman requesting they produce a 'softer' ink for the Kelmscott Press.

9 June 1895: Ellen Terry ordered a copy of the Kelmscott Press edition of *The Life & Death of Jason*.

11 June 1895: Morris visited Charles Grayson to settle the final details of his mother's estate.

18 June 1895: Morris was at Kelmscott Manor where he had 'been rather guzzling on peas and cucumber & strawberries'.

8 July 1895: Morris was scheduled to give another speech in support of the candidature of George Lansbury at St Stephen's Hall, Boyson Road, Walworth.

13 July 1895: An unsigned review of *The Wood Beyond the World* appeared in the *Spectator* (pp. 52–3). The reviewer claimed that the book was a socialist allegory on the relationship between capital and labour.

17 July 1895: Morris travelled to Blythborough to see the church on behalf of SPAB. Of Blythborough he wrote: 'a poor remnant of a village with the ruins of a small religious house and a huge 15th century church.'

18 July 1895: Morris began his article 'The Present Outlook of Socialism in England'. It was not to be finished until 23 November 1895.

19 July 1895: Morris wrote a letter to the Thames Conservancy relating to the proposed rebuilding of the Lock-Keeper's Cottage at Eaton Weir near Kelmscott.

20 July 1895: A letter from Morris (dated 16 July) responding to criticism of the *Wood Beyond the World* was published in the *Spectator*: 'I had not the least intention of thrusting an allegory into "The Wood Beyond the World;" it is meant for a tale pure and simple, with nothing didactic about it.'

24 July 1895: Morris recorded in his *Diary* that he had just been sent a thirteenth-century French Horae from Rosenthal.

25 July 1895: In the morning Morris visited the Grange where he showed the Horae to Burne-Jones. Morris and his family later travelled down to Kelmscott Manor. *Of Child Christopher and Goldilind the Fair* was finished by the Kelmscott Press. There were 600 copies on paper and 12 on vellum.

26 July 1895: Morris and Jenny were prevented from walking to Buscot Wood due to 'a savage Bull'.

27 July 1895: In the afternoon Morris was visited by Ellis at Kelmscott Manor. The latter spent three days at the house.

3 August 1895: Morris returned to London from Kelmscott Manor.

4 August 1895: Morris went to the Grange where he found Georgiana Burne-Jones – who had been ill – 'much better'. He also worked on the floriated initials for *The Earthly Paradise*.

5 August 1895: Morris recorded in his *Diary* that he had bought the thirteenth-century Horae from Rosenthal for £450. Engels died.

6 August 1895: Morris finished the rough draft of *The Waters of the Wondrous Isles*. He then took the manuscript round to the Grange where he read extracts to Georgiana Burne-Jones.

8 August 1895: Morris joined his family at Kelmscott Manor.

10 August 1895: A review of *The Tale of Beowulf* by Theodore Watts-Dunton appeared in the *Athenaeum* (pp. 181–2). Blunt wrote in his *Diary*: 'To Kelmscott for a couple of nights and had much interesting talk with Morris.'

12 August 1895: Burne-Jones went to see Sir Arthur Church to discuss the problems that he and Morris had been having with the staining of the sheets of the *Chaucer*. Cockerell recorded in his *Diary* that Burne-Jones 'had rather an encouraging interview'. The most useful advice they received was to try and bleach the sheets in the sun. This they attempted to do in the garden of Sussex Cottage. Unfortunately, they had problems when it rained so Morris was obliged to rent a greenhouse.

13 August 1895: Morris wrote in his *Diary*: 'Cockerell came by aft: train bringing early 12th century book of Rosenthal's 29 pictures: not very good … refused it.'

15 August 1895: Blunt visited Merton to examine the progress on his tapestry.

16 August 1895: Morris returned from Kelmscott Manor. The new ink for the Kelmscott Press supplied by Gebruder Janecke and Fr. Schneenman was used for the first time. Three days later Morris wrote to Emery Walker saying it 'worked well: I shall use no other now'.

18 August 1895: Morris gave a talk 'about the Socialist Party' at a meeting sponsored by the HSS at Kelmscott House, Hammersmith.

19 August 1895: Morris and Georgiana Burne-Jones travelled down to Kelmscott Manor.

23 August 1895: Georgiana Burne-Jones left Kelmscott Manor. During her stay she wrote: 'Topsy looks very happy, and is so sweet down here … but I feel the added years in Janey and Topsy and me, so that it seems like visiting something that is not quite real.'

24 August 1895: The *Athenaeum* printed a letter from Morris (dated 13 August) on the subject of the tapestry collection at the South Kensington Museum. *The Poetical Works of Percy Bysshe Shelley* was finished by the Kelmscott Press. There were 250 copies on paper and 6 on vellum.

25 August 1895: In a letter Swinburne told Theodore Watts: 'I have just read the *Well at the World's End*. The living charm of its loveliness is wonderful.'

27 August 1895: Morris entertained Emery Walker to supper.

28 August 1895: Morris travelled down to Kelmscott Manor. His journey was spoiled, as he wrote to Georgiana Burne-Jones, 'when [as] we passed by the once lovely little garth near Black Bourton, I saw all my worst fears realized; for there was the little barn we saw being mended, the wall cut down and finished with a zinked iron roof. It quite sickened me when I saw it… Now that I am grown old and see that nothing is to be done, I half wish that I had not been born with a sense of romance and beauty in this accursed age.'

31 August 1895: The *Athenaeum* published another letter by Morris on the subject of the tapestries in the South Kensington Museum.

8 September 1895: Morris had breakfast at the Grange before travelling to Rottingdean with Burne-Jones.

10 September 1895: Morris travelled down to Kelmscott Manor.

11 September 1895: Morris wrote to Webb to reassure him that a rumour that Jane had died was completely untrue: 'Janey has, it is true been bothered with boils & blains like Job; but is getting better of them and is in good spirits.'

13 September 1895: Morris travelled to Taplow from Kelmscott Manor to attend the 'Wayzegoose' of the staff of the Kelmscott Press: 'This time there *was* a goose at the feast; but as there was *no apple sauce* I rejected my portion in dudgeon after the first mouthful.' A photograph was taken of the group that attended this event. Morris travelled back to Kelmscott House with Walker.

14 September 1895: Cockerell visited Kelmscott House before leaving for Switzerland. Morris spent the afternoon with Webb.

15 September 1895: Morris gave an unnamed lecture at a meeting sponsored by the HSS at Kelmscott House, Hammersmith.

19 September 1895: Morris wrote to an unknown recipient declining an invitation to investigate the Morris family history: 'I have no ancestors, and don't think I should care if I had; it would be enormous trouble to hunt up photos of myself and this generation of my people. The last generation having been recorded (if at all) before the days of photography and after those of art... Besides I don't think I approve of the whole affair. What I offer the public is my work, I don't want them to know anything else about me.'

23 September 1895: Morris recorded in his *Diary*: 'May home – she and Steele to dinner.' He also finished one of the borders for *The Well at the World's End*.

24 September 1895: Morris had dinner with Walker and Catterson-Smith.

25 September 1895: Morris travelled down to Kelmscott Manor with Mrs De Morgan.

October 1895: 'William Morris in Unpublished Letters on Socialism: A Poet's Politics' by W. G. Kingland appeared in *Poet Lore* (vol. 7, pp. 473 and 543).

2 October 1895: Morris travelled to London for the day in order to visit the Grange and to view a thirteenth-century psalter at Ellis & Elvey's.

6 October 1895: Morris was chairman at a lecture given by Shaw at a meeting sponsored by the HSS at Kelmscott House.

7 October 1895: Morris travelled down to Kelmscott Manor.

8 October 1895: Edmund Hort New visited Morris at Kelmscott Manor in connection with the two illustrations he was preparing to illustrate Morris's 'Gossip about an Old House on the Upper Thames' (*c.f.* November 1895).

9 October 1895: Morris recorded in his *Diary* that he took a 'little walk in [the] field with Jenny & New'. 'Do People Appreciate the Beautiful?: A Chat with William Morris' appeared in *Cassell's Saturday Journal* (no. 628).

11 October 1895: Morris returned to London from Kelmscott Manor to act as chairman at a meeting of the HSS at which Shaw spoke on 'The Political Situation'.

14 October 1895: Morris travelled down to Kelmscott Manor. The *Daily Chronicle* published a letter from Morris (dated 12 October) on the proposed restoration of Rouen Cathedral.

17 October 1895: John Carruthers visited Morris at Kelmscott Manor.

18 October 1895: Morris, Carruthers and Jenny visited Buscot wood.

19 October 1895: Morris returned to Hammersmith accompanied by Carruthers and C. Smith.

22 October 1895: Morris returned to Kelmscott Manor.

24 October 1895: Morris was visited by Newman Howard, his accountant, to discuss his finances. Rossetti's *Hand and Soul* was finished by the Kelmscott Press. There were 225 copies on paper and 10 on vellum for sale in Britain. In addition 350 copies on paper and 11 on vellum were produced for distribution in America. In the States the book was sold by Way & Williams. This was the only book by an American publisher to carry the Kelmscott Press imprint.

26 October 1895: Jane wrote to Blunt: 'I am always inventing plots for novels, and if I ever find myself anywhere in peace I should develop them, but I daresay they would be bad and would not sell.'

30 October 1895: Morris delivered 'What We Have to Look For' at a meeting sponsored by the Oxford and District Socialist Union at the Central School (later the bus station), Gloucester Green, Oxford. He slept the night in York Powell's rooms in Christ Church College.

31 October 1895: Morris and York Powell visited Christ Church Library to view two medieval books. Morris later returned to Kelmscott House. Jane and Jenny had returned from Kelmscott Manor on the same day.

November 1895: An illustrated article entitled 'Gossip about an Old House on the Upper Thames' appeared in the *Quest* (no. 4). Fifty copies were later issued in boards by the Birmingham Guild of Handicraft. Another article entitled 'The Kelmscott Press of William Morris' by Ernest Dressel was published in *The Book Buyer*.

1 November 1895: Morris granted Joseph Batchelor permission to call his antique handmade paper 'The Kelmscott Hand Made' as long as it did not include the Kelmscott Press watermark.

11 November 1895: According to Cockerell in his *Diary* it was on this day that 'W. M. wrote an account of his aim in starting the Press for Mr. Edelheim of Philadelphia'.

20 November 1895: Morris wrote to Hans Ey: 'I admit that I have been a great admirer of Chaucer, and that his work has had, especially in early years, much influence on me; but I think not much on my style.'

21 November 1895: *Poems Chosen Out of the Works of Robert Herrick* was finished by the Kelmscott Press. There were 250 copies on paper and 8 on vellum.

25 November 1895: Morris travelled down to Rottingdean.

26 November 1895: Morris wrote to Jenny from Rottingdean: 'I am all right; without pains, & shall be much better (if I don't over-eat or over-drink myself) when I come back on Friday.' A letter by Morris on the 'Trinity Almshouses' (dated 25 November) was published in the *Daily Chronicle*.

27 November 1895: Morris was reading Hasting Rashdall's *The Universities of Europe in the Middle Ages* and Jane Austen's *Pride and Prejudice*.

29 November 1895: Morris returned to London from Rottingdean.

1 December 1895: Morris gave a lecture illustrated by lantern slides at a meeting sponsored by the HSS at Kelmscott House, Hammersmith.

7 December 1895: Arthur Gaskin visited Morris to discuss the drawings for *The Shepheardes Calendar*. The *Daily Chronicle* published a letter by Morris (dated 5 December) on the proposed restoration of Peterborough Cathedral.

13 December 1895: The *Daily Chronicle* printed another letter by Morris (dated 12 December) on the subject of the proposed restoration of Peterborough Cathedral.

14 December 1895: The *Times* published a letter from Morris (dated 12 December) concerning a plan to rebuild the north-west tower of Chichester Cathedral. Morris delivered 'The Woodcuts of Gothic Books' at a meeting sponsored by the Technical Education Department of the London County Council at the Bolt Court Technical School, Fleet Street, London. According to Cockerell this 'was the last lecture he gave with his old vigour'.

19 December 1895: Morris bought the thirteenth-century manuscript book, the Brabant Psalter, from Ellis & Elvey for £375.

21 December 1895: Morris was forced to cancel a dinner engagement with Richmond due to his health: 'I am done up & of no avail this evening.'

24 December 1895: Sergius Stepniak was struck down by a train on a level-crossing near his home at Bedford Park. The official verdict was that his death was 'accidental' but there were rumours of suicide.

Christmas 1895: 'The Kelmscott Press: An Illustrated Interview with Mr William Morris' by I. H. I. Temple Scott was published in *Bookselling* (pp. 2–14).

26 December 1895: Jane wrote to Blunt: 'Stepniak's accident was a great shock to us. I did not know him personally, but many friends and neighbours knew him well, and were devoted to him.'

27 December 1895: The last of the designs for the Kelmscott *Chaucer* was finished.

28 December 1895: Morris made his last open-air speech in the drizzle outside Waterloo Station at the funeral of Sergius Stepniak. Jane had written earlier: 'my husband has consented to speak at the burial, he dislikes doing so, but Kropotkin wished it for various reasons, so he gave in.' A report of this speech appeared in the *Times* on 30 December. Morris did not attend the subsequent funeral at Woking Crematorium.

End of 1895: Georgiana Burne-Jones recorded that Morris told her husband: 'The best way of lengthening out the rest of our days now, old chap, is to finish off our old things.' Burne-Jones is also recorded as saying: 'Sad to see even *his* enormous vitality diminishing.'

Beginning of 1896: In the *Memorials* Georgiana Burne-Jones recalled her husband saying: 'Last Sunday, in the very middle of breakfast, Morris began leaning his forehead on his hand, as he does so often now. It is a thing I have never seen him do before in all the years I have known him.'

1 January 1896: Morris walked with Jenny to the Grange to see Burne-Jones. In the evening he went to Emery Walker's.

2 January 1896: Morris attended a meeting of SPAB and wrote two pages of *The Sundering Flood*.

3 January 1896: Morris gave a speech at the New Year's meeting of the London SDF at Holborn Town Hall, London. Hyndman wrote: 'He was ill at the time, and I fear that even coming to this meeting was an overtasking of his strength.'

5 January 1896: In the morning Morris went to the Grange. He later lectured for the last time at the Clubroom at Kelmscott House. His subject was 'One Socialist Party'. In his *Diary* he wrote: 'all sorts of people at [the] evening lecture. Couldn't sleep. Got up and worked at the *Sundering [Flood]* between 1–4 am.'

7 January 1896: Morris wrote in his *Diary*: 'Began Chaucer binding again. Early to bed. Slept till 1am then no more.'

8 January 1896: Morris's *Diary* entry reads: 'To Grange and read *Sundering [Flood]* up to p. 45 to Georgie who really approved of it.'

9 January 1896: Morris wrote to Louis Edwin Van Norman stating: 'I have *not* changed my mind on Socialism.'

13 January 1896: Morris's *Diary* entry reads: 'Seedy. Did nothing all day.'

16 January 1896: In the morning Morris went for a walk with Jenny. He attended a meeting of SPAB in the afternoon.

17 January 1896: Morris wrote in his *Diary*: 'Walked to Grange and read *Sundering [Flood]* to Georgie. Nothing else – seedy.'

24 January 1896: In a letter to Hiram Price Collier, Morris declined an invitation to go to the USA on the grounds of age. However, he added: 'I have always reckoned on a kind reception from the "otherside kindred" if ever I should cross the water.'

30 January 1896: Cockerell wrote: 'W. M. at S.P.A.B. and Gatti's (for the last time).'

31 January 1896: Morris made his final public address at a meeting of the Society for Checking the Abuses of Public Advertising at the Society of Arts, John Street, Adelphi, London. He seconded the first resolution.

February 1896: Morris began work on *Kilian of the Close*. Shaw stated: 'From being a man who was never idle or listless, he suddenly, to his own dismay, found himself sitting about doing nothing and quite at a loss, his voice weakened and his energy scattered.'

3 February 1895: In the afternoon Morris travelled down to stay at Rottingdean.

4 February 1896: Morris wrote in his *Diary*: 'At Rottingdean... Walk in the morning and a short one in the afternoon.'

5 February 1896: Morris wrote to Cockerell from Rottingdean: 'I have been out both yesterday and today. I think I am better.' *Poems Chosen out of the works of Samuel Taylor Coleridge* was finished by the Kelmscott Press. There were 300 copies on paper and 8 on vellum.

8 February 1896: Georgiana Burne-Jones arrived at Rottingdean to stay with Morris.

9 February 1896: Morris's *Diary* entry reads: 'Did nothing but go out twice.

First time only down [the] street.'

11 February 1896: Georgiana Burne-Jones returned to London.

12 February 1896: Emery Walker went to stay at Rottingdean with Morris for a couple of days. Morris wrote to Tom Mann declining an invitation to attend his five-lecture series on 'Socialism and the Labour Problem': 'I am decidedly unwell and must keep very quiet.'

13 February 1896: Morris wrote in his *Diary*: 'Had a good walk with Walker to High Barns. Talked to old Shepherd. Went into Church in afternoon and read *Sundering [Flood]* to him in evening.' Jane wrote to Blunt: 'My husband has been unwell all winter, but the last few weeks there seemed fresh cause for anxiety he looked so very ill, and the worst is that no doctor has discovered anything very wrong with him.'

14 February 1896: Morris and Emery Walker returned to London from Rottingdean. Morris wrote in his *Diary*: 'Nothing else. Seedy.'

18 February 1896: Jenny returned to London.

22 February 1896: Burne-Jones accompanied Morris on a visit to the eminent physician, Sir William Broadbent: 'He examined me, partly bare, for about 3 quarters of an hour. And said that sugar there *was* in my water, but not so much as to be serious and expected to get rid of it by rigid diet, eggs, milk, puree of meat, at first, and when my stomach can stand it un-fat flesh meat.'

25 February 1896: Shaw called on Morris at Kelmscott House.

26 February 1896: Morris's *Diary* entry reads: 'Went to Broadbent. He though I was [the] same. Not impressed. He gave me some pills... I don't feel any better – so weak.'

27 February 1896: Various friends visited Morris at Kelmscott House. In his *Diary* he wrote: 'Fried a piece of flesh meat and ate it with pleasure.'

2 March 1896: *The Well at the World's End* was finished by the Kelmscott Press. There were 350 copies on paper and 8 on vellum.

4 March 1896: Morris again visited Broadbent: 'He cannot find me better.'

5 March 1896: Morris wrote in his *Diary*: 'Got up the garden and back and up the Mall and back. Very feeble.'

6 March 1896: Morris told Blunt: 'I am ... far from well. I seem to have broken down altogether, & have been under the doctor's hands a fortnight, and am still dreadfully weak & helpless, digestion all gone to pot.'

7 March 1896: Jane was in bed suffering from rheumatism.

8 March 1896: Morris's *Diary* entry reads: 'Felt better today. Began Chaucer title. Walker, Hyndman, Furnivall, Lushington [and] Rowley called.'

11 March 1896: Morris visited Broadbent: 'he thinks me much better.'

14 March 1896: *Sire Degrevaunt* was finished by the Kelmscott Press. There were 350 copies on paper and 8 on vellum.

23 March 1896: Morris's *Diary* entry reads: 'poorly and weak'.

25 March 1896: Morris once again visited Broadbent: 'he thought me going on well.' He also wrote to Bernard Quaritch: 'I am certainly getting better, but the recovery is likely to be slow.'

April 1896: Morris's article 'The Present Outlook of Socialism in England' was published in *The Forum*, pp. 193–200.

8 April 1896: Morris wrote to Ellis: 'As to my health; just at present I don't seem to be getting on at all, am no stronger than I was a month ago.'

19 April 1896: Bax visited Morris at Kelmscott House.

20 April 1896: In a letter to Blunt, Jane wrote: '[M]y husband has been ill for 3 months ... he is only just able to take a little journey to Kelmscott, he refuses to go anywhere else – he is improving slowly but is very weak still and not in the least like himself.'

22 April 1896: Morris and Jane travelled down to Kelmscott Manor: 'Got there about 8 not tired by journey, but ill-tempered when I got there.'

24 April 1896: In the evening Walker came to stay for the weekend with Morris at Kelmscott Manor.

26 April 1896: Morris and Walker went for a walk as far as the Want-Ways at Kelmscott but had to give up as Morris was too tired to go on.

27 April 1896: Walker left Kelmscott Manor. In a letter to Webb, Morris wrote 'I don't seem to mend a bit; am weak and belly-achy.'

1 May 1896: Cockerell bought an English Bestiary of 1140 from Jacques Rosenthal on Morris's behalf. The book cost £900. Ellis came to stay for a few days with Morris at Kelmscott Manor. Jane wrote to Blunt: 'My husband is no better for the change, except that he coughs less. The weakness is the same, he can only walk a little way outside, and generally goes no further than the garden.'

4 May 1896: Morris wrote to Webb: 'I am not getting on; I say that in all calmness: I am afraid I am rather weaker than stronger, and am bothered with belly ache and pains in the limbs.' Cockerell brought the Bestiary to Morris at Kelmscott Manor. According to Mackail '[Morris] was delighted with it beyond measure'.

5 May 1896: Morris left Kelmscott Manor. Cockerell wrote: 'I travelled to London with Morris… He never saw Kelmscott again.'

7 May 1896: In the morning Morris visited the Grange. *The Earthly Paradise* (volume 1) was finished by the Kelmscott Press. There were 225 copies on paper and 6 on vellum.

8 May 1896: The Kelmscott Press finished *The Works of Geoffrey Chaucer*. There were 425 copies on paper and 13 on vellum. The book contained 87 woodcuts by Burne-Jones, a woodcut title, 14 large borders, 18 different frames for the illustrations and 26 large initial words designed by Morris.

9 May 1896: Morris wrote in his *Diary*: 'Hogg to see me – says I am much better (don't feel it).'

10 May 1896: Morris visited the Grange to show the Bestiary to Burne-Jones.

18 May 1896: Morris arranged for presents to be given to the workmen on the completion of the *Chaucer*.

22 May 1896: Morris visited Broadbent: 'didn't seem to think very well of me.'

26 May 1896: The Morrises went to stay with Blunt at Newbuildings Place in Horsham, Sussex. Blunt was to write: 'he does not believe in any God the Creator of the World, or any Providence, or, I think, any future life. But he is not a pessimist, and thinks mankind "the crown of things", in spite of man's destructive action and his modern craze of ugliness.'

28 May 1896: Morris wrote in his *Diary*: 'Better, did a little border. Went for a walk to the wood in the afternoon. Was driven out a bit to see an old farm house. Very beautiful.'

29 May 1896: Morris visited Shipley Church: 'fine Norman Tower and Nave but quite spoiled by restoration regardless of expense.' Blunt wrote in his *Diary*: 'The new piece of tapestry he [Morris] has made me, Botticelli's Spring, is up and is very decorative and brilliant in the drawing-room, though the faces are hardly as good as they ought to be.'

30 May 1896: Morris returned to London. By this time he weighed only 10st 7lbs.

June 1896: An unsigned review of *Old French Romances* appeared in *Nation* (pp. 88–9).

1 June 1896: The Kelmscott Press issued a 'List of Publications' illustrating the Golden, Troy and Chaucer types.

2 June 1896: The first two copies of the Kelmscott *Chaucer* came from the binders. Morris's copy is in the library at Exeter College.

3 June 1896: Morris went to see Broadbent about his health. The latter recommended he see Frederick William Pavy, a specialist in diabetes. Burne-Jones gave the second copy of the Kelmscott *Chaucer* to his daughter for her birthday. Georgiana Burne-Jones recalled: 'The joke of a surprise present was repeated by his packing up the big volume in a parcel of shape so disguised that no one could guess at its contents.'

4 June 1896: Morris visited the Grange. Burne-Jones told him of a Punch and Judy show held the day before to celebrate the joint birthdays of Margaret Burne-Jones and her son. Georgiana Burne-Jones recalled him saying '"I say, old boy, I saw a play yesterday you would have liked – Punch!" "Yes," said Morris, "I like Punch."' Jane reported that Morris had lost two pounds in weight during the last fortnight: 'this state of things has rather alarmed both doctors and a third specialist is to be consulted as soon as possible, meanwhile he is not in bad spirits fortunately.'

5 June 1896: Morris went with Burne-Jones to see the exhibition of English manuscripts organized by the Society of Antiquaries at their rooms at Burlington House. Morris had lent four leaves of a Psalter to this exhibition and was amazed to find them placed alongside the book from which they had been removed. He was later to buy this book (*c.f.* 6 July 1896). He also admired another Psalter: 'Duke of Rutlands book a marvel of marvels. Must try to get it.' Mackail records that this particular endeavour was 'in vain; and this last pleasure was denied him.'

6 June 1896: In the afternoon Morris went to be examined by Frederick William Pavy. Pavy ordered a holiday in Folkestone.

9 June 1896: Jane wrote: 'the fits of prostration are startling from time to time and the loss of flesh goes on.' She visited Dr Playfair who said in his view 'the disease was being William Morris and working 18 hours a day'.

12 June 1896: Morris's weight had fallen to 10st 4lbs. Later he and Jane travelled down to stay at the Norfolk Hotel in Folkestone. On the way Morris learned of the death of Middleton: 'I did like him very much ... we had a deal to talk about, and much in common as to our views of things and the world, and his friendliness to his friends was beyond measure.'

13 June 1896: In his *Diary* Morris wrote: 'Went to Harbour in morning, and walked about. In the afternoon drove to Hythe and went into church.' Jane wrote to Blunt: 'My husband has been worse, he lost flesh this week to an alarming extent, 2½ lbs; and was so weak and low that I thought he would not be able to come.'

14 June 1896: Morris wrote to Webb: 'Every morning we drive down to the Harbour (it is too far for me to walk there) and then I toddle about, and sit down, lean over the chains, and rather enjoy it, especially if there are any craft about.'

18 June 1896: Morris and Cockerell took the ferry to Boulogne for a day trip to France. Jane wrote: '[It was] a sort of test of what he can do, he was not very tired afterwards.' Swinburne wrote a letter to Burne-Jones in response to news of Morris's illness: 'I am so grieved and alarmed by what you tell me of dear old Morris... [I knew] he was seriously ill; but somehow I had never realised it – he always seemed to me such an embodiment of health and strength.'

20 June 1896: Morris weighed himself at the station: '10–7lb. (gain of 3lbs in a week).' Jane wrote to Blunt: 'he is rather stronger this morning after being much down at heart last night.'

21 June 1896: Morris wrote to Cockerell: 'I have *gained* 3 lbs weight since I have been down here.'

23 June 1896: Blunt spent the day with the Morrises in Folkestone. Georgiana Burne-Jones arrived on the same day.

24 June 1896: *The Earthly Paradise* (volume 2) was finished by the Kelmscott Press. There were 225 copies on paper and 6 on vellum.

27 June 1896: Jane wrote to Blunt: 'Georgy Burne-Jones has passed the last four days with us – she proposed having a nurse, which gave great offense – she considered that his food was not always as carefully selected as it ought to be, which is true enough, but no nurse could force him to eat what he refuses to look at.'

30 June 1896: Morris and Jane took Walker to visit Lympne Court: 'The Court is a most exceedingly beautiful house. Knocked about as a farm-house but quite unrestored.'

Summer 1896: 'A Visit to William Morris', by W. Irving Way, appeared in *Modern Art [Boston]*, vol. 4, pp. 78–81.

1 July 1896: Morris wrote to Webb: 'I don't know if I am any stronger, but I am pretty sure I am not weaker: per contra except for my breakfast, I take no interest in my food, and can hardly eat butcher-meat at all, especially beef.'

3 July 1896: Morris wrote to Lord Aldenham offering £1,000 for his Psalter.

6 July 1896: Morris and Jane returned to London from Folkestone. In his *Diary* Morris wrote: 'to Broadbent Janey with me. He thought me a little better (I'm not). Ordered me a sea voyage with a medical man whom he will provide.' Morris purchased the Windmill Psalter from Lord Aldenham for £1,000.

7 July 1896: *Laudes Beatae Mariae Virginis* was finished by the Kelmscott

Press. There were 250 copies on paper and 10 on vellum.

13 July 1896: Morris sent a signed copy of the Kelmscott *Chaucer* to Swinburne. Morris described himself as 'so ill & weak that it is impossible for me to do any work'.

14 July 1896: Swinburne wrote to Morris thanking him for the copy of the Kelmscott *Chaucer*: 'Watts-Dunton says it is and must be the most beautiful book ever printed.'

19 July 1896: Morris's lecture 'How We Live and How We Might Live' was read – 'to a very small audience' – by R. Catterson-Smith at a meeting sponsored by the HSS at Kelmscott House, Hammersmith.

21 July 1896: Jane wrote to Blunt: 'my husband is trying to rest all he can, he starts early tomorrow.'

22 July 1896: Morris set off on the SS *Garonne*, an Orient liner, on his last voyage to Norway, accompanied by Carruthers and Dr Dodgson, a doctor recommended by his consultant Sir William Broadbent. The ship was making a special trip to observe the solar eclipse.

23 July 1896: Morris was seasick: 'though with little excuse, as the sea was very good.'

25 July 1896: The *Garonne* steamed up the Norway Firths after what Morris described as 'a perfectly calm run from Cuxhaven'.

27 July 1896: Morris wrote to Webb from Bergen: 'the victualling is abundantly abominable, the eggs & milk e.g. having a strong "scientific" flavour. The wine rather good though.' Carruthers sent an optimistic report of Morris's progress to London.

August 1896: Maud Herapath visited Kelmscott Manor: 'This afternoon I went with Mr Henderson and Mrs MacNaught for a long walk. We went chiefly with the object of calling on the great William Morris. We did not find him at home as he is somewhere in Iceland [*sic*] but his daughter was there and she showed us over the place. The house is lovely for its oldness but oh! *so so* artistic & grubby. The tea was laid out in a barbaric fashion was a loaf on the table and a dirty jam pot that had been broken open through the paper at the top and the spoon looked too sticky to touch. We did not accept the tea but sat in a row in the plain *painfully* plain dining room & stared at Miss Morris and wondered why she dressed in such a sloppy way with no stays.'

18 August 1896: Morris returned to Tilbury from Norway. However, on the voyage back he had suffered severe hallucinations and imagined that the ropes on the deck of the ship were coiled snakes. His decline was not immediately apparent to Jane. But she was later to report that 'he became so alarmingly ill that he had to go to bed and stay there for a few days'.

20 August 1896: Morris wrote to Jenny: 'I am so distressed that I cannot get down to Kelmscott on Saturday; but I am not well, & the doctors will not let me; please my own dear forgive me, for I long to see you with all my heart.' Around this time Kelmscott House was turned into a nursing home and even the knocker was muffled. Morris took offence at this and demanded the muffler be removed on the grounds that 'folks would think he was having a baby'.

21 August 1896: *The Floure and the Leafe* was finished by the Kelmscott Press. There were 300 copies on paper and 10 on vellum.

24 August 1896: *The Earthly Paradise* (volume 3) was finished by the Kelmscott Press. There were 225 copies on paper and 6 on vellum.

26 August 1896: Morris declined an invitation from Thomas Wardle to visit him at his home in Swainsley: 'I am quite unable to do so, for at present I cannot walk over the threshold, being so intensely weak.'

27 August 1896: Morris dictated four and a half pages of *The Sundering Flood* to Cockerell.

28 August 1896: Morris wrote in a letter to Shaw, dictated to Cockerell, 'as might have been expected am much the worse for the voyage & in fact very ill'. Jane wrote to Blunt that Morris 'gets up now to the library – but is still in a very weak condition, his lungs are unsound – he will always have to live a very careful life in future when he has pulled through this attack'.

End of August 1896: Dodgson wrote to Cockerell telling him that Morris's lung trouble was tubercular and his condition was critical.

1 September 1896: Morris wrote to Georgiana Burne-Jones at Rottingdean urging her to 'Come soon, I want sight of your dear face'.

4 September 1896: Cockerell wrote: 'W. M. began designing Empty [a woodcut] for The Water of the Wondrous Isles.' Blunt visited Kelmscott House but was unable to see Morris due to his ill-health.

8 September 1896: Morris dictated the last dozen lines of *The Sundering Flood* to Cockerell.

9 September 1896: Morris made a new will in the presence of Jane, Cormell Price and Mary De Morgan. Jane, Ellis and Cockerell were appointed executors. One of the central provisions of the will was financial support for Jenny's nursing care for the remainder of her life.

12 September 1896: Cobden-Sanderson wrote: 'Morris is dying, slowly. It is an astonishing spectacle. He sits speechless, waiting for the end to come.' But he was reported to have said to Mary De Morgan: 'I cannot believe that I shall be annihilated.'

14 September 1896: Morris wrote his last surviving letter to his daughter Jenny: 'I wish my hand were not so pen feeble, & then I could write you a proper letter; but as it is I must ask you let this scrawl pass. I like your letters very much darling; please write me another, & pardon me if I can't answer it, or only in this fashion.' The letter bears a postscript: 'I believe I am somewhat better.'

Mid-September 1896: Morris was declining noticeably, having hallucinations in which he believed he was composing Dean Farrar's *Life of Christ*.

21 September 1896: Arnold Dolmetsch entertained Morris by playing pieces by English sixteenth-century composers on the virginal.

25 September 1896: Jane wrote to Blunt: 'Some days he can't go in his chair into the garden. The doctor says the lung is improving, but he is still very ill indeed.'

28 September 1896: Blunt visited Kelmscott House: '[Morris] came in like a man risen from the grave, and sat a few minutes at the table, but seemed dazed and unable to follow the conversation. Miss De Morgan was there and his wife, waiting on him... [H]e seemed absorbed in his misery.'

30 September 1896 (Wednesday): Cockerell visited Morris and found him having increasing difficulty breathing. Morris was visited by Georgiana Burne-Jones in the morning and her husband in the afternoon. Detmar Blow, Cockerell and Emery Walker stayed up the night with him. By this point he was imagining he was back on the *Garonne* off Norway.

October 1896: A review entitled 'Mr. Morris's Poems' by Andrew Lang appeared in *Longman's Magazine*.

1 October 1896 (Thursday): In the morning Morris was visited by his sister Isabella. He was by now wandering and restless. Mary De Morgan and Detmar Blow sat with him through the night.

2 October 1896 (Friday): Georgiana Burne-Jones visited Morris in the morning, followed by her husband in the afternoon and Webb at 6 pm. A professional nurse, called Gillespie, and Emery Walker stayed up with him all night. Although Morris was not in any great pain, Burne-Jones considered his 'weakness was pitiful'.

3 October 1896 (Saturday): Morris died peacefully at eleven-fifteen in the morning at Kelmscott House. Cockerell recorded that Morris was shown the first bound copy of the Kelmscott Press edition of *The Floure and the Leafe, and the Boke of Cuipe, God of Love, or the Cuckoo and the Nightingale* 'an hour or two before [his] death'. Almost his last words were 'I want to get mumbo-jumbo out of the world'. The family doctor pronounced that he had 'died a victim of his enthusiasm for spreading the principles of Socialism'. Another doctor stated that 'the Disease is simply being William Morris, and having done more work than most ten men'. Georgiana Burne-Jones who – along with Jane, May, Detmar Blow, and Mary De Morgan – was by his bedside said he died 'as gently, as quietly as a babe who is satisfied drops from its mother's breast'. Mary De Morgan and Emery Walker travelled to Kelmscott to break the news to Jenny. Later in the day Fairfax Murray made two drawings from the body.

4 October 1896: Glasier wrote in his *Diary*: 'Socialism seems all quite suddenly to have gone from its summer into its winter time. William Morris and Kelmscott House no more!'

5 October 1896 (Monday): Blunt visited Jane. He found her lying on a sofa upstairs as usual. 'I am not unhappy', she said, 'though it is a terrible thing, for I have been with him since I first knew anything. I was 18 when I married – but I never loved him.' Blunt found Morris in his coffin – 'a very plain box' – lying in his little bedroom downstairs. The coffin was covered with an embroidered cloth 'and a small wreath of leaves and sad-coloured flowers'. Shaw wrote to Ellen Terry: 'Happy Morris! he is *resting*.' Obituaries appeared in the *Times*, the *Daily Chronicle*, the *Daily News*, the *Standard*, the *Pall Mall Gazette*, the *St James's Gazette* and the *Westminster Gazette*.

6 October 1896 (Tuesday): Morris's remains were transported by a privately hired train to Lechlade station. Cunninghame Graham recalled that there were 'no red-faced men in shabby black to stagger with the coffin to the hearse but in their place four countrymen in moleskin bore the body to an open cart festooned with vines, with alder and bullrushes'. The coffin was of unpolished oak with wrought-iron handles. His body was buried in the churchyard at Kelmscott. Cunninghame Graham wrote: 'dust to dust fell idly on my ears, and in its stead a vision of the England which he dreamed of filled my mind.'

SELECT BIBLIOGRAPHY

It is outside the scope of the present volume to provide a complete bibliography of all the books that have been written on Morris. Readers requiring further information in this area are highly recommended to consult Gary Aho's *William Morris: A Reference Guide* (1985) and David and Sheila Latham's *An Annotated Critical Bibliography of William Morris* (1991). The latter work is regularly updated through supplements published in the *Journal of the William Morris Society*. The following select bibliography lists the most readily available books on Morris, influential specialist and critical works by subject, and the books on his family and friends which have proved particularly useful in compiling *The William Morris Chronology*.

Works by Morris

Aho, Gary (intro.), *Three Northern Love Stories and Other Tales* (Bristol: Thoemmes Press, 1996).

Boos, Florence (ed.), *William Morris's Socialist Diary* (London: The Journeyman Press, 1985).

Briggs, Asa (ed.), *William Morris: Selected Writings and Designs* (London: Penguin, 1962).

Ennis, Jane (intro.), *Sigurd the Volsung* (Bristol: Thoemmes Press, 1994).

Faulkner, Peter (ed.), *William Morris: Selected Poems* (Manchester: Carcanet Press, 1992).

——— (intro.), *Hopes and Fears for Art and Signs of Change* (Bristol: Thoemmes Press, 1994).

Fitzgerald, Penelope (ed.), *The Novel on Blue Paper* (Journeyman Press, 1982).

Henderson, Philip (ed.), *The Letters of William Morris to his Family and Friends* (London: Longmans, 1950).

Kelvin, Norman (ed.), *The Collected Letters of William Morris*, 4 vols. (Princeton University Press, 1984–96).

Latham, David (intro.), *Poems By the Way* (Bristol: Thoemmes Press, 1994).

LeMire, Eugene (ed.), *The Unpublished Lectures of William Morris* (Detroit: Wayne State University Press, 1969).

——— (intro.), *The Hollow Land and Other Contributions to the Oxford and Cambridge Magazine* (Bristol: Thoemmes Press, 1996).

Magnusson, Magnus (intro.), *William Morris Icelandic Journals* (London: Mare's Nest, 1996).

Miele, Chris (ed.), *William Morris on Architecture* (Sheffield: Sheffield Academic Press, 1996).

Morris, May (ed.), *The Collected Works of William Morris*, 24 vols. (London: Longmans, Green & Co., 1910–15; reprinted Bristol: Routledge/Thoemmes Press, 1991).

——— (ed.), *William Morris: Artist, Writer, Socialist*, 2 vols. (Oxford: Basil Blackwell, 1936).

Morton, A. L. (ed.), *The Political Writings of William Morris* (London: Lawrence and Wishart, 1973).

Peterson, William S. (ed.), *The Ideal Book: Essays and Lectures on the Arts of the Book by William Morris* (Berkeley: University of California Press, 1982).

Poulson, Christine (ed.) *William Morris on Art and Design* (Sheffield: Sheffield Academic Press, 1996).

Salmon, Nicholas (ed.), *Political Writings* (Bristol: Thoemmes Press, 1994).

——— (ed.), *Journalism* (Bristol: Thoemmes Press, 1996).

——— (intro), *The Well at the World's End* (Stroud: Alan Sutton, 1996).

——— (ed.), *William Morris on History* (Sheffield: Sheffield Academic Press, 1996).

Talbot, Norman (intro.), *The Waters of the Wondrous Isles* (Bristol: Thoemmes Press, 1994).

——— (intro.), *The Glittering Plain and Child Christopher* (Bristol: Thoemmes Press, 1996).

Wilmer, Clive (ed.), *'News from Nowhere' and Other Writings by William Morris* (Harmondsworth: Penguin, 1993).

Biographies and surveys

Aho, Gary, *William Morris: A Reference Guide* (Boston: G. K. Hall, 1985).

Bradley, Ian, *William Morris and his World* (London: Thames & Hudson, 1978).

Dore, Helen, *William Morris* (London: Pyramid, 1990).

Faulkner, Peter (ed.), *William Morris: The Critical Heritage* (London: Routledge & Kegan Paul, 1973).

——— , *Against the Age: An Introduction to William Morris* (London: Allen & Unwin, 1980).

Forman, H. Buxton, *The Books of William Morris described, with some Account of his doings in Literature and in the Allied Crafts* (London: F. Hollings, 1897).

Glasier, John Bruce, *William Morris and the Early Days of the Socialist Movement* (London: Longmans, Green & Co., 1921; reprinted Bristol: Thoemmes Press, 1994).

Henderson, Philip, *William Morris: His Life, Work and Friends* (London: Thames & Hudson, 1967).

Latham, David and Sheila, *An Annotated Critical Bibliography of William Morris*

(London: Harvester Wheatsheaf, 1991).

Lindsay, Jack, *William Morris: His Life & Works* (London: Constable, 1975).

MacCarthy, Fiona, *William Morris: A Life for Our Time* (London: Faber & Faber, 1994).

Mackail, J. W., *The Life of William Morris*, 2 vols. (London: Longmans, 1899).

Parry, Linda (ed.), *William Morris* (London: Philip Wilson, 1996).

Poulson, Christine, *William Morris* (London: The Apple Press, 1989).

Thompson, E. P., *William Morris: Romantic to Revolutionary* (London: Lawrence & Wishart, 1955).

Thompson, Paul, *The Work of William Morris* (London: Heinemann, 1967).

Vallance, Aymer, *William Morris: His Art, his Writings and his Public Life* (London: George Bell & Sons, 1897).

Works on Morris's friends and acquaintances

Allingham, H. and Radford, D. (eds.), *William Allingham: A Diary 1824–1889* (Fontwell: Centaur Press, 1967).

Blunt, Wilfrid Scawen, *My Diaries* (London: Martin Secker, 1919).

Bryson, John (ed.), *Dante Gabriel Rossetti and Jane Morris: Their Correspondence* (Oxford: Clarendon Press, 1976).

Burne-Jones, Georgiana, *Memorials of Edward Burne-Jones*, 2 vols. (London: Macmillan, 1904).

Christian, John, *Edward Burne-Jones* (London: Arts Council, 1975).

Cowley, John, *The Victorian Encounter with Marx: A Study of Ernest Belfort Bax* (London: British Academic Press, 1992).

Crane, Walter, *An Artist's Reminiscences* (London: Methuen, 1907).

Doughty, O. and Wahl, J. R., *The Letters of Dante Gabriel Rossetti*, 3 vols. (Oxford University Press, 1965–7).

Faulkner, Peter (ed.), *Jane Morris to Wilfrid Scawen Blunt* (Exeter University Press, 1986).

Fitzgerald, Penelope, *Edward Burne-Jones: A Biography* (London: Michael Joseph, 1975).

Gaunt, William and Clayton-Stamm, M. D. E., *William De Morgan* (London: Studio Vista, 1971).

Grierson, Janet, *Isabella Gilmore: Sister to William Morris* (London: SPCK, 1962).

Hyndman, H. M., *The Record of an Adventurous Life* (London: Macmillan, 1911).

Lang, C. Y. (ed.), *The Swinburne Letters*, 6 vols. (Yale University Press, 1959–62).

Laurence, Dan H. (ed.), *Bernard Shaw Collected Letters 1874–1950*, 4 vols. (London: Max Reinhardt, 1965–88).

Lethaby, W. R., *Philip Webb and his Work* (London: Oxford University Press, 1935).

Lubbock, P. (ed.), *Letters of Henry James* (London: Macmillan, 1920).

Marsh, Jan, *Jane and May Morris: A Biographical Story 1839–1938* (London: Pandora, 1986).

Meynell, Viola (ed.), *Some Friends of a Lifetime, Letters to Sydney Carlyle Cockerell* (London: Jonathan Cape, 1940).

—— (ed.), *The Best of Friends, Further Letters to Sydney Carlyle Cockerell* (London: Rupert Hart-Davies, 1956).

Street, A. E., *Memoir of George Edmund Street* (London and Edinburgh: John Murray, 1888).

Surtees, Virginia (ed.), *The Diaries of George Price Boyce* (Norwich: Real World, 1980).

—— (ed.), *The Diary of Ford Madox Brown* (Yale University Press, 1981).

Waters, Bill, and Harrison, Martin, *Burne-Jones* (London: Barrie and Jenkins, 1973).

Architecture

Dufty, A. R., *Kelmscott: An Illustrated Guide* (London: Society of Antiquaries, 1984).

Hollamby, Edward, *Red House* (London: Architecture, Design and Technology Press, 1991).

Pevsner, Nikolaus, *Pioneers of the Modern Movement* (London: Faber & Faber, 1936).

Watkinson, Ray and Hollamby, Edward, *Red House, A Guide* (London: William Morris Society, 1993).

Art and Design

Baker, Derek, *The Flowers of William Morris* (London: Barn Elms, 1996).

Clark, Fiona, *William Morris: Wallpapers and Chintzes* (London: Academy Editions, 1974).

Dufty, A. R., *Morris Embroideries: The Prototypes* (London: Society of Antiquaries, 1985).

Gillow, Norah, *William Morris Designs and Patterns* (London: Bracken Books, 1988).

Marillier, H. C., *History of the Merton Abbey Textile Works* (London: Constable, 1927).

Parry, Linda, *William Morris Textiles* (London: Weidenfeld & Nicolson, 1983).

—— , *Textiles of the Arts and Crafts Movements* (London: Thames & Hudson, 1988).

—— (ed.), *William Morris: Art and Kelmscott* (Woodbridge: Boydell & Brewer, 1996).

Stansky, Peter, *William Morris, C. R. Ashbee and the Arts and Crafts* (London: Nine Elm Press, 1984).

—— , *Redesigning the World: William Morris, the 1880s and the Arts and*

Crafts Movement (Princeton University Press, 1985).
Vance, Peggy, *William Morris Wallpapers* (London: Bracken Books, 1989).
Watkinson, Ray, *William Morris as Designer* (London: Studio Vista, 1967).

Kelmscott Press
Cockerell, Sydney (ed.), *A Note by William Morris on his aims in founding the Kelmscott Press, together with a short history of the Press* (London: Kelmscott Press, 1898).
Dreyfus, John, *Morris and the Printed Book* (London: William Morris Society, 1989).
Dunlap, Joseph, *The Book that Never Was* (New York: Oriole Editions, 1971).
Franklin, Colin, *Printing and the Mind of Morris* (Cambridge: Rampant Lions Press, 1986).
Isherwood, Andrew, *An Introduction to the Kelmscott Press* (London: V & A, 1986).
Needham, P., *William Morris and the Art of the Book* (London: Oxford University Press, 1976).
Peterson, William S., *A Bibliography of the Kelmscott Press* (Oxford: Clarendon Press, 1984).
———, *The Kelmscott Press: A History of William Morris's Typographical Adventure* (Oxford: Clarendon Press, 1989).
Robinson, D., *William Morris, Burne-Jones and the Kelmscott Chaucer* (London: Fraser, 1982).
Sparling, H. Halliday, *The Kelmscott Press and William Morris Master-Craftsman* (London: Macmillan, 1924).

Literature
Coleman, Stephen and O'Sullivan, Paddy, *William Morris and News from Nowhere* (Bideford: Green Books, 1990).
Hoare, Dorothy M., *The Works of Morris and Yeats in relation to Early Saga Literature* (Cambridge University Press, 1937).
Hodgson, Amanda, *The Romances of William Morris* (London: Cambridge University Press, 1987).
Marshall, Roderick, *William Morris and his Earthly Paradise* (Tisbury: Compton Press, 1979).
Oberg, Charlotte, *A Pagan Prophet: William Morris* (Charlottesville: University Press of Virginia, 1978).
Tompkins, J. M. S., *William Morris: An Approach to the Poetry* (London: Cecil Woolf, 1988).

Morris & Co.
Harvey, Charles and Press, Jon, *William Morris: Design and Enterprise in Victorian Britain* (Manchester University Press, 1991).

Politics

Arnot, R. Page, *William Morris: A Vindication* (London: Martin Lawrence, 1934).

———— , *William Morris: The Man and the Myth* (London: Lawrence & Wishart, 1964).

Meier, Paul, *William Morris: The Marxist Dreamer* (Sussex: Harvester Press, 1978).

Frow, Edmund and Ruth, *William Morris in Manchester and Salford* (Salford: Working Class Movement Library, 1996).

Stained Glass

Harrison, Martin, *Victorian Stained Glass* (London: Barrie and Jenkins, 1980).

Robinson, R. and Wildman, S., *Morris & Company in Cambridge* (Cambridge University Press, 1980).

Sewter, A. Charles, *The Stained Glass of William Morris and his Circle*, 2 vols. (New Haven: Yale University Press, 1974–75).